Democracy in the Balance

DEMOCRACY
IN THE BALANCE
Culture and Society in the Middle East

Mehran Kamrava
California State University, Northridge

CHATHAM HOUSE PUBLISHERS

SEVEN BRIDGES PRESS, LLC

NEW YORK • LONDON

Democracy in the Balance:
Culture and Society in the Middle East

SEVEN BRIDGES PRESS, LLC
P.O. BOX 958, CHAPPAQUA, NEW YORK 10514-0958

Publisher: Patricia Artinian
Managing editor: Katharine Miller
Production supervisor: Melissa A. Martin
Cover design: Steven Brower Design
Composition: Bang, Motley, Olufsen
Printing and binding: Versa Press, Inc.

LIBRARY OF CONGRESS CATALOGING-IN-PUBLICATION DATA

Kamrava, Mehran, 1964–
    Democracy in the balance : culture and society in the Middle
East / Mehran Kamrava.
        p. cm.
    Includes bibliographical references and index.
    ISBN 1-56643-063-1 (pbk.)
        1. Democracy–Middle East. 2. Democracy—Social aspects
—Middle East. 3. Political culture—Middle East. 4. Popular
culture—Middle East. 5. Middle East—Social conditions.
I. Title.
JQ1758.A91 K35   1998
306.2'0956—ddc21
                                                    98-8990
                                                    CIP

Manufactured in the United States of America
10 9 8 7 6 5 4 3 2 1

To Melisa

Contents

Tables and Figures, ix
Foreword by Peter Avery, xi
Preface, xiii

1. The Social Origins of Democracy   I
   The Debate over Democracy, 2
   Democratization and Political Crafting, 9
   Civil Society in Comparative Perspective, 16
   Democracy in the Middle East, 31

2. Social Forces and Institutions   40
   Social Forces, 41
   Social Institutions, 49

3. Social Classes   82
   Urban Social Classes, 90
   Rural Social Classes, 117

4. Social Change   131
   Causes of Social Change, 134
   Manifestations of Social Change, 145

5. Popular Culture   168
   Islam, 170
   Culture of Confusion, 176
   Culture of Wasted Energies, 184
   Culture of Virility, 189
   Rural Culture, 196

6. Political Culture 201

Islam, 204
The Cult of Personality, 213

7. Conclusion 224

Notes 232
Bibliography 266
Index 292

About the Author 300

Tables and Figures

Tables

1.1 Stages in Democratic Transitions   22
1.2 Nature and Chronological Involvement of Transition Actors   23
2.1 Ethnic Composition in Middle Eastern Countries   57
2.2 Religious Composition in Middle Eastern Countries   68
3.1 Urban and Rural Classes in the Middle East   91
3.2 Sectoral Employment of Economically Active Industries   94
3.3 Population Based in Urban Areas   99
3.4 Annual Urban and Rural Growth   100
3.5 The Ruling Families in the Countries of the Gulf and the Arab Peninsula   105
3.6 Expatriates: Percentage of Population and Origins   115
4.1 Population and Settlement Patterns in the Middle East   138
4.2 Annual Tourism Statistics for Selected Middle Eastern Countries   145
6.1 Regime Types in Different Regions of the Globe   220

Figures

3.1 Sociocultural and Economic Divisions within Society   86
3.2 Class Structure in More Integrated Economies   88
3.3 Class Structure in Oil-Dependent Economies   89
4.1 Cultural Disposition within Each Class   150
4.2 Sociocultural and Economic Composition of Middle Eastern Societies   150

Foreword

by Peter Avery

THIS LUCID, explanatory study of the complexities of modern Middle Eastern society and politics is particularly distinguished by its author's consistently maintained thesis that the latter spring out of and are fashioned by the former. Society's modification, culturally speaking, often, alas, negative from foreign intrusion (notably the West) is not ignored because in a work as comprehensive as this one, it cannot be. Thus Kamrava spans, in a manner that would have intrigued the late Ernest Gellner, three disciplines: history, political science, and social anthropology. He demonstrates that democracy is a social as well as a political phenomenon, "entailing not only a set of democratic institutions and political arrangements but also a supporting social and cultural context." It might, of course, be said that democracy obviously does this. Unfortunately, however, the degree to which democracy and its problems can be properly explained in terms of cultural and social environment has in current studies too often been obscured by the monodisciplined approach. This study, therefore, is as timely as it is valuable, not least in its convincing attempt to relate failures in the establishment of democratic institutions in the areas with which the book is concerned to unachievement of that "fusion between state and society" on which a democratic system ultimately depends.

The pessimism about the future of democracy in Middle Eastern societies that, albeit with reluctance, the author expresses in his concluding observations, need not be entirely shared. It is nevertheless justifiably prudent, especially in view of his sensitivity to the "deep cultural schizophrenia running rampant throughout" those societies. Here the negative effects of foreign intrusion referred to above come to mind. But here too the author's insightful understanding of the peoples about whom he is writing, and their often betrayed aspirations, becomes manifest. To date, as he points out, even when voting has been ostensibly free and elections apparently "truly democratic," the average citizen has had little stake in a system for which "he or she had [not] fought" and which has all too frequently been a matter of "the same group of elites who rotate in and out of office."

Needless to say, at this juncture consideration must be given to revolution, that breaking of molds to which even the most cowed and pacific of peoples can ultimately be driven. It is in his discussion of the revolutionary solution that one of the more arresting features of the book emerges—a very enlightened contribution on Islam. This part of Kamrava's discussion is all the more important because it is remarkably free of anything that smacks of the prejudiced and sometimes panicky cant from which talk of Islam today no more escapes than it might have in medieval Christendom.

It is hoped that enough has been said about a work that would so eminently stand on its own without any foreword and how indispensable this major study is, concerning not only the problem of democracy in the Middle East today but also the region's many other social and political complexities, about which greater understanding is so urgently needed.

Cambridge, March 1998

Preface

THIS BOOK examines the social and cultural forces that have hindered the emergence and widespread evolution of democratic polities in the Middle East. Democracy, whether in the Middle East or elsewhere in the world, must have a firm basis in culture and society in order to function. A democratic polity must not only be made up of a group of democratic mechanisms and institutions—elected officials, democratic constitutions, elections, and so forth—but also, more important, it must rest on a solid body of social and cultural premises that gives the system social meaning and cultural resonance. Democracy, in other words, must necessarily be supported by civil society. In turn, examining the precise nature and evolution of civil society requires, almost more than anything else, a careful study of political culture in particular and other society-based dynamics in general.

But looking at social forces is by nature an imprecise and tricky venture; in fact, consideration of social and cultural influences is potentially damaging to one's entire analytical framework. I say more about this dilemma in chapter 1. It is important to note at the outset, however, that social and cultural analysis of the sort undertaken in this book is not endorsed by all students of the social sciences. Apart from the quantitative/qualitative dichotomy that currently divides the discipline, there is more subtle and ultimately more substantive disagreement among social scientists, especially the comparativists, as to exactly where in the state-society equation their focus of analysis should be. Some argue from a "neostatist" perspective, seeing the state as the primary locus of power and thus the final arbiter of a society's life and its many nuances; others look at society and its systemic relationship to a larger whole, which also includes the state; and still others point to the importance of the relationship between the two separate entities of state and society.[1] It is in this last category that my arguments seem to fit most comfortably, and therefore I have chosen to focus on the latter half of the state-society equation. Neostatists and proponents of the systems approach may find the theoretical underpinnings of this work deficient in one way or another, but I hope to convince them at least of the merits of social and cultural analysis in the following chapters. To their possible charges of my overreliance on such inexact phenomena as, for example, political culture or civil society, I plead guilty and present the following pages as justification.

The reasons for my particular choice of emphasis are simple: despite considerable advances in the study of the Middle East as a whole, especially on the nature and role of Middle Eastern states, little has been written on Middle Eastern societies per se, with most of the socially based literature on the region focusing on such specific social or cultural phenomena as Islam, tribalism, or ethnicity. I hope to contribute to this body of literature by filling the noticeable gap in sociological analyses. I say more about this later, especially in regard to some of the more precise differences between the argumentative methodologies of this work and those of similar publications now in circulation.

I have come to this project through an intellectual journey that started in graduate school. My first serious academic exposure was to Iran and from there, for reasons that should not require much explanation, I became interested in the study of revolutions, Third World development, and ultimately the larger discipline of comparative politics. This book, therefore, is a culmination of a paradigmatic odyssey, bits and pieces of which are found in my previous publications. If I refer to them on occasion, it is not for self-promotion but out of necessity and in the interest of space.

A Note on Methodology

The particular nature of this project warrants a few words about the research and argumentative methodologies employed throughout the book. My argument that current social and cultural forces thwart democratic possibilities in the Middle East is not new. Scholars, particularly those from the "orientalist" camp, if indeed there is one, have long maintained that the Middle East is not, for one reason or another, "ready" for democracy. Elie Kedourie, for example, points to a "native autocratic tradition" that he claims has persistently undermined repeated historical attempts at introducing constitutional rule in various Middle Eastern countries.[2] Less indicting of the Arab tradition is Bernard Lewis, who comes close to accepting Kedourie's position. After pointing to Islam's penchant for egalitarianism and compromise and ridiculing the likes of

T.E. Lawrence, who considered Semites loath to compromise, Lewis asserts, "That there is a pre-disposition to autocratic government among Muslim peoples is clear enough; that there is an inherent capacity for any other is yet to be proved."[3] Lewis offers several additional explanations for the demise of democracy in the Middle East, chief among them its imported nature, the lack of support by domestic and colonial elites once they are installed in office, and the lack of appropriate social and economic factors (58–61). "The parliament of Cairo was imported in a box," writes Lewis, "to be assembled and put into use without even a set of do-it-yourself instructions. It responded to no need or demand of the Egyptian people; it enjoyed the backing of no popular interest or body of opinion" (60). Finally, the late Albert Hourani may be of similar mind, not so much for what he has said about the absence of Middle Eastern democracy but for his obvious exclusion of the subject, especially in his later writings.[4] Given the depth and breadth of Hourani's panoramic view of Middle Eastern history, his neglecting to mention democracy's absence is nearly as telling as if he had explored it. By not examining the opposite side of the coin, Hourani involuntarily draws himself close to the camp to which Kedourie and Lewis voluntarily belong.[5]

By maintaining that democracy in the Middle East is at present highly implausible, if not outright impossible, I come perilously close to the conclusions of Kedourie, Lewis, and, by implication, Hourani. Samuel Huntington offers a different "non-orientalist"—or, more accurately, "neo-orientalist"—perspective, but he reaches similar conclusions, claiming, among other things, that Islam impedes the spread of democratic norms and denies legitimacy to democratic institutions.[6] Thus there would seem to be hardly any room for yet another rehash of old arguments so meticulously presented by giants of the discipline. I believe, however, that my perspective is different, not necessarily in its conclusions but in the argumentative and analytical methodologies used to reach those conclusions. Originality is often defined in one of two ways: it involves either the presentation of facts and figures previously unknown or the development of new interpretations for facts and figures that may already be common knowledge. My sense of the improbability of democracy in the Middle East may not be original, but my *interpretation* of why this is so is original. At the most basic level, I approach the subject from an angle that has yet to be explored, one that most broadly falls somewhere under the rubric of political sociology. H.A.R. Gibb,[7] Kedourie, Lewis, and Hourani, to name only a few of the more renowned scholars in the field, have all viewed the Middle East through historical lenses, looking at the region and the social and political phenomena entangling it from the perspective of the past. Without delving into the essence of their rich literature, a quick survey of some of their publications' titles reveals their general perspective: Hourani's most celebrated works are *The Emergence of the Modern Middle East, Europe and the Middle East, Syria and Lebanon,* and *A History of the Arab Peoples;* Gibb's major contributions include *Studies on the Civilization of Islam, Mohammedanism,* and *Modern Trends in Islam;* among Lewis's most recent works are *The Shaping of the Modern Middle East, The Arabs in History,* and *Islam and the West;* and two of Kedourie's more recent histories are *Politics in the Middle East* and *Democracy and Arab Political Culture.* Huntington and other latter-day orientalists, however, argue from a perspective that may best be described as cultural geography, assigning certain valuative characteristics to the cultures of particular areas of the world. Every region of the globe, Huntington argues, has a certain religiocultural flavor that greatly determines its receptivity to democratic norms and practices.[8] Thus to Huntington, the Middle East, with its Arab culture and Islamic religion, is inhospitable to democracy.[9]

While inevitably drawing on some of the historical and political perspectives offered by these and other authors, I concentrate in this book on the profound importance of the social and cultural forces that continue to undermine democratic possibilities in the Middle East. The task I have set for myself in the following chapters is simply to engage in an analysis of these forces that would explain, even if only partially, the absence of democracy in the region. I am well aware that some of my conclusions may come uncomfortably close to those of the orientalists who are these days fashionably maligned, sometimes justifiably, for their cultural reductionism.[10] My arguments differ from those of that school, however, because they are placed in a *sociological,* not an *orientalist,* framework. In simplest terms, I apply traditional social scientific methodologies, especially drawn from political science and sociology, to reach certain conclusions. If my conclusions are similar to those of many orientalists, it does not necessarily mean that I have replicated their methods of analysis or general approach. The same applies to Huntingtonian cultural geographers, who engage not so much in social and cultural analysis as in crude categorizations of the globe into religious and ideological camps.

I take political culture in general and civil society in particular as the starting points of my analysis, arguing that these two interrelated and potentially complementary phenomena are pivotal to any viable process of democratization. This argument is the premise of chapter 1, in which I

state that a meaningful analysis of democratization cannot ignore the social and cultural contexts of democracy. While political crafting and institutional arrangements are indispensable to democratic transitions, so are
democratic political cultures and civil society organizations. A political
"window of opportunity" is only half of the story; the other half has
largely to do with cultural receptivity and acceptance.

With the overall theoretical approach to the study thus articulated, I
focus in succeeding chapters on the different social and cultural characteristics and forces found throughout the Middle East. Chapter 2 looks at
social forces and institutions; chapter 3 focuses on social classes; chapter
4 examines social change; chapters 5 and 6 focus on popular and political
culture respectively; and the book's main arguments are summed up in
chapter 7, the conclusion.

My general methodology of gathering information for the book took
me to several Middle Eastern countries beginning in 1992, when I began
the "fieldwork" phase of the research. In each country, I usually started in
the capital city and worked my way to as many close and distant villages,
towns, and cities as time and funds allowed. In order to get a sense of the
cultural lives and mind-sets of people belonging to the different social
strata in each place I visited, I tried to spend as much time as possible
with people of different backgrounds and social standings—from the rich-
est and most affluent to those considered marginal and fringe elements;
from university professors and intellectuals to the semiliterate and illiter-
ate. As a single male, I occasionally had more difficulty interacting with
and observing women, although I tried to get around that by making sure
that a local male, preferably a family member of the female interviewee,
was present. I rarely took notes while in the presence of those I inter-
viewed but almost always wrote down my observations and impressions
immediately after I had left them. This type of research, which may appall
disciples of quantitative methods, is what I found worked best for the task
at hand. Empiricism may indeed be the most "scientific" method of proving a particular hypothesis, but the very thesis of this book—that a democratic political culture does not exist in the Middle East—makes the strict
adherence to such a methodology both inapplicable and pointless.

Acknowledgments

The research and completion of this work would not have been possible
without the generous assistance of many individuals, both inside and outside the Middle East. Aware of the Iranian (as well as the Middle Eastern)

penchant for hyperbole, I will keep my acknowledgments brief, though this by no means lessens the depth of my gratitude to the countless individuals I met and befriended in the Middle East for their trust and confidence and for their tolerance of my inquisitiveness. Atef Hosni and his family were especially helpful in acquainting me with the subtler aspects of life in Egypt, and I consider myself fortunate to be one of their friends. My family's love and support have always provided the much needed sustenance for my work. I also gratefully acknowledge the financial assistance of the Fred P. Gattis Foundation through the provision of a grant that enabled me to conduct research in Egypt, Jordan, and the Israeli-occupied territories in the summer of 1992. I was also awarded the J.S. Seidman Fellowship in International Studies when I began work on this book, and for that I am most thankful to Dr. P.K. Seidman. Practically all the other research that has gone into the book, including the purchase of books, subsequent research trips to the Middle East, and the hiring of research assistants was made possible by this generous fellowship. A number of individuals also rendered invaluable assistance, both directly and indirectly. The staff of the Burrow Library at Rhodes College were instrumental in locating and acquiring many sources. I am especially grateful to Annette Cates for helping me borrow countless books and articles from other libraries. Long after I left graduate school, Peter Avery continues to be my mentor and to share with me his amazing and insightful appreciation of Arab and Iranian cultures. Much of my curiosity about Middle Eastern culture is rooted in what he taught me.

My good friend Edward Artinian, the founder of Chatham House Publishers, Inc., passed away months before this book assumed its present form. Nevertheless, I remain grateful to Edward for agreeing to take on this project, for his wisdom and advice, his jokes, and his friendship. I shall remember him fondly.

I am also thankful to the many students in my courses on the Middle East at Rhodes College and at California State University, Northridge. Over the years, many were directly involved in the evolution of this book from lecture notes and unorganized ideas. They are too numerous to name individually, but I remain grateful to all of them for their support, criticism, and many intellectual contributions over the years. Sharing with them the ideas I have expounded in the classroom or those that are contained here has always been an intellectual challenge, and in the process they made me a better teacher.

Finally, I wish to thank Melisa Çanli, who came into my life as I was finishing this book. As an excuse for a date, I asked her to read chapter 5, and to my delight she returned it full of red marks and suggestions. She has been a tough critic and a source of inspiration ever since, and, now that she is my wife, I cannot imagine how I wrote the other chapters without her input and loving support. It is to her that I dedicate this book.

1. The Social Origins of Democracy

HE DEBATE over democratic rule has come to the fore of scholarly debate, and the recent global wave of democratization has resulted in the publication of a number of highly significant theoretical and empirical studies on the subject.[1] By all accounts, democracy indeed seems to be on a global march, with a phase having started in southern Europe in the mid-1970s, spilling over to Latin America in the early to mid-1980s, and finally engulfing eastern Europe in the late 1980s and early 1990s. Considerable scholarly energy has been expended on looking into the dynamics of democratization in Africa and the Middle East, with some authors promising an imminent flourish of democracy in those regions; at the same time, others go so far as to argue that African and Middle Eastern democratic openings have already started taking place.[2] Nevertheless, in this and the following chapters I argue that prospects for democratization and the successful implementation of democratic rule in the Middle East are far from certain, particularly in light of a number of social, cultural, and economic factors that undermine democratic openings in the region. My claim is based not only on the existence of certain empirical, antidemocratic circumstances in the Middle East, or at least across most of the region, but also on a larger theoretical concern in the study of democracy itself. I examine in this chapter the theoretical issues relating to the phenomena of democratization and democracy and argue that, all things being equal, social and cultural forces are just as important in effecting and helping to sustain democratic rule as are success-

ful political crafting and institutional engineering. This is not to maintain a socially and culturally deterministic or reductionist position but simply to assert that in attaining the birth and longevity of democratic polities, factors within society and culture are just as important, if not in some cases more so, as political and institutional ones. Such democratically supportive social and cultural phenomena, this book argues, are not presently found in the Middle East, or if existent, they are mostly subdued under the larger weights of economic and political forces. Democracy is not unattainable, but at present the region does not offer as many of the social and cultural requisites to cultivate and then to sustain it as are found elsewhere in the world.

The Debate over Democracy

Before delving into the theoretical debates involved, it may be useful to consider briefly some of the basic premises of democracy and democratization.[3] Most notably, there is widespread consensus among scholars about the definition of a democratic system and the process of democratization; the general varieties of systems labeled democratic; and the recent appearance of "waves" of democratization on both a regional and global basis.

Definitions of Democracy

The logical starting point is to define a democratic system, and in this respect most scholars, at least those writing in the West, have adopted Joseph Schumpeter's classic definition:[4] "The democratic method is that institutional arrangement for arriving at political decisions in which individuals acquire the power to decide by means of a competitive struggle for the people's vote."[5] Schumpeter saw democracy in what one scholar has called a "narrow" sense,[6] perceiving it simply as a mechanism for choosing among different political leaders at election times. Subsequent scholars such as Robert Dahl and Samuel Huntington have similarly defined democracies, or "polyarchies," as Dahl prefers to call them. To Dahl, a system is democratic if it has at least two inseparable features: free and fair political contestation and participation. A democratic system, he maintains, is "substantially popularized and liberalized, that is, highly inclusive and extensively open to public contestation."[7] Huntington's definition is equally minimalist. He views a political system as democratic "to the extent that its most powerful collective decision makers are selected through fair, honest, and periodic elections in which candidates freely compete for votes and in which virtually all adult population is free to vote."[8] Other variations of the definition emphasize the social components of democracy. David Held, for example, calls attention to the extent of citizens' "democratic autonomy," which, he believes, requires "both a high degree of the accountability of the state and a democratic reordering of civil society."[9] Georg Sorensen's perceptions of democracy are likewise socially grounded; he argues that "in the very broad concept, democracy is not only a political but also a specific social and economic system."[10]

Clearly, democracy is a political as well as a social phenomenon, entailing not only a set of political institutions and arrangements but also a supportive social and cultural context. The definitions given by Schumpeter, Dahl, and Huntington are politically reductionist.[11] The requirements set by each of these authors for a system to be democratic are necessary but insufficient. Democracy does involve an appropriate set of democratic institutions and constitutional guarantees that enable people to use the ballot box freely and effectively, but the simple ability to vote for one's political leaders does not make a democracy. There must be larger societal factors at work. A democratic system is one in which there is not only a consensus but also a high level of fusion between state and society that is both institutional and normative. Institutions such as political parties, grassroots movements, and various other citizen action groups establish links through which society can effect its demands on the state. But even if the institutional opportunities are there, society must *want* to get involved in the political process. In other words, the state-society nexus must be not only institutional but also cultural. Such a political democratic imperative on the part of society must be more than merely episodic, elite-based, or somehow manipulated. There must be an inherent vernacular, a subconscious, tacit understanding of everyday political language in the mass culture. Large and diverse strata within society (i.e., not just elites or workers) need to have a long-term, vested interest in the maintenance and functioning of a democratic system if it is to be classified as a true democracy. Otherwise, a liberal democratic system in which there are state institutions but little societal support would end up operating in a social and cultural vacuum. Thus the state may be democratic, but its functions, operations, and political turnovers are largely inconsequential to much of the population. This kind of system is what I have termed a *quasi democracy*, or pseudodemocracy, as opposed to a *viable democracy*, because of its elite-dominated, socially isolated nature.[12] Such quasi-democratic systems exist in almost all regions of the Third World: Jamaica and the Dominican Republic in the Caribbean; Costa Rica and

Honduras in Central America; Kenya, Botswana, and the Gambia in Africa; Taiwan and the Philippines in East Asia; India, Pakistan, and Bangladesh in South Asia; and Turkey and Lebanon in the Middle East.

Democratic Varieties

The nature and extent of state-society interaction, therefore, directly determines the precise kind of democratic political system. Classical theorists have long made a clear distinction between *direct* and *representative* forms of democracy. In the former, citizens personally take part in political deliberations and lawmaking, but in the latter, they relegate such duties to their designated representatives.[13] More recent classifications of democratic rule have categorized its varieties into presidential versus parliamentary, majoritarian versus representational, two-party versus multiparty, and consociational versus consensus.[14] While most of these classifications are self-explanatory, consociational and consensus democracies need further explanation. According to Arend Lijphart, who has written much on the subject, the main difference between them is a matter of degree. He defines a *consociational democracy* as one "that is responsive to the challenge of a culturally fragmented or plural society (that is, a society that is sharply divided along religious, ideological, linguistic, cultural, ethnic, or racial lines into virtually separate subsocieties with their own political parties, interest groups, and media of communication)."[15] *Consensus democracies* are similarly suited for divided societies, although the political emphasis is on *incentives* for broad power sharing rather than *requiring* the various communities to cooperate politically. Moreover, consensus democracies encourage "segmental autonomy," whereas consociational democracies demand it.[16]

Georg Sorensen, however, points to three different typologies, classifying them into the categories of restricted, elite-dominated, and mass-dominated democracies. Restricted democracies, he asserts, "are political systems with some democratic elements but also with limits on competition, participation, and liberties. Frequently, they are characterized by the presence of elite groups whose members reserve the right to interfere in the democratic process in order to protect their interests."[17] Elite-dominated democracies are "frozen," "unwilling to transgress the narrow limitations imposed on them by the elite factions who engineered the transitions to democracy in the first place."[18] Finally, mass-dominated democracies are "systems in which mass actors have gained the upper hand over traditional upper classes. They push for reform from below, attacking the power and privilege of the elite."[19]

All of these typologies are valid, depicting various political and ideological shapes that some democratic systems, and at times nondemocratic ones as well, have assumed around the globe. The hard realities of the political world are often too complex and intertwined to fit neatly into distinct categories analytically devised on paper. Nevertheless, these typologies accurately reflect the overall functions and nature of political systems that are either generally perceived or perceive themselves to be democratic.[20] At the same time, however, it is important to emphasize the role of civil society in particular and political culture in general as prime factors that differentiate between what I see as the two main forms of democracies, viable and quasi democracies.

Political culture, as mentioned earlier, is made up of collective norms and values that people hold in regard to political institutions, principles, and practices.[21] Civil society, in the narrow sense, is a specific manifestation of political culture that tends to develop when there is a popular desire by society to organize and articulate itself along democratic lines.[22] Viable democracies are those in which there is a socially based, cultural imperative to maintain the democratic parameters of the political system. These democracies are not limited to particular groups of elites or specific strata within society, nor could their very existence be easily threatened by populist demagogues or threats of violence from within or abroad. They are democracies in which the elaborate democratic institutions of the state are seen not as artificial constructs but as natural fixtures of the overall social and political order. Thus acceptance of and adherence to the democratic "rules of the game" become second nature to the citizen who, as a result of the prevalence of civil society organizations, is accustomed to thinking and behaving democratically. Civil society and the various grassroots organizations that bring it about are therefore the linchpins in a viable democracy.

Not all democracies, however, have the luxury of resting on the resilient support of civil society. In fact, many of the democratic systems in the Third World, especially those predating the latest wave of democratization, are a completely different variety. Most of them are based not on strong, active civil societies but on a kind of elite consensus that does not always translate into a cohesive and unified mass-political culture. These are quasi-democratic systems that are democratic in name and appearance only, not in substance or spirit. They have all the institutions and mechanisms necessary to insure society's free and unhampered participation in the political process, such as political parties, elections, parliaments, and liberal democratic constitutions. But most segments of society have other nonpolitical preoccupations that prevent them from developing normative bonds with the political system. The trials of economic survival for the lower classes and the challenges of remaining affluent for the upper classes frequently outweigh the normative imperatives of political democracy. This is not to assert that the impulse toward attaining political liberties is thwarted there and not elsewhere. Calls for ending dictatorship and breaking the chains of oppression are part of the political history of every developing country. The cause of democracy has seen plenty of bloodshed, in the Third World as well as in the First and Second Worlds. But in many parts of the Third World, especially in places where the genesis of democracy was more a product of elite consensus than of social and political dynamics, the social resonance of democracy is somewhat subdued. The masses did not rise up to demand democracy (as many have in parts of Latin America and eastern Europe)—the elite simply bargained for it. Thus, insofar as the general masses are concerned, participation in the political process is far more perfunctory than it is a product of a genuine sense of civic obligation. Even if voting is free and elections are truly democratic, the average citizen has little stake in them; this is not a system for which he or she has fought, and, at any rate, it is always the same group of elites who rotate in and out of office.

Elitism is only one aspect of quasi-democratic systems. A second feature that separates them from genuine viable democracies is the lack of serious attention to the civil rights and liberties of disenfranchised groups within their societies. Quasi democracies are often elite-engineered systems, and what the elites are most interested in is the right to participate freely in the political process. Often overlooked are the rights of the downtrodden and minority groups, especially if those groups happen to be subject to widespread social and cultural prejudice. The political system may be meticulously observant of such democratic rituals as elections and party politics, but it is just as likely to overlook the intricacies of respecting civil and individual rights. The system, in short, may be *democratic*, but it is not *liberal*. In the elite's scheme of a top-down democracy, the lowest echelons of society are likely to be left out of the democratic equation in the participatory rituals of the system as well as in the privileges and guarantees that come along with it. It is no accident that throughout Central America's quasi democracies—Mexico, Honduras, El Salvador, and Nicaragua—as well as elsewhere in Latin America (especially Bolivia, Peru, and Ecuador), indigenous Indian peoples are often subject to harassment by the authorities, and their civil rights are routinely violated.[23] In Pakistan some of the most extreme violations of human rights took place during the tenure in office of the country's first freely elected government, headed by Zulfikar Ali Bhutto.[24] Even the government of Bhutto's daughter, Benazir, carried out a systematic process of Islamization that was hardly compatible with the tenets of democracy. Freedom of speech and other civil liberties are significantly curtailed in Bangladesh, as was made evident by attempts to prosecute the author Taslima Nasreen for her allegedly antireligious novella, *Shame*. The persecution of the Tamil by the state in Sri Lanka, another quasi democracy, is also a case in point. In Turkey, eradicating the "Kurdish problem" is not only government policy but also popularly condoned by the Turkish majority.

In addition to its indifference to the intricacies of a liberal democracy, the quasi-democratic system gives new meaning to the term "career politician." The jockeying for political office and position is particularly intense at the cabinet and parliamentary levels, and often members of the same family or the same clique dominate one specific cabinet portfolio or parliamentary seat for years, even decades. Senators may indeed be elected repeatedly, but this is a result less of brilliant campaigning than of voter apathy and popular cultural deference to elites. Political parties, accordingly, are essentially old-boy networks instead of meaningful mechanisms to facilitate popular political expression and input into the system. With the entire system thus reeking of elitism, sometimes even the highest political offices become the preserve of the same cast of characters.

South Asian quasi democracies have been particularly susceptible to family dynasties. A peculiar gender specificity is at work there, with the mantle of power often passing from fathers to daughters or from husbands to wives. A prime example is the legacy of the Gandhi family in India, supposedly "the world's largest democracy." Jawaharlal Nehru first served as prime minister from 1947 to 1964. His daughter, Indira Gandhi, occupied the same office from 1966 to 1977 and again from 1980 until her assassination in 1984, and the torch was then passed to her son Rajiv, who served from 1984 to 1989. Rajiv's Italian-born wife, Sonia, was then offered the presidency of the Congress Party, but she at first refused, accepting only in 1998; and attempts at recruiting her son, Rahul, were unsuccessful. According to news reports, however, her daughter, Priyanka, may be pursuing political office in the near future.[25] Sri Lankans seem to have a similar affinity for voting members of the same family into the prime minister's office. Solomon Bandaranaike served from 1956 until his assassination in 1959; his wife, Sirimavo, then served from 1960 to 1965 and again from 1970 to 1977. (She was, incidentally, the world's first female prime minister.) Their daughter, Chandrika Kumaratunga, assumed the same office in August 1994. Pakistan's Benazir Bhutto, whose father served as prime minister from 1971 to 1977, occupied the same position from 1988 to 1990 and again from 1993 to 1997. And in Bangladesh Prime Minister Khaleda Zia achieved political prominence after the 1981 slaying of her husband, the country's president, General Ziaur Rahman.[26]

Mexico is another example where, for the past seventy years, political power has been concentrated within an elite-dominated democracy by the Revolutionary Institutional Party (PRI).[27] Mexico is, admittedly, often considered more of a bureaucratic-authoritarian state than a quasi democracy.[28] Nevertheless, there have been regular presidential elections, and the political process has long maintained a semblance of democracy. Yet the PRI has been dominant since the 1920s and has supplied all twelve of the country's elected presidents. In 1994, when Luis Colosio, the party's front-runner candidate for the presidency, was slain, he was succeeded by one of his former associates and deputies, Ernesto Zedillo, who went on to win the country's national presidential elections. Whatever democracy, if any, does exist in Mexico, it does not seem to go beyond the institutional parameters of the PRI.

The Middle East's two quasi democracies, Lebanon and Turkey, are also elite-dominated. In Lebanon's supposed consociational democracy, the term "political boss" (za'im) has long been part of the lexicon of everyday language, and the country is often mocked as being run by "twenty families."[29] In 1982, when the country's president-elect, Bashir Gemayel, was assassinated, he was duly succeeded by his brother, Amin. Turkey is often hailed as the Middle East's other democracy or, depending on the analyst's perspective, the region's only democratic regime. Again, however, the formal institutions of democracy have not been complemented by a democratic civic spirit there. Turkish democracy is both highly elitist and rigidly restrictive. The rotation of the same groups of faces in and out of office has become an ingrained aspect of Turkish politics. By 1997, for example, President Süleyman Demirel had held the office of prime minister seven times. Cabinet ministers and other partners in the coalition government are equally prominent career politicians who have little in common with the average Turk in, say, Erzurum. Even opposition figures tend to come from the elite, as the religious activist Necmettin Erbakan exemplifies.[30] But the restrictive nature of Turkish democracy is even more pronounced than its elitism. There are several crucial aspects of Turkish politics that one simply does not question. Most significant, Turkey's democratic system has no tolerance for those questioning the character or methods of the country's modern founder, Mustafa Kemal Atatürk. The system may be democratic, but Atatürk remains a sacred figure, and questioning the wisdom of some of his actions is considered both a sacrilege and a political offense.[31] Even more thorny is the issue of the Kurdish population in the southeast, where the government has long been engaged in a full-blown military campaign against this ethnic minority. Turkey's democracy seems intolerant of any solution to the "Kurdish problem," short of the Kurds' unconditional submission to Ankara. Thus when Kurdish deputies to the parliament demanded an explanation for the government's actions, they were duly arrested and imprisoned.[32] This is symptomatic of a larger indigenous ethnocentrism that is concentrated in the country's western region. Whatever democracy exists in Turkey seems limited to its western half, since eastern Anatolia, especially the Kurdish regions in the southeast, is largely left out of the Istanbul-Ankara-Izmir power triangle.

In quasi democracies, therefore, democracy has a different meaning for the political elite than it does for the average citizen. Civil society is either nonexistent or does not reach beyond the immediate confines of elite circles. The elites may indeed abide by an elaborate set of democratic rules, but those rules are not the same ones that society has developed in its relations with the state. *Politics,* in other words, may be democratic, but the *political culture* is not. And a political culture that is either largely undemocratic or only halfheartedly democratic is one easily swayed in different directions. In the absence of civil society, popular public perceptions can become especially vulnerable to storms of dogmatism and ideology and to movements that offer quick salvation and a sense of conviction lacking in incumbent politicians. History is full of examples of democratic experiments that have collapsed, sometimes with tragic consequences, under the weight of nondemocratic cultures. Witness the fall of the Weimar Republic and the rise of Adolf Hitler, or the political ascent of Juan Perón in Argentina.[33]

Democratization and Political Crafting

Not all scholars and students of democracy agree, however, with the premise of the argument made above—that democracy requires a significant social and cultural component. In fact, the most recent studies on the subject have focused predominantly on the *political* dynamics involved in democratic transitions. At least at the start, they maintain, it is primarily through political crafting that democracies are brought about. This line of analysis has been convincingly argued by Giuseppe Di Palma and Samuel Huntington, who does, however, include a particular cultural axiom in his arguments.[34] Political culture and its particular democratic derivative, civil society, are not seen by either Huntington or Di Palma as important ingredients in the initial establishment and later evolution of a democratic polity. Di Palma argues that a democratic political culture, while beneficial, is not a necessary precondition for democratization.[35] Such a political culture, he asserts, will evolve as the democratic game itself progresses. A "rooted democratic culture and social tolerance fostered by limited class inequalities or by ethnic and national homogeneity will augur well for a democratic transition." "Genuine democrats," however, "need not precede democracy" (30). Democracy rests on a "borrowed or presumptive legitimacy" and on the prospects of an alternative more appealing than those offered by nondemocracies (31). Democratic rules must therefore be implemented, and political actors need to be convinced that these are the only rules available. This, in fact, is the biggest challenge to new democracies: to convince otherwise nondemocratic actors to play by the rules of the democratic game. And this can only be achieved by the successful negotiation of a democratic pact and the actual performance of the new democratic system. Still, nondemocratic actors need not be totally converted—what is necessary is for their values and behavior to be affected and modified (111). Di Palma's recommendation is straightforward: "If you wish to set up an attractive democratic game, do not delay. The proof of the pudding, especially for those who have not yet developed a taste for it, is in the eating" (79).

Huntington's arguments about the importance of political culture to democracy are more specific. On the one hand, he maintains, a democratic political culture is not a prerequisite for the establishment of a democratic political system. On the other hand, as argued in his more recent writings, there are some cultures that are inherently antidemocratic and thwart the possibility for democratic openings. Most transitions to democracy, according to Huntington, have tended to take place in one of three global "waves," the first two having been mostly reversed. The first wave of democratization occurred between 1828 and 1926 but was reversed from around 1922 to 1942. The second wave took place between 1943 and 1962 and was reversed from about 1958 to 1975. The third wave of democratization, which is currently in progress, started in 1974.[36] Each of these waves, Huntington states, was the result of historically specific political and economic dynamics. In the nineteenth century, a number of national democratic institutions emerged as the result of a historical phenomenon (26). The second wave of democratization, which occurred after World War II, was largely the result of the Allied occupation of such previously nondemocratic countries as West Germany, Austria, Japan, and Korea (18). In the third wave, democratization developed not so much by foreign imposition as by the political transformation of elites, their replacement by others, or a combination of both ("transplacement") (114). Nowhere in his analysis does Huntington make room for the integral role of democratic political culture.

Huntington argues, however, that while a specific culture may not be particularly favorable to democracy, others may be "profoundly antidemocratic" (300). Huntington points to Islam and Confucianism as two examples of nondemocratic cultures that, he asserts, "would impede the spread of democratic norms in the society, deny legitimacy to democratic institutions, and thus greatly complicate if not prevent the emergence and effectiveness of those institutions" (298). Confucianism emphasizes the primacy of the group over the individual, authority over liberty, and responsibilities over rights. "Confucian societies," therefore, "lacked a tradition of rights against the state; to the extent that if individual rights did exist, they were created by the state" (300). Islamic doctrine can be as receptive to democracy as it is antithetical to such a political system. The peculiar mixture of religion and politics in the Middle East, however, has made Islamic cultures decidedly antidemocratic. "To the extent that governmental legitimacy and policy flow from religious doctrine and expertise, Islamic concepts of politics differ from and contradict the premises of political democracy" (307). But Huntington tempers his discussion of cultural obstacles to democracy by concluding that cultures, dynamic as they are, change and will not remain indefinitely antagonistic to democracy. Ultimately, he believes, it is poverty, not culture, that may be the principal obstacle to democratic development. "The future of democracy depends on the future of economic development," he warns. "Obstacles to economic development are obstacles to the expansion of democracy" (311).

Huntington's assertions regarding the cultural incompatibilities of Islam and Confucianism with democracy are important and worthy of serious examination, but they must be considered in conjunction with his later claims in the highly controversial article, "The Clash of Civilizations?"[37] This is essentially a work of cultural geography and entails a bold synthesis of some of the ideas that had appeared in his book *The Third Wave* and earlier essays.[38] One of the most striking claims of "The Clash of Civilizations?" is that Islamic and Confucian societies are likely to emerge as the next great enemies of the West. Ideological or economic priorities, according to the article, already have or will soon cease to be sources of division and conflict and will be replaced by the new fault lines of civilizational identity.[39] "The central axis of world politics in the future is likely to be ... the conflict between 'the West and the Rest' and the responses of non-Western civilizations to Western power and values" (41). The most likely civilizational conflict, Huntington states, will be between an alliance of Confucian and Islamic civilizations and the West.

> Those countries that for reason of culture or power do not wish to, or cannot, join the West compete with the West by developing their economic, military and political power. They do this by promoting their internal development and by cooperating with other non-Western countries. The most prominent form of this cooperation is the Confucian-Islamic connection that has emerged to challenge Western interests, values and power. (45)

Within a larger scholarly context, Huntington's assignment of anti-democratic cultural traits to Islam and Confucianism becomes somewhat suspect. As the following chapters demonstrate, the current predicaments of Middle Eastern cultures, *in conjunction with the specific forms of political and economic dynamics in the region,* render the appearance of viable democratic systems there unlikely. In this respect, Huntington's conclusion is not without merit; what is questionable, however, is the intent behind the conclusion and the inferences drawn from it.

What is emerging in the Middle East is not indicative of clashing civilizations but rather the product of profound social and cultural changes that have left people hopelessly lost and disillusioned. In such supposed ultraconservative societies as Iran and Saudi Arabia, as well as in the ostensibly more liberal Turkey and Tunisia, one is just as likely to find men with shoulder-length hair, leather jackets, and John Lennon-style glasses as those whose bushy beards attest to their piety and devotion to religion. If civilizations are indeed clashing, they are doing so within the Middle Eastern psyche itself and throwing into confusion a cultural order once emotionally and politically more stable. What is emerging from all of this is a new form of socially grounded political discourse through which the state caters to the ebb and flow of popular sentiments. The volatile verbal barrages that Middle Eastern politicians are so fond of spewing out should not be confused with deeper manifestations of civilizational identity. The agendas of the state and the sensibilities of the masses have seldom been parallel, and the instances when the two have dovetailed were only temporary. There is a deep cultural schizophrenia running rampant throughout Middle Eastern societies, and most states, especially those with few or no ideological convictions—Turkey, Jordan, Kuwait, Bahrain, Qatar, Egypt, Tunisia, and Morocco, for example—find themselves performing endless balancing acts in order to stay one step ahead of their societies. Other states more convinced of having found the Right Path—Iran and Algeria, to mention two extreme examples—stick forcefully to their guns and shove their ideological and cultural agendas down their societies' throats. The result is what in the West has come to be known as "Islamic fundamentalism," replete with a host of bloody and menacing manifestations. This ideology is a product not of clashes *between* civilizations but rather from *within* them, and of clashes between civilizations and the states that seek to govern them.

The Politics of Crafting

While Di Palma and (to a lesser extent) Huntington de-emphasize the significance of cultural factors in the transition to democracy, they both highlight the importance of political crafting to the establishment and successful operation of a democratic system. As Di Palma sees it, "Democratization is ultimately a matter of political crafting."[40] This crafting is the most important aspect of the transition to democratic rule: "Reaching democratic agreement is sufficient to usher in a fruitful period of implementation and institutionalization, with all that the period holds in store for democratic stabilization" (134). The initial impulse toward democratization, according to Di Palma, comes from within the nondemocratic state itself because it has "a proclivity to deteriorate through self-exhaustion" (35). Such states, he claims, often either face internal paralysis and incapacitation or, alternately, liberalize a little and hence give rise to expectations they cannot control. It is at such an impasse that a democratic compromise between elements of the old regime (the "right") and proponents of democracy (the "left") seems to be the most viable option. "The challenge is how to reconcile those forces and interests to a democratic compromise while, at a minimum, removing those structures that are incompatible with political democracy" (36). Between the countervailing forces of the right and the left is a center "with an implicit bias for democracy, or more simply, with a bias for strategic moderation. This strategic objective of the center is the immediate reconstitution of an open and diverse political community. Its moderating behavior is crucial, though not sufficient, in determining the outcome of the crisis" (49). It is only at this point that some social factors may come into play. The deepening of the political crisis occurs, Di Palma argues, simultaneously with a steady gathering of momentum by elements of civil society, and thus democracy shows itself as an increasingly more appealing option.

> Disagreement is likely to manifest itself precisely when democracy gathers credit as a potential way to resolve the regime crisis. For at the same time, a diverse civil society will be gathering greater self-confidence and a more central role, parties will be reconstituted, barriers to their reconstitution will be lowered, organizations reflecting various cleavages in society (class, regional, ethnic) will begin agitating, and the season of elections will approach. (39)

The ultimate task for democratization, then, is to strike a balanced, acceptable pact between the various transition actors involved, and its success can be tested by holding democratic elections. Moreover, regardless of which actors come into power—whether from the right, the left, or the center—they cannot be oblivious to the agendas and priorities of the other actors. "Though democracy is about uncertainty," Di Palma warns, "there is a minimum of corporate identities, vital to the functional and institutional interests of some transitional actors, not easily subjected to uncertainty. They are not the objects of a competitive game; rather they define the boundaries of the game" (89–90).

Huntington's analyses of the dynamics of democratization are also politically grounded; in fact, he assigns an even less critical role to political culture than does Di Palma. Huntington points to three developments in structural and institutional crises within authoritarian regimes as the most important catalysts for democratic transition: the transformation of political elites, from which reformers emerge among authoritarian leaders and, for various reasons, press for an opening of the political process; the replacement of the old elite through state-sponsored elections or other political events in which they lose and have to relinquish power (as in the Philippines and throughout eastern Europe); and transplacement, in which the combined actions of government and opposition actors bring about a democratic system.[41] In all three instances, the actual transition to a democratic system is most feasibly achieved through the successful negotiation of a democratic pact. "How were democracies made?" His answer:

> They were made by the methods of democracy; there was no other way. They were made through negotiations, compromises, and agreements.

They were made through demonstrations, campaigns, and elections, and through the nonviolent resolution of differences. They were made by the political leaders in governments and oppositions who had the courage both to challenge the status quo and to subordinate the immediate interests of their followers to the long-term needs of democracy. They were made by leaders in government and opposition who withstood the provocations to violence by opposition radicals and government standpatters. They were made by leaders in government and opposition who had the wisdom to recognize that in politics no one has a monopoly on truth and virtue. Compromise, elections, and nonviolence were the third wave democratization syndrome. In varying degrees they characterized most of the transformations, replacements, and transplacements of that wave. (164–65)

Within this formula the role of political culture or other social dynamics is at best secondary. Huntington never explicitly explores the sociocultural imperatives that compel social actors to seek a democratic solution to their unhappy political predicament. He simply states that "the leaders of key political forces and social groups in society bargained with each other, explicitly or implicitly, and worked out acceptable if not satisfying arrangements for the transition to democracy" (166). Huntington does argue that "some cultures appear to be more favorable to compromise than others" (171), but, as previously mentioned, his concern is more with antidemocratic cultural traits than with the development of those that enhance and facilitate democratic possibilities.

This summary does not, admittedly, cover all the pertinent aspects of Di Palma's and Huntington's arguments, much of which focus on the stability of the democratic system *after* transition has been successfully completed. But it does describe the role that the two theorists assign to civil society in the process of a democratic transition. My debate with their analyses does not revolve around the importance of political crafting to democracy—clearly, political crafting plays a highly crucial role during all stages of the transition to and the establishment of a democratic political system. Where I differ with Huntington and Di Palma is in the exact stage at which I see civil society and its constituent organizations playing a determining role. As demonstrated, neither Huntington nor Di Palma attributes great significance to civil society as a—not the only—catalyst for democratic yearning before the actual political transition is set in motion. I maintain, however, that civil society, which is narrowly defined here as society's democratic self-organization, is in fact instrumental both in effecting the initial popular impulse toward democratic change and in determining the overall flavor of the subsequent democratic system. Ultimately, the question to ask is from where did the imperative to democratize come? If it comes largely from above, that is, as a result of mostly elite bargaining and negotiations, the resultant political system may be a quasi democracy, one in which the institutions and mechanisms of democracy are not necessarily complemented by accompanying social and cultural bonds. If, however, the impulse toward democratization comes from below, that is, as a result of the democratic agitations of groups and strata within society, then the political system that eventually emerges from the chaos (i.e., the disruption of old patterns of state-society relations) will probably have a powerful civil society component. Apart from its political characteristics, such a system would be socially and culturally resonant as well. For a political system to be a viable democracy and not become quasi-democratic, civil society must *precede* democratic political crafting. Democracy, as Di Palma maintains, may not be a "hothouse plant" and it may be easily transplanted into different national contexts given the right kind of political crafting.[42] But the outcome, while democratic, may not necessarily have social and cultural resonance. Democracy, as argued here, has a strong social and cultural component. Understanding how it is created and sustained, therefore, is as much a matter of sociological investigation as it is of political analysis.

Civil Society in Comparative Perspective

As the diversity of scholarly opinion indicates, the examination of democracy and democratization requires a sharper focus. Concurrent with political analysis, attention must be paid to the exact juncture at which civil society appears and the precise role it plays. In some democratization processes, civil society either does not initially play a determining role and emerges later, or it does not appear at all, even well into the life of the supposedly democratic country. Examples of countries in southern Europe are most instructive in this respect. In Greece, Portugal, and Spain during the mid-1970s, when each country witnessed a democratic transition, civil society was nascent only at the time of the change and caught off guard largely by the collapse of the old order and its transformation into a democratic one.[43] Today democracy seems to be stable in each of these countries, where it is built on a strong foundation of civil society.[44] Turkey, on the other hand, is an exception. While its transition to a democratic system has long been completed, Turkey's social and cultural transformation has not yet taken place.[45] Civil society, in other words, has not evolved and is not expected to develop anytime soon.[46] Thus the Turkish political system is at best quasi-democratic and highly susceptible to populist and demagogic movements from below.[47] This is not, however, what has happened in most of the democratic transitions in eastern Europe and South America, often where civil society appeared first and then eventually led to democratic political change. In such countries as Poland, Hungary, the former Czechoslovakia, Argentina, and Brazil, civil society preceded, sometimes by many years, the actual political transformation of authoritarian structures into democratic ones. From the start, then, the political system in each of these countries began as a viable democracy, sustained not only by democratic institutions but also by a democratized and democratizing society.

Democratic transitions are set into motion by the workings of two general dynamics that can be broadly classified as either structural or valuative. All democratic transitions involve structural transformations, for without such changes the actual institutional mechanisms of democracy, ranging from interelite pacts to constitutional guarantees, would not come about. In such instances, democratization is often initiated from above and then set into motion as a direct result of nuances and developments that are indigenous to the state. State breakdown or weakness compels old political elites to open up the political process to accommodate other contending elites. When the democratic transition is complete, the new elite face the task of democratic consolidation, which involves not only structural and institutional engineering but also popularizing the norms of democracy within the larger population. In a few Third World democracies, the new system enjoys high levels of valuative consolidation despite having been the result of negotiated pacts among elites. Argentina, Brazil, Chile, and South Korea all fall into this category (as do Greece, Portugal, and Spain), for in all of them democracy was initiated from above and became culturally accepted and popularized (sooner in some cases and later in others) among the various social strata. For whatever reason, democratic elites, however, do not always actively try to consolidate or succeed in consolidating democracy culturally; therefore, the resultant democratic system becomes more elitist instead of evolving into a truly representative democracy. This has occurred in many ostensibly democratic countries of the Third World, such as Kenya, Tanzania, Zambia, and Madagascar in Africa; Costa Rica, Colombia, and Venezuela in Latin America; Taiwan, India, Sri Lanka, Bangladesh, and Pakistan in South and Southeast Asia; and Lebanon and Turkey in the Middle East.

Democratic transitions initiated from above, in short, face the *potential*, not the inherent, danger of resulting in elitist, quasi-democratic polities that have all the institutional and structural trappings of democracy but lack a strong valuative component that would give them resonance among the different strata of society.

Not all democratic transitions are initiated from above, and those that are a result of societal nuances in general and civil-society agitations in particular cannot help but have a strong valuative component when and if they eventually succeed in establishing a democratic order. In these transitions, the impulse to democratize begins not within the state but with nonstate groups and actors, some of whom ask specifically for democratic rights while others may have demands that are limited to particular issues. In either case, in the predemocratization era certain societal actors begin to demand greater space and political autonomy, and many of them over time join organized or semiorganized grassroots movements that become civil-society organizations. If these organizations, which by definition must operate democratically from within, demand and succeed in creating a democratic polity, they themselves then become the societal and valuative supports on which the new system rests. In a way, the new democratic polity is already culturally consolidated *before* the actual democratic transition takes place; otherwise, civil society organizations could not have gained enough support and momentum to force the authoritarian state to agree to democratic concessions. And once broadly based, increasingly popular grassroots organizations have succeeded in bringing about a democratic polity, they are not about to take their newly won liberties for granted or to allow democratic rights to be practiced primarily by specific elite groups. They strive to be active in the political process and to ensure the democratic and representational integrity of the system.

Civil society–driven viable democracies are comparatively rare, but they have occurred in recent years in Poland, Hungary, and most notably, South Africa. These democratic systems are not only representative of broad strata of society but also highly self-conscious. Eventually, citizens begin to take such democratic systems for granted, as happens in most long-established democracies. But in the years immediately following the democratic transition, when their energy is maintained by the very newness of the system, they are far more vibrant than quasi democracies could ever hope to become. In viable democracies, membership levels in political parties tend to increase, voter turn-outs are relatively high, elections—not only national elections but also regional and local ones—are often engaging, serious contests, the media is free and by and large vigilant, and frequently a growing array of issue-driven grassroots organizations springs up to facilitate increasing levels of popular political input.

Democratic transitions that result in viable democracies are most frequently initiated from below, that is, through pressure exerted on the state by various autonomously organized social groups. In such instances, the state and society have few cultural links (or none at all) to bind them together, their interrelations being based largely or exclusively on coercion by the state and submission by society. The state, therefore, is praetorian par excellence, having virtually no popular ideological legitimacy and relying heavily on a mammoth bureaucracy and a brutal police force to stay in power. Not only is the state's ideology devoid of any meaningful resonance among the populace—often, as in the former communist bloc, state actors themselves do not really believe in its validity—but also the state has no other means of, or at least not the wherewithal for, establishing some extrainstitutional links with society. State actors do not have charisma; state policies are not populist; and the political culture on which the state relies and which the masses experience have nothing in common. The valuative chasm between state and society is wide and seemingly unbridgeable. This gap translates into and is further magnified by the pursuit of state policies and agendas that, if not outright offensive, are insensitive to the needs of the masses. Such states often go against the cultural grain of their societies by trampling on deeply held religious and traditional beliefs, fomenting nationalist anger, forming alliances with unpopular international actors, and/or pursuing economic policies generally perceived as ruinous. These state models perfectly describe the former bureaucratic-authoritarian states in South America and the communist ones in eastern and central Europe. Most contemporary African and Middle Eastern states, however, have managed to devise a variety of cultural, noninstitutional means to solidify and complement institutional ties with their respective societies. In Africa most nominally democratic regimes, and even some overtly authoritarian ones, have allowed just enough political space to contending social forces to blunt their potentially disruptive nature, although not always successfully.[48] A vast majority of Middle Eastern states have been highly effective in placating social opposition by playing up to (and into) whatever culturally resonant forces happen to dictate popular norms and values—they adopt religion and make it official (hence *Islam rasmi*, "official Islam"), the leader becomes a father to the nation and relies on a patriarchal cult of personality, government nepotism becomes a normal method of co-option into the system, and so forth.

In addition to political dynamics, society also experiences its own changes in transitions to democracy. The lack of viable cultural and functional links with the state prompts social actors to look to themselves for providing organizational alternatives to those official agencies of the government that they perceive as useless, corrupt, coercive, and manipulated. These are most frequently well-educated members of the middle class who, although direct products of government economic policies, nevertheless cannot be co-opted by the state. Through social change and economic development, these middle-class professionals have reached a comparatively high level of affluence, but their elevated social status makes them all the more alienated from the state, which they view only in an adversarial light. Thus they form politically autonomous groups and organizations that not only are independent of the state but also are meant to replace some of the state's specific cultural and functional operations. For example, if the state does not allow open expression of political thought, these organizations provide a forum for it (the Civic Forum in the former Czechoslovakia is a case in point). While the state may ridicule or suppress religion, some organizations may be devoted to spreading religious gospel and other teachings (e.g., Base Ecclesiastical Communities in Latin America). While the state's glorification of the workers may be hollow propaganda, some groups may try to do something to enhance work conditions and wages (Solidarity in Poland is an example). These organizations are the building blocks of civil society; they are autonomous, self-organized, and political in consequence, if not in original intent. But they must also have an additional characteristic, one that is of great significance: they must be democratic in their internal workings as well as in their larger political goals. Forming a politically autonomous organization in itself is no indication of a burgeoning, democratic civil society. Most states can easily dismantle or assimilate such organizations through repression or corporatist modifications. A civil-society organization must have overt democratic goals, no matter how specific or narrowly defined those goals may be, and it must press the state for greater accessibility to the political process instead of simply asking that particular demands be met. Civil-society groups may come perilously close to corporatist ones, but they must at all times remain focused on achieving the larger goals of democracy. This is no minor feat, for it involves not only democratically committed intellectuals but also, more important, an internal, psychic transformation of the authoritarian self into a democratic one. Democratic intellectuals must establish links of their own with the larger population to gain popular acceptance of their ideals—they must sell the idea of democracy to the people—and that is neither easy nor, under authoritarian circumstances, always possible. I argue later that the social mechanisms and conditions necessary for the emergence of civil society, at least based on the criteria presented here, are conspicuously absent from the Middle East.

Stages of Democratization

It is only logical that a transition to democratic rule involve different stages and that in each stage a different set of factors and dynamics be at work. Transition stages, of course, often overlap, and nuances involved in one stage often spill over into the next. Given the determining influence that the timing of civil society's emergence plays, however, it is important to distinguish the characteristics of each transition stage. Where the democratic impulse emanates from below, social actors begin to agitate not just for political space but specifically for democratic liberties. They either organize themselves into new organizations that are specifically set up to further their demands, such as Solidarity in Poland, or they reformulate the nature and the message of existent organizations to express their agendas (the Catholic Church in both Latin America and eastern Europe is an example). As with most spontaneous revolutions, their demands, which are met with increasing acceptance in society, begin to snowball, and the state is gradually confronted with a serious political crisis that it cannot easily contain. Soon negotiations are the only viable option available to the political elite, resulting in an actual transfer of power through elections, followed by an institutional consolidation of the new order through the ratification of a constitution, the appointment of new policymakers and bureaucrats, and so forth. The important point is that this kind of society-initiated democratization is the result of the workings of civil society, which has set in motion the political dynamics that culminate in the replacement of the old order with a new democratic one. Thus social actors, the most important of whom, politically speaking, are the primary components of civil society, have a vested interest in maintaining the integrity of the new system. It is precisely for this reason that the incoming democratic regime is a viable one.

But the stages involved and the precise chronology of events in democratic transitions from above are quite different (see table 1.1, p. 22). In such instances, state actors are first faced with some unsettling development that is often their own doing, an indigenously initiated problem with which they cannot deal effectively. Their inability to handle this difficulty is compounded by the untenable institutional and structural predicaments that such regimes have often forced themselves into, so that soon a situation of paralysis and dysfunction evolves, initially localized to the state. The structural weaknesses of the state are then exploited by various social actors who seize the opportunity to press on the state specific demands that may or may not be democratic. Negotiations follow and a *controlled* transition process begins, one that assures the state parties that the incoming order will not be harsh in its prosecution of them. The negotiations have an air of democracy about them, and all the parties gather around the negotiating table with claims of acting in democracy's interests. Thus the outcome of the negotiations is ostensibly democratic, with elections, a liberal democratic constitution, and all the other necessary trappings. But there are no popular mass elements involved in these negotiations—no electrician-*cum*-national hero, no struggle per se, no grand rethinking of

TABLE 1.1

STAGES IN DEMOCRATIC TRANSITIONS

	Transition from below	*Transition from above*
Catalyst:	Civil society	Internal political turmoil
Process:	Shake-up Crisis Negotiation and transition Institutional consolidation	Crisis Negotiation and transition Institutional consolidation
Probable outcome:	Viable democracy	Quasi democracy

national priorities and cultural dispositions. It is the elite who negotiate, and it is the elite who win—those who belong on the government's side and those who claim to represent the masses. The system they usher in cannot be anything but elitist, even if it is democratic. Such a system is quite likely to end up as a quasi democracy, a quintessentially elitist political system wrapped in a thin democratic disguise.

A number of significant questions arise. Exactly what actors, it is important to ask, are involved in the democratization process and at what stage? What ties, if any, do these actors have to their respective constituents within the state or within the larger society? What exactly is civil society and how does it come about? And, once established, how does civil society become routinized? These questions are addressed in the remainder of this chapter.

Social Actors and Democratization

Four general kinds of actors, slight differences and/or overlaps notwithstanding, are involved in almost every democratic transition. What differs from one case to another, and what eventually determines the nature and overall direction of the transition, is the exact point in the process at which each actor becomes involved. The four kinds of actors are *intellectuals*, who at first act as representatives of the larger society; specific *political actors* from the state; various other *state institutions*, the influence of which may not be direct but is nevertheless consequential; and *social institutions*, for which intellectuals claim to be acting. In one form or another, each actor is found in virtually every transition process (see table 1.2). In one kind of democratization, therefore, social actors take the

TABLE 1.2

NATURE AND CHRONOLOGICAL INVOLVEMENT
OF TRANSITION ACTORS

Viable democratic transitions		
Intellectuals	►	Grassroots movements and political parties, tied directly to the masses
Political actors	►	Weakened, eager to compromise
State institutions	►	Military, political parties, etc., willing to negotiate
Social institutions	►	Religion, family, etc., democratizing and/or democratized
Quasi-democratic transitions		
Political actors	►	Compelled to reform
Intellectuals	►	Seeking democracy; weak ties to the masses
State institutions	►	Retaining many privileges and nondemocratic traits
Social institutions	►	Not always fully democratized

lead in the transition process from the very start, while in another they come into play at a later date when, by its own initiatives, the regime has signaled its willingness to change and be transformed. State and society, in other words, take primary and secondary roles in different kinds of democratizations, and this role is played by specific groups and institutions within them.

Intellectuals are the particular product of one of society's constituent institutions. As I discuss in chapter 2, every society is made up of a number of institutions that bestow on their members a corporate sense of identity and a specific sense of belonging. A number of social institutions are universal and can be found in all societies (e.g., the family, religion, an educational system), while some are specific to particular societies (e.g., race, tribe, ethnicity). As a distinct group within society, intellectuals are products of the educational establishment who, by virtue of the status they have attained, often formulate and express some of the nuances within society that may have otherwise remained uncommunicated.[49] Their role in Third World societies is especially crucial, and all the more so in democratic transitions because they are often the ones who formulate democratic demands and serve as the state's contacts with the rest of society. This mediating function is accomplished through various grassroots movements or political parties, such as Solidarity in Poland, the Civic Forum in the former Czechoslovakia, and the New Forum in the former East Germany, that are independent of the state. But a number of important qualifications need to be made. Not all intellectuals seek democracy, and despite the rhetoric of many, the likes of the Czech Republic's Václav Havel are rare.[50] But even if there are genuinely democratic intellectuals who wish to see real democracy in their country, few enjoy the luxury of having meaningful cultural ties with the rest of their society. In most Third World countries, intellectuals, as an elite social group, are often isolated and detached from other social institutions, operating in a world of their own that is alienated from the general cultural texture and norms of the larger society. It is one thing for intellectuals to yearn for democracy; it is quite another to give social resonance and meaning to that yearning.

The ties that intellectuals have with the rest of society, therefore, are an important determinant in the precise nature of a democratic transition. In transitions brought about as a result of pressure from below, where intellectuals have spearheaded an increasingly popular social movement to overturn a dictatorial state, intellectuals possess strong ties to the rest of society. These ties, more than anything else, are normative and valuative: the intellectuals' call for political democracy has real and tangible meaning for the other social classes whom they address. The intellectuals are, in other words, operating within a civil society in which their calls for democracy are occurring simultaneously with a social and cultural transformation of a receptive society. Ad hoc, unofficial groups spring up at the grassroots level and make the abstraction of democracy a tangible reality at the local level. As Solidarity and the "Beer Drinkers' Party" in Poland show, some of these grassroots movements later become actual political parties in the democratic era. This is the crucial axiom of civil society that turns successful democratic transitions initiated from below into viable democracies. At a time when intellectuals are pressing for democratic openings, society is also undergoing its own democratic transformation, and the two complement and reinforce each other. The emerging democratic system cannot help but have a strong social and cultural component.

Civil Society

The most apparent manifestations of civil society are found in such grassroots pressure groups, which may be diverse in their intentions and compositions; in fact, they may have nothing in common insofar as their stated purposes and agendas are concerned. But they all have one crucial common denominator: to press the state for greater political space—*they demand democracy.* The social and political autonomy of such organized groups is of critical importance, but it is not enough. If we were to end the discussion here, backgammon players in the teahouses of the Middle East or beer lovers in Poland and the Czech Republic would have to be considered as progenitors of civil society; they are not. Nor is civil society made up of just any group that manages to exert pressure on the state for political cooperation or even space. Under this definition, most corporatist institutions pressing demands on the state, such as labor or the Catholic Church in Latin America in the 1960s and 1970s, would also have to be considered as components of civil society, and that is not always the case. Civil society gives rise to a very specific kind of organization—one that is *social* in origin and composition but *political* in its broader agendas and impact. It is an organization formed from the autonomous initiatives of politically concerned individuals. These social actors are united by a common cause, often rallying around a specific issue (greater political space or less literary censorship, for instance). But regardless of the cause, if the actors' demands on the state were met, they would either directly or indirectly result in greater accessibility to the political process.

In his pathbreaking study of civil society, Ernest Gellner offers a similar, organizationally based definition of the phenomenon in its "simplest, immediate and intuitively obvious" form:

> that set of diverse non-governmental institutions which is strong enough to counter-balance the state and, while not preventing the state from ful-

filling its role of keeper of the peace and arbitrator between major interests, can nevertheless prevent it from dominating and atomizing the rest of society.[51]

Gellner sees civil society as first and foremost a liberator from the tyranny of social and cultural rituals. But in addition to its social and cultural ramifications, civil society has a more pointed political function. Because civil-society organizations and groups are agents of democratization, the cumulative effect of their pressures on the state could overwhelm political leaders with exhausted legitimacies and limited, noncoercive means of governance.

The point to bear in mind here is the chronological order in which civil society and democratization take place. First, there are social pressures for democratic openings, which then crystalize into civil-society groups that are democratic in nature. If these groups coalesce or mount on their own a political challenge that the state cannot fend off, then a successful process of democratization takes place. Once democratization occurs, it provides a more hospitable environment for additional civil-society groups to take shape and evolve, but democratization would not have taken place had it not been for the early formation of some established civil-society groups.

How does civil society come about? A number of complementary social and political forces need to be present simultaneously for civil society and the groups representing it to emerge. A praetorian political system is a prerequisite, for democratic yearnings must first be formulated and then rejected by state authorities before groups begin to look to alternative nonstate agencies for political expression. More specifically, the praetorian state and the larger society must operate in different, mutually exclusive cultural realms. The average citizen must feel not only disenchanted with the state but also disenfranchised from it. No norms or values attach to the state with which he or she can identify, and there is a stark contrast between his or her cultural orientations and whatever it is the state stands for. Such a state might seem to operate in a world of its own, detached from the cultural contexts of its society, apparently unaware of or insensitive to social and cultural needs emanating from below. With the exception of Tito's somewhat charismatic rule of Yugoslavia, the former communist states of eastern and central Europe fit this model perfectly, as do the many bureaucratic-authoritarian regimes that dotted Latin America in the 1960s and 1970s. Other possible configurations might involve a society that is religious at its core, while the state is either aggressively secular or deliberately antireligious; a society in which industrialization has not progressed to the point of superseding agrarian life, while the state pretends to be industrially advanced and highly modernized; a society that wants to be autonomous, while the state seeks to penetrate and change it; or a society that wants to express itself politically and to participate in the system, while the state subdues and controls it. At every turn, the state and society diverge and conflict with each other. Nothing but animosity and distrust exists between them—no political culture that could be manipulated by politicians and accepted by the people, no halfhearted democracy to placate the demands for real participation, no charismatic leader who could find devotees among the masses.

But this is only the political half of the equation, one based on a clash of perspectives between the state and those who regard it as at best apathetic and at worst adversarial to their hopes and aspirations. The political roadblocks created by the state compel these individuals to form civil-society organizations of their own in an attempt both to replace some of the specific functions of the state and to provide themselves with channels of democratic expression. Who exactly are these individuals who come together to form civil-society organizations? And what social and cultural imperatives prompt them to do so? The answers lie in the particular formation of social forces that the state is seeking to thwart. The pivotal role of intellectuals in the flowering of civil society has already been discussed. Intellectuals alone are not enough, however, because every society has its own intelligentsia, no matter how minuscule and socially powerless it may be. If civil society is to develop, the intelligentsia must have three particular characteristics. First and foremost, it must be committed to the principles and practices of democracy to the extent of having internalized them. Simple rhetoric and heroism do not make a democratic intellectual; he or she must be a believer in and a practitioner of democracy in everything from urging it on those at work to discussing it with family members or others with different viewpoints. Equally important is the social resonance of intellectuals in terms of both the message they have and their accessibility to the rest of society. Elite intellectuals, in other words, cannot be too *elite* in their social standing, but must be close enough to the population to be heard and understood, if not followed by them. Finally, intellectuals must find for themselves an institutional forum, no matter how informal, through which they can meet and circulate ideas, solidify their links with one or more social classes, and bring direct or indirect pressure on the state. Such institutional forums may range from ad hoc clubs and syndicates (e.g., a writer's association or the Civic Forum) to full-blown grassroots organizations (CEBs) and political parties (Solidarity).

For the voices of civil society's intellectuals to resonate requires certain social preconditions, chief among them a homogeneous national culture and a spirit of tolerance. Without a standardization of culture, social actors cannot fully comprehend one another, let alone unite to achieve the goals for which civil society stands. "The old segmentary societies of various kinds," Gellner explains, "highlighted and fortified the boundaries between the segments by accentuated cultural differentiation: people spoke, ate, dressed, etc., differently according to their precise location in a complex, intricate social structure."[52] Their possibilities for unification under civil society were thus minimized. Civil society requires cultural uniformity on a national level, whereby people are bound not by segmentary, exclusivist institutions that differentiate but by associations that are instrumental and effective.[53]

National cultural homogeneity is necessary but not enough. In addition, civil society requires the psychological transformation of the individual on a personal level and of the larger collective whole—be it a syndicate, political party, or an entire nation—to which he or she belongs. Communicating through the same idiom that is free of ritualized subcontexts is an essential prerequisite to forming voluntary associations and groups. Thus people who come from different parts of the country and have different accents may form an association in which their unified goals for the organization are emphasized, despite their differences. In countries with a semblance of national culture, that is how most organizations of workers, teachers, merchants, and writers are formed and operate. But taking an active part in an organization alone, while important, is inadequate for a burgeoning civil society. What must take place is an internalization of democratic norms and mores on an emotional, personal level. What must happen first is a democratization of the individual, and then individuals, and on and on from there to the larger community, until a critical mass of like-minded aspirants for democracy begin to exert pressure on the state.

Here the contest intensifies. Civil society presses democratic demands on the state and its various institutions, and much of the outcome of the transition depends on the precise manner in which these state institutions react to pressures from below. In this respect, the politically grounded analyses of Huntington and Di Palma have much to offer, especially regarding the role of the military.[54] The state and its various institutional arms must be vulnerable enough to democratic pressures from below for a viable democratic transition to take place. The specific political actors who are in official state positions at the time of democratization must have already been weakened—the reasons for this differ in each case—and thus they are eager to compromise with the opposition. Moreover, the different auxiliary institutions on which the officeholders' powers are directly or indirectly based (i.e., the military, the official political party, the bureaucracy) must also be willing to relinquish some of their privileges. The state need not be in complete paralysis for a viable democratic transition to occur, but it must be weak enough to compel those in official positions to come to the bargaining table. The situation in quasi-democratic transitions is often different because not all state institutions are sufficiently weakened to go along with a fully open democratization process. In some instances, state institutions, especially the military, demand extensive guarantees in the posttransition period and exert considerable influence afterward (the state institutions of Turkey, Peru, and Venezuela are examples). But transition processes do not always succeed, even partially, and in these cases the resistance of state actors has proven critical. Sometimes elements within the state are unwilling to yield to any democratic opening and thus seek to abort the democratization process altogether.

Some examples of successful, partial, and aborted democratic transitions better illustrate the point. In most of the former communist states of eastern Europe during the mid- and late 1980s, such crucial arms of the state as the Communist Party and the bureaucracy were in a state of near, if not complete, paralysis, but the army, which had not undergone the extensive atrophy of the other two institutions, still maintained much of its coercive capabilities. Nevertheless, when the democratic transition process gathered steam and began threatening the very existence of the communist state, the army did not, and in some instances could not, intervene in the political process. This sequence of events is markedly different from what happened in Algeria in the early 1990s, when the country witnessed a bloody reversal of the democratization process that had begun in the late 1980s.[55] When President Chadli Bendjedid ratified the country's liberal democratic constitution in 1989 and promised open parliamentary elections, the military scornfully looked on as its once-extensive powers were greatly reduced, while the Islamic Salvation Front (FIS), whom the military considered "antidemocratic," gained strength. When the FIS won a majority of seats in the 1992 parliamentary elections, the military duly stepped in, removed Bendjedid from power, annulled the elections, and reasserted itself as the dominant institution of the state. The military either had not been weakened enough or was somehow unwilling to accept the uncertain possibilities of a fully democratic transition.[56] Between these two extremes—one a viable transition and the other an aborted one —falls the Turkish situation. The Turkish army has always considered it-self to be the ultimate guardian of the Turkish Republic and the protector of the legacy of the country's modern founder, Atatürk.[57] Consistent with their sense of mission, the army launched a coup in 1980 in reaction to what it saw as the inability of politicians to maintain domestic order, and then it handed power over to elected civilians in 1983. Because this was a controlled transition, initiated and directed from above, the military re-tains extensive powers in today's Turkey, imposing severe limits on the country's democratic system.[58] The overall flavor and nature of Turkey's political system, at best a quasi democracy, is very different from the viable democratic systems of Poland and Hungary, both of which were largely the result of pressures from below.

Democracy and Culture

It seems only appropriate to conclude this section with a reminder about the centrality of political culture. A successful democratic transition does not simply end with careful and coercion-free negotiations, even if state institutions are genuinely willing to relinquish power to groups having emerged from grassroots movements. That step merely signals the end of the *transition* process, not the continued operation of a democratic polity. It is fully conceivable for previously authoritarian political structures to become democratic; however, such a transition process in itself does not give currency to the spirit of democracy among all social actors or even among all intellectuals.

How a democratic political culture originates and civil society flour-ishes depends on each specific case, but there are some universals. To be-gin with, there must be a democratically committed core of intellectuals. Not every university student or professor is an intellectual, and not every intellectual is a democrat. In the Third World, in fact, only recently have a number of intellectuals rejected the prevailing ideologies of communism, socialism, nationalism, or some other "ism" and instead embraced the tenets of democracy.[59] Democratic intellectuals must convince the masses to endorse democracy, and there needs to be a genuine, popular impera-tive for a democratic political system. It is ironic that the most brutal au-thoritarian dictatorships are often the best catalysts for the growth of popular democratic yearnings. The insanity of Nazism in Germany, the horrors of fascism in southern Europe and of bureaucratic-authoritarianism in South America, and the fallacies of life under communism in eastern Europe were all instrumental in instilling in the average citizen under those regimes a fundamental yearning for democracy. Democracy becomes culturally popular when all the other "isms," especially those with a penchant for bombastic chauvinism, exhaust themselves and fail to provide the salvation they promise. But not every authoritarian system drives its citizens to the opposite extreme and makes democrats of them. Few political systems, in fact, exhaust all their legitimacy as those mentioned above did. Most systems in the world today are successful in at least one or two of the functions that give them some legitimacy. Some systems effectively manipulate certain popular sentiments (nationalism is a favorite); others are economically successful enough to keep the middle class preoccupied or complacent; and still others acquiesce just enough to placate potential opposition activists. Most political systems manage to retain enough power to resist pressures for democratization.

Contrary to Di Palma's assertion, democracy is indeed a hothouse plant. It involves civil society and all the intricacies that come with it. Intellectuals must abandon demagoguery and agree to disagree. Sloganizing needs to give way to civil discourse; democracy has room for ideologues, not demagogues. More important, democracy requires civil society. Democracy must become culturally resonant and routinized, enough so that it eventually becomes a subconscious part of daily life and social, cultural, and political activity. There *is* a difference between culturally based viable democracies and culturally vacuous quasi democracies. Rarely does a democratic system devised from political crafting alone result in a congruent, democratic political culture. And such a culture is not one that appears overnight with ease or frequency. The prevailing norms of a society that govern its politics must become democratic; social classes must advocate those norms; and any nondemocratic forces and traits in social life and cultural thought must be devalued or abandoned. Only then can democracy—in the full sense of the word—be discussed.

Democracy in the Middle East

From the rigid preconditions for democracy spelled out above, the current prognosis for the appearance of democratic transitions in the Middle East does not seem positive. The following chapters show that the requisite social and cultural dynamics for the emergence of democratic movements and the maintenance of viable democracies are largely absent from the region—or, if present, are suppressed by the greater weights of economic or nondemocratic political priorities. Civil society, as defined and outlined earlier, has not found a hospitable environment in Middle Eastern societies, and its absence is reinforced by social and cultural forces that, for the time being at least, remain undemocratic, or even antidemocratic. As they now stand, Middle Eastern societies have neither the social classes and institutions nor the cultural disposition to give widespread credence to democratic norms and practices. It is the forces of primordialism, informality, and autocracy that have shaped and continue to shape the parameters of life in Middle Eastern societies—not proceduralism, formal politics, and democratic thought. The social institutions found in the region are even less amenable to democratically committed intellectuals or the more complex emergence of civil society. Islam, tribalism, the family, and informal gathering places have hardly served as facilitators for democracy, and the social institution that has the best chance of developing and then popularizing democratic ideals, namely, the intellectuals, has been more interested in sloganizing and name-calling than in giving popular currency to the tenets of democracy. The intellectuals' ties with their societies remain largely severed, while most social classes are absorbed in their insular worlds, having little contact with those stationed above and beneath them. In Gellnerian phraseology, Middle Eastern societies remain "segmentary"; they have yet to develop homogeneous national cultures.

The cultural forces at work in the Middle East have not helped the cause of democracy. Rapid, fundamental social change in some countries has upset any semblance of balance and tranquility their societies may once have had, and even the more conservative states of the Arabian peninsula have witnessed discontinuities in their traditions. Thus Middle Eastern cultures have been subject to much wrenching and disillusioning change, sending the average citizen in a troubling search for answers and remedies. Huntington's thesis about the clash of civilizations may not hold true on a global basis, but anyone from the Middle East will readily attest to the constant clash of cultures that he or she must contend with in the most mundane aspects of life—from watching television or listening to music to choosing an outfit and a style of appearance. Even one's manner of speech betrays his or her cultural dispositions, and one is often most concerned about escaping from or fitting into a distinct cultural category. Absolutisms of all kinds have emerged as the great cultural victors, tearing societies at the seams and leaving those in between bewildered and lost. The political culture, steeped in tradition and orthodoxy on the one hand and manipulated and machinated on the other, has had little inclination or opportunity to become democratic. The Middle Eastern state, for its part, has managed to carve out just enough of a social and cultural niche to impede possibilities for the development of meaningful civil-society organizations.

Civil Society in the Middle East

The proposition that civil society does not exist in the Middle East is likely to elicit sharp criticism from authors and scholars who have devoted entire journals and books to challenging this very point.[60] Most notable among them are Augustus Richard Norton and a group of collaborators who have deftly argued in *Civil Society in the Middle East* that such organizations not only exist but also are thriving.[61] Middle Eastern regimes are "facing persistent crises of government," they argue, and old political remedies are no longer yielding traditional results.[62] Thus, "the new language of politics in the Middle East talks about participation, cultural authenticity, freedom, and even democracy," according to Norton.

> No doubt, the defining flavor of the 1990s is participation. Like Coca Cola, "democracy" needs no translation to be understood virtually everywhere, yet the vocabulary of democracy is more succinct than the institutional variations that democracy may assume. There is no reason, a priori, that one variant or another of Western democracy is especially adaptable to other locales. Instead, scholars must be alert to the possibility that the Middle East will evolve its own characteristic style of democracy, no doubt with an Islamic idiom in some instances. (5)

Norton points to the flourishing of autonomous organizations, syndicate groups, and political parties as indications of a feverishly active civil society. The number of political parties in some of the region's countries are impressive indicators of a "blossoming civil society": 46 in Algeria; 43 in Yemen; 23 in Jordan; 19 in Morocco; 13 in Egypt; 11 in Tunisia; and 6 in Mauritania (9). More impressive, however, is the abundance of professional associations, businessmen's groups, and cultural clubs found especially in Algeria, Egypt, Iran, Israel, Kuwait, Turkey, Yemen, and in the Israeli-occupied territories (15). Of particular note is Kuwait's *diwaniyyah*, "a gathering place in leading citizens' homes where men (and in recent years a few women) gather to socialize and share views on a range of topics from sports to politics" (16). Other scholars seem more skeptical about the prospects of civil society in Kuwait, calling it "a work in progress" by "quasi-autonomous associations" that operate in a system that has "controlled participatory institutions."[63]

Other contributors to Norton's volume are equally enthusiastic about the existence of civil society in the region. Saad Eddin Ibrahim cites not only political parties and syndicates but also professional organizations that engage in "politics by proxy"—Kuwait's University Graduates Society, Qatar's Jassrah Cultural Club, and the United Arab Emirate's Association of Social Professions.[64] In Jordan, another contributor claims, there is a "growing vibrancy in the civic realm," as demonstrated by "greater respect for human rights, far greater freedom of expression, the emergence of political parties, the development of political satire (particularly in the theater), and the multitude of conferences, lectures, panel discussions, and meetings on a variety of topics." Nevertheless, she argues that what has been occurring there is at best a state-led process of "managed liberalization," not a full-scale democratization process.[65] Civil society has similarly evolved in Palestinian communities, states another author, where it is made up of political shops (*dakakin siyasiyyah*), voluntary cooperatives and mass organizations, and various Islamist groups. In fact, these "social formations," when combined, could support "an infrastructure of political and civic institutions that would support a Palestinian state, whenever that state arrives."[66] These and other similar observations lead Norton to conclude the following:

> Though scholars of the Middle East may debate civil society existentially, rhetorically, conceptually, culturally, and ontologically, the simple fact is that civil society is today part of the political discourse in the Middle East. Scholastic debates notwithstanding, civil society is the locus for debate, discussion, and dialogue in the contemporary Middle East.[67]

Ibrahim is more blunt in his defense of Middle Eastern civil society:

> Some Middle East area observers contend that the lagging democratization of the Arab world is due to the absence or stunting of its "civil society" and its corresponding "political culture." Some orientalists and mongers of ethnocentrism may go so far as to totally dismiss even the potential for the evolution of an Arab civil society, and hence any prospect of genuine democratization. Propagators of this point of view often forget the long arduous, and occasionally bloody, march of civil society and democratization in their own Western societies.[68]

One need not be an "orientalist" or a "monger of ethnocentrism" to question the viability of a civil society or a democratically hospitable political culture in the Middle East. Even some authors in Norton's book question whether civil society exists in all Middle Eastern countries, although their concept of the phenomenon is somewhat less than rigid.[69] One of the contributors cites Syria as an example where prospects for the evolution and growth of civil society are dismal. The Syrian state, he asserts, has been successful at stifling a civil society, employing in the process the help of the bourgeoisie. Syrian "elites have opted, so far successfully, to control the revival of civil society through a merely political decompression calculated to preserve, not transform the state."[70] Another author cites the decreasing autonomy of political parties in Egypt and the tendency of both state and social actors to punish dissenters as factors that inhibit the potential growth of a vibrant civil society there.[71] In Tunisia, it is argued in another chapter, the potential for civil society's growth remains uncertain, enjoying, on the one hand, "a vast network of associations that are training citizens in *civisme* and civility," while, on the other hand, state elites continue to resist opening up the political process.[72]

A further obstacle to the spread of democratizing tendencies in general and democratizing civil society organizations in Middle Eastern societies in particular is the character of the region's political economy, two aspects of which are especially crucial: the specific nature of class formation, especially insofar as the middle classes are concerned, and the larger role of the state in controlling and then distributing economic resources. Although the exact boundaries between the upper-middle class and the upper class, and between the lower-middle class and industrial workers or the lumpen proletariat, are not always clear, democracy nevertheless requires the existence of a sizable and democratically committed middle class, however broadly defined. Among the social classes, it is the middle strata who are not too preoccupied with the necessities of day-to-day survival, have not been economically bought off or incorporated into the regime's economic inner circle, and who have the potential for devoting attention to the political sphere and pushing political demands forward. But to push such demands implies a certain degree of autonomy from the state, if not outright rejection of its agenda. This circumstance partly accounts for democratization processes in western Europe and more recently in southern Europe and Latin America (but not, interestingly, in eastern Europe). In each of these three cases, a middle class that was largely autonomous and independent of the state gradually developed the elbowroom to press its various political demands, including the right to reconstitute the state periodically, if it so desired, and to ensure that those in positions of political power obeyed the rules laid out for them.

In the Middle East, however, such a politically autonomous middle class has not yet developed, although the middle class itself forms a sizable segment of society in each country. The very birth and subsequent evolution of the middle classes have been institutionally and systemically tied to the state in general and its structural growth and agendas in particular. Although there is a significant portion of the middle class not employed by the state, direct government employment through the civil service is a primary source of income for the vast majority. Those middle-class citizens not employed by the state (the *bazaaris* and others who are privately employed) have somewhat more autonomy, but they are still affected by the state's economic, industrial, and foreign-trade policies. The state's central role in the national economy leaves little room for total economic independence for even the often powerful *bazaaris*. While partially or completely dependent relationships between the employer (state) and employee (the middle classes) do not negate the possibility of pressures arising from below, they make such possibilities more difficult. When state employees and other members of the middle classes have rebelled, they have done so either through subtle and indirect means from within by resorting to corruption, nepotism, deliberate inefficiency, and other methods of obstructing the regime; or they have found solace in such uncompromising and undemocratic ideologies as communism, socialism, or the recent wave of Islamic radicalism.

It is important to note that in the countries of the Arabian peninsula, the situation is somewhat different. The concept and phenomenon of the middle class exists there, but such a class has a different connotation than in other Middle Eastern nations. An average middle-class family in Kuwait or the United Arab Emirates tends to have a higher standard of living than a middle-class family in Morocco, Syria, or Yemen. As chapter 3 demonstrates, the more affluent social classes in the Gulf countries have literally been bought off by the state, while the less fortunate, who have the potential to become oppositional, are predominantly made up of expatriate workers who are officially and systematically segregated from the national, political, and economic mainstreams of society. Democracy may yet develop in these countries as a result of social pressures from below, but the possibility is not great as long as the state can afford to act as a generous yet discriminatory benefactor.

Taxation—or, more precisely, the exact form that taxes in the Middle East tend to take—is a second impediment to democratization arising from the region's political economy. Comparative studies have shown that *direct* forms of taxation are not as prevalent there as in other parts of the world.[73] This assertion is challenged by those who claim that Middle Eastern states exact as much, if not more, revenues from their societies as states in comparable Third World countries. Therefore, the assumption goes, taxation exists in the Middle East and is often in fact quite heavy. This is indeed the case, and irrefutable statistical evidence clearly demonstrates that these states routinely levy heavy taxes on their societies.[74] What is important to realize, however, is that such state-derived revenues are seldom labeled or popularly perceived as "income tax." Although there is such a thing as a direct tax on income in practically every Middle Eastern country, most of the revenues that states exact from the social classes are in the form of hidden and indirect taxes. Tariffs on imported goods, licensing and a multitude of other fees, exorbitant luxury taxes, and other indirect means of taxing income are among the more common ways that states use to supplement their budgets. As a result, there is no widespread popular perception that because the state levies taxes on people's incomes, it must be held accountable for its actions. Middle Eastern states have, on the one hand, taxed their subjects through a variety of elaborate mechanisms, while, on the other hand, they have managed to avoid giving rise to the slogan "No taxation without representation."

But there are even more fundamental obstacles to the appearance and widespread growth of civil society in the region, obstacles that are found in more than a few select countries and that cannot be easily overcome with such relatively minor policy adjustments as political liberalization and accessibility to the state. The political forces that have undermined civil society's appearance include, among other things, not only repressive states but also, and more important, each state's effective manipulation of enough social norms to retain some crucial cultural resonance among its subjects. Thus leaders as diverse as Qaddafi, Khomeini, Sadat, and Saddam Hussein have in one form or another presented themselves as father figures who look after the best interests of their extended national families. Some leaders have met with more success than others in selling this patriarchal image to their nations, but all these men have found enough citizens willing to buy their paternal rhetoric to establish valuative links between them and their respective societies. Similarly, various shades of populism have been used to disguise more flagrant forms of opposition. The Iranian parliament (*Majlis*) is the scene of some of the liveliest political debates anywhere; members of the Islamist opposition have won seats in the Jordanian parliament; political leaders are ostensibly elected in Turkey; the Egyptian judiciary is remarkably independent; and the Kuwaiti regime plays up its less restrictive nature when compared with its neighboring monarchies. Moreover, Middle Eastern regimes invariably pursue economic policies aimed at elite co-option, thus giving rise to a social class structure in which status is often directly connected with the level of accessibility to the state.

But there are also social and cultural impediments to the birth of Middle Eastern civil society. Even in years of extreme regime crisis—Lebanon, 1975–90; Iran, 1978–81 and 1988–89; Iraq, 1990–91; Saudi Arabia, 1979, 1982, and 1990–91; Syria, 1982; Kuwait, 1990–91; Morocco, 1982 and 1990; Algeria, 1990–present; Tunisia, 1990–92; Libya, 1989–present; and so on—civil-society pressures from below have failed to materialize and overthrow the state. The reason is simple: the social and cultural ingredients necessary for a democratic civil society are absent. The social institutions that make up Middle Eastern societies—the family, tribalism and ethnicity, intellectuals, gathering places, and so forth—either have not been internally democratized (i.e., the family) or have failed to formulate a democratic corporate identity of their own (i.e., intellectuals). The social classes, whether in the more integrated economies of Turkey and Egypt or in the more oil-based ones of Kuwait and the United Arab Emirates, are divided not only economically but also culturally, and these multiple chasms impede the development of a collective sense of identity that could unite them in a democratic effort against the state. Of the social classes in the Middle East, invariably one or two relate to the state at some level—economically, politically, or culturally—and consider themselves to be the direct beneficiaries of carefully crafted state policies.

Even if all social classes manage to unite for a common cause, as they did under Khomeini in Iran in 1978, that unity is only temporary and masks deep valuative and cultural divisions stemming from protracted and uneven social change. If social change leaves anything behind, it is one's values and norms. The question who am I? becomes one of cardinal importance, the search for an answer a daily and conscious struggle. Middle Eastern popular cultures have become a hodgepodge of incongruities, inconsistences, and contradictions. The state's relationship to the divided or dividing society becomes manipulative and self-sustaining: it caters to the cultural orientations of some while alienating others (as in Iran and Turkey), or it plays a balancing act (as in Egypt, Jordan, and Morocco). In either case, the state retains some of its valuative links with certain segments of society. This aspect of the state-society nexus is further reinforced by a political culture that has as its cornerstones a personality cult, a lack of compromise, and a penchant for demagoguery. Finally, if a viable alternative to the regime has arisen, it has been from a socially and culturally overarching religion that has yet to accept any criticism by its adherents. Whether or not there is any merit to Huntington's assertion that Islam is inherently antidemocratic is a matter of debate. But this is only a small detail in the big picture. What matters is that a particular combination of political, social, and cultural characteristics have kept the forces of civil society at bay in the Middle East. Islam happens to be one of those forces; it is certainly not the only one. As the following chapters demonstrate, social and cultural dynamics that have little to do with Islam are as antithetical to democracy as are the current manifestations of the religion.

2. Social Forces and Institutions

HE SEARCH FOR premises, contexts, and causes of the unique nature of Middle Eastern societies has long preoccupied specialists of the region. Middle Eastern studies are replete with examples of astute scholarship that explore inner workings of society both on a larger regional scale and within each particular country.[1] In this chapter I will look at Middle Eastern society from an angle that, to my knowledge, has not previously been examined. My task here is both simple and complex: to decipher the maze of forces, institutions, strata, and nuances that make up the region's societies. Specifically, I examine several causal connections between these social forces and institutions on the one hand, and certain political proclivities and/or dynamics on the other. It is a matter of historical record that political autocracy has been a constant reality in the Middle East. But how has this absolutist tradition influenced or been reinforced by some of the social characteristics prevailing there? In a similar vein, are the features that dominate these societies conducive to the development of antistate or antidictatorial democratic pressures from below? And have these potential society-based impulses toward democratic pressures been politically vanquished by becoming authoritarian?

Although each Middle Eastern society is unique in its own right and steeped in national traditions, it shares with other societies in the region a number of salient characteristics, enabling one to examine these societies under the larger umbrella of "Middle Eastern." The subtle distinctions in national character and priorities, differing—often conflicting—political agendas and policies, and even linguistic and religious differences are all too often overlooked when regarding the strikingly parallel roles that various social forces and institutions play in each country. Some forces may establish a more compelling presence in one society than another, and the social stratum dominating one society's urban or rural arena may be only marginal in others. Nevertheless, it is possible to speak of "Middle Eastern society" per se and to point to various sets of social commonalities. The same, of course, applies to Middle Eastern cultures, states, and the relationships between states and societies.

I begin by examining the driving forces that, although not strictly *social,* have come to shape and significantly influence the region's social equation. These forces have had ramifications far greater than the immediate sociological, cultural, political, or economic parameters that originally defined them: kinship and ethnicity, nationalism, and a host of growing pains to which all Third World polities are prone. Within the complex and interdependent universe of society, certain nonsocial phenomena may have residual effects in a particular sphere of social activity, while their greatest impact may be in a domain that is only tangentially related to society. Society, for example, cannot escape the influences that such economic phenomena as individuals' upward mobility and employment in the civil service have on it. Such influences may be inconspicuously exerted on society, but they are not any less consequential. In their own way, phenomena of this kind have combined with various institutional and political arrangements to influence profoundly the Middle Eastern social setting. The city, which in the Middle East has historically been the primary arena for the most significant political and cultural developments, is particularly affected by the synergy of social forces.[2] It is in the cities that the ravages of social and economic change and the agendas of the state are most dramatically felt, and there the prevailing social and cultural norms are the most transient. Even the two other prevailing social formations, nomadism and rural settlements, have not fully escaped the influences of urban-based social forces. Many of the dynamics that shape life in urban society exert themselves on rural and nomadic formations as well, although with considerably less pronounced and somewhat different consequences.

Social Forces

The phenomena that affect Middle Eastern society are a group of powerful forces that, although not specifically social in character, significantly hold sway over some of the patterns of social relations and conduct. Indeed, those forces continue to exert a compelling influence on society's overall agendas, conduct and operations, and composition. The most significant of these social forces arises from three conflicting yet reinforcing phenomena: political autocracy; the processes of economic and social development; and the persistence of a number of primordial loyalties and attachments. Although primordialism may have varying connotations in different national contexts, in the Middle East it entails the strength of successive circles of social affiliation, beginning with the most fundamental social unit, the family, and extending to the clan, neighborhood, larger community (including the tribe), sect, and eventually to the country. Regardless of the specific manifestations that primordialism has taken in particular Middle Eastern countries, it has often conflicted with the forces of economic development and/or the state's political agendas, which are invariably geared to safeguard its longevity. Because these forces have frequently conflicted, they have resulted in what one scholar has aptly called "distorted change" and ultimately neopatriarchal social relations.[3] The very forces that have pushed developing Middle Eastern societies toward change and modernity have reinforced the primordial tendencies that are by nature impervious to change. The authoritarian state promotes economic change and development, while at the same time it relies on and in turn exploits the already extensive primordial tendencies within society. Hence the contradictions of modern state agendas.

The state's relationship with prevailing social forces has often been a paradoxical one, marked by intermittent stages of co-option and conflict. The state has, on the one hand, tried to manipulate existent contradictory social forces, while, on the other hand, it has often failed to enforce fully its policies in the face of the same currents of social and cultural resistance. Some states have been particularly adept at representing themselves as the natural political extensions of existent social forces. To one extent or another, all Middle Eastern states rely on and exploit the patriarchal relationships found within the family and the larger community.[4] Consciously or unconsciously emulating the leadership style of the prophet Muhammad, political leaders invariably view themselves as having a paternal relationship with their country and thus project a patriarchal image of themselves to their citizens. The family-based monarchies of the Arabian peninsula—Saudi Arabia, Kuwait, Qatar, Bahrain, the United Arab Emirates, and Oman—and, to a lesser extent, the Jordanian and Moroccan monarchies are particularly dependent on linking their political legitimacy and survival to relationships with the lineal and familial networks in their respective societies. One observer has gone so far as to argue that the close ties between the prevailing social forces (namely, families and, by extension, tribes) and the state make such states seem like natural extensions of society.[5] Even though the correlation between the body politic and social forces is more artificial, being based, for example, on such concocted notions as divine kingship or the more socially accepted tribal ancestry, the extensive parallels between the political and social patterns greatly facilitate the state's legitimacy and its longevity.

Not all states, however, are capable of finding politically consonant social forces within society. Outside the Arabian peninsula, in fact, it is frequently difficult to find states that do not encounter extensive social resistance in carrying out their agendas, which are, admittedly, often decidedly different from those pursued by the smaller, wealthier, and politically more conservative sheikhdoms. Nevertheless, the social resistance faced by such states as Iran, Iraq, Syria, Lebanon, Tunisia, Algeria, the Sudan, and especially Egypt have as much to do with the nature of prevailing social forces in these countries as with the particular features of the policies their governments pursue. Subtle political differences notwithstanding, each of these states essentially relies on a mixture of carefully cultivated sociocultural norms and promises of economic performance in order to further its legitimacy and resilience. But the state's attempts to carve out a social stake for its survival and to implement its specific agendas often come into direct conflict with entrenched social forces. The professional ethos of the modern bureaucracy, which is one of the primary institutional mainstays of the state, revolves around procedural formalism, rational economic priorities, and merit-based, vertical political and economic mobility. The forces that govern social life, however, are seldom amenable to such dictates. Middle Eastern societies are characterized by high degrees of informalism, linear reliance on and patronage of kinfolk and other primary groups, and a good deal of concern with such noneconomic principles as honor and "face." Reflecting on this phenomenon in Egypt, Leonard Binder made the following observation: "The interests of the urban middle class are to be identified with their current largely bureaucratic functions, but their cultural values are still importantly traditional or rather derived from the life experiences of the rural middle class."[6] Thus because of the inherent contradictions between its social composition and its ostensibly modernizing mission, the bureaucracy can potentially become either dysfunctional or at best highly inefficient and ridden with corruption. In this and multitudes of other ways, the modern state finds its agendas and priorities socially resisted, undermined from within, or haphazardly enforced.

The development of the social forces that run rampant in the Middle East can be traced to a potent mixture of political, sociocultural, and economic factors endemic to the region. The internal dynamics of state-directed capitalism combine with existent social networks and the cultural norms that govern them to produce a number of nuances that exert countervailing influences on society. Like their counterparts in other contemporary Third World governments, Middle Eastern policymakers have long set out to expand the state's involvement in the economic sphere and to create new forces and relations of economic production.[7] This has meant organizing society along particular ideological and developmental lines and creating new sociopolitical orders to replace old ones. Some states, as in Egypt and Tunisia, have embarked on ambitious projects of bureaucratic growth and management, even though relatively well established bureaucratic structures already existed.[8] Indeed, mammoth bureaucracies have developed in every Middle Eastern country, charged with not only ensuring the political longevity of the regime but also coordinating and implementing the state's numerous economic development projects. Atatürk set the pace, followed by the Pahlavis in Iran, Nasser in Egypt, and an entire array of champions of modernization in the region. Whether under the aegis of state capitalism or that of the more rhetorical "Arab socialism," states such as Egypt (from 1957 to 1974), Tunisia (1962 to 1969), the Sudan (1969 to 1972), Syria (since 1963), Iraq (since 1963), and Libya (since 1969) have set out specifically to effect carefully engineered economic development.[9] That these state-led processes of economic change have largely led to economic *growth* rather than *development* and have failed to achieve some of their basic goals is a subject for another discussion. In almost all instances, however, the structural exigencies of state-led capitalism, led by Egypt, Tunisia, Algeria, and Turkey, soon became apparent, and successive Middle Eastern governments have sought to initiate corrective measures.[10]

While the state's rhetoric and agendas dictate one reality, actual economic and political circumstances control another. Social and political life is supposed to revolve around the developmental universe created by the state: everything has a logical order, its relationship to the others clearly defined. The state is to outline the economic agendas to be followed and the policies to implement them, the modern and merit-based bureaucracy is to carry out these policies, and thus the economic order of society changes as planned. In turn, the social and cultural orders, which may initially lag slightly behind the new economic order, will fall in line and also change accordingly. But the flaws of this logic, which became apparent to social scientists some time ago, have yet to be fully comprehended by many of the Middle East's political practitioners. As previously mentioned, some of the promises for economic development programs have failed to materialize in a number of Middle Eastern countries, including Algeria, Iraq, and Iran, where the real extent of such shortcomings has often been concealed by the infusion of petrodollars into the economy.[11] But state-led capitalism (or its derivative, Arab socialism) has had a number of other less quantifiable ramifications as well, particularly insofar as Middle Eastern cultures and societies are concerned. Specifically, the political agendas of the state and their practical application have had two particular consequences: they have strengthened, not weakened, the primordial ties of kinship and lineage (and, by inference, informality), and at the same time they have accentuated the actual processes and the dreams of modernity, embourgeoisement, and further economic mobility.

For most Middle Eastern societies, tribal ethos and values remain at the core of social organization and have long played pivotal roles in the family, other primary groups, and the informal relations that characterize them. Despite extensive efforts to break the hold of such informal relations and to replace the centrality of primary groups with allegiance to the state, the family—both immediate and extended—and the larger community continue to be of far greater significance to most Middle Easterners than the state could ever hope to become. The state's frequent inability to deliver the goods and to honor the lofty goals it promises (both militarily and economically), its ineptitude, mismanagement, and rampant corruption only help to erode any measure of popular approval of its officeholders or their agendas. The omnipresent authoritarian state has usually been viewed in an adversarial light by its citizens, particularly after intensely populist regimes (Nasser's Egypt, Khomeini's Iran, and Saddam Hussein's Iraq) turned out to be merely political machines exploiting popular sentiments. In response, people have clung to the social ties that were always trusted and relied on in times of hardship.

Although political socialization through the government is viewed with suspicion, nepotism is commonplace. Kinfolk of politicians can count on sought-after government jobs, even though their merits and qualifications may be deficient. While the state may offer minimal fringe benefits, high-powered friends and relatives are likely to offer more extensive advantages. "By entering into these primary relations," one observer notes, "which they do freely and spontaneously, individuals engage in an unlimited commitment to one another. They derive satisfaction from extensive affiliations and develop a sense of belonging."[12]

Naturally, the more eroded the political and economic powers of the state, the more extensive and pervasive primordial ties are likely to be.[13] In Lebanon, to cite an extreme example, the atrophy of the state in the late 1970s and early 1980s resulted in a dramatic heightening of such primordial forces as sectarianism and clannishness to the extent that the average Lebanese citizen was plagued by a "confessional mind."[14] But extensive state incapacitation is not a necessary precondition for the prevalence of primordial forces and informal relations. Reflecting on his visit to Iraq at the height of the Iran-Iraq war, Guilain Denoeux writes in his book on urban life in the Middle East how he was struck by "the true vitality of informal networks. . . . Even in that suffocating police state," he observes,

> where the pressure of formal cadres was truly terrifying, informal ties and loyalties survived in a dormant state, sustained by roots that reached deep into the region's past. In fact, as the fear of a possible Iraqi defeat gripped the population, and as the traumatic shock of Iran's repeated missile attacks spread throughout the Iraqi capital, informal networks rose to provide the social and psychological support that Saddam Hussein's totalitarian machine could not deliver.[15]

Informality is a natural derivative of established primordial loyalties, which in turn reinforce it. Some states thrive on and then perpetuate the existent informal relations found throughout society. Other states seek to limit the extensive powers of those informal organizations that may emerge as obstacles to some of their specific agendas; however, they often find their efforts undermined by entrenched social practices and interests. In an atmosphere in which the formal procedures and institutions are frequently ignored altogether, and when a greater degree of comfort, security, and mobility is obtained through informal connections, it is inevitable that various forms of informality would permeate social and political life. Although the state may pride itself on its strict adherence to legal and formal procedures, the norm is informality. Whether social or economic, informal relations continue to resist the onslaught of formalism. To this day, most business transactions in the Middle East remain private affairs between two parties, and many moneylending and notary functions have only recently been formalized through a banking system. The informal group also continues to be the mainstay of social interaction and political socialization. The formal outside world structured by the state is perceived as hostile and contrived, but the closed world of the informal group has managed to remain civil, familiar, and reassuring. In the segregated societies of the Middle East, men tend to socialize in mosques, teahouses, bazaar shops, and sports clubs, whereas women gather in private homes and bathhouses and at religious charity events.[16]

The results of such opposing influences as formality versus informality, political rhetoric versus performance, the push of modernity versus the pull of tradition, economic aspiration versus reality, and many other forces that simultaneously tear Middle Eastern societies in different directions have been numerous and often dramatic. The Iranian revolution, the assassination of Anwar Sadat in 1981, and the 1992 Algerian military coup d'état were spectacular manifestations of the forces at work beneath the surface. Far more extensive yet less discernible to the casual observer have been the deep social and cultural divisions that fragment these societies. Insofar as processes of economic development and modernization are concerned, the emphasis on social and cultural divisions rather than commonalities is not unique to the region and can be found in most other Third World societies.[17] Social formations in the Middle East, as well as in other parts of the Third World, may be simultaneously modern and traditional, old and new, capitalist and feudal, religious and secular. Dichotomies abound, with all-encompassing divisions and ever-present crises.[18] But unique to the Middle East are the peculiar ways in which these contradictory forces manifest themselves in society: the forces of modernity contend with those of tradition, neither being fully capable of supplanting or overcoming the other; the desire to become modern clashes with the often-restrictive weight of religious orthodoxy;[19] the economic imperatives of upward mobility and assimilation into higher social strata encounter resistance from stunted economic growth; the constraints of nepotism and many other obstacles are inherent to the system. What emerges is a society that is neither modern nor traditional. As one observer has expressed it,

> [It is] a quintessentially underdeveloped society. Its most pervasive characteristic is a kind of generalized, persistent, and seemingly insurmountable impotence: it is incapable of performing as an integrated social or political system, as an economy, or as a military structure. Possessing all the external trappings of modern society, this society nevertheless lacks the inner force, organization, and consciousness which characterize modern social formations. Indeed, modernization in this context is for the most part only a mechanism promoting underdevelopment and social entropy, which in turn

produce and reproduce the hybrid, traditional, and semi-rational structures and consciousness typical of neopatriarchal society.[20]

Just as existent social forces have a paradoxical relationship with Middle Eastern states, these forces also seem to have a double-edged effect on the extent to which a society is politicized. They foster or even facilitate a politically charged atmosphere in society, or, adversely, they may effect political apathy and preoccupation with nonpolitical matters. It is no accident that the prosperous states of the Arabian peninsula are politically stable. The states in these sheikhdoms are authoritarian and will not tolerate dissent, but this does not completely account for the politically docile nature of their societies. Nor can the general apathy be wholly blamed on the state's pacifying the populace with petrodollars. Societies in the throes of economic growth and accumulating wealth do not necessarily bother with politics. Instead, many become concerned with economics as an all-consuming domain of thought and activity. If political activity especially happens to be a punishable offense, society's learned behavior to be apolitical is reinforced over successive generations.

In other instances, social forces may politicize a society and help effect a politically charged social atmosphere. Nationalism is one such force. The import/substitution industrialization path to economic development, which most Middle Eastern states chose in the 1960s and 1970s, and which to this day continues to be widely practiced in Morocco, Tunisia, Egypt, Jordan, and Turkey,[21] may have contributed to the popular notion that some countries are dominated and run by multinational corporations, especially if their leaders are unpopular and have close affiliations with one or more foreign powers. These characteristics can thus heighten xenophobic, economically based nationalism. Although not enough to radicalize otherwise apolitical citizens, this kind and other forms of nationalism can gradually lead to mass politicization. Again, avowedly political factors such as state initiatives may prove highly significant in determining the ultimate outcome of this and other social forces.

The opposing pushes and pulls exerted on society by political autocracy, economic development, and primordialism help determine the essence of social life in the Middle East. Regardless of a particular country's social setting, the nonpolitical dynamics that shape the overall social "beat" can perhaps be traced to the presence and workings of these social forces. Their influences on society are exercised through the various institutions that compose it. Thus social institutions are important not only as constituent parts of society but also as conveyors of the nuances that

shape and determine everyday life. The important interrelationship of social forces and social institutions is exemplified by primordialism, which
makes certain institutions, such as the family, all the more pivotal in the
overall conduct of society.

Social Institutions

In its broadest sense, politics is made up of all the relationships that take
place within and between various social and state institutions. Within this
larger context, social institutions may be seen as a group of "intangible
phenomena that endow a community of people with a collective sense of
identity."[22] These common identities are based on shared experiences and
sentiments, ideologies, rituals, kinship and lineage, geographic identification, and other characteristics that bestow on people a collective sense of
"us." It thus follows that the nature, characteristics, and significance of
social institutions may differ from one society to another. By the same token, the functions and importance of the same institution within a given
society may vary over time, depending on the specific social and political
forces at work. Troubled times may see the growing importance of religion or the family, whereas a different social and political milieu may lead
to their steady erosion. It is possible, nonetheless, to note a number of
social institutions that together form the core of particular social formations.

   In Middle Eastern societies, the most important social institutions are
the family, tribe and/or ethnicity, religion, the educational establishment,
and various communal gathering places. Not only do they form the core
of societies but also, equally important, they function as the main social
venues through which political values and sentiments are formulated and
expressed. While they differ in importance to individuals in all social
strata, each institution plays a vital role in the overall life of society. More
important, as the following pages show, their very nature and functions
have made it difficult, if not impossible, for the state to subjugate them.

The Family

The most important institution in the Middle East is undoubtedly the
family, which serves as the font of countless social arrangements, cultural
norms, and economic interactions. Its primacy can be still be found in all
three patterns of living in the region—nomadic, rural, and urban—despite
the numerous challenges that the family has faced in recent decades.[23]
Some scholars point to the social pattern known as "familism," in which

the family "is central in practically all aspects of life" and "continually wields considerable power over Arab thought and sentiment."[24] This pervasiveness has not escaped the state's attention. As if the family as an institution needed any official sanctioning, the Egyptian Constitution of 1971, Article 90, explicitly states:

> The family forms the basis of society. It is built on religion, morality and patriotism. The state is concerned with the preservation of the authentic character of the Egyptian family and the values and traditions it represents, in addition to affirming and developing this kind of relation within Egyptian society.[25]

Even Turkey's staunchly secular constitution from 1982 specifically mentions the state's responsibilities to the institution of the family. According to Article 41:

> The family is the foundation of Turkish society. The state shall take the necessary measures and establish the necessary organizations to ensure the peace and welfare of the family, especially the protection of the mother and children, and the family planning education and application.[26]

The intent of including such statements in national constitutions goes beyond the state's simple determination to preserve the institution of the family. Instead, it signals the state's realization of this social institution's importance, and hence its attempt to manipulate the family for specific political and ideological purposes.

Much has been written on Middle Eastern families, and it is unnecessary to replicate a detailed list of their features and characteristics.[27] Some of these characteristics are so pervasive and socially and politically important, however, that they merit further mention. For the most part, the family is a highly cohesive institution that remains largely impenetrable to outside influences and encroachments. Although there may be signs of dissention and disagreement within the kinship group, the family invariably presents a united front against outside competitors, especially if the competitor happens to be the state. This solidarity is reinforced by a number of built-in mechanisms and features: the Middle Eastern family is "patriarchal; pyramidally hierarchical, particularly in respect to sex and age; and extended."[28] The authority of the father as patriarch is virtually absolute, mirroring a larger pattern of relationships between the national ruler and his subjects. Few Middle Eastern leaders have *not* viewed themselves as father to their country, and when necessary, most have imposed harsh discipline when their "children" have disobeyed. Yet political machinations of the family and its replication on a national scale have only served to strengthen the family's immunity to outside interferences.

Frequently, the unity of the family is further reinforced by its economic functions. In many instances, immediate and extended family members run a family-owned shop or work on a family-owned farm. The central role of the father, particularly because of his earning an income and distributing it to his wife and children, makes the patriarchal family a tightly knit economic unit. But nontraditional (and, by inference, nonpatriarchal) families may also serve as important economic units. Family enterprises are as important in the Middle East as they are in other parts of the Third World; in fact, in certain Middle Eastern countries they play an unusually prominent role in the national economy.[29] The economic importance of the family is amplified in the sector that by nature relies on the informal network of kinship for the sale, service, and distribution of the family's goods. Although exact statistics are unavailable and estimates vary widely, consistently high percentages of the labor force are believed to be employed in the informal sector in various Middle Eastern countries: 57 percent in Morocco; 36 percent in Tunisia; 36 percent in Turkey; 35 percent in Iran; and anywhere from 16 percent to 43 percent in Egypt.[30]

The same general dynamics at work within the patriarchal, nuclear family can be found within the family-owned enterprise. Usually, the patriarch is the proprietor of the business, providing the main capital or the goods to be sold. His employees are frequently drawn from a pool made up of his own children, his nieces and nephews, the children of friends, or neighbors. With the patriarch's retirement or death, usually one of his sons assumes the family business. Similar economic interests draw peasant families together as well, although in agricultural areas the primary capital is in the form of cultivable land.[31] Nevertheless, the cohesion of the family unit is not only preserved but also solidified by its corporate interests. Family unity is reinforced and its protection from outside influences—especially from the government—is vigilantly guarded.

The differences that separate nomadic, rural, and urban families from one another are mostly matters of degree rather than of substance. The greater the distance between the family unit and the forces of modernity and formalism, the greater its extent, cohesion, and resistance to outside forces. Thus the family is strongest and most extensive in areas farthest from the reaches of the state, particularly those regions inhabited by self-sufficient, politically autonomous bedouins and other tribal nomads. The same characteristics mark both the rural and the pseudo-urban family that has settled in the city without becoming fully urbanized. Although the kinship community is divided into several smaller units in the city, it continues to rely on extensive lineal networks for the provision of social services. The necessities of life in the city may require the replacement of family loyalties with ties to others, but the centrality of the family as one's continued source of reference and reliance remains basically unchanged. Even the nuclear family of the urban middle and upper classes exhibits similar features. In fact, the peculiar nature of social forces at work in the cities in many ways strengthens, rather than weakens, the prominence of the family as a key social institution and its importance to the body politic. The breakup of extended families into nuclear ones does not necessarily destroy the support mechanisms that underlie the functions of large kinship networks. Since access to sources of political, social, and/or economic power is privileged and limited, families often unite, either through marriage or through kinship ties, in order to further their corporate interests.[32] Marrying into the "right" family or maintaining cozy relations with a powerful but distant cousin becomes vitally important. At the same time, the ever-changing, seemingly hostile world outside serves only to emphasize the inviolability of the family. Because many of the other social and political relations found throughout society rely on the same top-down, authoritarian pattern as the family, they only reinforce that institution's autonomy and resonance. "The same patriarchal relations and values that prevail in the Arab family," one observer notes,

> seem also to prevail at work, at school, and in religious, political, and social associations. In all of these, a father figure rules over others, monopolizing authority, expecting strict obedience, and showing little tolerance for dissent. Projecting a paternal image, those in positions of responsibility (as rulers, leaders, teachers, employers, or supervisors) securely occupy the top of the pyramid of authority. Once in this position, the patriarch cannot be dethroned except by someone who is equally patriarchal.[33]

Thus the internal, self-generated powers of the family remain largely unabated in spite of the political agendas of the state and the forces of economic development and social change.

On a purely structural level, the top-down, authoritarian nature of the Middle Eastern family is often a valuable asset to the region's political establishments. The family does, however, become a political liability to the state when it instills in its members a sense of identity and loyalty that overshadows their loyalties to the state and its leader. The bonds of the family are the most difficult for the government to crack.

Tribal and ethnic identities play a similar though less emphasized role vis-à-vis the influence of state institutions. While the structure and hierarchy of tribes are important, their members' sense of distinctive identity and loyalty are politically more significant. Thus the institution of the tribe is as important as ethnic identity.

Tribes and Ethnicity

Tribes have long been an integral part of the Middle Eastern mosaic, intriguing classical as well as contemporary scholars. Yet from the writings of Arab historian Ibn-Khaldūn (1332–1406) to those of contemporary observers, there is little scholarly consensus over the precise nature of Middle Eastern tribes, their organization, and their functions.[34] Middle Eastern tribal units can be distinguished on two levels: the tribe and the confederacy (or, alternately, tribal chieftaincy).[35] The difference between them is one of extent rather than of function and nature. A tribe is basically made up of a number of extended families, whereas a confederacy contains a collection of loosely tied tribes. As one author has noted, "Several wandering units formed a subtribe, several of these a tribe, and some of the tribes occasionally a tribal confederation."[36] Leadership, social organization, and topographic and geographical settings are some of the critical factors that determine the "evolution" of tribes into a confederacy. Yet by its very nature, this evolution undermines the cohesiveness and solidarity that characterize tribes, and it eventually causes their social and political importance to diminish. In essence, the tribe outgrows and outsettles itself, becoming more and more just another component of a rapidly urbanizing society.

It is not uncommon to find both leaders and youths of a tribal confederacy attracted to the amenities and luxuries of urban life. Tribal elites often prefer to manage their affairs from a nearby town or even a provincial capital, to which they are drawn by the creature comforts of city life. Many of the tribes' youths are frequently drawn to cities in search of jobs in the informal or even the formal sector, for secondary or higher education, or better opportunities. Growth in the powers of the central authority, rapid urbanization, and social and cultural change have all contributed to the gradual disappearance of tribalism. Although it retains its basic foundations, tribalism assumes a more subtle expression.[37] Increasingly, the tribe becomes "a referent for social identity and loyalty."[38]

The social unit of the tribe thus gradually becomes the social phenomenon of ethnicity. What becomes a defining factor for the individual is not so much where he or she fits within the tribal structure but rather what social and cultural characteristics he or she retains out of his or her tribal heritage.

The relationship between tribalism and the state thus needs to be analyzed on two levels. On the one hand, analysis must focus on the continued role and political significance that tribes play as actual social institutions. Because of their institutional and organizational characteristics, the political importance of tribes needs to be examined on a structural basis. In fact, an accurate understanding of the state in the Arabian peninsula cannot be achieved without reference to patterns of tribal organization and hierarchy. On the other hand, the focus needs to be functional because, as mentioned earlier, in most other parts of the Middle East the political import of tribalism lies increasingly in its social and cultural ramifications and its role as a source of ethnic and cultural identity. The following analysis will show that while the structural significance of tribes as actual institutional sources of power has steadily declined, the political and cultural ethos associated with them continue to influence social and political life in important ways.

Although urbanization and its ramifications may have transformed the phenomenon of tribalism into ethnicity, tribes continue to exist as viable and important social units in most nonurban areas. Typically, Middle Eastern tribes have consisted of desert-dwelling nomads (called "bedouins" in the Arab world), although in recent decades, especially with the extension of central state authority over the countryside, many nomads have become settled cultivators.[39] Whether settled or nomadic, the tribe has at its core a series of highly evolved norms and institutions that maintain the solidarity of the tribal group. Primary among these are the bonds of kinship and lineage, with members of a tribe often perceiving themselves as members of the same extended family. Tribal social organizations may be seen as a series of kin-based, concentric circles, beginning with the nuclear family (*usra*), the extended family (*beit* or *ahl*), the subtribe (*hamula*), the clan (*ashira*), and the tribe (*qabila*).[40] These kinship ties may not be with actual blood relatives, although they nevertheless serve to strengthen the tribal group's cohesion. More commonly, tribal solidarity derives from a "myth of common ancestry," supported by political, social, ethnolinguistic (or folkloric), and territorial bonds.[41]

Concurrent with the importance of kinship bonds is the pivotal role of the tribal leader or chief. A chief exercises a moral, military, and political authority over tribal members.[42] Frequently, he has ascended to his position by virtue of his family's reputation and status within the tribal community, as well as by his ability continually to deliver the goods that the tribe needs. These necessities may be tangible, as in protection from other tribes or the state, or intangible, in the form of communal pride or a symbolic sense of belonging. Skills as a conciliator and a consensus builder, especially if there is conflict between some of the tribal families, are also important. The links between tribal leaders and their followers are often connected to various symbolic systems. Notions of a shared history, rituals, music, apparel, dwellings, and other forms of expressive art (folklore, dancing, music) all provide bonds between leaders and their followers.[43] The role of the chief and especially the political significance of the larger tribal group are emphasized in proportion to the group's population size and geographic reach. Naturally, the tribal group's and especially the larger confederacies' relationships with the state become concerns to those in power.

In addition to kinship ties and the role of the chief, a number of other factors also influence the structural and organizational characteristics of Middle Eastern tribes. Chief among them are the geographic location of the tribe, the agendas of the chiefs and other tribal notables, the nature of the economic activities in which the tribespeople engage, their religious and ideological dispositions, and the initiatives of the state. In particular, the effects of geography and economics on tribal structures can hardly be overstated. Except for a number of Iranian tribes, namely, the Lurs, Qashqais, Kurds, Turkomans, and Shahseven, that live in the relatively hospitable central plateaus of Iran and Turkey, most of the other tribal groups in the Middle East are desert-dwelling bedouins. The term *bedouin* comes from the Arabic word "bedwa," or desert. The aspects of leading a desert life are both varied and far-reaching. Desert life makes bedouins cherish certain values: chivalry, individuality, hospitality, simplicity, and tribal solidarity.[44] Bedouins also tend to be fiercely independent and resist outside attempts at social and political integration. Some observers have maintained that even the virtue of hospitality, which on the surface may seem to derive from altruism, ultimately fulfills a self-serving function because it strengthens the cohesion and solidarity of the larger group.[45] This independent spirit becomes all the more noteworthy when it is combined with a measure of economic prosperity, especially if the tribe is located on an important trade or pilgrimage route. "Traders and pilgrims on the move need transport, accommodation, and protection," remarks Ernest Gellner, thus emphasizing the importance of not only the tribe but also its leaders and chiefs.[46] In recent years, this economic importance has become an increasingly "modern" phenomenon, with the more prosperous tribes targeting the urban market. Tribespeople often sell sheep, dairy products, carpets, and various kinds of handicrafts to urban consumers either in the marketplace or from house to house. Some own and run small huts from which they sell produce, soft drinks, tea, and dairy products to nearby villages and occasionally to urban consumers.

The links between Middle Eastern tribes and the city are not limited to commercial or political contacts. Even more important are the social and cultural resonances of tribalism on urban societies. For most urbanites who view the city instead of the countryside as the focus of their social, economic, political, and cultural energies, the tribe is an ideal often romanticized but hardly a reality. To the urban world, tribalism and the norms and values attached to it become something of a "cultural construct,"[47] a vague though important reference point on select topics. This is not to imply that tribalism in itself has little importance or relation to the larger social setting. To the contrary, as we are approaching the end of the twentieth century, numerous tribal groups continue to evade the full force of government hegemony. The Kurds in Iran, Iraq, and Turkey, and the Berbers in most North African countries have so far been largely successful in resisting government efforts to integrate them into society.

What is important to realize, however, is that in the predominantly *urban* world of politics and economies, and in light of the dramatic growth of urbanization in the region in recent decades, it is necessary to look at ethnicity as a social institution as well. The sense of identity and the values that ethnicity bestow on people are often a direct product of the mores and norms of the nationally dominant tribes. It is no coincidence that the major *ethnic* groups, whether living in predominantly urban or rural areas, broadly correspond with their country's notable tribal groups. As table 2.1 shows, this parallel in tribal and ethnic divisions is particularly strong in Algeria, Egypt, Iran, Iraq, Jordan, Libya, the Sudan, Syria, and Turkey.

The problem of distinguishing between tribes and ethnic groups is further complicated by the difficulties involved in sociological classification. In a number of Middle Eastern countries, especially in Iran, tribes are often assumed to be ethnic groups. In an insightful essay on Iranian tribes, Lois Beck has elaborated on the connection between tribalism and ethnicity. "Ethnicity is a wider, more inclusive construct than is tribe," she argues, "and it can encompass different kinds of principles, structures, and organization." She explains,

TABLE 2.1

ETHNIC COMPOSITION

IN MIDDLE EASTERN COUNTRIES

Algeria	80% Arabs and Arabized Berbers; 20% Berbers
Bahrain	Majority indigenous Arabs; minority Saudi Arabians, Omanis, Iranians, Asians, and British
Egypt	90% Homogeneous Egyptians, Hamites, and Copts; 10% ethnic minorities: Bedouins, Nubians, Greeks, Italians, and Maltese
Iran	66% Aryan origin, Persians; 34% Turk-speaking Azerbaijanis and Qashqais and other ethnic minorities: Jews, Muslim Arabs, and Kurds
Iraq	80% Arab Bedouins and Madans; 15% Kurds; <.5% Turkomans, Persians, and Lurs
Israel	95% Semitic race; 5% Arab
Jordan	40% Palestinian Arabs; 5% Bedouins; largest group, original Arabs; smallest group, Circassians
Kuwait	40% Kuwaiti nationals; 60% others: Jordanians, Palestinians, Iranians, Iraqis, Omanis, Saudi Arabians, South Asians, and Afghans (changed after 1990–91 conflict with Iraq, when most Palestinians left)
Lebanon	93% Arab; <1% minority Assyrians; 6% Armenians; <1% Muslim Kurds; .5% foreign nationals
Libya	90% Muslims of mixed Arab-Berber ancestry; 4% Berbers; 1% Black Africans, Tebus, and Harratins
Morocco	99.1% Arab and Berbers
Oman	87.5% Arab; minority Iranians, Baluchis, Indians, Pakistanis, and East Africans
Qatar	33% ethnic Qatars; 25% Egyptians, Palestinians, and Omanis; 34% South Asians
Saudi Arabia	100% Arab
Sudan	33% Arabs; 3.2% Nubians; 6.4% Beja; 8.1% Nuba; 11.5% Dinka; 5.8% West African Muslims
Syria	90% Arabs; 6% Kurds; 4% other minorities: Assyrians, Turkomans, and Armenians
Tunisia	10% pure Arab; 90% Arab-Berber mixture
Turkey	85% Turks; Donme, Kurds
UAE	25% Adnani, Northern Arabs; 50% ethnic Iranians, Indians, Pakistanis, Palestinians, Egyptians, Iraqis, and Lebanese
Yemen	100% Arab

SOURCES: Compiled from Gregory Thomas Kurian, ed., *Encyclopedia of the Third World*, vols. 1–3, 4th ed. (New York: Facts on File, 1992); for Israel and Turkey, Gregory Thomas Kurian, ed., *Encyclopedia of the First World*, vol. 1 (New York: Facts on File, 1990).

Tribes were often ordered differently from ethnic groups, especially as regards their culturally defined boundaries. The term tribe emerges in reference to some form of sociopolitical organization, whereas the phrase ethnic groups emphasizes a culturally defined self-consciousness.... When key tribal (that is, sociopolitical) organizations and institutions were undermined or eliminated, usually under state pressure, people formerly encompassed by these systems may have adopted or enhanced other traits associated with ethnic groups, particularly a self-conscious sense of distinctiveness. Tribal groups are sometimes said to have transformed into ethnic groups, especially when the people involved, if they continued to evoke commonly held ideologies, were increasingly drawn under state control.[48]

This transformation of tribal organizations into ethnic identity, as Beck would argue, does not mean that tribalism and ethnicity are mutually exclusive and that the latter only emerges from the political demise, or "evolution," of the former. One useful way to distinguish between tribalism and ethnicity is to view them as two geographically distinct phenomena. Tribalism, in the Middle East at least, continues to be an important social and political institution in the countryside, whereas ethnicity plays a definitive role in the cities. Naturally, the two institutions are found simultaneously in a number of Middle Eastern countries, particularly in those with hegemonic ethnic cores (e.g., Iran, Iraq, Turkey, Syria, Egypt, Libya, Algeria, and Morocco). Most of the smaller Gulf countries (especially Bahrain, Kuwait, Qatar, and the United Arab Emirates) have sizable emigrant and expatriate populations. These expatriates are often politically disenfranchised and socially segregated, seldom integrating into the mainstream of society. Jordan is a slightly different case, for while the Palestinians, who make up anywhere between 40 and 75 percent of the Jordanian population, continue to view themselves as foreigners, they have at the same time been integrated enough into Jordanian society to constitute a separate ethnic group of their own. For all intents and purposes, the Palestinians are not foreigners living and working in Jordan as, for instance, Omanis in Kuwait may be, but they have become an integral part of the Jordanian population.

A sense of distinctiveness, as mentioned earlier, is at the heart of ethnicity. In provincial towns and metropolitan areas, ethnicity manifests itself in a number of ways. Most but not all symbolic means of identification that differentiate large numbers of urban dwellers from one another are manifestations of ethnicity, especially one's accent and dialect, dress, folklore, place of birth, ancestral heritage, and other attributes that separate an otherwise ethnically homogeneous population. At times, race and/or religion also become important determining factors in one's ethnicity, especially in instances where racial or religious heterogeneity happen to be the norm.[49] Religion and the mosque as the place of worship are so integral in defining most Middle Easterners' identities that they deserve to be studied as separate social institutions. But even where there is considerable religious homogeneity (almost all countries of the region except Israel, Lebanon, and the Sudan), there is still a notable degree of ethnic heterogeneity that escapes detection in official surveys and statistics. The figures in table 2.1 (p. 57) may represent ethnic background in relation to one's tribal ancestry, but they do not take into account the more subtle differences that people of diverse backgrounds may have, such as dialect and accent. Certainly, not everyone with a regional accent is a member of a particular ethnic group. But that difference in accent becomes important if the person happens to be a first- or even second-generation urbanite who has retained certain tribal and/or rural characteristics. Most Kurds, for example, may have lived in the more metropolitan areas of Iran, Iraq, Turkey, and Syria, but they nonetheless tend to retain much of what defines them as being Kurdish rather than Iranian (Persian), Turkish (Turk), or Iraqi or Syrian (Arab). The same holds true for the long-established Turks and Arabs in Iran.

Viewed from this perspective, the Middle East appears to be a region in which ethnic pluralism is the norm,[50] although it is important to note that few countries have not had hegemonic ethnic cores that once dominated both the social and the political arenas. The disintegration of Lebanon along ethnic and religious lines in the 1970s and 1980s and that of the Sudan in the 1980s and 1990s were as much a result of the lack of hegemonic ethnic cores in these countries as they were the result of dysfunctional political systems. Elsewhere in the region, Arabs, Turks, and Persians have jealously guarded their historic monopoly over politics, culture, and society in their respective countries. While this ethnic hegemony has often enhanced the processes of state building and political consolidation, those in power cannot afford to be completely indifferent to the political ramifications of ethnic pluralism. In fact, ethnicity has often been a governing factor in the political lives of Iraq, Jordan, Syria, Palestinian Arabs, and to a lesser extent Egyptians.[51] On occasion, ethnicity has been an important force in Israeli politics as well, with the Sephardi-Ashkenazi division often greatly influencing party affiliation and voting patterns.[52]

The difficulty in assessing the real impact of ethnicity on Middle Eastern politics derives from its elusive nature. More than a reality in itself, ethnicity's power depends on the popular perceptions of the majority regarding people with different ethnic backgrounds in their society. Although popular prejudices and biases toward one or two of the ethnic minorities exist within each Middle Eastern society, ethnic pluralism has hardly been a catalyst for the breakup of national entities for a number of political, cultural, and economic reasons. Politically, Middle Eastern states have often not hesitated to respond with brute force when confronted with ethnically based challenges. In 1982 Hafez Assad's bloody suppression of the Sunnis in Hama sent shock waves through not only Syria's non-'Alawi population but also ethnic minorities all over the region.[53] Other recent episodes of ethnic minority· suppression include the bloody though brief confrontation between the Kurds and the Turkomans; Iran's postrevolutionary government in 1979 and 1980; the Kuwaiti government's crackdown on Shia activists in the early and mid-1980s; and the massacre of Kurds and Shias by the Ba'athist regime in Iraq following the Gulf War.[54] Yet not all Middle Eastern states have had to resort to force to subdue ethnic uprisings because economic growth has often kept ethnicity from becoming a political issue. In nearly all Middle Eastern countries, spurts of economic growth and prosperity have subdued the potentially disruptive nature of existent ethnic divisions. Middle Eastern governments have been able to use increments of growth to pacify or gloss over ethnic cleavages while maintaining the privileged position of the ethnically dominant group.[55] It is telling that where ethnic divisions have degenerated into civil wars (Lebanon, the Sudan, and Iraq), it was only *after* the breakup of the state that the various ethnic minorities began to flex their political muscles. Political paralysis did not occur as a result of ethnic disunity but facilitated its expression once the restraint mechanisms of the state had been removed or substantially weakened.

Finally, the cultural romanticization of ethnic diversity has done much to depoliticize ethnic differences. Most Middle Eastern states have often successfully presented a romantic image of politically docile ethnic and tribal minorities to the larger society. For instance, a sense of nostalgia and a longing for the so-called simple, "clean" life of the bedouin characterize the sentiments of most urbanites in most Arab countries.[56] This carefully crafted, nonthreatening image of the various ethnic groups can potentially placate some of their assimilationist demands while at the same time reducing some societal friction and prejudice. Nevertheless, although the forces of tribalism and ethnicity tend to become politically blunted, they remain powerful enough to merit the continued attention of the state.

Religion

Religion in general and Islam in particular should be analyzed on two levels. First, every religion provides a system of values and a set of beliefs according to which its adherents are meant to live their lives. But beyond this valuative significance is the important role that religious institutions play. Whether they are temples, churches, or mosques, places of worship are important centers for social organization and mobilization. Thus as an institution, religion is a phenomenon that influences society with more than its values alone by providing internal organization and additional institutional mechanisms as well. It is important to note, however, that the significance of religion as both a system of beliefs and a social institution varies greatly, depending on the existence of numerous other social, cultural, or political variables. Throughout Latin America, for example, Catholicism steadily lost ground to the forces of economic development and social change in the 1960s and early 1970s, finding itself increasingly on the defensive and retreating into the confines of the church and doctrinal orthodoxy. It slowly reoriented itself in the 1970s and the 1980s, or at least some segments within it did, and gradually developed viable institutional components (e.g., Base Ecclesiastical Communities) through which it reestablished ties with some of the social strata that were becoming increasingly detached from it.[57] In essence, Catholicism had been transformed from an abstract cultural ideal for ethical well-being into a tangible social institution that affected people's lives and the way they organized and mobilized. A set of developments not unlike those in Latin America have appeared in the Middle East in recent decades and have greatly enhanced the significance of religion as a pivotal institution in society.

When looking at the role of religion—particularly that of Islam—as a social institution in the Middle East, one cannot help but be struck by its dramatic political radicalization in the recent past. The politicization of Islam, or, more accurately, its repoliticization, has frequently been referred to in the West as "Islamic fundamentalism" by the media, and it has assumed an image and a life of its own by most Western conceptions.[58] The semantics of this phenomenon will be discussed in a later chapter. For now, it is important to keep in mind that the repoliticization of Islam has resulted in its increasing significance as a social institution, although Islam by its very nature has always been a salient phenomenon. Islam, after all, began as a movement designed to shape a new community of believers (*umma*) politically and religiously.[59] Gradually over time Islamic rulers discovered it was beneficial to encourage their subjects to render unto them what was theirs and to relegate nontemporal matters to an emerging class of religious specialists. Whether calling himself a caliph, sultan, or even president, the caesar kept close tabs on the *imams* (or the *sheykhs* or *ulema*) and often found it necessary to remind them of his own superior abilities to interpret Islamic tenets when the situation called for it. Thus the once-solid marriage of Islam with politics and society had, by the early twentieth century, become largely one of convenience, dictated more by the mostly secular political, economic, and diplomatic realities than by the internal dynamics of Islam itself. Yet the social and political resonance of the religion remained and, especially in the realm of society, was not pushed completely into the background. Political Islam therefore became largely theoretical, an abstract to be studied and only seldom pursued. Such caesars as Atatürk; Reza Pahlavi and later his son Mohammad Reza, the shah of Iran; Nasser; Sadat; Bourguiba; Assad; Mubarak; and Saddam Hussein did not take kindly to the idea of an Islam with political agendas. Only when the caesar saw fit did Islam become a medium of political expression, and a heavily machinated one at that. As history has shown, not all Middle Eastern caesars have been successful at neutralizing Islam's political urges.

A similar though less thorough process of de-Islamization occurred in almost all Middle Eastern societies, with Saudi Arabia and parts of the United Arab Emirates as major exceptions. This process was differential and staggered both within individual countries and between them. Nevertheless, it occurred, whether because of the necessities of economic development, the effects of social change, the agendas of the state, or, as was most often the case, a combination of all three. As widespread as de-Islamization was and has been, several factors differentiate it from Islam's growing distance from politics. Although most Middle Eastern states have launched extensive campaigns aimed at secularizing the legal and educational systems, their efforts have not often been coercively enforced. As a result, such campaigns have been undermined by the more "traditional" strata of society whenever possible. The distance between these traditional classes and the state remains wide in such ostensibly "modernizing" countries as Algeria, Morocco, Tunisia, Egypt, Jordan, Syria, and Iraq. (Iran before 1979 would also fit into this category.) For the traditional classes, Islam and its values serve as more than mere valuative alternatives to the state. Indeed, for them Islam constitutes a whole universe apart and separate from that which the state is seeking to create.

Two factors have reinforced Islam's importance as a social institution, one inherent to the religion itself and the other a product of certain sociopolitical and economic developments in recent years. The first is the belief that Islam is a comprehensive blueprint for social order.[60] Of all the different social institutions found in the Middle East, Islam is the one that, ideally at least, subsumes, overwhelms, and dictates all the others. Islam governs the life of the individual, family, tribe, and larger community, dictating absolutes for even the most mundane and minute aspect of their conduct. Some of Islam's innumerable laws include regulations on what to eat, when to sleep, how to worship, when and how to clean oneself, when to engage in or abstain from sexual intercourse, when and how to defend against outside intruders, and how to behave in a socially, politically, and economically responsible manner.[61] How can the state possibly suppress, or even supplant, such an overwhelmingly thorough social institution? Realizing the continued and lasting resonance of Islam throughout their societies, even the most secular states have found it necessary to pay lip service to Islamic tenets.[62] The end result is that for a substantial number of Middle Easterners, Islam has remained a tangible social and cultural reality, a living mechanism influencing everyday life in far more profound ways than the state could ever hope to do.

The second factor influencing Islam's importance as a social institution is the decreasing legitimacy of most secular institutions, particularly those created or maintained by the government. In country after country in the Middle East, Islam has become a more pervasive force when the legitimacy of the secular state has begun to diminish. This has meant that former believers have rediscovered its necessity in the benefits and services it provides that the state cannot deliver. While almost all the states have strived to become bureaucratic-authoritarian, albeit most unsuccessfully, their failure in addressing the needs of their societies has not necessarily resulted in economic difficulties, although crippled economies were and have been instrumental in spreading fervid religious sentiments throughout prerevolutionary Iran and present-day Egypt. Where the state has failed—and this applies to almost all of them—has been in the moral-ethical and emotional-psychological domains. Most states suffer from debilitating, chronic moral bankruptcy. Leaders claiming to be modern-day messiahs, for example, turn out to be oppressive caesars, and crooked ones at that. The president and his wife patronizingly talk about their lean years in the village, but they live in palaces where opulence is fathomed by few and actually seen by even fewer. The government's bureaucracy and its official ideology are hardly any less corrupt. Within such a context, how could religion *not* grow in stature and social importance? As Fouad Ajami put it, the resurgence of Islam is, more than anything else, a "response to the blockage of ideas and the failure of state elites."[63] The secular alternative, especially that proposed by the state, has been fully discredited. The caesar's oppressive corruption is countered by the supposed piety of the *imam*, unless the *imam* is otherwise exposed. Thus the false, material world on which the caesar relies takes a psychological backseat to the real, seemingly pure world of Islam. It is now Islam that provides an alternative universe for an even greater segment of society, offering a source of refuge and an answer to the disillusioned who were once not so attracted to it.

But the resurgence of Islam as a medium of popular expression and a revitalized social institution does not spring from political factors alone. It is part of a larger, more universal phenomenon that is symptomatic of societies undergoing tremendous social, cultural, and economic changes. Islam's increasing importance in Middle Eastern societies is less an affirmation of Muslims' growing piety than a sign of societies in crisis—societies that are desperately seeking to discover what their identities are, what their traditions and heritages mean, what aspects of their nationality to take pride in and what to reject, how to perceive themselves in comparison with others, and so forth. In short, societies grappling to make sense of it all.

The peculiar observance of the Islamic dress code by a growing number of educated "modern" women presents an insight into their psyche. Throughout the Middle East, women have rediscovered the veil (or scarf). But on occasion one sees a woman in headcover wearing a skirt and no stockings. While this combination may not necessarily violate her modesty, it clearly defeats the purpose of the veil. In most cases, then, the veil has become less an indicator of ardent Islamic belief than a symbol of belonging, a signpost signaling the discovery of identity in an otherwise disillusioning world. Such apparent contradictions abound all over the region and among all social classes, manifested through such displays of identity as personal appearance (with the beard serving the same function for men as the veil does for women), lifestyle, language and other modes of discourse, art and music, and family and personal relations.[64] The growing pains associated with countries in the Third World—rapid urbanization, fundamental social change, disillusionment with Western values and cultural products, middle-class fetishes, and other similar ailments—only accentuate the sense of real and perceived crisis in society.[65] Gellner has eloquently placed this phenomenon of cultural rediscovery in a global context. "Developing countries," he writes, whether European ones in the nineteenth century or Third World ones in the twentieth—in general face the painful dilemma between Modernism and Populism. The former is the key to wealth and power, but involves a denial of the local identity and the recognition of the authority of an alien model. The latter implies an idealization of the backward masses, the Volk, nomad, etc. In fact, the painful dilemma between on the one hand development and self-transformation, and hence self-contempt and repudiation of local tradition, and on the other maintenance of cultural identity at the price of economic and military weakness, is the general formula for the predicament of "backwardness." Muslim societies can escape this fork. Popular idealization of the fellah or the bedouin is mainly perpetrated by foreign romantics. The society itself, on the other hand, can at this point identify with one or more important strand within itself, its own Great Tradition, which is simultaneously indigenous and yet appears, to a considerable extent at least, to be usable as a banner for modernity, as a spur, standard and chastisement of local slovenliness, superstition, lethargy, and immobility.[66]

It is important to note that although the tide of Islamic resurgence seems to be widespread in Middle Eastern societies, it is not by any means uniform or permanent. As a social institution and a system of values, Islam has found particularly fertile ground in countries where secular alternatives have ruled high and then discredited themselves. In Turkey, Iraq, Syria, Jordan, Egypt, Tunisia, Algeria, and Morocco, both the state and society consider themselves to be "modern," or at least "modernizing." On the societal level, it is predominantly in these very countries where Islam has been rediscovered as the panacea to sociocultural ailments, where people voluntarily and without state encouragement become attracted to Islam and observe its social and cultural dicta. In fact, most of these states not only discourage the spread of Islam but often harass the faithful for their zeal.[67] The state's underlying friction with and at times its open hostility to Islam only enhance the religion's social and cultural resonance. Witness the predicaments of the Egyptian and Algerian governments and their societies since the early 1980s and 1990s.[68]

The trend has been reversed in countries where the state has used Islam as its official ideology and mainstay of political legitimacy. In many of the societies that have officially adopted it as a social blueprint and the guideline to which all social relations and cultural norms must conform, Islam has lost much of its sway in the hearts and minds of its adherents.

In Iran the kind of Islam that in the 1970s seemed to be the answer to all social and political ills turned out to be in the 1980s, in much of the public mind, a tool for repression and war. In essence, Khomeini did much more to discredit Islam in the eyes of Iranians in less than a decade than the shah had done in more than thirty years. In Lebanon, where, not unlike the Druze and the Christians, the Muslims sought refuge in their religion against the country's disintegration in the 1970s and early 1980s, many later saw it as a catalyst for disunity and a more bruised image abroad. And in Saudi Arabia and the rest of the Gulf countries where Islamic edicts are forcibly carried out by the state, many citizens try to circumvent them whenever possible. As a social institution Islam becomes paramount when the state stands in subtle or overt opposition to it. By the same token, it declines as a social institution and valuative guideline when it is forced on society. In such instances, Islam may continue to have a strong emotional resonance for the individual, but only in his or her personal, private life. As an overall framework for social organization and a guideline for politics, however, Islam has largely discredited itself in virtually the same way that most of the secular alternatives had before.

Like Saudi Arabia, Israel traces its genesis to the very birth of its dominant religion. Judaism deserves separate discussion here because many Israelis see the pursuit of Jewishness and citizenship in the State of Israel as one and the same. Like Islam, Judaism permeates virtually all aspects of the believer's life, governing social and cultural spheres of activity as well as the political and religious spheres. But Judaism's historic experience has bestowed on many of its adherents a deep-seated moral and psychological desire to maintain actively the religion's resonance along social, cultural, religious, and political lines, even if it is necessary to take up arms. As one observer notes, "Jews ... have addressed *the Land* in song and speech; proclaimed that 'the atmosphere of the Land of Israel makes one wise,' and so on." The preoccupation of Jews as a people, the author continues, "has been to keep faith with itself when its Mythic Theme is dependent on a geographic locale, whereas it has become a world people."[69] For most Israelis, then, Judaism and the political movement Zionism are more than central notions of self-identity and life—they define their very historic existence, not in any ordinary sense but as "the chosen people." This does not overlook the divergencies or even social schisms in Israel along religious lines; in fact, such divisions have often become deep chasms between different religious communities, thereby affecting the electorate. But on the whole, Judaism as a social institution is perhaps

more powerful than Islam in maintaining a hold over its followers by profoundly shaping and molding the lives of its believers, and it does so more
or less independently of political or other outside influences. Judaism is
maintained through the force of its own internal dynamics, its own history, and the personal effect it has on its adherents. It is, after all, their
religion for which Jews were persecuted, that took them where they are
today, and for whose defense they are willing to fight and die when necessary. For Israeli Jews, their religion is a universe far more comprehensive
than any other social institution could ever become. Its centrality in Israeli
society has been further reinforced through the agendas and policies of
the state and the country's own political, diplomatic, and military experiences. Few worldviews or social institutions could hope to accomplish the
dominance and genuine devotion that Judaism has among Israeli Jews.[70]

A word needs to be said about minority religions in the Middle East
and their importance as social institutions to their respective followers.
Table 2.2 (p. 68) shows that all Middle Eastern countries except Israel are
either predominantly or entirely Islamic. There are, nevertheless, large
numbers of non-Muslims in Lebanon and the Sudan as well as smaller
numbers within each Middle Eastern country. The minority status of non-
Muslims causes them to cling to their religion as an important source of
identity, as the sole institution that defines their uniqueness compared
with others. Because Islam is usually the "official" state religion and a
pervasive social institution, religion becomes an equally defining factor for
the non-Muslim minorities. But the peculiarities of the Middle East tend
to complicate matters. With chants of "Death to Israel!" as official state
policy in Iran, Iraq, Syria, and Libya, it may not be prudent to advertise
one's Jewishness in those countries. Similarly, although to a lesser extent,
the region's numerous Christian sects may at times feel compelled to keep
their religious views to themselves in public gatherings and forums.

Two features tend to characterize the societal role of religion for the
religious minorities. On the one hand, religion, while pivotal in defining
the self, becomes increasingly private, less openly displayed but devoutly
followed in the confines of home, church, or temple. Thus religion does
not serve as a blueprint for social order or even a full-fledged guideline for
valuative conduct. The world outside compels one to act otherwise—if
not necessarily according to the tenets of Islam, then at least according to
the secular limits that society is willing to tolerate. On the other hand, the
very restrictions placed on religious minorities—if not by the state, then
by the larger Muslim society—encourage them to become cliquish and to

TABLE 2.2
RELIGIOUS COMPOSITION
IN MIDDLE EASTERN COUNTRIES

Algeria	Majority Sunni Muslims (Maliki and a small group of Hanafi)
Bahrain	60% Shia Muslim; ruling family is Sunni
Egypt	90% Sunni Muslim; 10% Coptic Christian
Iran	Majority Shia Muslims; small communities of Sunnis, Christians, Jews, and Zoroastrians
Iraq	50% Shia Muslim; 40% Sunni; 10% various Christian sects
Israel	82.97% Jews; 13.04% Muslims; 2.33% Christians; 1.63% Druze; 0.02% others
Jordan	80% Sunni Muslim; 6% Christian minority
Kuwait	60–70% Sunni Muslim; 30% Shia; small Christian minorities
Lebanon	33% Shia Muslim; 20% Sunni Muslim; 40% Christian; 7% Druze
Libya	Majority Sunni Muslims
Morocco	Majority Sunni Muslims
Oman	75% Ibadi Muslim; 25% Sunni Muslim
Qatar	Majority Wahhabi Sunni Muslim
Saudi Arabia	Majority Sunni Muslims; 5% Shia Muslim
Sudan	70% Muslim; 26% Animist; 4% Christian
Syria	70% Sunni Muslim; 12% 'Alawi; 15% Druze, Ismaili, and Christian minorities
Tunisia	Majority Sunni Muslims; Jewish, Christian, and other minorities
Turkey	99% Sunni Muslim; Christian and Jewish minorities
UAE	Majority Sunni Muslim; small minority Shia Muslims
Yemen	50% Zaydi Muslim; 50% Shafii Sunni

SOURCE: Compiled from Trevor Mostyn and Albert Hourani, eds., *Cambridge Encyclopedia of the Middle East and North Africa* (Cambridge: Cambridge University Press, 1988).

find solace and security in greater reliance on their fellow believers. This makes meaningful national integration more problematic, with religious divisiveness unresolved though subdued by social and political imperatives. Thus in Iraq, Syria, and Egypt, where there are noticeable communities of religious minorities, the absence of overt religious divisions or even hostilities does not mean the potential for such developments is not there. In fact, where the state has proven to be dysfunctional and no single religious or ethnic group is predominant (as in Lebanon and the Sudan), religious differences have added fuel to the fires of civil war.

Education

Schools and other educational establishments form another important social institution, bestowing not only a unique sense of identity but also a
set of values and norms on a segment of the population that is significant
politically, namely, the educated. As in other developing nations that are
in the midst of social change and are continuously defining and redefining
the boundaries of permissible or desirable social and political activity,
Middle Eastern educational establishments play a crucial role in the political socialization of the populace.[71] From their earliest years, students are
taught to glorify the ruling family or the leader and *his* political system, receiving what at best amounts to a warped education in the social sciences
and the humanities. Distortions in historical data are imparted as fact, and
rarely if ever is there a free discussion of such objectionable subjects as sociology or political science. Only a state-sanctioned version of history is
taught, emphasizing certain "glorious" eras and de-emphasizing or painstakingly justifying less flattering periods. Proper rituals for worshipping the
state's cult of personality form an integral part of the curriculum at all levels, even at the university level, although there is less indoctrination.

Government educational policies are designed to go beyond containing any troublesome university students—they are meant to inculcate the
regime's legitimacy, its raison d'être, among students of all ages in order
to ensure support from future generations. Strengthening the state's efforts is the social prestige attached to studying the practical, not the theoretical, sciences: medicine and engineering are emphasized rather than
philosophy or the social sciences because they are perceived to be of far
greater relevance to the country's development and its scientific and industrial accomplishments. Those few individuals who become men and
women of letters all too often specialize in such nonpolitical humanities
subjects as literature, theoretical philosophy, Islamic studies, or (relatively
distant) history.

Few authors in the Middle East explore, or dare to explore, the soul
of their countries, politically or otherwise, and an equally small minority
of writers devote themselves to examining the disconcerting mazes that
their national cultures have become. Sociological and cultural criticisms
are scarce, overwhelmed by publications on topics considered safe and
therefore popular. The works of the prominent Egyptian writer and essayist Muhammad Hussein Heykal, whose latest book is entitled *Weapons
and International Relations in the October 1973 War,* are prime examples
of the genre of literature that, often out of necessity, has become popular
among Middle Eastern authors.[72]

Despite their ceaseless efforts to control the education and thoughts of students, Middle Eastern governments have been no more successful at creating a politically supportive student identity than have other regimes in the Third World. University and even high school students throughout the region have long proven to be among the most difficult segments of the population, as demonstrated by sporadic or even orchestrated student uprisings in Iran (in the 1970s and early 1980s), Turkey, Egypt, and Algeria. Following government crackdowns and other forms of reprisal, many students have in recent years opted for more symbolic and less violent forms of political expression, as evidenced in the widespread adoption of the Islamic dress code and the growth of religious student organizations on numerous campuses. A number of factors, some unique to the Middle East and others endemic to the developing world in general, reinforce this politicization of students. By virtue of their elite social and educational status, some university students undertake a mission to alleviate the miseries and injustices they have witnessed around them. On the one hand, their sense of responsibility is fueled by the politically stifling atmosphere created by the government, thereby turning even the most elementary forms of political expression into melodramatic acts of heroism. On the other hand, there is the greater availability of banned literature on university and high school campuses. That educational institutions throughout the Third World are not hotbeds of political discontent and opposition may be more a product of careful government control mechanisms than of student passivity.

Student political activity in the Middle East has since the late 1970s been ideologically resuscitated by the rebirth of political Islam, arming students with a socially and culturally resonant blueprint for moral salvation as well as political liberation. The students, whose youth makes them susceptible to disillusionment and demagoguery, have become the most militant members of the so-called Islamic movement. For them religion provides ready and understandable answers to a multitude of confusing political, social, intellectual, and emotional issues. In countries other than Iran and Lebanon where religion did not have a political heyday in the 1970s and 1980s and thus did not become an instrument of regime repression, the political abstractness of religion appeals to those in search of answers, especially to students. Demagoguery and a culture of hero-worship—by no means unique to Islamic activists—are additional elements that increase the likelihood of student activism. This is not to imply that universities automatically transform students into Islamic political activists; to the contrary, a combination of political repression, economic demands, and social pressures often leave little room for students to venture into political activities, especially of an organized nature. Outbursts of student political frenzy and opposition, as in Iran in the late 1970s, Egypt in the early 1980s, and Algeria in 1991 and 1992, are few and far between. Nevertheless, a greater number of political militants or those with the potential to become militants are found among university and high school students than elsewhere in the society. The mind-set of particularly volatile students and the peculiar atmosphere prevailing on most campuses provide the right conditions for political and religious militancy.

In addition to students, intellectuals—the socially and politically more noticeable product of the educational establishment—deserve particular mention. After all, intellectuals should define the guiding conscience of a nation, critiquing and in the process refining their society's cultural frame of reference. Indeed, if the educational establishment as a social institution is supposed to endow people with a special sense of identity, that identity is most clearly expressed through intellectuals, who contemplate, write, and "predicate societal action."[73] Theoretically at least, intellectuals are that segment of the larger intelligentsia (i.e., academics, people of letters, and the well educated) who are politically aware and often view themselves as the future leaders of a political movement. Thus by definition, intellectuals are of far greater relevance to the overall social and cultural context in developing countries than in industrialized nations. As modernization transforms the industrial infrastructure and the cultural values that govern a society, intellectuals assume a special place of honor. In modernizing societies, intellectuals' support for or opposition to these values is at a more fundamental level because some values have either not been fully adopted by the general public, or their adoption or popular social acceptance can be easily challenged by other contending values. As the contention between opposing values becomes more polarized in modernizing countries, the greater the intellectuals' influence.[74]

It is within this context that the social role and importance of intellectuals in the Middle East should be viewed. As in other regions of the Third World, a clear distinction must be drawn between those Middle Eastern intellectuals who live and write in their own societies and those who live in the West. Each group is important in its own right, but there are significant differences. The writers and artists who observe, work, and reside in their native countries come closest to the theoretical definition of intellectualism presented above because of their influence and how they shape the dominant norms of their society. The expatriates, in contrast, can write without fear of losing their freedom or job security, and they often cast a broader net of critical scrutiny over their societies, occasionally writing about or critiquing fellow intellectuals in their native lands. Yet the very distance that buffers them from official sanctions is also their greatest handicap—they exert little influence over the societies they analyze and to whom they have devoted their careers. In the Middle East hardly anyone has heard of scholars renowned in the West such as Edward Said, Fouad Ajami, Hisham Sharabi, and Samir Amin, but almost everyone knows who the largely politically and socioculturally ineffectual Heykal and Fouad Zakariyya are.[75] One observer has written that

> There are serious ills in Arab popular culture. The tendency to avoid self-criticism and blame Arab problems on external conspiracies still prevails among many Arabs. Some still interpret the world according to their reading of the *Protocols of the Elders of Zion,* which unfortunately remains a best-seller in most Arab capitals, due to its promotion by regimes and political parties, including the Syrian Social National Party and various fundamentalist groups....
>
> Arab wounds are partly, and perhaps largely, self-inflicted. The nationalist and Islamist apologetic schools want to blame the outside world for all miseries in the region. Unless chauvinistic taboos are lifted, and unless Arabs show a willingness to examine themselves critically and mercilessly, the road to national recovery will be prolonged. In the words of Hasan Hanafi, "The current circumstances through which the Arab nation passes necessitate a reconsideration of everything: the beginnings, the introductions, and the axioms. No prohibitions and no taboos."[76]

Current intellectual trends within Middle Eastern countries are difficult to pinpoint, particularly at a time when no single event or movement of historical significance marks the political history of the region. After their psychologically troubling "defeat" in 1967, Arab intellectuals looked increasingly to Islam as the remedy for their disillusionment with secular ideological alternatives, a trend that was reinforced after the reassuring 1973 "victory." Simultaneously, the superpower rivalry of the cold war, disillusionment with a supposedly stale religious heritage, and the plague of Western imperialism attracted some intellectuals to communism and other ostensibly "progressive" ideologies.[77] But the current prognosis for intellectual activity is somewhat poor because it is undermined by a lack of certain social, cultural, and political preconditions. Society needs to be sufficiently troubled, and to be so under the right conditions, for an intellectual fervor to develop as well as to gain a meaningful social and cultural footing. The example of prerevolutionary Iran is most revealing. "Political Islam," whose genesis was the result of larger regionwide phenomena, grew as a specific ideological force in the 1970s in Iran, beginning as a deliberate attempt by a group of thinkers, especially Ali Shariati and Abolhasan Banisadr, to lay out a political alternative to the shah's secular dictatorship.[78] But their ideas flourished as a result of profound social and political disillusionment. Whether hailed or ridiculed for their controversial perspectives, the likes of Shariati were at least listened to in the hope that they might be the ones with the answers. Similar social and political preconditions are absent from most Middle Eastern countries today. Egypt and Lebanon, renowned for their critical thinkers, are both preoccupied with more tangible and pressing concerns than the luxury of philosophical thought and contemplation. Egyptians are learning how to cope with the harsh economic realities of the Mubarak era, while the Lebanese are piecing back together their fractured and war-torn nation. The intense intellectual activism of the 1960s and 1970s in Iran degenerated into disillusionment and was then banned and its leaders punished in the twists and turns of the 1978–79 revolution.[79]

The bleak assertions made here should not be construed as an argument that thinking, writing, and reflection in the Middle East are rare these days. After all, as the Arabic saying goes, "Egyptians write, the Lebanese publish, and Iraqis read." The rich intellectual tradition that began in the mid-1800s has retained some of its seminal vitality,[80] enough so that some writers speak of an Arab renaissance (*nahda*).[81] In Egypt the writers Naguib Mahfouz, Heykal, and Zakariyya continue to challenge the intellect with their expositions.[82] Turkey's Yasar Kemal is a prolific author and an outspoken critic of the government, being a thorn in the side of the Ankara regime for its mistreatment of the Kurds and frequent violations of human rights.[83] In Iran a far greater number of books have been published since the 1978–79 revolution than ever before, and a whole new host of figures have joined a literary circle once greatly limited in its composition as well as in its larger political and cultural significance.[84] Abdulkarim Soroush, an increasingly popular Islamic thinker in Iran, is slowly and subtly challenging the Iranian government's orthodox interpretations of Islam in his essays and lectures. But in these and other Middle Eastern countries, the cumulative social and cultural importance of contemporary literary figures has remained minimal in shaping the overall agendas and priorities of their societies.

The ideological and philosophical divisions, or the lack of a broad consensus, that mark contemporary Middle Eastern intellectuals was discussed earlier. But such divisions, which are to a certain extent an ac-knowledged fact of intellectual discourse, pale in comparison to the ef-fects of political co-option and even repression by regimes. Some Middle Eastern intellectuals, as one observer wryly notes, "choose to defend their integrity by going into exile."[85] Others, such as Mahfouz and Heykal, steer clear of more controversial political issues and limit their expositions to largely nonpolitical, or "safer," topics, whether they be history, social satire, or philosophy. A third group of intellectuals, however, either be-come literary or journalistic mouthpieces for the government, or some at the very least give a gloss of legitimacy to the regime through subtle criti-cism of the opposition. Hardly an issue of the revered *Al Ahram* appears without a column by one well-known essayist or another in which a posi-tion taken by the government is directly or indirectly endorsed and pre-sented in the guise of reason. The same type of manipulation goes on, of-ten with less subtlety, in other government-owned or controlled dailies in circulation from Rabat to Tehran and points in between. Whatever the reasons for this cooperation, these intellectuals have largely detached themselves from the rest of society and become tied to the state. Although they may not have quite sold their souls to the government, they have ceased being the conduits through which society can attain greater politi-cal and cultural involvement. Whether or not they are willing to admit it, these same intellectuals have perpetuated the vacuousness of the state.

Gathering Places

Apart from the educational establishment and such "natural" institutions as the family or the tribe, a number of other institutions routinely serve as informal gathering places throughout the Middle East. The depth of their social and cultural resonance have gradually transformed them into insep-arable parts of the social equation. Two such places, teahouses and mosques, are found in all countries of the region, albeit in different forms and with varying degrees of significance. Among the others—and not including specific institutions that may be unique to individual Middle Eastern countries—are the neighborhoods (*mahhaleh*), traditional sports clubs (in Iran called *zourkhaneh,* literally, "houses of strength"), and city parks and local squares (*maydan*).[86] The Iranian *dowreh,* or periodic reli-gious gatherings by women, are important social rituals that give their participants a sense of identity and purpose.[87] In quite a different manner, *hammams,* or public baths, play an important role in socialization, espe-cially among women, in Iraq and parts of the Maghreb, particularly Mo-rocco and Tunisia.[88]

A number of important qualifications need to be made here. In one way or another, many of these social institutions are essentially undergoing slow and gradual extinction as the forces of modernity push these vestiges of tradition into the fringes of social life. Yet this process is by no means universal and is subject to larger sociocultural and political nuances. Teahouses, for instance, may decline or increase in social stature and political significance, depending on the prevailing political climate. It is nevertheless undeniable that some traditional gathering places that once formed the very fabric of social life and were instrumental in formulating people's identities, their cultural frames of reference, and their social and political worlds, have lost some of their former resonance and strength. These and other similar institutions continue to exist and in fact are thriving because of some groups' needs, but the unmistakable trend has been toward their curtailment.

Before examining the nature and the current state of each of these social institutions, it is important to look at the factors that have traditionally (although to a lesser degree today) underlain their resonance and longevity. One of the paradoxes of Middle Eastern politics is that it can, given the right historical circumstances and environment, have very little to do with all the nuances of society. Middle Eastern societies often have internal dynamics and forces that enable them to operate at full potential in a universe unscathed by the intrusion of formal politics and governmental institutions. Society often has little need for the state. This, incidentally, is precisely what many Middle Eastern governments count on: *leave politics to us, and you can do almost anything you like.* The inherent informality of life in these societies both facilitates and reinforces some self-sufficiency insofar as formal politics is concerned. More specifically, in Middle Eastern societies there are certain institutions that serve as vital outlets for political expression and for politicking, not necessarily on a national scale but at least within and among one's peers. Teahouses and mosques serve precisely this kind of function. While they may be largely inconsequential on a national political scale (except in Iran), these gathering places are important local institutions that enable people to express their political opinions—in very different ways, of course—while socializing with their kinfolk, neighbors, friends, and associates. This is not to imply that mosques or teahouses are natural hotbeds of political discussion or activity. Nor is their social scope, as mentioned earlier, by any means uniform throughout the region or even within the same country. What is politically important about them is their *potential* role as centers of information, as gathering places through which local and intense mass mobilization, either in defense of or in opposition to the regime, can be achieved.

Teahouses—or coffeehouses, as they are called in parts of the Middle East—dot almost every city and town in the region, though their social function and importance varies considerably from one country to another. In Egypt and Jordan, and to a lesser extent in Algeria, Iraq, and Iran, teahouses have managed to retain a significant degree of social importance, serving as the locus for gatherings and entertainment for certain social groups. Rarely do women go to teahouses, and almost never alone or with other women. When they do go, women are usually in the company of a male relative and are there only to drink their beverage, not to hang around and socialize. Men, in contrast, may spend considerable lengths of time in a teahouse, frequenting one in their neighborhood where they can watch television (in past decades, they would listen to storytellers or the radio), play backgammon, smoke the waterpipe, or simply chat.

The social importance of teahouses throughout the Middle East has declined drastically in recent decades. In Iran, teahouse recitals of Firdawsi's *Shah Nameh* were once considered an elevated art form, and Cairo's teahouses have inspired many of Mahfouz's rich literary works. To this day, the Havana Cafeteria in Damascus remains a favorite watering hole of writers, essayists, and men and women of letters. But like other traditional gathering places of their genre, teahouses have lost much of their former audience and clientele, their social reach having progressively narrowed as the forces of change and modernity chip away at their stylishness, feasibility, and cultural resonance. The importance of teahouses—as well as those other informal gathering places, for that matter—lies in the political ramifications of their continued existence. Those who tend to congregate in teahouses often include people drawn from the lower economic stratum of society, those who express a greater ease with tradition than with modernity. They are frequently men working in the informal economic sector who, if not living hand-to-mouth, have few prospects. In Egypt they are often unemployed urban youths whose aspirations have been thwarted by the systemic shortcomings of the national economy; in Algeria, Iraq, and Iran they are mostly first-generation rural immigrants whose dreams of an affluent city life have yet to materialize. In one way or another, they are all economically and politically disillusioned, socially and culturally alienated. A demagogic leader could hardly hope for a more receptive audience. Teahouse patrons are potential recruits for extremist movements that promise immediate and easy salvation. It is precisely from among these ranks that the footsoldiers in Iran's

Islamic revolution and its war with Iraq were drawn, and it is here that the current extremist movements in Algeria and Egypt have found fertile breeding ground.

Mosques have played this recruiting role even more pointedly, although their influence has again varied greatly from one country to another as well as from one social stratum to the next. Middle Eastern mosques were traditionally one of the most important centers of social activity and scholarship (complemented by such other gathering places as the bazaar and smaller shrines and tombs [*imamzadehs*]), and were usually a mandatory element in each city.[89] Because of the historically intimate and at times conflicting relationship between religion and the state, the social and political importance of mosques has tended to oscillate widely within and between countries of the region. In recent years, mosques and other centers of religious activity have often been marginalized in times of economic prosperity and social continuity, only to reemerge as centers of dissent and even for mass mobilization during times of disillusionment and crisis. The classic example of mosques having turned into political nerve centers is in Iran immediately before and after the 1979 revolution. Recent developments in Algeria, Egypt, and, to a lesser extent, Jordan have given religious gathering places there somewhat of a political flavor as well.[90] The overt politicization of mosques and of Islam as a whole are recent and rather sporadic phenomena, and the political successes of Shiism in Iran have not yet been replicated in the predominantly Sunni Middle East. But few mosques in towns and cities are completely nonpolitical, the degree of their politicization often depending on the individual preacher and his style of sermons.

Themes covered in sermons can range from morality, elucidating a particular aspect of Islamic history, discussing a story from the Prophet's life, or even touching on more politically relevant issues that deal with power, national unity or fragmentation, military valor, righteous leadership, or the Palestinian cause.[91] But doublespeak is a popular cover for getting an intended message across. The following quotation from a largely apolitical sermon in Jerusalem is most telling:

> God, make Islam and Muslims victorious. God, make Islam and Muslims victorious. God, make Islam and Muslims victorious. Good God, support the power of Islam. Good God, support the power of Islam. Good God, support the power of Islam. And destroy the cunning unbelievers. Good God, make victorious all who walk in his path in order to raise the banner of Muhammad, may God bless and grant him salvation.[92]

Nevertheless, despite the unrelenting political messages found there and with the exception of Iran since the late 1970s, Middle Eastern mosques are largely places of solace, quiet prayer, and worship. Apart from prayer services held five times a day and especially on Fridays for the noonday prayer meeting and sermon, mosques are seldom places of mass congregation. The mosque usually has a clerical guardian who may also serve as its caretaker. Although Sunni clergymen are theoretically without any rank, the eminence with which they are held depends on such factors as how they are recognized by their congregations and peers for their scholarly and theological contributions, the size and historical importance of the mosque or seminary school (*madreseh*) with which they are affiliated, and the wealth and prestige of the neighborhood in which the mosque or school is located.

While it is rare that teahouses and mosques serve as centers for popular political mobilization, they have a leading role in hampering or at least undermining the regime's social and political agendas. Their perseverance points to the fundamental obstacles the modern state faces in enforcing its rule over society. Even though they are not necessarily antagonistic toward the state, as some mosques have become in recent years, these institutions have enough of a hold over society that they present a formidable problem. And although the scope of their social reach has been limited to specific classes within society, the informal patterns of interaction and behavior they perpetuate resonate across the social spectrum and govern many lives. In fact, these and other similar institutions are part of a larger dilemma for Middle Eastern states, that is, how to cultivate citizen loyalty to their own formal institutions, such as the military, the bureaucracy, the official party, and so forth. The lower and lower-middle classes may frequent teahouses and regularly attend mosques, but the upper-middle class and other "modernists" have their own gathering places and forms of entertainment. Sports clubs and American-style gyms have become popular with not only young people but also those larger segments of society who point to the West as their frame of social and cultural reference. In some countries, particularly Morocco, Tunisia, Egypt, Turkey, and Iran, there are gyms that double as social clubs, each with its own level of prestige, where the less traditional strata of society congregate, entertain themselves, and spend time. The al-Gazireh club in Cairo may be far more fashionable than any of the city's teahouses, but it nonetheless serves the same social and cultural function, albeit for a different class of people.

Conclusion

The informality of life that characterizes Middle Eastern societies is manifested most clearly in its various social institutions. By far the most resonant of them have proven to be the family, the tribe and its derivative ethnicity, and religion. Most other social institutions, namely, educational establishments and intellectuals, informal gathering places, and institutions that may be unique to particular countries, have declined in importance in recent years and have lost much of their former power and significance. The extended family has retained its strength and vitality despite the onslaught of social change and its attendant consequences, such as the emergence of the nuclear family and the generation gap. Likewise, religion remains deeply embedded in people's emotions and psyches, its hold seldom affected by fads and political nuances. Extremists like Sadat and Khomeini may come and go, but religion has remained a powerful constant in the people's daily lives. Insofar as the Middle East is concerned, the dichotomy between "traditional" and "modern" does not in any sense mean an aversion to religion by even the most modernized social classes. Islam is the lifeblood of most Middle Easterners, as are Christianity and Judaism to their respective adherents in the region. Religion in the Middle East is more than a source of moral certainty and righteousness in times of disillusionment and despair; it is the means for expressing identity and for being. The intelligentsia has been less fortunate, unable in any sense to help formulate a coherent language through which the troubled self can be expressed. Most resident intellectuals have been either silenced or co-opted, while expatriate intellectuals are little known inside their native countries. Informal gathering places continue to exist but attract only certain social classes: the nouveau riche frequent the social clubs considered prestigious and the rest go to teahouses and coffeehouses. These institutions may help each group develop its own identity, but in the process they only magnify the differences that separate the classes.

Of course, the functions, role, and significance of each of these social institutions is influenced by the prevailing broad forces that permeate the life and overall priorities of society. I identified in this chapter three such social forces in the Middle East: autocracy, primordial loyalties and sources of identity, and noneconomic and nonpolitical concerns. The larger consequences of these phenomena to the prospects for democracy are discussed in later chapters. Nevertheless, it is possible to make some cursory observations here based on the preceding analysis. In one form or another, primordial tendencies still exert considerable influence on Middle Eastern societies, and prevalent social institutions such as the family, religion, ethnicity, and even the educational establishment have proven to be highly rigid, uncompromising, and not at all conducive to the spirit of democracy. The patriarchal, male-dominated family has been authoritarian to the core, unyielding in its demand for blind obedience to the father and other elders. Any sign of dissent is perceived as a major threat to the cohesion of the family unit and, by inference, to the larger community. The nation, which is the ultimate community, is equally unlikely to welcome or to tolerate political nonconformity. The authoritarian dynamics of a father-child relationship are established in the greater arena of national politics with remarkably few changes. The leader, whether calling himself president or *imam,* passes himself off as the nation's father, often calling on his faithful "children" to chastise their unruly siblings. Most Middle Easterners have little difficulty with this arrangement because they have been culturally and psychologically accustomed to it most of their early and adult lives. The seeds of submission are sown early in the Middle East.

Religion and ethnicity have emerged as compelling and powerful sources of identity, familiar institutions from the comfort of which the hostile world outside can be confronted. Again, the current manifestations of religion and ethnicity, especially tribalism, do not foster social and cultural features that would welcome democracy. Both tribalism and ethnicity have long been manipulated by the political center and used as tools for acquiring popular legitimacy, fostering divisiveness, and pursuing other political ploys. Even if tribalism and ethnicity were to act as forces that encouraged democracy, the political realities of the region would guard against such a possibility. A similar process of political subjugation, at least during most periods of Middle Eastern history, has prevented Islam, as socially pervasive and culturally resonant as it may be, from becoming a pillar of antiauthoritarianism. In recent years, in fact, Islam's own doctrinal features and the political context within which they have been practiced have persistently turned that religion into a decidedly anti-democratic force, whether it has been at the service of or in opposition to the state.

The intellectual climate has not fared any better. As a general rule, Middle Eastern schools encourage rote memorization over critical thinking, obedience over independence, and tunnel vision over a broader outlook. High schools and universities are filled with robots who are taught not to rationalize but to internalize. Creative thinking is welcomed as long as it pertains only to the abstract, the distant, the nonthreatening. Those who are creative and employ this gift for the greater social good are often harassed by the state or chastised by the society; dispirited and resigned, they may alienate themselves from the rest of their environment. Few of them, at any rate, dare speak out, and fewer members of their societies hear them. Under the gloss of intellectualism, a vicious cycle of misunderstanding and ignorance is continually reinforced. Even if the dogmas that are generated in the process are meant to be democratic, their substance and manner of expression are often highly undemocratic. Not unlike the other social institutions with which it coexists, the Middle Eastern intellectual culture contributes little to the essence of democracy—if anything, it often undermines it.

In the final analysis, the gap between state and society in the Middle East remains hopelessly wide, each operating within a largely distinct valuative and institutional domain of its own. Society goes on leading its own life, governed by its mostly nongovernmental and nonofficial dynamics, while the state struggles to impose its cultural legitimacy and institutional hegemony. The ensuing patterns of state-society interaction have, among other things, greatly affected the various social classes, which are examined in the next chapter.

3. Social Classes

IN THE PREVIOUS chapter the social institutions through which people interact with one another and with the state were examined. These institutions, each based on certain values, loyalties, and functions, bestow on their members a common sense of identity and particular shared characteristics. The family, tribe and ethnicity, religion, education, and informal gathering places were highlighted as social institutions that have in one way or another been instrumental in shaping the lives of Middle Easterners. Whether because of their own peculiar pattern of development or because of the political environment in which they have evolved and presently operate, none of these institutions is particularly receptive to the principles or premises of democracy.

Conspicuously absent from the discussion were *economic* characteristics, which not only have great potential for fostering collective identities among masses of people but also could, within the right context, enhance or impede prospects for the growth and evolution of democracy. Simply stated, "class"—in its literal economic sense—was not identified as a social institution. The omission was not unintentional. Because of the peculiar social, economic, cultural, and political formations found in the Middle East, economic class consciousness has failed to develop in a way that would mobilize citizens into socially or politically cohesive units. The development of class consciousness has been at best fragmentary and episodic, although examples of labor and leftist movements are found in the recent histories of Turkey, Iran, and Egypt. Frequently, however, class consciousness has been diminished by more consuming sociocultural identities and values that have superseded loyalties based on economic status or the nature of one's employment. Thus by itself class cannot be relied on as a useful tool for the analysis of Middle Eastern societies. But the economic differences that set groups apart within their own societies simply cannot be ignored. What is needed is an analysis that would take into ac-

count the economic similarities of Middle Easterners, as well as their social and cultural characteristics. In order to complete the analysis of the
last chapter, I therefore examine here the various *social classes* found in
the Middle East and their possible ramifications for the larger political
system. Before delving into the task at hand, however, the concept of social class and its analytical utility should be clarified.

The concepts of class and class consciousness have been particularly
important in classical and neo-Marxist social analyses, which assigned a
central role to economic classes as constituent members of the social order. Specifically, class position determines the distinct consciousness or
worldview of its members. Marx himself claimed that on the basis of its
socioeconomic position, each class creates "an entire superstructure of
distinct and peculiarly formed sentiments, illusions, modes of thought and
views of life."[1] Class consciousness would lead to interclass conflict and
eventually to a dialectical process of historical progression. "The history
of all hitherto existing society," according to Marx in *The Communist
Manifesto,* "is the history of class struggles."[2] Recent elaboration of this
analysis has drawn a sharper connection between class and the state.
"Class structure and class relations," one neo-Marxist scholar has noted,

> are the major determinants of politics and the state, and class conflicts
> and class strategies lie at the center of social and political transformation,
> for it is only through such struggles that state power is attained and the
> will of the victorious social class(es) is imposed over society—although the
> dialectics of class struggle permit the state, from time to time, to become
> "relatively autonomous" of the contending class forces and their fractions
> and *appear* neither of the two main antagonistic classes.[3]

These definitions of class, it must be remembered, are invariably based on
the collective relationships that certain groups of people have with the
forces and relations of production (i.e., with decidedly economic phenomena), and their "subjective" and cultural characteristics are all essentially
derived from matters and relations that are economic to the core.

This strict, narrowly defined concept of class as an exclusive economic unit is devoid of analytical value in explaining Middle Eastern social formations, as well as those in other parts of the world. In Middle
Eastern societies at least, the historical resonance of social and cultural
forces, combined with their dominant roles in the daily lives of average
citizens, have resulted in the predominance of sociocultural determinants
of identity over others, including economic ones. Class consciousness has

thus been largely overshadowed by the pointed differences that have grown around differing tribal and ethnic identities, religions or degrees of belief, familial and kinship lineages, and traditional versus modern influences. Of course, class differences exist, and there have been historical instances of noticeable animosity between one economic group and another. Yet the differences that have separated classes from one another have not been always economic, but at times social and cultural as well. Similarly—and this assertion will find few takers among devout Marxists —these economic differences and even animosities have not been enough to account fully for the separateness of one social stratum from another. Complementing and occasionally mitigating these economic differences have been equally pervasive social and cultural forces governing the life of the group. Thus in the Middle East, the concept of class is a more complex construct, entailing a set of implied economic relations and an attachment to certain social norms and cultural forces. In examining Middle Eastern social classes, pointing only to the economic divisions that characterize society is inadequate. The degree to which one has undergone social change and the resultant alterations in one's social reality are equally important. What differentiates people from one another is not only their socioeconomic position or the nature of the sociocultural values they hold, but a combination of both.

As economic realities, classes indeed exist in the Middle East, but they have consistently failed to act as cohesive political forces by themselves. In a Marxist sense, while class membership may exist, class consciousness does not. A number of factors have impeded the development of this consciousness, chief among them such state policies as the co-option of elites and suppression of independent trade unions.[4] An equally important hindrance has been identifying more strongly with primordial institutions such as the family and tribe than with one's class.[5] In such ethnically and socially heterogeneous countries as Lebanon and, to a somewhat lesser extent, Syria, Iraq, Iran, Algeria, and Morocco, class distinctions have been superseded by, or at best compete with, other noneconomic means of differentiation.[6] Where states could afford it, they have simply bought political stability and social harmony with the infusion of vast amounts of money and petroleum revenues into their small, mostly homogeneous and highly manageable societies.[7] Thus in the affluent countries clustered around the southern rim of the Persian Gulf, class and class consciousness tend to mean very little, having been stymied by deliberate government policies. Conversely, other states' political and economic policies have been important, and these policies are dealt with in more detail later. Suffice it to say, Middle Eastern states have by and large been successful in containing or breaking up significant economic interests in their societies.[8] Even in the less prosperous countries that have a somewhat homogeneous ethnic makeup, namely, Tunisia, Egypt, Turkey, and even Iran, pronounced class differences have failed to translate into political grievances by themselves. The Iranian revolution was as much a product of social unease and disenchantment as it was a result of economic hardships, and Egypt's troubles in the 1980s and 1990s are based not only on economics but also on cultural disillusionment and malaise. At best, economic and class differences can provide additional tinder to already volatile social and cultural environments. In rare circumstances, as among some revolutionary groups in Iran, such differences may even serve as a basis for political solidarity. But class differences alone are neither sufficient stimuli for political action nor are they the only sources of identity. One scholar notes that

> the constitution of political forces relates to various and shifting bases of social solidarities, but, crucially, these varieties and shifts often result from changes in political and economic conjecture, including state structures and policies.... Communities and classes are not in themselves political forces. Under particular conditions political forces may be *constituted* on the basis of class or community, and this constitution is in itself a political process.[9]

The need to examine class and economic relations in the Middle East within a larger social and cultural context has long been appreciated by most students of the region. Even those who emphasize such historical dynamics as imperialism in order to explain the current social and political predicaments of the region (Said and Sharabi are two of the more noted scholars in this category) agree that the social and cultural ramifications of colonialism cannot be entirely ignored. Sharabi's elaboration on the concept of neopatriarchy, as mentioned in chapter 2, pays particular attention to the social and cultural effects of imperialism on today's Middle Easterners. He argues that "the disorienting impact of imperialism was perhaps most deeply felt in the cultural sphere."

> The colonization of consciousness (and the unconscious), seen in social and political terms, has perhaps influenced the development of the structure of neopatriarchy more than has military occupation or political domination. From this vantage point, the problem can no longer be regarded

as conventional modernization theory sees it—as simply that modernization threatens "traditional society," or that the hardships of development
rock an "underdeveloped" formation. Rather, the view must be taken that
patriarchal society has been forced to appropriate European economic
models and cultural paradigms under the distorting conditions of imperi-
alist domination, cultural subordination, and economic dependency.
Whence the lopsided character of "modernized" patriarchal (neopatriarchal) culture, with its pseudoscience, pseudoreligiosity, pseudopolitics, its
political helplessness and cultural disorientation, and its distance from
genuine modernity, that is, from authentic self-emancipation.[10]

In order to distinguish clearly between class as a purely economic
construct and the social as well as economic unit I have in mind, I focus
here on "social classes," by which I mean an amalgam of sociocultural
and economic features. The distribution of these social classes, and the
multifaceted divisions of society in general, may best be represented in a
diagram (see figure 3.1). Two axes of socioeconomic differentiation are
depicted: vertical divisions based on economics and horizontal ones based
on exposure to social and cultural change. A twofold division of society is
therefore reflected: the vertical axes represent the different economic
strata in society, while the horizontal ones denote different classes that
share certain norms and values. While the economic differences are based
on one's level of affluence and access to sources of economic power, the
sociocultural chasm is derived from the traditional-modern dichotomy,

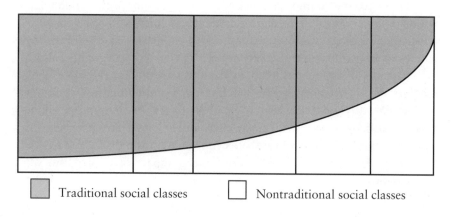

Traditional social classes   Nontraditional social classes

FIGURE 3.1
SOCIOCULTURAL AND ECONOMIC DIVISIONS
WITHIN SOCIETY

which in different societies means different things. Rapid economic development and its attendant consequences throughout the Middle East have greatly magnified existent differences between the various classes. As a result, there exists a complex maze of economic classes in every Middle Eastern society. Similarly, as chapter 4 shows, the effects of social change have not only been dramatic but also, more important, they have been unequally distributed, affecting some classes more extensively than others. Without replicating the arguments of the next chapter, it is worth mentioning here that fewer classes close to the bottom of the economic ladder have experienced social change than those higher up on the ladder. The significant point is that not everyone at the top experienced the same extent and breadth of social change; however, some people at the bottom of the ladder have become socially and culturally "modern," as have many of the rich. Thus wealth or poverty may or may not accord with belief in particular values, norms, and priorities. What constitutes a class and its sense of identity is not only its economic position, therefore, but also its social predicament and cultural norms.

It would be simplistic and indeed inaccurate to assume that all Middle Eastern societies have the same social class configuration or that the one model that differentiates between sociocultural and economic differences in the cities applies to rural areas as well. Specific delineations are needed to account for cross-national as well as intranational differences. Within each Middle Eastern society, sociocultural and economic formations must be divided into urban and rural areas. Within the larger region, there is a marked difference between the social classes of the oil-rich, demographically and geographically smaller countries of the Arabian peninsula (Saudi Arabia, Kuwait, Bahrain, Qatar, the United Arab Emirates, and Oman), and those of the countries whose economies happen to be somewhat more integrated and less dependent on oil, even if only slightly (Iran, Iraq, and Algeria).[11] Figures 3.2 and 3.3 (pp. 88 and 89) reveal the differences found in the social classes of the two broad groups of Middle Eastern countries. The social classes in the urban areas of countries with more integrated economies are somewhat more complex and sometimes cannot be readily distinguished from one another (see figure 3.2). Broadly, they include an upper class, an upper-middle class, a middle class, a lower-middle class, a working class, and the lumpen proletariat.[12] In the rural areas, class position depends mostly on one's relationship to the land. The rural classes are made up of an estate-owning upper class, owners of medium- to small-size farms, artisans and traders, landless peasants, and bedouins.

In less integrated, oil-dependent economies, both the urban and rural class structures are quite different because they are less complex but more rigid (see figure 3.3). The class structure in urban areas typically includes the royal family, a number of merchant families, an upper-middle class, a middle class, and a class of expatriates and immigrant workers. In the rural areas there is often a small though wealthy class of landowners, farm-

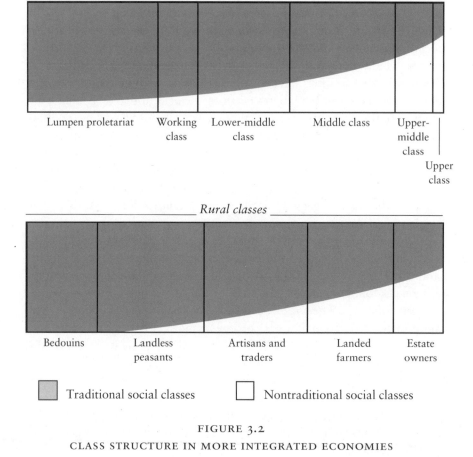

Urban classes

| Lumpen proletariat | Working class | Lower-middle class | Middle class | Upper-middle class |
| Upper class |

Rural classes

| Bedouins | Landless peasants | Artisans and traders | Landed farmers | Estate owners |

☐ Traditional social classes   ☐ Nontraditional social classes

FIGURE 3.2

CLASS STRUCTURE IN MORE INTEGRATED ECONOMIES

ers owning their own land, and tribal bedouins who often own some camels, horses, or sheep. Whether rural or urban or in economies that are more integrated or more dependent on oil, these classes have undergone varying degrees of social change and hold differing sets of values and norms. Not only are they economically divided from one another, but also they are socioculturally divided within themselves. These economic, social, and cultural differences are discussed in the next section.

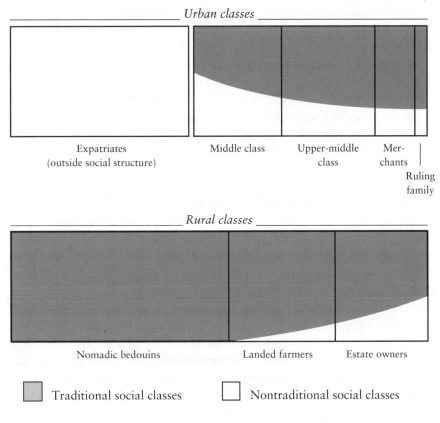

Urban classes

| Expatriates (outside social structure) | Middle class | Upper-middle class | Merchants | Ruling family |

Rural classes

Nomadic bedouins   Landed farmers   Estate owners

Traditional social classes   Nontraditional social classes

FIGURE 3.3

CLASS STRUCTURE IN OIL-DEPENDENT ECONOMIES

Urban Social Classes

Throughout the Third World, a number of important political, social, and economic factors have combined to make the urban social classes some of the most significant elements of national society. Urban classes display remarkable economic and sociocultural similarities throughout the Third World. Whether poor or wealthy, modern or traditional, religious or secular, tied to the civil service or privately employed, these urbanites inhabit the economic and political nerve centers of their countries. Regardless of the extent of their political power, economic affluence, or social and cultural priorities, these are the groups in society that, because of where they reside and what they do, embody the life and general conditions of the nation. "Urban bias" is more than a simple preference by policymakers in favor of the city: it is a reality that has made understanding Third World countries impossible without detailed focus on urban areas.[13] Within this context, exploring the composition of urban social classes assumes particular importance because most states strive for containment and control of these classes, and it is from them that recruits for the country's most sensitive political and economic positions are drawn. They become policymakers and bureaucrats, merchants and workers. They may also pose the biggest threat to the legitimacy and viability of the state. In the Middle East, the structure and composition of the urban classes may be less complex in some countries than in others, but their significance is paramount nevertheless.

Urban Classes in Integrated Economies

In Middle Eastern countries whose economies are somewhat less dependent on the export of oil, urban social classes tend to have a slightly different composition as a direct result of the limited role of petroleum. In countries with more integrated economies—or overpopulation, as in Iran, Iraq, and Algeria—there is little or no oil revenue to equalize or minimize preexisting economic differences. Governments have tried to effect general prosperity and economic growth through the expansion of the bureaucracy and speedy industrialization, but in the process they have only magnified class and economic disparities within their societies. Such differences have become more pronounced by the unimpeded flow of rural migrants into cities, which assume an even greater social and cultural significance because of the rural-urban divide. There are six broad social classes in the urban centers of Middle Eastern countries with more integrated and less oil-dependent economies (see table 3.1). They include the

upper, upper-middle, middle, and lower-middle classes; industrial workers; and the lumpen proletariat. Except for the working class, which remains relatively small, the size of the classes seems to be inversely propor-
tional to their economic level, that is, the upper class is a minority and the
lumpen proletariat is the majority. Each of these classes, as mentioned, is
subdivided by its social and cultural values.

The upper classes are often perceived as consisting of the wealthy
bourgeois and notables.[14] The bourgeoisie itself is not a monolithic group,
however, and can be further stratified into an upper class and an upper-

TABLE 3.1

URBAN AND RURAL CLASSES IN THE MIDDLE EAST

Class structure in more integrated economies

Urban classes	Rural classes
Lumpen proletariat	Bedouins and nomadic tribes
Industrial working class	Landless peasants
Lower-middle class	Artisans and traders
Middle class	Landed farmers
Upper-middle class	Estate owners and tribal leaders
Upper class	

Class structure in oil-dependent economies

Urban classes	Rural classes
Expatriates	Nomadic bedouins
Middle class	Landed farmers
Upper-middle class	Estate owners
Merchants	
Ruling family	

middle class. The upper class is made up of those who control the major
sources of economic and political power, as well as having tremendous
wealth and social prestige. Some authors have claimed that this stratum
contains only those in positions of political power and is therefore synonymous with the ruling class.[15] While not entirely inaccurate, this assertion
needs to be qualified. Regardless of their political rhetoric and ideological
dispositions, those at the highest levels of political power—presidents and
prime ministers, cabinet members and their deputies, high-ranking military commanders—also make up the dominant economic classes. Others

without political power, however, may come close to attaining the same level of wealth as those in power, such as owners of big estates (who may own entire villages), factory owners and wealthy industrialists, and import-export merchants. While the economic power of the upper class poses a potential threat to the state, the class itself is not antagonistic to the government. As long as the upper class remains politically neutral, its economic interests are not jeopardized. Of course, associating with those in power does not hurt; in fact, the heads of most monarchical and pseudomonarchical states, such as Sadat and Mubarak, the late shah, the Arabian peninsula rulers, and Kings Hussein and Hassan, thrive on bringing the wealthy into their political orbit by extending political privileges in return for support and complicity.

Immediately below this highest political and socioeconomic stratum is the upper-middle class. What differentiates it from the super rich is not necessarily its social and cultural norms but rather its lower degree of affluence and less direct access to sources of political power. Bankers, heads of government bureaus, directors and managers of state-run enterprises, lieutenants general and colonel, successful businessmen and contractors, and owners of medium-size workshops and small factories typically belong to the upper-middle class.[16] Despite its relatively small size compared with the classes below it, the upper-middle class exerts a considerable degree of influence in the economic, political, and cultural spheres. As the intermediate class between rulers and private citizens, the upper-middle class often functions as a conduit to the powerful. In the context of societies where family names and connections matter, members of the upper-middle class are often the ones who have the right connections, who can make or break careers, and who are in positions that everyone seeks. It is to the upper-middle class that society as a whole looks for political and economic patronage. Ironically, its role as patron is reinforced, not weakened, as a result of industrial growth and bureaucratic expansion. The uneven persistence of old customs and practices, coupled with the stunted processes of economic change and development, have increased the importance of connections and patrons. Within the bureaucracy, merits and qualifications may mean something, but having the right connections means much more. The same holds true for bidding on state or private contracts, obtaining visas to travel abroad, acquiring the necessary permits to import or export goods, and other kinds of activity for which the permission or blessing of a higher-up is necessary.

The upper-middle class plays an equally important social and cultural role both consciously and unconsciously. This is the intelligentsia, that sizable group that has been forcibly silenced or bought off into complicity through lucrative salaries and official patronage. Thus many writers and essayists, radio and television personalities, famous journalists and academicians—people in charge of crafting and influencing the society's norms and values—come from the upper-middle class. Their social and cultural roles, therefore, are often of great importance. But also important is the general station in life that the upper-middle class occupies. Their aspirations, while only a dream for many, are relatively realistic. Dreaming of becoming a successful and wealthy businessman is not as far-fetched as dreaming of becoming a prime minister or president one day.

The middle class by its very nature strives for higher mobility and enhancement of its economic powers, political connections, and social prestige. Its members thus emulate the upper-middle class's values and cultural norms, manner of speech, and means of entertainment. By far the largest segment of the middle class comes from the bureaucratic and other professional ranks, including salaried government employees, administrators and managers of small-scale enterprises, teachers and principals in junior and senior high schools, accountants, engineers, and industrial technicians. Table 3.2 (p. 94) contains data concerning employment in various economic sectors in the mid- and late 1980s. Not everyone in the middle class is a white-collar employee. Small-scale merchants and store owners are some of its most important members. Whether their stores and stalls are located in one of the more fashionable shopping districts or in the bazaar, these business owners are in a rather unique and enviable position. Because they are self-employed, their relative economic independence affords them great maneuverability vis-à-vis the state and other social classes. Frequently, these merchants see the government's regulatory policies as inimical to their interests and believe that the state should not interfere with economic matters. Their opposition to the state is reinforced by their more traditional values, and many experience disenchantment with the prevailing social and cultural environments. Their informal guilds and unions are convenient places to congregate, exchange information, and, if need be, organize for political reasons.[17] The crucial role that these merchants played in the Iranian revolution may never be repeated elsewhere in the Middle East, but certainly the potential for their alienation and political dissent is there.[18]

Merchants and store owners are not the only members of the middle class with the potential for political opposition. A number of factors have combined to make the entire middle class prone to volatility. Besides political and cultural forces, its economic woes are cause for concern. Begin-

TABLE 3.2

SECTORAL EMPLOYMENT

OF ECONOMICALLY ACTIVE INDUSTRIES

(IN PERCENTAGES)

Country	Agriculture, forestry, and fishing	Construc- tion	Manufacturing, mining, quarrying, and public utilities	Services[a]
Algeria	13.6	12.9	11.6	33.5
Bahrain	2.0	21.0	13.4	63.5
Egypt	42.7	4.7	16.6	36.0
Iran	24.9	9.4	12.3	36.4
Iraq	12.5	8.6	8.8	61.2
Jordan	6.2	10.7	7.7	75.5
Kuwait	1.3	15.4	9.0	72.9
Lebanon	19.1	6.2	18.9	55.8
Morocco	39.2	7.3	16.9	18.5
Oman	6.8	27.5	33.0	46.0
Qatar	3.1	20.1	11.9	64.1
Saudi Arabia	14.3	18.7	14.9	52.1
Syria	30.0	15.5	14.5	42.0
Tunisia	21.6	10.5	17.7	32.7
Turkey	45.3	4.9	13.7	27.8
UAE	5.0	24.8	10.4	59.8
Yemen[b]	53.2	7.6	8.7	30.5

SOURCE: Compiled from Gregory Thomas Kurian, ed., *Encyclopedia of the Third World*, vols. 1–3, 4th ed. (New York: Facts on File, 1992).

a. Includes those employed in trades, hotels, restaurants, transportation, communications, finance, and real estate.

b. Figures are averages from former North and South Yemen.

ning with the "oil bust" of the late 1970s and into the 1980s and 1990s, the once-healthy economies of Iran, Iraq, Syria, Tunisia, and Algeria (and even those of the Persian Gulf sheikhdoms) have suffered sharp reversals.[19] It is the middle class that has borne the brunt of this hardship and now finds itself under increasing economic and social pressures. Whether working in the public or private sectors, members of the middle class have painfully realized that their salaries have seldom kept pace with the rate of inflation. Living in the capital or other major cities, where housing and many consumer items (such as appliances and television sets) are particularly expensive, is especially difficult for them. Compounding this difficulty is what one observer has called the "tyranny of the face," or the Middle Eastern tendency to hide one's troubles from friends and associates in order to keep up appearances.[20] Thus even if a second job would alleviate some of the economic pressures on the family, the message this would send to others would make the average middle-class person think twice before accepting additional employment.[21] Instead, the tendency is to "beat the system" by relying on influential patrons, or, as the Egyptians are fond of doing, to complain privately but do little about the situation. But if there are enough grievances, the economic woes of the middle class may translate into political action.

In light of these recent economic difficulties and the unfavorable outcomes from change and development, the distinctions between the middle and lower-middle classes have become increasingly blurred, and the size of the lower-middle class has grown steadily. While spurts of economic growth and reversals of fortune might have had a faint equalizing effect on these classes, there are nevertheless particularly glaring differences in levels of income and purchasing power between them. The lower-middle class is primarily made up of grade-school teachers, low-ranking bureaucrats and secretaries, technicians and other relatively low-paid, blue-collar workers, shopkeepers, and office workers. Frequently, they are former workers in the industrial sector or second- or third-generation immigrants from the countryside who have succeeded in securing jobs with middle-class trappings. These jobs may not pay much, often not enough to support a family, but they carry with them a degree of social prestige because they rarely involve manual labor and are often located in offices or healthier work environments. This mentality is symptomatic of a larger perception of the lower-middle class: its members are seen as the last bastion of city life. Lower classes may live and work in the city, but they are not quite urbanized. The lower-middle class, therefore, represents the buffer between the city and the village, between two ways of life separated by vast social and cultural differences. It is the one class to which the country's economic well-being and sociocultural "prestige" do not extend. If the norms of the village are idealized, it is a distorted, academic version that is romanticized. Regardless of what demographics and economic realities dictate, the city as a cultural construct ends with the lower-middle class.

Industrial workers are a social class that may reside in the city, but they are generally not urbanized. Although the working class is by no means the only stratum of urban society that has yet to be fully urbanized, its pivotal role in economic development and increased size in recent decades make it a particularly significant social formation. It is mainly composed of skilled and technical workers who have regular (rather than seasonal) employment in factories or other industrial plants. Most observers of Middle Eastern economies see industrial laborers and other members of the informal economic sector as belonging to the same social stratum.[22] There are, however, notable social and economic differences that place industrial workers into a distinct class of their own in contrast to those who can be classified as lumpen proletariat. Whether through vocational training or on-the-job experience, industrial laborers have learned to work with machinery and industrial equipment and thus have acquired a technical skill that places them in relative demand and sets them apart from recent arrivals from the countryside. This technical know-how may sometimes be exaggerated: the ability to push a button, pull a lever, or perform other simple assembly-line tasks does not make one a technical wizard. But the perception of specialized skill is nonetheless there among the industrial workers themselves and the social classes above and below them.

In the Middle East, as in most other parts of the Third World, these industrial workers have often been in great demand because they form the backbone of industries. Some observers have even spoken of a "labor aristocracy," for many industrial workers are aware that their skills are sought after by employers and industrialists.[23] A labor aristocracy exists in the developing countries and even then only under specific circumstances. When oil-based industrial development reached unprecedented proportions throughout the 1960s and 1970s, Iran, Iraq, Algeria, and to a lesser extent Egypt could not have developed without the existence of a sizable class of industrial workers. (Saudi Arabia and other Gulf countries imported their needed labor.) Thus in many parts of the region, this class grew in size, economic importance, and social stature. By the 1980s, however, oil prices stabilized and then declined, and with them went the fortunes of industrial labor. Today, the industrial working class is only aristocratic in its own eyes and in those of the lower classes who wish to join its ranks.

The working class enjoys some privileges that the lumpen proletariat does not, such as job security and relatively steady employment. The lumpen proletariat may spend much of its time moving from one job to another, whereas industrial workers stay with the same employer for years or do not have great difficulty finding another one. This is largely because most industrial workers are employed in the formal sector of the economy,[24] and they are therefore less likely to be fired at the whim of an employer, since, in the Middle East at least, most of the larger industrial enterprises are wholly or partly owned by the state. With this comes a larger paycheck and a host of fringe benefits about which the lumpen proletariat can only dream: time off for national holidays and annual vacations, bonuses and pay raises, health insurance or other kinds of medical care, and, especially from state-owned enterprises, profit-sharing ventures, workers' councils, and, occasionally, free transportation to and from work. These privileges do not, however, translate into affluence or material comforts because they are often offset by the needs of one's (usually large) family, remittances to family and kin in smaller towns and villages, expenses of city living (especially housing), and the responsibility to provide temporary lodging and other forms of assistance to family and friends who are recent arrivals to the city. Yet despite all these financial strains, the working class is in every sense far better off than the lumpen proletariat.

The precise political role and significance of the working class in the Middle East have long been subjects of scholarly debate and disagreements. The spectacular sociopolitical events that have rocked the region over the past decade or so have prompted many observers to take a closer look at the question of labor.[25] Some have argued that the Middle Eastern working class remains a "significant social agent" with great potential for political opposition. "Mired in a profound economic and social crisis," Zachary Lockman comments,

> and under unrelenting pressure to restructure their economies in accordance with the prescriptions of the International Monetary Fund, regimes across the region have hesitated and equivocated for fear of popular reaction, and perhaps especially from worker reaction. However the current crisis unfolds, members of the urban working class broadly defined are likely to continue to have a role to play, whether as workers under their own banner or as a component of other groupings that will nonetheless be infused with the energy of working-class grievances and demands.[26]

Evidence for this conclusion can be seen in the growing maturity of the labor movement in Turkey,[27] instances of labor unrest in postrevolutionary Iran,[28] and the continuing difficulties of the Egyptian and other Middle Eastern governments with organized workers.[29] But not unlike the working class in other regions of the Third World when viewed in a broader context in which all existing social forces and institutions are considered, the working class in the Middle East has failed to play any decisive political role by itself. An organized and relatively skilled group, and one that can potentially develop its own identity, the working class cannot be completely ignored by either those in power or those pursuing it. However, as the history of the Middle East has demonstrated again and again, the most powerful agents for political change and mobilization have traditionally come from other groups, notably the military, the intelligentsia, and the clergy. And even if the rhetoric of these agents has included appeals to the working class, their real followers have come from the ranks of the more populous lumpen proletariat and lower-middle classes.

Finally, a mass of underprivileged proto- or lumpen proletariat are found in most Middle Eastern countries. This class is endemic to those countries whose economies have a larger, more integrated industrial base but cannot absorb all of the population within them. The relative impoverishment of the agricultural sector and the concomitant social and economic lures of the city have only expedited the growth of this underclass. It is difficult to approximate the size of the lumpen proletariat because its members have been excluded from official statistics. It does, however, form a sizable chunk of the urban population in Iran, Turkey, Iraq, Egypt, and Algeria, and its members are found in ever-increasing numbers in Syria, Jordan, Tunisia, and Morocco. Made up of immigrants who are caught between the rural communities they left behind and the city life to which they wish to assimilate, they inhabit a social and economic universe of their own, neither fully urban nor rural any longer, neither agricultural nor necessarily industrial. Table 3.3 reveals that a greater percentage of Middle Easterners lived in the cities in the 1990s than in the 1960s.[30] A similar trend is shown in table 3.4 (p. 100), which demonstrates that urban populations grew at a faster rate than rural ones. These numbers indicate not only higher birth rates in the cities, but also, more important, the steady stream of villagers into urban centers in search of jobs and better opportunities. Invariably, these rural immigrants end up working in the informal economic sector, frequently as maids and servants, coolies and hired hands, street vendors, or odd-job helpers at construction sites. Their employment is often seasonal, and as a result they have very little means to support themselves. Finding adequate housing is one of their biggest challenges, and Middle Eastern (as well as other Third World) cities have shantytowns and squalid settlements on their peripheries, such as "the City of the Dead" near Cairo, *Halab-abads* in Iran, and *Gecekondus* in Turkey. Few can afford to stay in cheap motels or hostels, but even these places are often unsafe and expensive. But housing is only one of their dilemmas. Most have no access to medical care; they are easy prey

TABLE 3.3

POPULATION BASED IN URBAN AREAS

(IN PERCENTAGES)

Country	1960s[a]	1980s[b]	1990s[c]
Algeria	88	44	56
Bahrain	n.a.	81	84
Egypt	41	48	45
Iran	37	54	60
Iraq	51	73	75
Israel	81	90	93
Jordan	46	67	71
Kuwait	78	95	97
Lebanon	n.a.	60	87
Libya	26	67	80
Morocco	32	47	48
Oman	n.a.	n.a.	13
Qatar	n.a.	88	91
Saudi Arabia	39	76	80
Sudan	40	21	25
Syria	40	51	52
Tunisia	40	54	59
Turkey	34	47	69
UAE	41	78	84
Yemen	5	23	34

SOURCES: Compiled from Ecomonitor, *World Economic Factbook 1994/95* (London: Ecomonitor, 1994), and Gregory Thomas Kurian, ed., *Encyclopedia of the Third World*, vols. 1–3, 4th ed. (New York: Facts on File, 1992); for Israel, Gregory Thomas Kurian, ed., *Encyclopedia of the First World*, vol. 1 (New York: Facts on File, 1990).

a. Algeria, 1966; all others, 1965.

b. Bahrain, 1981; Israel, 1986; Lebanon, 1970; Qatar, 1985; all others, 1988.

c. All figures, 1994.

for criminals and swindlers; and many are hopelessly naive about the harsh realities and complexities of city life. Even after years of city living and employment, few can hope to own a parcel of land or the dwelling in which they reside.[31]

Economic differences notwithstanding, classes are also separated by equally vast social and cultural differences. The cultural divide, however, runs *across* social classes, not between them. This divide is nearly impossible to quantify but is pervasive nonetheless. It involves people's outlooks and values, their cultural points of reference and customs, their habits

TABLE 3.4
ANNUAL URBAN AND RURAL GROWTH, 1985–90
(IN PERCENTAGES)

	Annual urban growth	Annual rural growth
Algeria	3.90	n.a.
Bahrain	3.94	2.29
Egypt	3.52	1.67
Iran	4.57	2.16
Iraq	4.46	0.90
Israel	n.a.	n.a.
Jordan	5.08	1.72
Kuwait	4.42	−3.18
Lebanon	2.92	−1.58
Libya	5.35	0.16
Morocco	4.12	1.19
Oman	7.00	2.95
Qatar	4.48	1.56
Saudi Arabia	5.11	0.47
Sudan	4.18	2.53
Syria	4.51	2.61
Tunisia	2.86	1.78
Turkey	3.05	1.05
UAE	3.26	3.26
Yemen	7.43	1.77

SOURCE: Compiled from Gregory Thomas Kurian, ed., *Encyclopedia of the Third World*, vols. 1–3, 4th ed. (New York: Facts on File, 1992).

and culture. The nature of this division is more complex than a simple dichotomy of tradition versus modernity, an old versus a new way of life, or progressive versus conservative outlooks. It revolves around the extent to which people's norms and values change, the specific nature of the values that change, and the direction in which they change. Social change, as discussed in the next chapter, affects some members of society more profoundly than others, regardless of their economic predicaments and levels of affluence. Thus the results of "distorted change" may be staggered and uneven not only within the same social class but also within the individual person. The person, his or her social class, and the society at large all become "schizophrenic," entangled in complex and intertwined yet contradictory layers of identity.[32] This is a crisis from which no one is immune. The poor and the upper class experience cultural schizophrenia, although a broad pattern concerning their general values is discernible. The wealthier the person, the more likely he or she is to have experienced social change and therefore to hold values that vary from those considered "traditional." Thus the degree to which the values of social classes have changed is inversely tied to their level of affluence.

Admittedly, such labels as "conservative" and "modern" do not do justice to the complex nuances that characterize cultures in general and variations in cultural beliefs in particular. Some of the people lumped together as "modern" may hold distinctly traditional values, especially ones that revolve around personal beliefs and ways of living. Others may have public and private selves, adhering to one set of norms in the company of others while abiding by another set at home. Nevertheless, there are indeed broad cultural similarities and differences that can be discerned from society. The general cultural breakdown of urban social classes in Middle Eastern countries with more integrated economies is represented in figure 3.2 (p. 88). Subtle differences and variations notwithstanding, few members of the upper class hold values that society at large considers traditional; slightly fewer people in the upper-middle class adopt supposedly modern norms; the middle class as a whole is divided rather evenly; and progressively greater percentages of the lower-middle class, working class, and lumpen proletariat remain socially and culturally conservative.

The term "modern" needs to be clarified in light of its inherent relativity. While there is usually a corpus of norms and values considered conservative by all social groups, what it means to be modern carries different connotations for different classes of people. Generally, those in the upper and upper-middle classes equate modernity with Western-oriented or influenced values, modes of expression, lifestyles, and kinds of employment. For the middle and lower-middle classes, however, as well as for industrial workers and lumpen proletarians, being modern has a less ideational connotation. The lesser one's earning abilities, the more superficial the understanding of modernity one is likely to have. Most people in these categories, therefore, are likely to equate modernity with owning the material goods that are associated with leading a modern life rather than internalizing and living by decidedly nontraditional values. Modernity in this instance, then, is often perceived as owning a color television, wearing jeans, and smoking American-made cigarettes.

Upward mobility is relatively easier in more integrated Middle Eastern economies compared with those with more rigidly stratified socioeconomic structures. A number of factors account for this difference. In countries with integrated economies, social and class standings tend to be less inherited and more meritocratic. Moreover, since members of different social classes may hold the same set of values, most of the obstacles in moving up to another class are only economic. The cultural adjustments are therefore less arduous. There is, in fact, an added incentive to improve one's economic lot since such progress is compatible with preexisting beliefs and values. The middle class, which by nature is made up of "high-need achievers" with sufficient capital to improve their status, are particularly prone to benefit from periods of economic growth and prosperity.[33] Urban-based industrialization and the spread of educational establishments from which the middle and lower-middle classes have benefited the most often provide further avenues to move into higher social strata. There is, however, a down side to the middle-class status. Recessions and high inflation are likely to hit the middle and lower-middle classes hardest, with some members dependent on fixed government salaries that seldom rise with the rate of inflation. Thus beginning with the global recession of the 1980s and the concurrent Middle Eastern oil glut, the middle and lower-middle classes have found their savings and pockets increasingly depleted.[34] This partly accounts for such manifestations of distress as religious radicalism, the loss of state legitimacy, political apathy, and increased government inefficiency.

Urban Classes in Oil-Dependent Economies

In the countries whose economic development depends exclusively on oil revenues, urban and rural class structures have assumed a decidedly different pattern than those in countries with more integrated economies. With the exception of Libya, where oil has been almost the sole source of revenue, most Middle Eastern nations in this category are located in the Arabian peninsula. But a cursory look at these countries reveals that what separates them from the rest of the region is not only their source of economic growth but also a host of noneconomic factors such as historical development, demography, political evolution, and social and cultural setting. These diverse features have combined to give the Gulf countries a distinct flavor of their own. Since the widespread discovery of oil in the region in the 1940s and 1950s, their similarities have been reinforced by a combination of massive economic windfalls from oil and relatively small and homogeneous populations. With an approximate population of 18 million, Saudi Arabia remains by far the most populous of the group, followed by Kuwait (2 million); the United Arab Emirates, which consists of a federation of seven city-states of varying sizes (2 million); Oman (1 million); Bahrain (500,000); and Qatar (400,000).[35] The particular patterns of economic development followed by policymakers in the Gulf region have invariably resulted in "rentier states," or governments that channel to the local population revenues generated from renting oil resources.[36] The immense wealth thus generated has had two reinforcing effects on social and political structures. First, rentier states have both dramatically augmented the wealth of the ruling families and enabled these families to use their wealth as powerful sources of patronage and loyalty. As a result of this patronage, coupled with the tribal heritage of each of these countries, subjects view their ruling families as almost natural extensions of the social order. Second, small populations and extraordinary wealth have enabled these states to avoid the mass poverty and misery suffered by the lumpen proletariat elsewhere, while at the same time enhancing the affluence of the middle and upper-middle classes. This is not to imply that poverty does not exist in the Gulf peninsula, but the poor there are seldom locals, with most belonging to the sizable pool of expatriate workers from nearby countries. The political heritage of the Gulf countries, which, until a few decades ago, was essentially a history of tribal entities and de facto British protectorates, has also greatly shaped their present social and cultural settings.[37] It is because of this heritage that ruling and merchant families have become integral parts of the social order.

Throughout the Gulf countries, the ruling families are of great political, economic, and social importance. With the possible exception of the al-Thani family in Qatar, who have by and large failed to develop a corporate identity of their own,[38] most of the ruling families in the peninsula view themselves and are viewed by the larger society as extensions of the social and political elite who govern the country. As a result, few Saudis resent the naming of *Saudi* Arabia after the Saud family because many believe the country would not exist had it not been for its founder, Ibn Saud. Similarly, the Kuwaiti proverb that "Kuwait is al-Sabah and the al-Sabah is Kuwait" offers insight into the psychological connection that many Kuwaitis see between the very existence of their country and its royal family.[39] This intimate connection between the ruling family and the state is due to a number of mutually reinforcing factors. Beginning in the mid-nineteenth century, many ruling families came to power when, under the leadership of a capable tribal leader, they conquered the area they currently govern by defeating contending tribes or securing the allegiance of others. In a few other places, such as Oman and Sharjah, ruling families gained power through the protection of the British, who then had an imperial presence in the region. Thus throughout the peninsula there is seldom a marked distinction between the history of the ruling family and that of the country as a whole. Table 3.5 outlines the tribal affiliation and the year in which each ruling family came to power.

This historical nexus is further reinforced by the ability of the ruling family to bestow gifts and favors on its loyal subjects. Political co-option and service to the state are among the more recent forms of patronage practiced by the ruling families, but their effects are limited because the highest echelons of the civil service and the military are already occupied by members of the royal family. One kind of patronage is found largely in Saudi Arabia, where both the size of the ruling family and its purse are unusually substantial. High-ranking members of the ruling family, who often hold the most sensitive government posts, frequently disburse money to their constituents from personal or official funds that are specifically set aside for this purpose. In the old tribal tradition, royal princes regularly hold informal gatherings called *majles,* at which they listen to the grievances of their constituents and frequently give some kind of reward (monetary or otherwise) to their visitors.[40] It is not always clear where their funds come from, and this blurred distinction strengthens the relationships between Saudi princes and all sections of society.[41] The second form of royal family patronage, practiced both in Saudi Arabia and elsewhere in the Gulf, is the granting of business contracts or donating of parcels of land to prominent merchants and other loyal servants. Merchants often compete for lucrative contracts for construction and development projects. Since many royal princes have entered into business and are involved in a number of projects themselves, winning a business contract is an especially prized form of patronage. Thus many merchants and prominent individuals vie to win the appreciation of the king or emir, often eagerly rendering their services without remuneration when called on. In turn, they may receive a lucrative contract, land, or favorable consideration in future endeavors. When receiving a royal "gift" of this nature, merchants often make their own gifts to the royal family.[42]

Patronage, of course, would not be possible without the ruling families' tremendous wealth, which is derived from three primary sources of income: stipends, land holdings, and various business ventures.[43] The nature and precise amount of stipends, where they come from, and whom they go to have been controversial and secretive issues. Only in the Kuwaiti constitution is it stipulated that the emir gets a regular stipend based on oil revenues (12 million Kuwaiti dinars in 1962, the year of the country's independence).[44] It is nevertheless common knowledge that the emir and his inner circle decide how much of the country's revenues go to his

TABLE 3.5

THE RULING FAMILIES IN THE COUNTRIES OF THE GULF AND THE ARAB PENINSULA;
THEIR TRIBAL AFFILIATIONS SINCE 1985

The United Arab Emirates

	Abu Dhabi	Umm al-Quwain	Dubai	al-Sharjah	Ajman	al-Fujaira	Ras al-Khaimah
Ruling family	al-Nahyan	al-Mualla	al-Maktum	al-Qawasim	al-Qawasim	al-Sharqi	al-Qawasim
Tribal affiliation	Bani Yas	al-Mualla	Bani Yas	al-Qawasim	al-Qawasim	al-Sharqiyun	al-Qawasim
Beginning of rule	1855	1820	1894	1790	1820	1892	1790

	Bahrain	Saudi Arabia	Oman	Qatar	Kuwait	South Yemen	North Yemen
Ruling family	al-Khalifah	al-Saud	al-Bu Said	al-Thani	al-Sabah	Political party	Military rule
Tribal affiliation	'Anazah	'Anazah		Bani Tamin	'Anazah	Various blocs within the political institution	Various blocs within the military institution
Beginning of rule	1783	1902 1792	1755	1878	1754	1968	1962

SOURCE: Khaldoun Hasan al-Naqeeb, *Society and State in the Gulf and Arab Peninsula* (London: Routledge, 1990), 102.

personal purse and how much is allocated to the national budget. In turn, the family princes are paid a stipend, the amount of which varies according to the line of succession, the degree of their involvement in politics, and whether or not they simply ask for more. Thus there may be great disparities in the wealth of siblings and cousins within the same royal household.[45] This lack of distinction between the personal wealth of the ruling family and the national revenues of the country has served to reinforce the centrality of the ruling family, especially the ruler within it. The maintenance of the ruling family in power is not only a matter of preserving the state's tribal, national heritage; it also has a strong economic component. As Jacqueline Ismael explained in her book on Kuwait:

> The power of the ruling family is based upon dependence of the community on oil revenues and the ability of the ruling family to manipulate these revenues. The wealth of the nation has filtered down to the population from the ruling family, friends of the family, servants, and so on to the periphery of the population. What has emerged within the indigenous population is a stratification system essentially based on distance from the ruling family.[46]

Since most of these revenues come from the sale of oil, the extent of the ruling families' wealth has varied according to their countries' oil reserves and the degree to which they have been able to manipulate the revenues derived from them. For example, Bahrain's oil resources are among the smallest in the region, and, consequently, the al-Khalifah family is not as fabulously wealthy as most ruling families.[47] Nevertheless, in Bahrain and even in the small United Arab Emirates, the wealth of the ruling families is substantial by any standards, enhanced by their ownership of valuable properties and business ventures. Ruling families are among the biggest landowners in the region.[48] This is significant because of the dramatic increase in land value as a result of the region's construction boom in recent decades. In a number of instances, governments have implemented policies that deliberately inflate land prices, benefiting not only royal princes but also commoners owning land in commercial areas.[49] Similarly, members of the ruling families are the largest investors in the private sector and sometimes even represent foreign companies bidding for government contracts.[50] Although there is a distinct class of merchants in each country, some members of the ruling family have become highly successful businessmen. An example is the late emir of Dubai, Sheikh Rashid, who administered the emirate much as he did a large corporation.[51]

The second social class that benefits in material wealth and social prestige in the Gulf countries is the merchant class. A distinction should be made at the outset between traditional trade merchants and the new, growing class of modern entrepreneurs who have also become inseparable fixtures of the Gulf countries' social order. Most of the modern entrepreneurs have risen from the ranks of the middle class and have only recently accumulated their wealth. They owe their ascendance directly to the rise of oil revenues and, like the discovery of oil itself, are themselves a relatively recent phenomenon. Perhaps the most flamboyant of this new breed of entrepreneurs is the Saudi businessman Adnan Khashoggi, whose lifestyle and penchant for publicity have won him considerable attention in the Western media.[52] There is, however, a distinct class of merchants whose roots go well beyond the economic boom generated by oil revenues. Before oil, most of these merchants engaged in a form of "speculative trade" (*mudarabah*) involving pearls, gold, precious stones, and herbs and spices.[53] The importance of their role to the rest of society and their relative affluence assured them a place in the social hierarchy even after the ruling families acquired power and oil was discovered. As Michael Fields explains, the intimate historical and nowadays business connections between royal princes and the various merchant houses magnify the merchants' social and economic status throughout the region:

> The merchant families are part of the Arabian establishment. They dominate Arabian commercial life and they have been responsible for as many economic innovations as the governments. They have established most of the new Arabian investment banks, light industries and high-technology service companies. In the Gulf states, which have a tradition as trading communities, the merchants are the most valued constituents of the ruling families; their senior members are consulted on most important domestic political issues. In both Saudi Arabia and the Gulf states merchants serve the ruling families in government.[54]

This is despite, or perhaps because of, their minority status: there are only about thirty or forty "big, highly diversified" merchant families throughout the Gulf region.[55]

The merchants' economic activities are by no means limited to trade in one specific commodity or service. The most popular and profitable activity is importing Western-produced consumer goods and automobiles, but most merchants have a variety of jobs such as managing shipping and travel agencies, currency exchange, insurance brokerage, real estate development, hotel management, and light manufacturing. Where possible, Fields reports, they try to ensure that their various business operations are complementary (7–8). Some of the wealthiest merchants' businesses involve low overhead costs and inconspicuous façades: big property investors, bulk-food importers, bankers, and exchange dealers (119). Despite their tremendous wealth and highly profitable ventures, most merchants fifty and older have by and large retained conservative social values and traditional business practices. An increasing number of younger merchants have either studied abroad and are familiar with modern (i.e., Western) managerial techniques, or they have somehow come into contact with and acquired a taste for them. But older merchants are often reluctant to embrace new concepts of accounting that are imported from the West; they seldom have mid-ranking managers and specialists in their businesses; and they make most of the decisions regarding purchases and investments (296–98).

These merchants' refusal to embrace "modern" techniques, however, has not hindered their ability to command large profits. The overall national, social, and economic contexts are of great significance in this regard. As long as the gain is not ill-gotten, Islam does not impose any general restrictions on the accumulation of wealth, with the exceptions of *khums* (charity to the poor) and *zakat* (alms tax). Because the prophet Muhammad was himself a merchant, today's merchants in the Gulf region—as well as those in other parts of the Middle East—are unashamed of large profits. Through an elaborate, internalized philosophy of their own, they see nothing wrong with making as much money as possible from every transaction. As Fields puts it, "If the buyer pays too much, then more fool he.... The moral responsibility for setting the right price is seen as resting with the buyer, as does responsibility for the ethical considerations of the deal" (92).

The merchants form a relatively small stratum of society in Gulf countries, whereas the upper-middle class is sizable, consisting primarily of entrepreneurs, contractors, and high-ranking civil servants. Entrepreneurs, as previously mentioned, are distinguished from merchants by their modern affluence and distance from the ruling families. The categorization of the "upper-middle class" needs to be qualified, for the Gulf region's upper-middle class is significantly wealthier than the same class in the rest of the Middle East. A typical upper-middle-class family in the Gulf region is likely to have an opulent mansion, a number of servants and attendants, two or even three automobiles, sizable savings, and frequent vacations abroad. These luxuries are often beyond the reach of the average Middle Eastern upper-middle-class family. The Gulf regions' upper-middle class occupies the same social position in relation to other classes and is of equal political importance to its counterparts in other Middle East countries. Although it is not overtly political, the upper-middle class's political passivity and affluence lend tacit support to the political establishment. Thus keeping this class economically (and therefore politically) content is an important governmental task, and many of the state's policies are specifically designed to achieve this goal. Members of the upper-middle class throughout the Middle East show deference to those with more wealth and power and condescension to those below them.

Unlike the merchant families, who have long-established, historical ties to the Gulf and the Arabian peninsula, the entrepreneurial stratum is a relatively recent development that resulted from the region's overall economic growth after the discovery of oil. This class derived from "an accident of geology (oil)," and "education, government service, and the economic boom in the 1970s."[56] The new-found wealth of the Gulf nations enabled these enterprising businessmen to put their intuitive and entrepreneurial skills to use and tap into the new opportunities and consumer markets that were being created. Because of the sudden, massive infusion of petrodollars into the region's economies, the highly underdeveloped societies of the Gulf were literally able to buy themselves into modernity by acquiring the latest manifestations of material wealth. One author remarks that "on every indicator of the standard of living, the population of Kuwait improves yearly its consumption of luxury commodities."[57] Ostentatious displays of wealth, such as the purchase of gold-plated cars and mansions lined with Italian marble, are some of the more extreme results of this windfall of riches. More prevalent has been the development of opportunities to invest capital in various business ventures, most of which involve the importing of consumer goods and foodstuffs from abroad. The society's insatiable appetite for everything Western, from television sets and cassette recorders to canned fruit and bottled water, has made it possible for a new breed of merchants to prosper. The concurrent construction boom has also led to the prospering of medium-scale contractors who oversee the many projects under way. Although they operate on a scale smaller than merchants and royal princes, such contractors often manage to make handsome profits. This entrepreneurial stratum's relative material affluence and distance from the political center makes it part of the upper-middle class.

Unlike his Western counterpart, the Persian Gulf entrepreneur is almost always assured of making a profit and can often start his venture without a huge investment.[58] In his examination of these new merchants, Saad Eddin Ibrahim makes the following observations about the Saudi Arabian entrepreneur:

> Since there is no risk, the only thing that differentiates one entrepreneur from another is his ability to assemble a "group" as partners in a private company. The ideal group consists of individuals who are blood relatives or close friends but who are strategically located in Saudi social and governmental structures. (9–10)

This is particularly true of contractors who bid on construction projects, and many of them initially have very little understanding of the construction industry as a whole. Government contacts are often essential in securing contracts. Once a contract is secured, the contractors then hire architects, engineers, suppliers, and workers. Basically, the contractors function as economic brokers through whom the oil-generated wealth is funneled down to the rest of society, and in this respect their role in society is of great importance. Along with the social classes above them, they supply the brainpower and managerial skills that make economic growth possible. But economic *growth* is not the same as economic *development*, the former being no more than enhanced purchasing power, while the latter entails more fundamental progress such as the construction of machinery and factories capable of making it.[59] Thus in terms of lasting technological progress and industrial development, the role of the upper-middle class must not be exaggerated. Made up of entrepreneurs, contractors, and ranking civil servants, the upper-middle class remains part of the services sector, a sector that, as in other parts of the Third World, is neither materially productive nor completely parasitic—it falls somewhere in between.[60]

The next social class in the Gulf states of the Arabian peninsula is the middle class, the majority of whose members are also wealthier in absolute terms than their counterparts elsewhere in the Middle East. That this class is at the bottom of the social and economic scale, that is, those who are part of the indigenous population, only demonstrates the immense wealth of the Persian Gulf states. Apart from its material affluence, the middle class has few other distinguishing features from the same social class elsewhere in the Middle East. In oil-dependent economies, most members of the middle class are employed in the bloated civil service, which is deliberately overstaffed in order to provide employment to every citizen.[61] As table 3.2 (p. 94) indicates, the services sector, of which the state bureaucracy is a significant component, is considerably larger in the Gulf states compared with other parts of the Middle East: 63.5 percent in Bahrain, nearly 73 percent in Kuwait, 64.1 percent in Qatar, and nearly 60 percent in the United Arab Emirates; but only 33.5 percent in Algeria, 36 percent in Egypt, 36.4 percent in Iran, and approximately 28 percent in Turkey. The overwhelming concentration of the middle class in the bureaucracy results from an awareness by both the state and the middle class that government employment is among the few opportunities available. Most of the unskilled as well as the skilled jobs (teachers, physicians, engineers) are taken by immigrant workers, and most government positions (and various kinds of fringe benefits) are reserved for citizens. As a result, throughout the region and especially in Kuwait, the governments have created an elaborate welfare system designed to keep consumption levels high and political grievances low.[62] It is precisely for this reason that the middle classes in the Arabian peninsula differ from those in other parts of the Middle East. The economic hardships of the integrated economies make the middle classes prone to political opposition and therefore they are potential sources of trouble for the state, whereas oil-dependent economies have largely placated the middle classes' economic and political grievances. Regardless of its nation's type of economy, the middle class is not politically oppositional per se. In the oil-dependent economies of the Gulf region, it has even less reason for antagonism because its political edge is blunted by lucrative benefits and the government's policies of appeasement.

As in the rest of the Middle East, the various social classes in the Arabian peninsula are not only economically divided from one another but also socioculturally differentiated within themselves. Values that are considered "traditional" and "conservative," however, tend to be more prevalent in the Gulf region. The cultural dichotomy of society into modern and traditional indeed exists, but the more conservative values remain dominant and they are psychologically less traumatizing and disillusioning. From a cultural perspective, the societies of the Gulf and the Arabian peninsula are in less turmoil because their values, associated with tradition and heritage, have not been as thoroughly discredited as in other parts of the region. In fact, the emirs and the general populace who hold conservative views of the world look with condescension on the failures and miseries that the supposedly progressive ideas of Nasser, Saddam Hussein, and Khomeini have brought on their respective countries.[63] Many support mechanisms give the Gulf societies their conservative flavor and uncanny ability to modernize economically while at the same time preserving the values of generations past. The continuing strength of the bedouin heritage is a major factor, especially because it is reinforced by the political manipulations of those in power. The economic miracles experienced by each of these oil-based countries have only enhanced the legitimacy of political establishments, which in turn justify themselves by specific reference to the past, particularly their tribal and Islamic past. If the Saudi king's title, "Guardian of the Two Holy Mosques," is a political ploy designed for domestic consumption, it is so far a largely successful one.

But the perseverance of traditional and conservative values in the Arabian peninsula goes beyond the successful combination of political and economic developments. It is also a direct product of the manner in which economic change and growth has come about. In countries with more integrated economies, economic growth and its accompanying processes of social change have been piecemeal, drawn out in phases or in prolonged spurts. Iran, Iraq, Algeria, and Egypt, for example, all grew in the 1960s and then again from about 1973 to the early 1980s. While in some cases this growth was a direct result of petrodollars, these economies had more channels for the revenue to filter down to the masses. To benefit from this growth and to get a piece of the economic pie, many people had to change their habits, lifestyles, values, and priorities. Peasants migrated to the cities and joined the lumpen proletariat; the middle class changed its occupations and rearranged its priorities; the upper classes sought ways of getting richer; and those in power justified their policies and their reigns by disseminating Western material goods and their attendant values. This was a widespread change, engulfing not only different classes of people but also different generations within the same class. Thus the social change that swept the Middle East beginning in the 1950s and 1960s was as much a cultural revolution as it was an economic one. But the manner of economic growth, its intensity, and its scope have all been different in the Gulf region, and consequently so have the resultant changes: the conservative states bought legitimacy through the massive infusion of wealth into their economies; the merchants latched on to the ruling families; the upper and middle classes benefited immensely; and those who labored in the factories and on construction sites were imported from abroad. Through it all, the social order was disturbed the least. The most dramatic changes occurred over the life of only a generation or two, and in such a way as to keep the evolving social values consistent with what they had been. Social classes became wealthy almost overnight and without the need to greatly compromise the traditional

values they had held. Even in instances where one's values were changed
—and they changed for many people in the Gulf—such changes remained
consistent and were not psychologically traumatizing. Culturally based
frictions have, therefore, been minimized, which contributes not only to
social harmony but to political stability as well.

As pervasive as traditional, conservative values may be in the Gulf, a
dichotomy along the crude lines of "traditionalism" versus "modernity"
exists, as represented in figure 3.3 (p. 89). However, the line dividing them
is the opposite of that reflected for social classes in countries with more
integrated economies in figure 3.2 (p. 88): in the societies of oil-dependent
countries, the greater one's wealth and proximity to the political establishment, the more likely one is to remain socially and culturally conservative.
The middle class, whose historic connections to the ruling family are most
tenuous and whose social status came about as a direct result of the economic changes, is almost equally divided between those with traditional
values and those with modern ones. But beginning with the upper-middle
class and moving up the economic ladder to the merchants and then to the
ruling family, the percentage of the tradition-minded rises significantly. The
emir and his inner circle are highly traditional, if not from genuine conviction, then certainly because of the political prudence of maintaining an appearance of strict piety and social conservatism. For the ruling family and
all other classes in the Gulf societies, Islam remains a vital point of reference
at all times, and its strictures are observed in even the most mundane aspects of life. This is not to imply that life has simply stood still or that all
values are holdovers from an era gone by. Indeed, Kuwait, Bahrain, and
Dubai have some of the most cosmopolitan societies found anywhere in the
Third World. What differentiates them from other societies is the relative
ease with which they resolve potential conflicts arising from different social
values. From all appearances, the conflict has been settled largely in favor of
tradition and conservatism.

The Expatriate Factor

A discussion of social classes in the Middle East would not be complete
without examining the sizable number of expatriate workers and residents throughout the Gulf region. An initial distinction must be made between the Palestinians, most of whom originally migrated to the region in
search of not only jobs but also a place of residence, and other migrants
who continue to move to the area for the sole purpose of securing employment. From the start, then, the Palestinians wanted to settle permanently in the Gulf region because they did not have a country to which

they could return. At the same time, determined to keep their national identity alive and dreaming of one day returning to their country, Palestinians have often resisted assimilation into other cultures, and they are among the most politicized people in the Middle East.[64] This problem has been compounded by the political agendas and policies of the various countries hosting Palestinians; only Syria and Jordan have granted them full property ownership rights.[65] The exact number of Palestinians in the Gulf countries is unknown, although many have risen to prominent bureaucratic and administrative positions, especially in Kuwait. None of the Gulf states, however, has granted citizenship privileges to the Palestinians as a whole; only in rare and exceptional cases has a Palestinian been made a full citizen of any of the Gulf countries. In Kuwait, restrictive citizenship laws have meant that a significant percentage of the population born inside the country is considered non-Kuwaiti,[66] which becomes a significant handicap in light of the many restrictions that the Kuwaiti government places on them. Consider the following:

> Non-Kuwaiti is a status distinction that permeates the entire social structure of Kuwaiti society and places manifold disabilities upon the population so classified. Non-Kuwaitis have no legal rights in Kuwait. A non-Kuwaiti cannot secure a working permit or residency without the guarantee of a Kuwaiti national who is responsible for the non-Kuwaiti in all legal and financial dealings. . . . A non-Kuwaiti must leave the country once unemployed. Furthermore, non-Kuwaitis have no access to the welfare system that Kuwaitis have. . . . Within the civil service, which was made up of 59.8 percent non-Kuwaitis in 1976 only Kuwaitis obtain permanent appointment and are entitled to a pension.[67]

Whether in Kuwait or elsewhere in the Gulf countries, Palestinians as noncitizens cannot own property and, like all other expatriate laborers, must leave once their employment is terminated or when retirement age is reached. Despite their long-term residence patterns and preponderant numbers, the Palestinian population in the Gulf region faces formidable obstacles and constant uncertainty. The PLO's pro-Iraqi stand during the Gulf War did not help the Palestinians' predicament, although their situation may change in response to progress in the Palestinian-Israeli peace process, especially should it result in the creation of a Palestinian Authority in the West Bank and the Gaza Strip.

Non-Palestinian migrants form the second category of expatriates. Beginning in the 1960s and 1970s, unprecedented economic growth resulted in acute shortages of both skilled and unskilled labor in virtually all Gulf countries. Consistent with the massive dislocation of Palestinians after the 1967 war and the growing economic hardships facing the Indian subcontinent, Egypt, and the former Yemens, floods of expatriate workers and immigrants streamed into the Gulf countries, in some instances eventually surpassing the numbers of the native population. By the late 1980s, prior to Iraq's invasion of Kuwait, approximately 55 percent of all migrant workers in the Gulf were estimated to be from other Arab countries and most others from Pakistan, Bangladesh, and India.[68] While reliable statistics are unavailable, most estimates put the number of foreign expatriates in the Gulf at around 44 percent of the region's total population.[69] Table 3.6 presents a rough breakdown of the percentage of expatriate workers to the total population in five Gulf countries. In addition, there were unspecified numbers of technicians, primarily from South Korea, and Egyptian soldiers and other military personnel from Iraq throughout the 1980s. After Iraq's invasion of Kuwait, however, almost all Iraqi migrant workers as well as many Kuwaiti ones left for their respective countries. The invasion and its political fallout have had profound effects not only on the lives of migrant workers in the Gulf but also on the official policies made by the host countries toward the expatriate population as a whole.

Prior to the Iraqi invasion, there was a subtle, though by no means universal, division of labor among expatriate workers based on their country of origin. Most Palestinian and Egyptian migrants tended to be skilled and were thus able to secure relatively good positions in the ser-

TABLE 3.6

EXPATRIATES: PERCENTAGE OF POPULATION
AND ORIGINS

Gulf country	Percentage of total population	Country of origin
Bahrain	30	Pakistan, India
Kuwait	60	Pakistan, India, other Arab nations
Qatar	73	Pakistan, India, Iran
Saudi Arabia	n.a.	No permanent immigration
UAE	58	Pakistan, India, Iran

SOURCE: Compiled from Gregory Thomas Kurian, ed., *Encyclopedia of the Third World*, vols. 1–3, 4th ed. (New York: Facts on File, 1992).

vices and manufacturing sectors, many finding employment as teachers, physicians, and engineers.[70] Most migrants from Yemen (former North and South Yemen), Bangladesh, and Pakistan, however, brought few skills with them and often ended up working as manual laborers or doing other kinds of menial jobs. Many Indians who could speak English were more marketable and employed as secretaries or clerks. Following the 1978–79 revolution and the war with Iraq, a number of Iranians also migrated to the Gulf region, and their vocations ranged from store or restaurant ownership to manual labor.[71] A growing number of female migrants from the Philippines and Thailand have also made their way to the Gulf area, with most finding employment as domestic servants. Although hiring East Asian maids has become quite fashionable in upper- and upper-middle-class circles, the number of female migrants remains negligible compared with the number of male migrants.

Beginning in the late 1980s, a number of Gulf countries became uneasy about the growing numbers of potentially troublesome migrant groups, especially Palestinians, Lebanese (particularly those with Shia backgrounds), and Iranians. This unease peaked during and immediately after Iraq's invasion of Kuwait, when many Palestinians sympathized with the Iraqis. Subsequently, anti-Palestinian sentiments were sanctioned at the highest levels—by the emir of Kuwait himself—and the governments of Saudi Arabia, Kuwait, and the United Arab Emirates all initiated measures to curb the number of Palestinian and other Arab immigrants.[72] Since the government of Yemen had refused to side with the Allied forces, many Yemenis were also harassed and forced to return home. One estimate puts the total number of migrants who were forced out of Iraq and Kuwait during and after the invasion at approximately 2.5 million.[73] Jordan, Yemen, Egypt, and the Israeli-occupied territories bore the brunt of this mass eviction, their fragile economies taxed even more by the sudden influx of returnees and the termination of the remittances previously sent from the Gulf countries.[74]

Since the war, migrant workers from Egypt, which actively took part in the liberation of Kuwait, and Southeast Asian countries have been given preferential treatment in finding employment there. Palestinians have been particularly targeted with suspicion and resentment, especially in Kuwait, which maintained a more liberal attitude toward them before the war.[75] Residence requirements have been toughened in many instances, and most governments in the region have passed laws requiring that priority be given to their own citizens for employment and promotions. Various studies have indicated that patterns of migration to the region are influenced as much by political and diplomatic considerations as they are by financial and economic ones.[76] The general unpredictability of Middle Eastern politics is likely to have continuing effects on the makeup and overall character of the expatriate population. Palestinian, Yemeni, and Iranian migrants are most likely to experience greater difficulties in securing employment and long-term residence. Even before the Gulf War, many of the region's governments and employers preferred hiring Southeast and East Asian laborers over others for both political and economic reasons. Asian migrants tend to accept lower salaries; their pronounced ethnic differences with the indigenous population makes them less likely to seek long-term residence; and they represent a diversified supply source.[77] As for the Palestinians, both in the Gulf and in the rest of the Middle East, their numbers, residence, and employment patterns could change significantly, depending on developments in Israel and the occupied territories.[78]

Rural Social Classes

Differences are also found between the composition of rural social classes in the countries that have relatively integrated economies and those in countries with smaller demographic bases and greater dependence on oil revenues. Broadly speaking, there have been more extensive social, political, and economic changes in the rural areas of countries with integrated economies, and consequently their class composition is both more complex and less permanent. In fact, it has often been official policy to break up the traditional economic and political authority structures in the rural areas and then replace them with government-approved ones. These changes, combined with the more integrated nature of the national economy, the relative poverty of rural areas, the general neglect of agriculture, and the larger social and economic ramifications of urban bias, have forced on the rural social structures in most countries tremendous upheavals in recent decades, leaving them in a constant state of flux. Through specific economic policies, the governments of Iran, Turkey, Iraq, Syria, Egypt, Tunisia, Algeria, and Morocco have sought to suppress tribal, ethnic, and other sources of rural identity, to neutralize those classes (such as feudal ones) whose economic priorities may be antithetical to the state's, and to replace rural values and sources of authority with loyalty to the state. Land reform has been the preferred method of achieving this goal, and the region saw land redistribution or seizure campaigns throughout the 1960s and 1970s.[79]

An opposite set of dynamics has been at work in Gulf countries, where regimes have a vested interest in maintaining the traditional character of the social order. Rural change has therefore been less pronounced, not necessarily because of these countries' particular pattern of economic growth but rather because the political legitimacy of the state has depended on maintaining and manipulating as many traditional sources of social authority as possible. The infusion of petrodollars into their economies and the resultant growth have necessarily changed some aspects of rural life, even in the most conservative Gulf countries. What distinguishes this type of change from what has occurred in the rest of the Middle East are the political and cultural imperatives behind it: other Middle Eastern states encourage and direct rural change; the Gulf countries either discourage it altogether or at the very least ensure that any rural values that bolster their own legitimacy remain intact.

Differences in rural class composition in the two regions distinguished here are part of a larger pattern of demographic distribution. In all Gulf states, with the possible exception of Oman, a much smaller percentage of the population lives in rural areas compared with the rest of the Middle East. As shown in table 3.3 (p. 99), urban-based populations were uncharacteristically high in all countries of the Arabian peninsula in the 1990s: 84 percent in Bahrain, 97 percent in Kuwait, 91 percent in Qatar, 80 percent in Saudi Arabia, and 84 percent in the United Arab Emirates. In contrast, in other parts of the Middle East, at most slightly more than half of the population lives in the urban areas, and the percentage of rural population remains quite significant. With the exception of Saudi Arabia, which is relatively unique because of its large size, its geographic diversity, and its multiple major cities, most Gulf countries are essentially city-states, containing one large metropolitan area and vast expanses of sparsely populated desert. The differences with other parts of the Middle East are quite telling. Iran, for example, is estimated to have as many as 45,000 villages.[80] Consistent with this, fewer people engage in rural-based economic activities in the Gulf states than in other Middle Eastern countries. As we saw in table 3.2 (p. 94), only 2 percent of the economically active population of Bahrain work in the agricultural and fisheries sector, as do only 1.3 percent of Kuwait's, 6.8 percent of Oman's, 14.3 percent of Saudi Arabia's, 3.1 percent of Qatar's, and 5 percent of the United Arab Emirates', compared with 42.7 percent in Egypt, 24.9 percent in Iran, 39.2 percent in Morocco, 30 percent in Syria, and 45.3 percent in Turkey. Based on these observations, a number of conclusions can be reached. From a political perspective, the Gulf countries have an easier task in their efforts to control and influence rural areas than do other Middle Eastern countries. This advantage is reinforced by the more peripheral economic role of the countryside in the Gulf than elsewhere in the Middle East, where domestic agriculture has not yet been completely supplanted by imports and city-based industries. Finally, although the village communities remain a significant part of the demographic and economic landscape in most of the Middle East, few countries in the Gulf region have notable rural communities per se, with most consisting of smaller and more diffuse bedouin groupings. The following sections examine these differences in greater detail.

Rural Classes in Oil-Dependent Economies

As shown in figure 3.3 (p. 89), three broad classes inhabit the nonurban areas of the Gulf region: a small class of estate owners; farmers who own small plots of land, fishermen, and others earning an income from a sea-related trade; and tribal bedouins. Estate owners are the least numerous; they often reside in urban areas and function as absentee landlords. Most often those with sizable landholdings in the rural areas are either descendants of former tribal leaders or somehow intimately tied to the current holders of power. Many are members of the ruling family itself, and others belong to the merchant families. Rarely does an individual who holds significant parcels of land reside in their vicinity. The geography of the area has a lot to do with the relative absence of a rural-based landed class. Apart from isolated oases that dot the desert, the area is simply not conducive to large-scale agricultural ventures. Only in Saudi Arabia has the government embarked on an aggressive campaign to encourage the agricultural sector, but the campaign has so far failed to yield profitable long-term results. More significant, the campaign's essentially urban character has prevented it from altering the country's rural landscape and social order.[81]

The second class of nonurban inhabitants consists of those who own the sources of economic production from which they earn a living. Few people in this category can be considered wealthy by any standards, and most earn only enough money to support themselves and their families. Within this class are two subgroups. The first includes those who live in the coastal areas and work in subsistence fishing (or in rare instances the construction of *dhows,* sailing vessels endemic to the region) or other forms of sea-related trade. Most are descendants of pearl divers and *dhow* builders who once inundated the region.[82] A few of these seafarers have earned additional income by smuggling goods across the Gulf to Iran and returning with individuals seeking to leave the country. For the most part, however, their incomes are not far above subsistence level. Members of the second subgroup live inland and on even less income, relying almost exclusively on animal husbandry, yields from palm groves, petty trade, and sometimes small-scale farming. Most are former bedouins who have settled into small rural communities. In a number of instances, especially in Saudi Arabia, their settlement is the result of deliberate government policies aimed at incorporating bedouins into the modern society, usually through employment in the oil fields or recruitment into the National Guard.[83] Thus modern life has gradually encroached on their world, with most households enjoying such amenities as electricity, running water, and at times even an automobile. But their settled way of life has done little to alter substantially their bedouin values, such as strong kinship bonds, chivalry, attachment to the desert, and hospitality.

By far the largest percentage of the rural population consists of those desert-dwelling bedouins who have resisted the temptation to acclimatize to the modern world. The majority have a nomadic lifestyle and live in tents. They maintain strong tribal loyalties, at the apex of which is often the ruling family. While most have horses, camels, sheep, and goats, they are rarely concerned with earning more money than they need, which is consistent with their general values. Their lives have changed nevertheless, for they live in countries that have undergone rapid and fundamental processes of economic growth. The spread of transportation networks and the increased number of cars have been particularly influential in changing most bedouins' lives. Of Saudi Arabia, Ibrahim observes that "the motor vehicle has had a tremendous effect on the life of the Bedouin." It has, he writes,

> opened up new cultural and economic vistas to the nomads. Now they go to the cities more often; listen to the radio at all times while roaming the desert; and they deal with car agents, mechanics, and gasoline dealers. The increasing use of trucks in the desert has been accompanied by other equally dramatic changes in the infrastructure basic to the exploitation of the desert.[84]

Some bedouins even find temporary employment or enlist in military service in the cities, after which they return to their tents. In the process, their core values may remain unchanged, but the newfound material trappings often greatly alter their lifestyle. Ibrahim's observations are again worth quoting:

Reverting back to a nomadic life-style ... is not going back to traditional nomadism. The tent, the camel, the sheep, the horse, and the sword are all still there. But cascading over them are the truck, the radio, and the machine gun.... The traditional Bedouin diet of milk, dates, and meat has been supplemented by Uncle Ben's Converted Rice and canned food. (7)

Such changes notwithstanding, the overall rhythm of life and values in nonurban areas of the Gulf countries remain largely conservative and tradition-oriented. For the most part, acute labor shortages have lured expatriate workers rather than creating an influx of rural inhabitants into the cities and the oil fields. Quite unlike other Middle Easterners, bedouins in the Gulf find few compelling incentives to assimilate socially, politically, or economically into the urban mainstream. The strength of and romantic attachment to bedouin values lessens the appeal of city life. Even those tribes that have been induced to settle because of government incentives pride themselves on their ability to hold on to their bedouin and nomadic roots. Thus few set out to become permanent residents of the cities, and those who do migrate tend to stay for temporary periods. The larger social universe they exist in makes their lives for the most part simple: they have few reasons to become urbanized but many reasons to remain what and where they are; their internal social stratifications are few because of the great distances between tribes; they adhere to a religion they consider to be universal and remain loyal to the ruling family; and they seldom find their economic lot to be so arduous as to force them to move to the city. They are, therefore, at a relative advantage when compared with rural populations in Middle Eastern countries with more integrated economies.

Rural Classes in Integrated Economies

Rural class composition in integrated economies is more complex and, consequently, so are the interrelationships. The relations between the rural classes and the urban arena in general and the state in particular are also more complicated in these countries, not even resembling the seemingly natural bonds that bind bedouins and ruling families in the Gulf countries. Indeed, while some rural groups have been co-opted by the state, a majority of these inhabitants remain outside the state's authority, and some have even shown great potential for political opposition. Their political positions are by-products of the diversities that characterize their occupations, social and cultural frames of reference, and lifestyles. Broadly defined, five distinct social classes can be distinguished among these rural inhabitants, beginning with a wealthy class of landowners who have managed to retain large-scale holdings despite official land reform and redistribution campaigns. Next are farmers who own small to medium-size plots of land. While their farms are seldom large enough for substantial agricultural production, they are of sufficient size to provide modest income, and therefore bring their owners social prestige and stature. Following the farmers is a significant segment of artisans, traders, and those who provide such rural services as moneylending, transportation of locally produced goods, management of small shops, and repair of tractors and automobiles. Next are landless peasants, many of whom migrate to cities to settle permanently or seasonally in hopes of escaping their rural poverty. The final group is made up of tribal bedouins who have maintained their nomadic lifestyle and values.

Before examining the composition and characteristics of each class, it is important to note that the kind of irrigation system found in different village settings plays a significant role in determining the nature of the prevailing social organization. The distinction between rain- and river-irrigated rural areas in the Middle East has directly affected not only the nature of the local classes but also the extent to which central authority has been involved in local affairs. In river-irrigated areas, such as Egypt and Iraq, the state takes a more active role in regulating access to and distribution of water and other resources, thereby creating greater government control, central planning, and teamwork.[85] More important, the state forges close ties with the dominant local elites, who are thus drawn closer to the national political elite. Borrowing a term originally used by Gaetano Mosca, Leonard Binder has called this group the "second stratum,"[86] as is discussed later. While major river systems invite the intervention of the central government (and the greater the significance of the river, the more extensive the depth of state intervention, as in the Nile and the Tigris-Euphrates basins), locally based systems of irrigation that rely on rain or underground canals, such as the Iranian *qanats,* allow for more autonomy from the state. Social organization in rain-irrigated areas, such as Iran, Turkey, Syria, Yemen, and parts of North Africa, thus tends to be not only more autonomous from central authority but also marked by relative isolation and diversification.[87]

Another important factor in determining the prevailing social organization is how a particular irrigation system directly affects the nature and characteristics of local rural elites. Land ownership and tenure have always been and will continue to be the most important determinants of one's class standing within the rural hierarchy.[88] In some Middle Eastern countries, the state has made a concerted effort to break the hold of large-scale ownership through land seizures or redistributions, while in other countries landholders have been steadily co-opted into the ranks of the regime itself and have become urbanized in the process. The prevalence of land reform schemes does not necessarily mean their automatic success. Throughout the region, in fact, land reform campaigns have not been fully successful in redistributing or seizing all that was targeted for redistribution. Too often, as has happened in Iran, old patterns of rural power relations and ownership have been reestablished once the promotional campaign for the government's latest scheme ends.[89] In Turkey, in fact, the state has largely been unable to carry out any meaningful land reforms in eastern Anatolia because landholders have effectively used the country's quasi-democratic system to preserve their own privileges.[90]

One transformation that has taken place has been in the form of turning former feudal lords into prosperous capitalist farmers. Their land assets may have been reduced, and they may no longer enjoy all the social and economic fringe benefits of being feudal lords, but their holdings are still large enough to allow them to live comfortably and employ numerous peasants. Modernization has forced them to sharpen their commercial skills, and the focus of their social values and economic activities is now the city instead of the village. Many have indeed become absentee landlords who often reside in the provincial city nearest the village in which their land is located. In one way or another, most have been able to place various constraints on their governments' agrarian policies and regulation of land holdings. "Because of their growing wealth and increasing awareness of shared interests, because of urban business, and because of their potential to boost exports, they have been able to reduce state autonomy vis-à-vis the still dominant rural sector."[91]

Land ownership is not, however, the only feature that characterizes today's Middle Eastern rural nobility. Through avenues provided by the state, many rural elites have become part of the national political machinery. Whether because of sudden historical changes, as in the Egyptian and Iranian revolutions of 1952 and 1978 respectively, or by gradual co-option into and penetration of the state, as in Turkey and Morocco, some members of the rural nobility have found themselves either directly in power or pretty close to it. Because national political power is essentially urban-based, these new holders of power quickly become fully urbanized, and most of their ties to the countryside are intentionally or unintentionally severed. In Egypt, Binder claims, most members of the postrevolutionary regime came from within this "second stratum," many of whom traced their family roots to nearby villages and rural communities. "The rural nobility is not the ruling class of Egypt," he argues, "but [it] provides the pool of qualified persons from among whom the important and not-so-important officials are chosen. It is the second stratum in Egypt."[92] Under radically different circumstances, similar social openings have taken place in Turkey, Morocco, and Iran, where former rural notables have been able to capitalize on their prestige and reputation not only to further their local interests but also to carve out a niche for themselves among the national elite. Although they may have lost their sizable landholdings by moving to the cities, many still retain the norms of the village and, more important, have close relatives in the countryside. They remain pillars of rural society while becoming respectable professionals and businessmen in the cities.[93] Whether absentee landlords or part of a new breed of powerholders, the position of these landowners in the overall hierarchy of the rural community does not change a great deal.

While geography and politics may have put some distance between large-scale rural landowners and the village community, land redistribution programs have had the result of swelling the ranks of farmers with small to medium-size plots of land. They differ from capitalist farmers in degree rather than in kind and often have the means to support only members of their immediate family.[94] Mostly geared toward the urban market, these farms tend to be apple orchards, orange groves, patches of watermelons or cantaloupes, or vegetable gardens. Family members often transport and sell the produce themselves, since the volume is not particularly large, from roadside stalls run by the women and children. Frequently, members of the extended family work the land, and therefore most farmers have neither the means nor the need to offer employment to the landless pool of peasants. Nevertheless, most farmers are able to send their children to nearby towns or cities for a better education, thereby unwittingly encouraging a cultural generation gap between them and their offspring. After having been exposed to the values of the city, not many youths choose to return to the farm. Many remain in nearby towns and assume bureaucratic and clerical positions, frequently visiting their birthplace and maintaining close ties with relatives. Those who return often open small stores and run them with the help of younger relatives. The farms nevertheless remain in family hands even after the death of the family patriarchs. Unlike their fathers, the younger generation may prefer to manage the land from a distance instead of working on it, but seldom will they relinquish it altogether. Land is, after all, a source of both social prestige and economic security.

Artisans, petty traders, mechanics, religious clerics, shopkeepers, moneylenders, drivers, and other members of the services sector make up the third class of rural inhabitants. Although their vocations may somehow be related to agriculture, these individuals have jobs that connect them to the larger operations and life of the village, and the larger the rural community, the greater the need for more diverse tradespeople. Their incomes vary from meager to sizable; for example, a rural mechanic may live more comfortably than the local clergy. Nevertheless, most tend to be economically on a par with owners of small and medium-size farms because many own the primary source from which they earn their livelihood—be it a store, truck, or roadside stall. But because they seldom own cultivable land and their economic activities traverse the urban and rural arenas, these tradespeople are often more directly affected by what goes on in the cities than are farmers. This is clearly the situation for those rural inhabitants whose livelihoods depend on the tourist industry. In countries with a lot of tourism, such as Morocco, Tunisia, Jordan, Turkey, and especially Egypt, many former peasants and farmers forgo farming for the occasionally more lucrative tourist trade, selling handcrafts, artifacts, and souvenirs to tourists. Most make a decent living and often hire extra help. When there is a slump in tourism, however, as has been the case throughout the region since the early 1990s, tourist trade merchants suffer the most because they seldom have other sources of income.

By far the largest segment of the rural population is a group whose economic lot is abysmal. These are the masses of landless peasants who work as farm laborers or hired help in the services sector. Though some may have small plots of land, their holdings are not sufficient to support even a small family. Therefore most must seek employment elsewhere. Poverty, malnutrition, and exploitation are constants in their lives. James Bill and Robert Springborg sum up the peasants' predicament:

> In predominantly agricultural societies, these are the individuals who work the land under a variety of arrangements that only alter the degree of their poverty, dependence, disease, and ignorance. The peasant class, located at the very bottom of the social structure, has very little power and is thus exposed to exploitation by all the other classes in society. For the individual peasant, this usually means abuse at the hands of landlord, merchant, and government official. Peasants have also suffered from manipulation by the clerics and from the raids of tribesmen.[95]

Many work as farm hands, or, if they can, head to cities and join the lumpen proletariat. Younger peasants are among the most frequent migrants, for they have the least at stake in the rural community and the most to gain by leaving their surroundings. Many migrate seasonally and try to maximize their earnings by alternating employment at the farm, factory, or construction site. It is therefore not uncommon in many parts of the Middle East to find what John Waterbury has called the part-time or shuttle peasant, one "with a hold on the land and on the city, on village life and migration, on agricultural and nonagricultural sources of livelihood."[96] Like rural tradespeople employed in the services sector, peasants in the countryside find that their well-being depends heavily on the health of the urban economy. The effects of inflation and unemployment are felt almost instantaneously in the villages, and members of the lumpen proletariat are among the first to suffer. Most eventually return home in such instances and rely on the traditional networks of support provided by family and kin. Although they may stay there for short periods of time, their unemployment further taxes the already fragile rural economy.

The deplorable conditions in which peasants live have prompted many observers to comment on their potential opposition to the state.[97] Even more commonplace have been attempts by would-be revolutionaries throughout the Middle East, as in other parts of the world, to mobilize peasants with political goals. Seldom are these revolutionaries from the peasantry itself, coming instead from urban, educated, middle-class backgrounds with the hope of finding converts to their cause. Yet despite their dedication and peasant-reform ideologies, few such activists have ever succeeded in mobilizing peasants to a meaningful extent, except in isolated instances in China and parts of Latin America.[98] The Middle East has been no exception, for at least in recent decades, the region has witnessed no peasant-based rebellions of any kind. Even the loosely governed provinces of the former Ottoman Empire, where central authority was diffused and peasant exploitation rampant, did not see widespread peasant revolts. There was widespread peasant avoidance of government officials and policies instead of insurrection, banditry instead of political opposition, and intersectarian violence among cultivators instead of collective action against the state.[99] It was only in the early decades of the twentieth century, when the burgeoning countries were weak, that notable peasant uprisings occurred in Iran (the Jangali movement from 1915 to 1921 in the north), in Iraq (the 1920 revolt in the Middle Euphrates area), and in Turkey (Sheikh Said's 1925 rebellion in the eastern provinces).[100] But in the past decades, the central authority of the state has been forcefully reestablished in even the remotest areas. Such ostensibly peasant-based insurrections as Oman's Dhofar revolution from 1965 to 1975 and the Polisario movement in southwestern Morocco are fundamentally urban in character and contain few, if any, peasant elements.[101] Even in Algeria's war of independence, in which the peasantry played a significant role, rebellions would not have been possible had it not been for the initiatives of urban-based intellectuals.[102]

The factors that thwart peasant political action in the Middle East today go beyond the effective, repressive abilities of the state. By themselves, peasants have neither the physical means nor the educational background to develop a unified identity through which they can make economic or political demands. The hungry and the destitute rarely rebel on their own; however, when they do act, it is usually in support of those who rebel on their behalf.[103] If an actual peasant uprising were to occur, it would most likely originate with farmers of small and medium-size plots of land. By virtue of their relative economic affluence, social stature, and education, the farmers can articulate peasant grievances and organize demonstrations. But such rebellions have never been common occurrences in the Middle East. In fact, certain national developments far beyond the countryside need to happen first: an acute economic crisis that threatens the livelihood of landowning farmers and their relationship with other markets, the emergence of mobilizational links between landless peasants and farmers or outside agitators; and a conducive political atmosphere made by the timidity or vulnerability of the state.[104] Since the region has not experienced some or any of these developments, peasant rebellions remain rare. Far more prevalent, however, are the less dramatic, everyday acts of foot-dragging, avoidance, and, at most, isolated acts of sabotage aimed at oppressive village notables. Other kinds of resistance may include destroying tax records or squatting on the landlord's property.[105]

Finally, tribal nomads and bedouins also inhabit the rural areas of Middle Eastern countries. In terms of geographic location, social organization, and class composition, there are few distinguishing features between bedouins in the Gulf region and other nomadic tribes in the Middle East.[106] Perhaps the most noticeable difference is the degree and nature of their allegiance to the state. States in the Gulf often identify themselves as essentially bedouin in character and, at least in rhetoric if not in substance, play up their nomadic heritage. Nomadic tribes therefore tend to develop a greater affinity with the state and to vest it with more cultural legitimacy than they would otherwise. But this symbiotic relationship is not maintained elsewhere in the Middle East, where the valuative and institutional gaps between the state and tribal groupings remain wide.[107] Beyond this political difference, however, there are few larger characteristics to distinguish nomadic bedouins from one another.[108] Some bedouins rely on raising camels for their livelihood and roam deep into the desert. They are found in some of the most arid parts of the Middle East: the Arabian peninsula, the Syrian Desert, the Sinai, parts of the Sudan and Somalia, and the Great Sahara. A second group of bedouins are pastoralists who raise sheep and cattle and move less often and less far into the desert. A third group, both semipastoralists and semicultivators, engage in land cultivation during farming seasons and roam the desert in others. They are virtually settled in village communities, where they often have huts made of bricks and mud to which they return seasonally.[109] The latter two groups of nomads are found in the less arid areas of Iran, Turkey, Iraq, and Egypt.

Rural social classes are not immune from the valuative and cultural chasms that characterize urban residents, and they too are marked by internal cultural and economic divisions. Figure 3.2 (p. 88) depicts the segmental as well as the internal divisions. Broadly speaking, the greater one's economic affluence, the more likely one has been exposed to "modern" ideas circulating in cities, and from them has developed a nontraditional social outlook. Conversely, traditional values become stronger the farther one gets from the urban, economic, and cultural mainstreams; most bedouins and tribal nomads hold values that few urbanites share. Indeed, perceptions of modernity vary from one social class to another, and even the most modern of rural classes may be perceived as provincial by city dwellers. There is general understanding in the village that the closer one's values are to those prevalent in the city, the more modern one must be, while in the cities the more Western one's values, the more modern he or she is considered to be. In remote areas, modernity is defined as having amenities such as running water and electricity, whereas for the wealthier farmers and landholders, modernity has a more cultural connotation. Many have internalized the values of the city by preferring to listen to the country's newest pop artists instead of local folk songs or by conducting their lives and relationships in the manner of urbanites.

Conclusion

As in other parts of the world, social classes in the Middle East cannot be understood as merely economic phenomena because they embody important social and cultural characteristics that also determine their composition, priorities, and relations with others. Because of the economic growth these countries have experienced and the nearly singular role of oil revenues in some nations, two broad patterns of social class composition can be discerned. Generally, the countries of the Arabian peninsula as well as Libya have smaller populations and extremely rich deposits of oil, hence their extensive reliance on oil revenues for continued growth and stable, prosperous economies. Another by-product of the oil industry is the development of a rather artificial class structure in which the various indigenous classes tend to gravitate toward the wealthier end of the scale. Thus the society includes a superwealthy ruling family, prosperous merchants, an upper-middle class, and a middle class—all of whom are more affluent than similar classes elsewhere. Massive wealth has enabled these countries to eradicate almost all poverty among their citizens and to import migrant workers to provide for their societies' and economies' various needs. Poverty, of course, does exist in the oil monarchies of the Persian Gulf, although it affects not the indigenous citizens but migrant laborers, few of whom, despite years of residence, ever attain full citizenship in their adopted countries. The class structure in the rural areas is also relatively simplified, being made up of estate owners, farmers, and bedouins, who are by far the largest of the three rural classes. A number of historical, social, and political factors have combined to bridge the cultural distance between these nonurban groups and their states, especially those headed by an emir.

Class composition is more complex in Middle Eastern countries with more integrated economies. Even so oil-rich a country as Iran or Iraq has too large a population and too established an economy to follow the Gulf countries' pattern of economic growth. In the less affluent countries, urban social classes are made up of an upper class, upper-middle class, middle class, lower-middle class, working class, and the lumpen proletariat. It is from these countries, especially Egypt, Jordan, and in recent years Iran, that laborers set out in search of better jobs in the Gulf. Each class is exploited by the one above, and the city as a whole exploits the countryside. Rural social classes include a reformed feudal class, which may have lost much of its land but has retained enough of it to live comfortably, farmers with small and medium-sized plots of land, traders and artisans, landless peasants, and nomadic bedouins. The country loses most of its youths and young adults to the city. The reality of limited prospects at home and the potential opportunities in the cities result in a steady exodus of villagers, but their aspirations of becoming urbanized are often shattered by insurmountable sociocultural barriers and economic hardships. Mobility from one class to another nevertheless occurs and is eased somewhat by cultural commonalities that people with different economic backgrounds may have. Subtle and complex cultural differences notwithstanding, and regardless of their economic status, social classes and even families may be broadly divided into those with traditional values and others with more modern ones.

Whether they are from countries with oil-dependent or integrated economies, from rural or urban regions, social classes are slaves to a larger sociological drama that influences their core values, interrelationships, and their very being. Social classes are shaped and affected by the far-reaching changes that societies experience, many of which they neither set into motion nor control. Classes, in other words, are recipients of social change, whether they embrace or renounce it.

4. Social Change

OCIAL CLASSES and institutions do not remain static; they change, as do the larger social and cultural contexts within which they operate. In fact, all societies undergo constant and far-reaching transformations that can be analyzed collectively under the rubric of "social change."[1] By nature, social change is context-specific, involving different catalysts, nuances, and consequences depending on the particular social and cultural milieu within which it takes place. Similarly, social change elicits different reactions from the various institutions and classes of society as well as from those in positions of political power. In the Third World, these responses to social change, whether by policymakers or ordinary citizens, have on the whole been sharp, and in the Middle East they have been especially pointed.

At the most fundamental level, social change refers to "the alteration of a social system over time."[2] It entails changes in the underpinnings of society, thus altering the habits, worldviews, values, customs, and overall lives of those it affects. Social change, therefore, is not just any ordinary alteration in one's cultural surroundings: it involves a thorough and intense process of transformation over a reasonably long period of time.[3] Wilbert Moore, a pioneer in the study of social change, emphasizes the process's depth and extent. "Social change," he argues, "is the significant alteration of social structures (that is, of patterns of action and interaction), including consequences and manifestations of such structures embodied in norms (rules of conduct), values, and cultural products and symbols."[4] As living organisms, societies change constantly. What is often conveniently called social change is actually a natural process of transformation to which all societies are subject, regardless of where they stand on an evolutionary scale or the levels of technological or political sophistication they have attained. "Change," wrote Moore, "is as characteristic of man's life in organized systems as is orderly persistence."[5] But what is an innate propensity to change does not necessarily make the change itself less tumultuous and disorienting. Even in its most innocuous form, social change is fraught with tension and confusion, upheaval and turmoil, instability and uncertainty.

What matters is the broader social and cultural context within which change occurs. Simply stated, some societies can handle transformation better than others. The crucial difference between the more adaptable societies and those that are less so lies in the extent to which they have previously experienced change. The more a culture and society have been subjected to change, the more likely they are to perceive future transformations as nonthreatening and inevitable. To them, change was once foreign, and it was met with great resentment and hostility. But they gradually developed mechanisms for dealing with the disconcerting sociocultural and psychological ramifications of change and are now, for the most part at least, accustomed to it. Thus cultures and societies in the West, where, because of the Industrial Revolution and its dramatic consequences, social change spread rapidly and thoroughly, are better prepared structurally to meet the challenges of continuing change than non-Western cultures and societies, in which long-held truths, traditions, habits, and ways of life have more recently been affected by contending, sometimes disparate axioms.[6] In non-Western and especially Third World countries, the effects of social change are greatly magnified, not necessarily because of their greater intensity but rather because their social systems on the whole are less adept at absorbing and dealing with change. It should be no surprise that in these arenas social change may even assume the character of all-out revolution.[7]

The origins, process, and outcome of social change depend on a number of variables that significantly affect its impact on society. Specifically, social change may occur in a gradual, evolutionary fashion, as is most often the case, or it may take place through cataclysmic, revolutionary events. Government policy initiatives, such as the implementation of family planning and child-welfare laws, and the cumulative effects of industrialization and technological growth, such as the construction of roads or the introduction of electricity, radio, and television, are among the most common catalysts for gradual social change, the full effects of which become evident only after a substantial length of time. In other instances, social change comes about as a result of far more intense, concentrated events that have a revolutionary character. In fact, revolutions are themselves highly condensed episodes of complete political and social transformation.[8] More specific examples of sudden, revolutionary social change can be found in virtually all postrevolutionary countries, especially given their penchant for carrying out "cultural revolutions" and carving out new, "revolutionary" social and political orders.[9]

The two general patterns of social change, gradual and sudden, are not mutually exclusive. Revolutions are merely condensed forms of political and social change; they build on previous changes and facilitate future ones. Because revolutions are not everyday occurrences, most social changes arise from piecemeal and gradual alterations in the economic, political, and social realms. On rare occasions, however, history has witnessed monumental revolutions: France in 1789; Russia in 1917; China in 1949; Cuba in the 1950s; Algeria in 1962; and Iran in 1978. Societies caught up in these and other revolutions were radically transformed. They also experienced change resulting from factors besides the revolution. Given the Middle East's history of coups-*cum*-revolutions (Egypt in 1952; Libya in 1969; and both Syria and Iraq throughout the 1960s and 1970s), distinguishing between revolutionary change and gradual social change is not an easy task. Sometimes there are distinct noticeable changes, such as those that accompanied the Algerian and Iranian revolutions.

Also important in determining the nature and direction of social change is society's relationship with the state, because the prevailing political atmosphere has a direct bearing on the effectiveness and extent of that change. Specifically, it is important to determine if the various changes taking place within society are directly or indirectly supported or opposed by the state. If they are not supported by the state, can these changes undermine the very basis upon which it is based and eventually subsume it? And if they are politically supported, does that enhance their acceptability among the various social classes or make them seem suspect and thus inconsequential?

Other forms of social change may arise from nonstate and nonpolitical factors and contribute to the erosion of the state's powers. To a great extent, this variable determines the pervasiveness of social change and influences the degree to which the different social classes are affected by it. Thus the pivotal role of the state in relation to social change cannot be ignored.

With these considerations in mind I examine the causes, processes, and manifestations of social change in the Middle East in this chapter. Much has been written on the causes and catalysts of the region's social change, and there is no need to detail the convincing arguments of others.[10] I shall, however, briefly note some of the crucial factors and developments that have set these far-reaching changes into motion.

The primary foci of social change in the Middle East have traditionally been revolutions "from above" and "from below," industrialization and technological advancements, and cultural modernization. The ramifications of social change, meanwhile, have generally included rampant urbanization, the appearance of new social classes, a general distortion of social norms, and widespread social afflictions such as alienation and the generation gap. Indeed, these changes have profoundly affected the prevailing political and popular cultures, not to mention the overall political landscape.

Causes of Social Change

The pivotal instrument and originator of social change throughout the Middle East has been the state. Every country in the region has developed its own form of government, and all of them have made social engineering a primary objective. In every country, the edifice of the state looms over society, seeking not only to govern but also to regulate and direct the behaviors, thoughts, and actions of its citizenry. Despite their differing ideologies and agendas, all Middle Eastern states have in one way or another fostered some kind of change. Most of the states outside the Gulf have embarked on specific programs of change, through land reform, family planning laws, literacy campaigns, and other concerted efforts. Not all state-initiated social changes have been planned, however. In such countries as Turkey, Tunisia, and Morocco, where comparatively liberal and noninterventionist social policies are pursued, the state is still capable of influencing some of society's more mundane aspects. But even where states have harbored an ideological hostility to change, as in most of the Gulf oil monarchies, social change has not been completely absent. And although these states have painstakingly limited the nature and extent of most changes, their own policies have gone a long way toward reshaping prevailing social relations and cultural norms.

None of the states' transformative powers would have come about, of course, had it not been for the phenomenal growth during the "fat years," from 1974 to 1981.[11] The Middle East experienced a tremendous burst of oil-generated economic growth, the residual effects of which also benefited oil-poor Egypt, Syria, Jordan, the Yemens, and Morocco. Oil began flowing in commercial quantities from Iran at the beginning of the twentieth century, then later from most of the other Gulf countries: Bah-

rain in 1922; Kuwait in 1946; Qatar in 1949; and the emirates of Abu
Dhabi (1962), Dubai (1969), and Sharjah (1974).[12] An oil bonanza was
not to occur until later, however, when the price of a barrel of oil rocketed
from $2 in 1974 to $40 in 1979.[13] There was staggering per capita economic growth from 1970 to 1979, ranging from Saudi Arabia's astronom-
ical 38 percent, to Syria's 15.2 percent and Egypt's 12.4 percent.[14] Not to
be outdone, those countries without oil, namely, Turkey, Jordan, and especially Egypt, adopted "open-door" economic policies and eagerly encouraged foreign infrastructural investments.[15] Morocco, Turkey, and Tunisia borrowed heavily from international financial institutions.[16] In real
terms and allowing for inflation, the national revenue of all Arab countries grew at an impressive 5.2 percent annually in the 1970s.[17] The states
then embarked on intensive programs of infrastructural development,
general welfare, and economic diversification.[18] Government bureaucracies and service sectors grew to mammoth proportions, as did the middle
and upper-middle classes. The provision of free education and health care
became the norm, with the oil-rich Gulf states providing the most extensive welfare coverage for their citizens.[19] At the very least, each state
sought to create a safety net that would keep the burgeoning middle
classes out of poverty.[20] The state everywhere became the chief architect
of structural transformation, assuming that only *it* could carry out the
monumental changes that the times demanded.[21] As Alan Richards and
John Waterbury point out:

> The Middle Eastern state took upon itself the challenge of moving the
> economy onto an industrial footing, shifting populations to the urban ar-
> eas, of educating and training its youth wherever they lived, raising agri-
> cultural productivity to feed the nonagricultural population, redistributing
> wealth, of building a credible military force, and doing battle with inter-
> national trade and financial regimes that held them in a thrall. These were
> goals widely held, if poorly understood, by citizens at large. There were
> no impediments then to the expansion and affirmation of the intervention-
> ist state.[22]

By the time the global recession and oil slump occurred in the 1980s,
the social ramifications of the former economic growth could not be reversed or even stopped. Almost all Middle Eastern states cut their development projects, curtailed their welfare programs, and Iran, Turkey, Morocco, Tunisia, and Egypt instituted austerity measures.[23] There were
budget deficits and other economic shortcomings even in free-spending

Saudi Arabia, where such sacred cows as defense spending and private loans to individuals and businesses were significantly curtailed.[24] But like its other oil-rich neighbors, Saudi Arabia continued to accumulate wealth in the 1980s, despite the economic downturn and slump in the oil market.[25] While the recession took a substantial toll on governments and individuals, however, the economic and politically generated social changes of the earlier years could not be reversed, having set into motion dynamics that had assumed a momentum of their own.

The most striking consequences of economic and industrial growth have been the dramatic population growth of the region's cities, making such Middle Eastern capitals as Cairo, Tehran, and Baghdad among the largest and most populous in the world. Social change is a catalyst for as well as a result of urbanization. Rapid industrial growth and its many direct and indirect consequences—the building of factories and the appearance of new employment opportunities; the expansion of road, transportation, and communication networks and the resultant increase in physical mobility; the increased demand for both skilled and unskilled laborers; the changes in demographics and family structure; and individuals' rising expectations and, in many instances, enhanced social status—all lead to rampant urban growth, which in nearly every Third World country goes unchecked and unplanned. Primary metropolitan centers have a virtual monopoly over all political, sociocultural, and economic power and activity. Hence crowded and poorly equipped "megacities" have developed, which despite their impressive size and modern façades, lack the necessary infrastructure to handle their burgeoning populations. As a result, shantytowns and squatter settlements are as characteristic of the Third World as giant, sprawling cities.

But this is at best only a partial process of urbanization, for an increase in the number of urban residents does not necessarily result in their assimilation into the overall urban environment through adoption of norms that prevail there. As noted in chapter 3, few migrants who flock to the cities from the countryside ever become fully urbanized. They retain many of their old habits and customs, often only slightly modifying them to adapt to their new surroundings. This cultural and emotional estrangement is reinforced by two additional factors. First, most existing urban residents, especially those in the middle and upper classes, consider themselves culturally, economically, and intellectually superior to the less sophisticated arrivals from the countryside. Most migrant workers, after all, end up working as servants, chauffeurs, gardeners, garbage collectors, or coolies for the urban wealthy. Second, what magnifies this blatant division is the actual physical segregation of most migrants from the rest of the city, because many tend to live and work in specific neighborhoods and remain virtually separated from the larger urban environment.[26]

The pace of urban growth since 1980 has been phenomenal.[27] As shown in table 4.1 (p. 138), the overall population of Middle Eastern countries grew at an average rate of 2.9 percent from 1980 to 1990. The average rate of rural population growth, however, was only 1.3 percent, compared with 4.85 percent for urban areas. During the same time span, an increasingly higher percentage of Middle Easterners lived in the cities than in rural areas. The demographic shift has been quite uneven, resulting in an even greater increase in the size and population of each country's largest city. For example, nearly 20 percent of all urban Iranians and 11 percent of the country's total population live in Tehran; Beirut contains 68 percent of Lebanon's urban population and 58 percent of its total population; nearly 30 percent of Iraq's urban population and 22 percent of all Iraqis live in Baghdad; and in Egypt some 37 percent of the country's urban population and 16.5 percent of its total population live in Cairo. This increase in urban population levels results from the combined effects of migration from rural areas and natural (birth rate) increases. V.F. Costello has written that

> the sequence of events for many major cities appears to involve firstly rapid growth resulting from migration and then within less than a generation a much higher rate of natural increase in the city than in the rural areas because of the youth of the immigrant population and lower death rates. Migration in absolute terms is important in Baghdad, Tehran, Cairo, and other major cities, but it is also an important primer for future urban natural increase.[28]

All of this urban growth has taken place with virtually no attention from the central governments. One observer has commented that in the Middle East "there are national plans for everything except the city."[29] The resultant phenomenal, unchecked growth of cities has had a number of important consequences within each country and for the entire region. City quarters and neighborhoods where people with similar social, economic, and cultural backgrounds tend to concentrate assume particular significance and become important arenas for socialization. These quarters are often segregated by the modern versus traditional values duality that prevails in the larger society, with some districts rivaling cosmopolitan European capitals and others remaining bastions of traditional norms

TABLE 4.1

POPULATION AND SETTLEMENT PATTERNS IN THE MIDDLE EAST

		Population estimate		Population growth per year		Population of largest city			
	Year	Rural %	Urban %	Rural %	Urban %	Year	(in thousands)	Percentage of national urban pop.	Percentage of total national pop.
Algeria	1980	56.6	43.4	2.1	4.6	—	—	—	—
	1990	48.3	51.7	1.1	4.4	1992	3300	23.4	12.5
Bahrain	1980	19.6	80.4	3.6	5.2	—	—	—	—
	1990	17.1	82.9	1.8	3.5	1990	130	30.4	25.2
Egypt	1980	56.2	43.8	2.2	2.6	—	—	—	—
	1990	56.1	43.9	2.4	2.4	1992	9000	37.3	16.5
Iran	1980	50.4	49.6	1.8	4.8	—	—	—	—
	1990	43.1	56.9	1.9	4.8	1992	7000	19.5	11.4
Iraq	1980	34.5	65.5	1.1	4.6	—	—	—	—
	1990	28.2	71.8	1.2	4.2	1992	4200	29.9	21.8
Israel	1980	11.4	88.6	-0.8	2.8	—	—	—	—
	1990	8.4	91.6	-1.0	2.2	1992	2000	43.2	39.8
Jordan	1980	40.1	59.9	0.2	4.0	—	—	—	—
	1990	32.0	68.0	0.9	4.4	1990	1020	37.4	25.4
Kuwait	1980	9.8	90.2	-3.7	7.7	—	—	—	—
	1990	4.2	95.8	-3.6	4.8	1992	1100	58.0	55.9
Lebanon	1980	26.6	73.4	-5.1	1.2	—	—	—	—
	1990	16.2	83.8	-4.6	1.7	1992	1600	68.0	58.0

Libya	1980	30.4	69.6	-0.7	7.0	—	—	—	—
	1990	17.6	82.4	-1.6	5.0	1992	2900	69.9	58.7
Morocco	1980	59.0	41.0	1.2	4.0	—	—	—	—
	1990	53.9	46.1	1.8	3.6	1992	3000	24.2	11.4
Oman	1980	92.4	7.6	4.8	8.9	—	—	—	—
	1990	89.0	11.0	3.4	7.4	1990	70	44.0	4.7
Qatar	1980	14.4	85.6	2.5	6.5	—	—	—	—
	1990	10.1	89.9	—	4.0	1990	329	100.0	89.4
Saudi Arabia	1980	33.2	66.8	0.8	7.7	—	—	—	—
	1990	22.7	77.3	0.2	4.8	1992	2200	17.9	14.0
Sudan	1980	80.0	20.0	2.8	4.1	—	—	—	—
	1990	77.5	22.5	2.5	4.3	1992	2100	34.5	8.0
Syria	1980	53.3	46.7	2.5	3.9	—	—	—	—
	1990	49.8	50.2	2.9	4.3	1992	1900	27.8	14.2
Tunisia	1980	49.7	50.3	1.5	3.7	—	—	—	—
	1990	44.0	56.0	0.8	3.2	1992	1900	39.3	22.5
Turkey	1980	56.2	43.8	1.3	3.1	—	—	—	—
	1990	39.1	60.9	-1.8	5.1	1992	7000	18.7	12.0
UAE	1980	28.5	71.5	10.1	15.8	—	—	—	—
	1990	19.1	80.9	-0.7	4.3	1990	260	21.0	16.4
Yemen	1980	79.8	20.2	2.3	7.4	—	—	—	—
	1990	71.1	28.9	2.4	7.0	1990	360	15.7	3.9

SOURCE: Compiled from United Nations, *Statistical Yearbook, 1990–91* (New York: United Nations, 1993).

and practices.[30] But the old quarters, often literally called "the old city" (e.g., the *Misr al-Qadimah* in Cairo), are not where migrants are found. They reside in districts of their own, often located on the city's periphery: the *bidonvilles* (from the French words *bidon* [metal can] and *ville* [city]) in North Africa; City of the Dead in Cairo; *gecekondus* (built overnight) in Turkey; and *halababad* (tin city) in Iran. As elsewhere in the Third World, the consequences of urban growth on social change have been dramatic. Consider the following: new classes have been formed (such as the lumpen proletariat) and the composition of old ones altered; both migrants and established urbanites have had to learn to coexist where they work and to relate to one another; new norms and values have been born either from a hodgepodge of existent and borrowed ones or created anew; rural communities have lost many young males and some young females, while cities have grown disproportionally; and society as a whole has been transformed.

Another important catalyst for social change in the Middle East has been the diffusion of Western culture. Although the region has had a long history of contact with the outside world, its exposure in recent decades to Western norms and values has exerted a profound influence on its societies and cultures. Any foreign values to be adopted must have the lure and luster of the West. They *must* bear an American or European stamp; otherwise, they are deemed not prestigious, unworthy of emulation and psychic internalization. Daniel Lerner noted the same phenomenon more than thirty years ago. "What America is," he wrote, "to condense a rule more powerful than its numerous exceptions—the modernizing Middle East seeks to become."[31] The nontraditional middle classes, whose social and cultural norms are the most transient anyway, are especially infatuated with Western culture. Their attempts to draw closer to the Western world are most apparent in their consumption patterns, in which Western brand names and labels are preferred to all others. Contrary to what some Middle Eastern scholars and laities think, this is not a by-product of imperialism alone or the result of sinister diplomatic machinations by the Western powers.[32] It is part of a deliberate effort by Middle Easterners themselves to seek, learn, and emulate popular Western values. Middle Easterners turn American or European cultural products—pop stars, movies, fast-food chains—into icons and institutions. Their resulting vulnerability to Western commercial exploitation occasionally leads to rather absurd incongruities. Even if he were alive, it is doubtful that the reggae singer Bob Marley would have had much to do with the naming of a youth hostel after him in the Egyptian city of Luxor.[33]

Because the resultant societal and cultural changes have been uneven and "distorted," they have only enhanced the stimulus for (or the reaction to) change among the various classes. The social and cultural division of Middle Eastern societies into traditional and nontraditional (modern) segments, as discussed in the last chapter, is a direct result of stunted and distorted social change. Clearly, some groups have more exposure to social change than others because the instruments and effects of modernization and cultural diffusion are unevenly spread throughout society. But even if the degree and nature of the exposure to modernization were uniform, people would probably respond differently to the same stimuli; every social group does. Exactly what accounts for these responses depends on one's physical environment, personality, socialization, political orientations, and economic position. The net result in the Middle East has been the appearance of a sharp cultural dichotomy, dividing society into antithetical halves, "modern" versus "traditional." Modernity to some has meant almost complete acceptance of Westernization. They have held on to deeply ingrained traditional values associated with religion or family, for example. But other, less resonant values, such as family size, tastes in home decoration and music, preferences for travel and dress, have been modernized. For this group even religion tends to be ritualized and often perfunctory—they go through the motions and continue to observe its basic tenets, more from the psychological comfort it provides than from sincere belief. The more traditional individuals or groups are often seriously religious, viewing religion not as an abstract to be observed when convenient but as an actual blueprint for existence. Just as "the West," with all its connotations, is the core of the modern individual's social and cultural frame of reference, Islam is fixed at the center of the traditional person's life. With each social group certain of the rightness of its values, traversing the social divide is extremely difficult and psychologically troubling.

Amid the social changes and ensuing divisions, the state has played a crucial role in promoting social and cultural diffusion. A number of Middle Eastern states initially welcomed the infusion of values from abroad, adopting social and cultural Westernization as mainstays of their political legitimacy. The promotion, whether subtle or blatant, of Western values and cultural practices was, in fact, an integral function of numerous states until the 1980s, when the tide of Islamic radicalism made its continuation politically imprudent. The specific reasons for this deliberate Westernization were basically the same from country to country. Most saw it as a middle-class obsession, a process conducive to Western-oriented economic growth, and an internationally prestigious achievement.

Frowning on Western values would have seemed backward and narrow-minded—not an image that most Middle Eastern leaders wanted to project in the 1960s and 1970s. The shah of Iran, Sadat, and Tunisia's Bourguiba were prime examples of such rulers, followed closely by Jordan's King Hussein and Morocco's King Hassan. When the wave of religious radicalism swept over the region, however, the states became suddenly pious, seeing their very survival threatened by the policies that they had aggressively promoted in the past. Iran became a bastion of Islamic extremism and promoted social change of a different order by zealously eradicating the vestiges of Westernization from the shah's reign. But the Iranians had had a revolution and could afford to be brash about it; the other states were not as fortunate. They had to perform a delicate balancing act by simultaneously appealing both to the newly pious, often anti-Western groups and to those that were Western-oriented. In one form or another, all Middle Eastern states in the recent past have tried to give themselves an Islamic, non-Western gloss in order to defuse any potential for domestic opposition. President Mubarak has carefully distanced himself from the legacy of the Sadat era, which many Egyptians viewed as corrupt and banal.[34] Elsewhere in the region, Qaddafi, Assad, and Saddam Hussein have all presented more pious images of themselves, and in 1993 Jordan's Islamist political parties participated and won a number of seats in the country's first parliamentary elections since 1967.[35]

But the current of popular Islamic radicalism has yet to be reversed. Except for the Islamic Republic of Iran, whose very extremism has evoked the opposite reaction among many Iranians, no Middle Eastern state has so far effectively stemmed the tide of religious radicalism in society. In fact, the tension between the state and Islamic radicals reached volatile levels in Turkey, Egypt, and especially Algeria in the 1990s.[36]

Tourism and the media are other sources of cultural diffusion, and both have been additional instruments of social change in the Middle East. The role of the media in diffusing culture has been somewhat compromised by its historical subservience to the state. In its earliest inception in the 1870s and the 1880s, the press served as a vehicle for liberal thought among a small circle of intellectual elites, and Beirut and Cairo remain important centers of publishing and scholarship to this day.[37] But the growing centralization of state power throughout the region, beginning in the 1950s, resulted in the press's steady loss of independence, for it was increasingly viewed as yet another means through which government policies could be justified and the national interest served.[38] Within this centralized context, most Middle Eastern governments have been able to direct, if not curtail, the social and cultural functions that the media play. Wanting to satisfy the traditional as well as the nontraditional elements of their societies, Middle Eastern states have been forced to adopt ambivalent, at times contradictory, attitudes toward the media. While it has had to cater to the tastes of the nontraditional groups, the media at the same time has had to be careful not to offend the sensibilities of the more traditional strata of society. For even in the most "liberal" Middle Eastern states, such as Turkey and Tunisia, especially during the constrictive and politically charged atmosphere of the 1980s and the 1990s, this has meant *reinforcing* existent social and cultural norms instead of deliberately effecting their change. Writing on the Arab press, William Rugh has commented that

> by giving considerable time and space to literature, Arab media help to reinforce Arab cultural identity. The same function is performed by the electronic media in carrying a great deal of Arab music as well as dramas on traditional themes. The music is both traditional and modern, and is performed by local artists and artists known throughout the area, such as Um[m] K[u]lthoum. In many Arab countries such programs take up hours of prime time on television as well as on radio. Similarly, readings from the Koran are broadcast regularly by stations all over the Arab world, and in some places religious commentaries or advice on proper moral and ethical behavior are featured on radio and TV.[39]

Wanting to keep the nontraditional segments of their populations content as well, Middle Eastern states have not completely banned Western shows or Western-style programming. The role of the electronic media in facilitating the diffusion of other cultures and thus social change has sharply increased in recent years. After years of strictly "revolutionary" programs, Iranian radio and television resumed Western-type music in the mid-1980s. In Kuwait the country's two television channels carry a Kuwaiti version of the American children's show *Sesame Street* called *Iftah ya Sisim (Open Sesame)*.[40] In Egypt one of the most popular prime-time evening shows on television in 1993 and 1994 was the American soap opera *The Bold and the Beautiful*. And Oprah Winfrey's celebrated interview with Michael Jackson on American television in March 1993 was broadcast and widely watched in Morocco.[41] In a recent study of broadcasting in the Arab world, Douglas Boyd makes the following observation about programming on Kuwait's two television channels:

144 / DEMOCRACY IN THE BALANCE

[T]he majority of programs are U.S. and European programs and made-for-television films. Officials are not concerned about the cultural effect of imported programs because they believe that it is up to the viewer to make a choice between what is offered on the two services. They indicate that even if imported programs from the United States and Europe were not offered on Kuwaiti television, they are available in local cinemas or on videotape for home video systems.[42]

Throughout the region, the centrality of the electronic media has been magnified by the increasing accessibility of radio and television in even remote areas and of videocassette recorders and satellite dishes in the cities. Satellite cable technology is now readily available in most Middle Eastern cities. In some areas of the Gulf, weather conditions make it possible to receive up to twelve different television signals, often from the neighboring countries, and international or transnational radio broadcasts are even more prevalent.[43]

The social and cultural impact of tourism has been less direct and less evenly distributed within the region. As a general rule, the oil monarchies of the Persian Gulf do not welcome foreign tourists. Saudi Arabia, and recently Oman, in fact, do not grant tourist visas to visitors, while other Gulf countries place numerous legal and physical restrictions on potential tourists. There are, however, a handful of Middle Eastern countries that have well-developed tourist industries, especially Egypt, Morocco, and Tunisia, and rely on tourism as a major source of revenue. As table 4.2 indicates, the majority of the tourists have been American and European, with only a few coming from other Arab countries, notably Saudi Arabia. But the numbers can be deceiving, and the real social and cultural impact of tourism must not be exaggerated. In the popular destinations of Israel, Egypt, Morocco, Tunisia, Turkey, and Jordan, the extent to which locals come into contact with tourists varies greatly within each country. Tourists rarely spend extended periods of time in nontourist areas, and thus only a portion of the local population comes into contact with them on a regular basis. The locals who do encounter them are often near the bottom of the economic ladder, from taxi drivers to souvenir salesmen and "guides," and often depend exclusively on the tourist trade for their livelihood. Of these, only the young adults, who are by nature impressionable and desirous of a different lifestyle, may be readily influenced by the norms and values of the tourists they assist. The locals' economic dependence on the tourists and the foreigners' frequent neglect of local customs or sensibilities (e.g., not observing the Islamic dress code or ignoring the

TABLE 4.2

ANNUAL TOURISM STATISTICS

FOR SELECTED MIDDLE EASTERN COUNTRIES

IN THE 1980S

	Egypt	Morocco	Tunisia	Turkey	Jordan
Tourism receipts ($ millions)	1,784	1,102	1,234	2,355	621
Number of tourists (in thousands)					
USA	169.0	100.7	10.4	196.3	54.7
France	119.9	401.4	401.1	n.a.	n.a.
Germany	116.3	162.8	277.7	299.5	n.a.
UK	n.a.	n.a.	99.5	n.a.	n.a.
Saudi Arabia	138.9	n.a.	n.a.	n.a.	286.3
Spain	n.a.	198.1	n.a.	n.a.	n.a.
Greece	n.a.	n.a.	n.a.	213.2	n.a.
Egypt	n.a.	n.a.	n.a.	n.a.	717.5
Total (in millions)	1.529	2.180	2.003	2.615	1.890

SOURCE: Compiled from Gregory Thomas Kurian, ed., *Encyclopedia of the Third World*, vols. 1–3, 4th ed. (New York: Facts on File, 1992).

Egyptian custom of returning a favor with a *bakhshish* [gift]), tend to create resentment and dislike for the tourists. It is precisely for these reasons that a number of tourists in Cairo and in the southern, conservative cities of Egypt have been attacked in recent years.[44]

Manifestations of Social Change

Whatever the specific cause of social change, its manifestations are numerous, varied, and often fraught with contradictions. On a very general level, the most apparent consequences of social change are structural and infrastructural, altering not only the physical environment in which societies live but also, as a result, the societies' own internal structures and stratifications. In terms of infrastructure, social change is caused by and in turn reinforces urban growth and urbanization. Along with other factors, urban-based industrial growth leads to the appearance of new social classes and institutions and to alterations in existing ones. A lumpen proletariat is born, its membership made up of former peasants and would-be industrial workers. An industrial working class also develops as a result of modernization and industrial growth, and in turn the ranks of white-collar technocrats in the middle and lower-middle classes swell. These wide-ranging changes lead to radical transformations in social institutions by either reducing or enhancing their resonance among the different strata of society. Some cling to religion while others abhor it; some reject the vestiges of ethnic identity while others still take pride in them; some families remain intact while others disperse; and some remain "traditional" while others strive after vaguely defined trends of "modernity." Society is thus highly disjointed, confused, and fragmented. Coping with these changes and appropriately modulating the self to adapt to constantly shifting milieus becomes a consuming preoccupation.

Within this overall context, the many varied manifestations of social change in the Middle East can be analyzed on three levels. A broad level of analysis can focus on the region as a whole, examining those social and cultural ramifications of change that are found in virtually all Middle Eastern countries. But a more in-depth analysis that would take into account the different patterns and consequences of social change within the region is also needed. Specifically, there are pronounced differences in the level and nature of the social change that has taken place in the oil monarchies of the Gulf, where change has been subject to greater political scrutiny and restriction than in the rest of the Middle East, where the phenomenon has occurred more haphazardly and with fewer deliberate restrictions. Such variables as political history, human geography, and the availability of economic resources have resulted in differing levels of social change throughout the region. The deciding factor has been the degree of society's autonomy from the state. In the countries outside the Gulf area, where societies have proved themselves to be less penetrable politically, social change has assumed an independent dynamic, spreading throughout society under its own momentum. While social change there has not been completely immune from state policies and initiatives, it has not been as intricately influenced by them. But in the smaller states to the south of the Persian Gulf, where the economic and political powers of the state seem enormous compared with the manageable size and composition of the population, social change has been far more susceptible to political nuances. While some social change in these countries has occurred independent of state control, governments have made it a point to manipulate or even control much of the social and cultural transformation of society. It is thus analytically useful, in fact necessary, to examine social change separately in these two areas of the region.

Social Change in the Middle East

Social change, it was noted earlier, involves both a cultural and a structural transformation of society. Social classes and institutions change, as do the values and norms that underlie them. In the Middle East, the most significant consequence of social change has been an ongoing dichotomization of society into traditional and modern spheres. This broad division has been an effect of and a perpetuator of rampant urban growth and the resultant mélange of city, peasant, and bedouin ways of life; wild oscillations in the strength and popularity of values and their constant revision; and the precarious and unique role that religion plays. Social change has, in essence, magnified existent contradictions in society and given rise to new ones. It has led to the creation of social classes that have little in common and compete over values and scarce resources. It has also polarized various social norms and led to the creation of new, intermediate ones that are neither traditional nor modern. The resulting social and cultural ambivalence has thus created a situation ripe for the growth of fetishes, absolutist values, and extremist ideologies.

In his pioneering work published four decades ago, Daniel Lerner claimed that Middle Eastern societies can be divided into the three subcategories of traditional, transitional, and modern. What differentiated each group was their level of "psychic mobility" and degree of "empathic capacity," a high level of which, he argued, is "the predominant personal style only in modern society, which is distinctively industrial, urban, literate and participant."[45] Defined as the "capacity to see oneself in the other fellow's situation," empathy is "an indispensable skill for people moving out of traditional settings" (49). This, Lerner concluded cautiously but optimistically, was the

> direction of change ... in all Middle East lands.... Everywhere the passing of traditional lifeways is visible; the secular trend is toward mobility—physical, psychic and social mobility.... In every Middle East country the transitional people exhibit more of those characteristics we have already identified with the participant style: urbanism, literacy, media consumption and empathic capacity. (83)

In his equally influential book published in 1964, Manfred Halpern argued along similar lines, maintaining that "almost every individual in the Middle East is now in motion, even those who are still standing still."[46] Halpern identified in the principal locus of history the "new middle class," who, after a succession of phases and battles, had emerged victorious in its "political struggle" against the traditional ruling class (74).

In the 1980s Hisham Sharabi presented a more sobering account of social change. He saw the central feature of Middle Eastern societies not as progressively merging trichotomies or successive struggles but as "neopatriarchal." Sharabi pointed to a crucial difference between the *façade* of modernity and its *reality*. Societies in the Arab Middle East, he argued, may have a "modernized consciousness" (modernism), but not the necessary "structure" (modernity), and they have not undergone the complete "dialectic of change and transformation" that this consciousness requires (modernization). What has resulted is a "distorted inauthentic modernity" that he called "neopatriarchy."[47] "Neopatriarchal society," he argued, "as 'modernized,' is essentially schizophrenic, for beneath the manifest modern appearance there exists another latent reality. Between this latent reality and its outward form there is opposition, tension, contradiction."[48]

> Neopatriarchal society as a dependent, nonmodern socio-economic structure represents the quintessentially underdeveloped society. Its most pervasive characteristic is a kind of generalized, persistent, and seemingly insurmountable impotence: it is incapable of performing as an integrated social or political system, as an economy, or as a military structure. Possessing all the external trappings of modernity, this society nevertheless lacks the inner force, organization, and consciousness which characterize truly modern formations. Indeed, modernization in this context is for the most part only a mechanism promoting underdevelopment and social entropy, which is turn produce and reproduce the hybrid, traditional, and semi-rational structures and consciousness typical of Neopatriarchal society.[49]

The best neopatriarchal society can do is to "convert models into fetishes"—in dress, art, ideology, organization, etc.—and to engage in "mimetic translations of Western models."[50]

The authors cited here, as well as the many others who have written on social change, have shed invaluable light on the subject. Without seeking to refute their arguments, I propose to look at the cultural and structural ramifications of social change in the Middle East from a slightly different perspective, aspects of which have been discussed in previous sections.

Chapter 3 outlined how each social class, regardless of its economic standing, is culturally subdivided into traditional and modern camps. It is generally believed that such elements of social change as urbanization and universal education lead to greater social cohesion and national integration. This is only partially true, for while the growth of urban areas may erode the strength of such traditional institutions as the village community, it leads to a plethora of other divisions that undermine prospects for sociocultural, political, or economic integration among the different social classes. In fact, in a region like the Middle East, where such values as religion, the family, and ethnicity have resonance far greater than any simple abstract norms, social change has in many instances helped strengthen, rather than weaken, their hold over individuals and entire groups. The spread of literacy, for example, allows more people to read secular books or to gain employment in the modern economic sector, but it also enables more people to read the Koran, to learn more about their tribal heritage, and to become more articulate in their demands and identities. In contrast, other groups are increasingly attracted to the new, the innovative, and the foreign. In fact, certain "modern-oriented" social groups—financiers and businessmen, physicians and engineers, technocrats and contractors, university students and professors—owe their professions to the rapidly changing sociocultural and economic milieus. They may not necessarily be the products of modernity, for many have existed in Middle Eastern societies for generations; however, because their professions often require them to look critically at tradition, most tend to be attracted to modernism.

This broad schism needs a sharper focus, for within each social class there are people who fall somewhere between tradition and modernity, not quite belonging to either sphere and yet traversing both. In every society, there is a larger body of interrelated and reinforcing norms and values, that is, culture. In the Middle East, the cultural milieu has been divided into the two spheres of modernity and tradition, some of which overlap (see figure 4.1, p. 150). This overlapping is a result of attempts by some people, whether intentionally or unintentionally, to reconcile the various opposing elements that are present in their culture. Within every social class, there is thus a group with an odd, and at times inconsistent, mélange of norms that overlap both traditional and modern ones. Because their norms are so uniquely situated between two diametrically opposed domains, this group suffers from an internalized confusion of values. They may go to great lengths to justify to themselves the internal logic of their values; in fact, many may successfully convince themselves that their value system is quite logically consistent. But there are instances when the

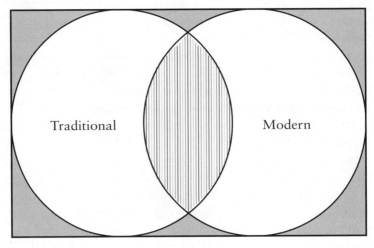

FIGURE 4.1
CULTURAL DISPOSITION WITHIN EACH CLASS

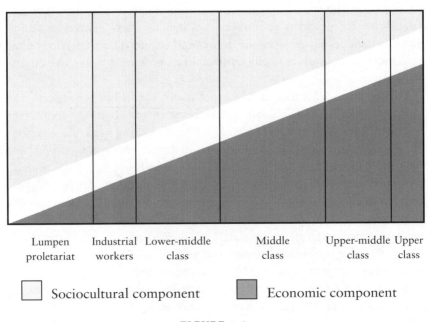

| Lumpen proletariat | Industrial workers | Lower-middle class | Middle class | Upper-middle class | Upper class |

Sociocultural component   Economic component

FIGURE 4.2
SOCIOCULTURAL AND ECONOMIC COMPOSITION
OF MIDDLE EASTERN SOCIETIES

mix of tradition and modernity does not turn out logically, when the half-hearted adoption of aspects from both cultures corrupts their essence and leaves the person emotionally and psychological unfulfilled. For all its certainty, it is precisely this segment of the population whose values are most precarious and therefore vulnerable to tides of moral absolutism.

These are the people whom Lerner calls "transitionals" and Sharabi labels "neopatriarchal." For both Lerner and Sharabi, this group has rather specific economic and class characteristics: Lerner sees it as having decidedly middle-class features,[51] while Sharabi argues that it is the hybrid class of the "petty bourgeoisie."[52] I maintain, however, that having overlapping and at times conflicting values is not class-specific and can be found within virtually all social classes. It is true that by virtue of their economic position as social conduits through which goods and services are dispersed to the rest of society, the middle classes' norms and values are likely to receive the greatest stress from the pull of tradition and the push of modernity. However, the middle classes are not the only ones doing some soul searching about culture, nor are all their members bogged down by an unending struggle over values. Perhaps fewer people at the top and bottom of the economic scale are uncertain about their values or have values that cross the domains of tradition and modernity. Their economic circumstances largely help to decide their social and cultural priorities (see figure 4.2), yet there are as many wealthy businessmen who enjoy seemingly modern lifestyles but remain traditional in such aspects as family relations or religion, as there are lumpen proletarians whose traditional lives are mixed with an attraction to modern music, ideologies, and ways of life.

Social Change in the Gulf Monarchies

Several factors distinguish between the nature and manner of social change in the smaller sheikhdoms of the Gulf and that in other Middle Eastern countries. Most notably, social change in countries of the Arabian peninsula has been highly controlled and politically directed, with the state playing a more defining role in the implementation and direction of change than elsewhere in the Middle East. Thus social change there has been comparatively circumscribed in range and scope. This would not have been possible had it not been for the decisive roles states have been able to assume in relation to their societies. As the self-appointed vehicles of much of the change occurring within society, the Gulf states have been able to manage their transformation by following cautious and politically prudent guidelines. Social changes are, as a result, planned and selectively implemented according to the dictates and policies of the state. The consequences could not have been more uneven, with some aspects of life, such as wealth, having changed beyond recognition in a matter of a few generations, while other aspects, such as personal status, especially women's, have remained stagnant for centuries.

In the Gulf region, social change confronts an inherent inertia that is not as pervasive or even possible elsewhere. Social change has taken place within the context of a fixed social and cultural mosaic, one in which, as noted in chapter 3, *tradition* is not only a historical memory but also a living blueprint for the present and a guideline for the future. Because of the region's unique political heritage and the continuous interplay of such forces as tribes, royal families, and religion, tradition permeates and defines its political as well as social universes and exerts a force that resists change. It is this built-in resistance to fundamental change, the culture's tendency to "maintain as much of its former condition as is practically possible however determined the attempts to alter its shape," that one scholar describes as a widespread presence of "homeostatic forces" in the Gulf societies.[53] Inertia is further reinforced by the conduct and policies of the state, specifically those of the royal family, for whom tradition is the cornerstone of legitimacy. But the connection between tradition and the body politic goes beyond political rhetoric and propaganda. The state, which is essentially made up of a hegemonic tribe, is in fact the product of a successful interplay of various forces, and although significant historical changes have taken place since its inception, it still seems largely "natural" in relation to society.[54] Moreover, for the ruling families to maintain exclusive political power has meant owning or dominating most of the productive economic resources as well. With political and economic power thus centralized, and keenly aware of the potential damage of uncontrolled change to its very survival, the state has sought to dictate the pace and direction of social change.

Two broad patterns of social change have emerged: one that is directly controlled by the state and another that is the unintended result of those controlled changes. The first category of social change has been made possible by the omnipresence of the state in relation to society and its monopoly over the political and economic resources that can effect change. The welfare states of the Gulf go beyond simply pacifying their populations; they also ensure that unwarranted societal and cultural changes are minimal.[55] An extreme example is Oman, where almost all potential catalysts for change—from the spread of education to most economic ventures—have been subject to careful political scrutiny and control by both the pre- and post-1970 coup regimes.[56] But Oman is not unique in its almost paranoid aversion to change. It was, for example, specifically stated in the third Saudi Development Plan that the state must try to "ensure that the new conditions in which people live will not force unwanted social change." The plan further stipulated that "the extended family, neighbourhood groups and traditional relationships are still the dominant features of the social structure . . . [with] the people essentially retaining their customary life-style, values and personal networks."[57] To achieve this managed transformation, states have isolated certain spheres of activity in which they have implemented change, while guarding others from even the slightest alterations. Such arenas as the military, economy, industry, education, and infrastructure cannot change fast enough, while great pains are taken to ensure that social norms, legal dicta, and political practices are not altered in any way.

A telling example is the legal status of women. Most countries of the Muslim world place restrictions on the husband's right under traditional Islamic law to be polygamous. In the Gulf states, however, the traditional law remains unchanged, and a man may have as many as four wives regardless of the consent of his present wife or wives.[58] The unwillingness to change the legal status of women highlights the larger issue of the state's attitude toward the institution of the family. Nowhere in the Gulf have there been changes to traditional laws relating to the family, "with a single exception in Kuwait, where a law allowing an orphaned grandchild to inherit has been promulgated."[59] "Emphasis," therefore, "is usually placed upon the economic category as the least controversial and the most immediately helpful in enhancing the power of the state and its ruler."[60]

One of the ways that Gulf states have sought to limit social change has been by ensuring that their societies' contact with the outside world does not go beyond what is necessary for economic and industrial growth. Except for Oman and Kuwait, Gulf states do not routinely issue tourist visas to foreigners, and their radio and television broadcasts are highly restricted and controlled.[61] They have also gone to great lengths to control the diffusional effects of migrant labor, often by segregating expatriate workers from the indigenous population. There are thus "enclave" industrial areas where expatriates live and work near major cities and economic centers: Shuiba (Kuwait), Umm Said (Qatar), Jebel Ali (Dubai), Ruwais (Abu Dhabi), and Yenbo and Jubail (Saudi Arabia).[62] According to Roger Webster, "blocks of flats, high-density housing developments, barrack blocks for construction gangs, whole streets of shops, restaurants and cinemas inhabited, managed and patronized solely by immigrants now dominate large areas of the principal cities of the Gulf from Kuwait to Muscat."[63] To ensure further that the potential for social change is reduced, there is a general preference to invite expatriate workers from outside the Middle East instead of from other Arab countries or Iran. Unlike workers from Iran or the Arab world, non–Middle Eastern laborers are easily distinguishable by their looks, seldom speak the language, are specifically there for economic reasons, and rarely develop political demands along the way. Within their enclaves, these workers rarely mingle with the local population, and therefore the potential for social change is reduced.[64]

Despite the state's careful political and economic planning, some unintended social and cultural changes have taken place. Controlling the media or limiting tourism may minimize diffusion, but economic growth and Western-oriented industrialization militate against complete social and cultural isolation from the outside world. Employment patterns, consumer habits, geographic mobility, and even family relations all change as a consequence of modernization in the economic arena, which inevitably effects further changes in norms and values. In spite of the state's skepticism and suspicions, as well as its deliberate attempts to thwart it, social change occurs in Gulf societies, albeit at a much slower and cautionary pace. One observer has concluded that social change

> comes about not because of any great desire for change per se, but rather as an unintended consequence of changes in the political systems, economies, bureaucracies, or communications systems that the local rulers were either powerless to resist (since they represented the fundamental interests of the more powerful Westerners), or that they saw as being worth some measure of social strain (since they simultaneously enhanced the power of the rulers).[65]

State efforts at curtailing the effects of diffusion have also not been completely successful. Even isolating the migrant workers has not fully contained it, for there has already been a significant integration of Middle Easterners from outside the Gulf into these societies. And despite such control mechanisms as industrial enclaves, the overwhelming number of migrants compared with the local population makes them prime agents of social change, even if they come from other Arab countries. According to one calculation, for example, approximately 90 percent of workers employed in the United Arab Emirates in the 1980s were expatriates, and 85 percent of the country's army was made up of mercenaries.[66] As a substantial majority of the labor force, the expatriates' values and norms are bound to influence those of the local population, whether or not there are subtle differences in those values. One can only imagine the role of expatriate teachers who numbered 7,274 out of a total of 8,658 in Oman during 1983 and 1984.[67] Although Oman's overwhelming reliance on foreign teachers may be an extreme example, Egyptians and Palestinians make up most of the professional teachers employed elsewhere the region.

The reluctance for social change has led to varied and at times ironic consequences. In areas where change has occurred, traditional institutions (e.g., the tribe or the ruling family) and cultural patterns (e.g., religion) have proved so resilient and flexible that they have absorbed and incorporated change and, in many instances, have remained unaware that any change has in fact taken place.[68] Coupled with the selective manner in which social change has occurred, this institutional adaptability has produced tremendous cultural incongruities and societal anomalies. What may be politically prudent at one time may later be socially unacceptable, and economic necessities may run counter to the more inflexible edicts of traditional culture and society.

Bedouin nomads and women, who embody unwavering traditionalism, have been especially subject to social and cultural contradictions. Backed by the powers of the state, society perpetuates idealized images of these groups that are no longer consonant with the realities of the modern era. Women in the Gulf, for example, enjoy one of the highest standards of living anywhere in the world, but they continue to be subject to laws and customs developed over a thousand years ago.[69] In an era when a Saudi Arabian pilot has orbited the Earth onboard an American space shuttle, Saudi women are forbidden to drive cars. And after the Western world rushed to liberate it from Iraqi occupation, Kuwait did not include women in the extension of voting rights to its population. Bedouins find themselves in equally precarious positions. On the one hand, they are pulled by the strength of tradition, while on the other, they are pushed by the forces of the modern economy.[70] But the bedouins' dilemma runs deeper than questions involving economics; there is an additional psychological and emotional component. Just as women in the region may not have a satisfactory answer to the question of what it means to be a Saudi, a Qatari, or a Kuwaiti woman, bedouins also would likely be at a loss if a similar question were asked of them. For their own purposes, the political elite may consider the bedouin status an esteemed and prestigious one, but nontraditional groups of society are likely to perceive them as unsophisticated, even pariahs.[71] Their very identity is at stake—an identity on which the political legitimacy of the state indirectly rests.

Does this mean that a sociocultural crisis of catastrophic proportions is imminent in the Gulf? Khaldoun al-Naqeeb argued that such a crisis was indeed approaching, particularly in light of the "mobility closure" that the rising social classes invariably experience.[72] He pointed to the "structural crisis" of Gulf societies and to such "pathological symptoms" as Islamic radicalism, the reassertion of tribal identities, and the preoccupation with luxury goods and consumerism. "The confusion of values and lack of standards," he maintained, "are the most serious of these symptoms in their effect on Gulf and Peninsula societies, which are undoubtedly the result of the decline of the socialist and Arab nationalist current following the defeat of June 1967, when society lost its spirit."[73] Today the symptoms that al-Naqeeb emphasized are still there, and in some ways they are stronger now than when he identified them in the 1980s, but the promised "structural crisis" has yet to materialize. Certainly, the Iraqi occupation of Kuwait, which, if anything, was caused by a structural crisis inside Iraq, does not qualify for what al-Naqeeb may have had in mind. The reasons for the postponement of such a crisis appear to be twofold. First, the immense wealth that Gulf states pump into their societies, which in many instances is tantamount to giving money away, serves as a powerful opiate in assuaging the destabilizing effects of social contradictions. This is not to imply that souls and intellects are bought and sold through the political economy of oil. But the fulfillment of superficial demands for luxury and consumer items goes a long way in soothing the psychological dilemmas that might have otherwise arisen in other arenas of life.

The second factor mitigating against the development of an all-out crisis is the role and nature of the ruling family. As seemingly natural extensions of prevailing social and cultural phenomena, the Gulf's ruling families embody, and in fact magnify, some of the very contradictions and inconsistencies that mark their societies. In order to remain symbolic representatives of the entire spectrum of their societies, they have had to appease and manipulate the many conflicting forces that social change has unleashed in their societies. These families, therefore, have had to represent simultaneously all aspects of the modern and the traditional, the urbanite and the bedouin, the religious and the secular. This difficult and delicate balancing act is often handled with remarkable deftness, and successful examples of it are found in literally all Gulf states. It was an inability, or more accurately an unwillingness, to strike such a balance among the forces of social change that in 1970 led to the deposition of Oman's Sultan Said by his son Qabus, the country's present ruler.[74] In their pivotal roles as the source and symbol of social change, the ruling families have been able to play a moderating function, representing a measure of historical continuity and resonance, and, more important, providing a base of psychological comfort against the ravages and uncertainties of uncontrolled change. In this respect the Gulf states have a decided advantage over other parts of the Middle East. As contrived as they may be, the Gulf states have at least a measure of historical legitimacy to their populations, and the ruling families function as vital bulwarks against the flood of change. Elsewhere in the Middle East, many states lack such popular consent, at least on a lasting basis, and the ruling elites, unable to control social change, are often swept aside by it. Political upheavals and revolutions in Iran, Egypt, and Algeria have all been the result of the state's inability to withstand and manipulate the forces of change. Every state, regardless of its institutions and powers, has to carve out a working relationship with the changing norms and structures of society. Because of their unique political evolution and their position vis-à-vis the various strata of society, the oil monarchies of the Gulf have been far more successful in handling these changes and holding on to power than have other Middle Eastern states.

Social Change Elsewhere in the Middle East

Social change in most Middle Eastern countries is neither easily containable nor even manipulable. As previously discussed, the comparatively simple and straightforward relationship between state and society in the small sheikhdoms of the Arabian peninsula is not found elsewhere in the Middle East. In fact, most states in the region at best have an uneasy relationship with their societies, and at worst there exists a deep-seated animosity. The reasons for this often acrimonious connection have to do with the following characteristics: the governments often have barely enough resources of any kind to stay in power, least of all legitimacy; the exercise of power does not rely on societal intermediaries or cultural imperatives but rather on arbitrary and nondemocratic structures that largely are sustained through coercion; populations are large and their growth uncontrollable; and state policies can rarely penetrate society beyond the most superficial level. In short, these societies are politically unmanageable. To rephrase the title of a book by Joel Migdal,[75] the Gulf states are strong and their societies weak, whereas other Middle Eastern states are weak and their societies strong. Of course, this power imbalance has had a direct bearing on the social change occurring outside the Arabian peninsula.

Within the context of the larger relationship between Middle Eastern states and societies, much of the social change has taken one of two forms: it is either created by society or imposed on society. Because the state's powers over society are limited, an overwhelming degree of the change has been generated within society and has had a momentum of its own. The best the state can hope for usually is to influence the minor details rather than the overall direction of the change and to ensure that it is not swept aside by the tide of change. On occasion, though, the state musters up enough power not only to control society effectively but also to force far-reaching and fundamental social changes. These are instances of "revolutions from above," moments in history when the reshaping of society becomes the sole driving force of the state and its stewards. For all their reluctance to subject themselves to the state's rule, Middle Eastern societies have been particularly vulnerable to episodes of state-sponsored social engineering. Power has seldom remained static, but often tilts back and forth between the state and society. The very instability of the state-society nexus lends itself to such radical shifts. "Semitotalitarianism" seems to be the most appropriate term for these particular eras in Middle Eastern history, for they have been neither completely totalitarian experiences on a par with fascism nor have they been as clearcut as simple authoritarianism. Examples of semitotalitarianism include the reigns of Atatürk in Turkey, Reza Shah in Iran, and Nasser in Egypt; the Iranian "White Revolution"; and the periods following the Algerian and the Iranian revolutions.

While intrinsically political in nature, revolutions from above are condensed and highly controlled episodes of social change. When initiating revolutions, states aim for more than political and institutional consolidation by working to instill in society an entire set of social and cultural values that will facilitate specific goals. The intent is nothing less than a complete reshaping of society and development of a new identity for the masses. Society is thus revolutionized not because of its own internal dynamics but through the efforts of the state.

The example for such a revolution was first set in Turkey by Mustafa Kemal Atatürk, who launched an ambitious campaign of national transformation that lasted from his assuming power in 1922 until his death in 1938. But because Turkey's overall class structure was unchanged during his rule, a number of scholars have questioned the truly revolutionary character of Atatürk's reign.[76] It is undeniable, however, that his rule brought with it a number of fundamental changes in Turkish culture and society. As James Bill and Robert Springborg state, "He began a program of social, cultural, and political modernization that shook the country to its roots. His program struck at the foundation of the conservative religious culture of the day and stressed national, secular, and modern goals."[77] The six principles of "Kemalism," introduced in May 1931, were republicanism, nationalism, populism, secularism, statism, and revolutionism (or reformism), and they represented radical departures from the social and political patterns to which Turks had previously been accustomed.[78]

Inspired by Atatürk's accomplishments, a host of successive Middle Eastern leaders tried to emulate his example; few, however, were as successful as he, for in their efforts to replicate the "Turkish paradigm," many were unwilling to resort to Atatürk's level of coercion.[79] Reza Pahlavi's goals for Iran were somewhat less ambitious than Atatürk's, but his reign was no less revolutionary within the Iranian context.[80] Reza Shah sought to instill in Iranian culture such principles as statism, modernization, and secularism. His son, Mohammad Reza, went somewhat further, seeking not only to alter the traditional cultural norms that he saw as inimical to his rule but also to eradicate an entire social institution, namely, feudalism. Thus was introduced the so-called White Revolution, a government-initiated program that began as a land-reform campaign but soon grew to encompass a wide variety of additional social and economic changes as well. The nineteen principles of the revolution ranged from the nationalization of forests and water resources to the provision of free education and the elimination of corruption.[81] The shah was convinced that it would take nothing less than a revolution to achieve the social changes that he deemed necessary:

> If our nation wished to remain in the circle of dynamic, progressive and free nations of the world, it had no alternative but to completely alter the archaic order of society, and to structure its future on a new order compatible with the vision and needs of the day. This required a deep and fundamental revolution which would put an end to injustice, tyranny, exploitation, and reactionary forces which could impede progress. This revolution had to be based on spiritual principles and religious beliefs, and the preservation of individual and social freedoms. (101)

Gamal Abdel Nasser, who would probably have resented being grouped with the Pahlavis, transformed Egyptian culture and society by promoting agrarian reform, transforming and partially leveling class structure, encouraging meritocracy instead of entitlement, and heightening the people's sense of nationalism and pride. The Nasserist revolution from above, instigated by the earlier "revolution" of the Free Officers in 1952, thus set into motion profound changes that reverberated far beyond Egypt's borders. Soon followed the Ba'athist revolution in Iraq in the 1960s and 1970s, which resulted in that country's radical social and economic transformation and caused innumerable changes to Iraqi social norms and practices.[82] Not to be outdone, Libya and Syria embarked on similar changes implemented by their "revolutionary" governments.

Another form of revolution from above has appeared in the aftermaths of "revolutions from below," which occurred in Algeria and Iran. Mass-based revolutions are themselves radical and highly compressed manifestations of social change that are often brought about by a state's inability to contain festering societal, cultural, and political contradictions. But these revolutions result in further social change once they succeed, giving birth to states whose central preoccupations become the changing of social norms and values. In order to bring about "ideologically reconstructed national identities," postrevolutionary states embark on campaigns of social and cultural purification, unleashing reigns of terror on their subjects, if necessary, in order to ensure total acceptance of the revolutions' norms.[83] The "cultural revolutions" that often follow are little more than campaigns designed to inculcate the new powerholders' values into the larger populace.[84] For Algeria's postrevolutionary leaders, the popular inculcation of ostensibly socialist values was particularly challenging, especially given their citizens' profound religiosity. Most of their early efforts concentrated on demonstrating the philosophical compatibility of Islam with socialism, at times even asserting that the prophet Muhammad himself was the founder of socialism.[85] In Iran the task of the founders of the Islamic Republic was no easier, nor was their response to cultural dissenters any milder, as the new regime attempted to eradicate all sociocultural vestiges of Pahlaviism and replace them with its own values. The new regime has thus instituted a pluralist and inclusionary system—a radical departure for Iran—through which it hopes not only to consolidate its own power base but also to ensure the resonance of its values.

Despite the frequency with which semitotalitarian states have appeared in the Middle East and carried out revolutions from above, much of the social change in the region has been without overt political impetus and has occurred almost independently of state initiatives. Launching a social and cultural revolution is not an undertaking on which most states are willing or able to embark. It involves considerable resources and energy, zealous and determined leadership, and passionate belief in some principles or in a cause. Indeed, only in rare historical moments have states set out to create new social orders. Far more frequent, though perhaps less obvious, are the changes that occur with less fanfare and with more subtlety, changes that are more gradual and whose cumulative effects become manifest gradually rather than suddenly. This kind of social change occurs largely at its own behest. It is often triggered by factors that have little or nothing to do with politics, and is frequently a by-product of or a reaction to other changes occurring simultaneously in society. This is the kind of change against which the state in the more populous, less manageable societies of the Middle East is almost powerless. From Iraq in the east to Morocco in the west, these states often find themselves observing social change rather than dictating its course and outcomes. Even in Iran, where the Islamic Republic has tried to curtail the intrusion of foreign values with the popularization of its own revolutionary norms, the regime's restrictive and conformist policies have failed to halt unwanted social and cultural changes. The American pop star Michael Jackson is as popular as ever there, and the clash of values and norms still takes place along the traditional-modern axis. Other examples of this kind of self-generated change include rampant population growth and other demographic shifts across the region, many of which continue unabated *despite* government efforts to reverse the trends.[86]

Changes within the family have been the most conspicuously felt, particularly in light of that institution's centrality to life in the Middle East. Industrial growth and development, the partial integration of women into the economic workforce, the necessity to migrate to new places of employment and residence, and other similar developments have resulted in changes to the functions and internal hierarchy of the family. According to recent studies, intergenerational relationships are moving toward increased emotional interdependence (rather than complete independence), and most Middle Easterners seem to be withdrawing from the disconcerting changes of the larger society and seeking refuge within the family circle.[87] At the same time, nuclear families, having become the norm in even the Gulf sheikhdoms, are becoming even more prevalent because of economic necessities and demographic shifts.[88] While these changes have not been as sweeping as may first be suspected, they have nevertheless been quite significant. The bewildering cultural predicament of the region, suspended between the poles of tradition and modernity, has resulted in the creation of a distinctively Middle Eastern type of family. One observer has summarized the family's predicament as follows:

The contemporary Islamic family finds itself confronting cultural, social, and economic diversity and changes linked to the development of the society of which it is a part. Its situation is culturally ambiguous, and this produces parallel and sometimes contradictory attitudes and behavior patterns. The conflict between old and new, between tradition and modernity, has made its home in the heart of the family. The new has penetrated not enough to triumph but quite enough to transform its problem altogether.[89]

Another significant area of change has been the position of women, whose role and status in Middle Eastern societies have been subject to countless social, political, and economic nuances. Much has been written on this topic,[90] although some aspects of these changes bear repeating. A starting point is to acknowledge that there have been profound changes for women in recent decades, facilitated by the spread of employment opportunities and education, legal reforms, and government policies and campaigns. Whether through deliberate "revolutions from above," as in Kemalist Turkey and elsewhere, through legal changes of the kind that were enacted in Tunisia, or from the sociocultural ramifications of economic transformation, as especially in Egypt and Iran, women have benefited from tremendous changes of all kinds from previous generations to the present.

Four broad catalysts for such changes can be identified. First and foremost is the widespread entrance of women into the workforce and their consequently enhanced economic independence within the family unit. Most studies agree that women's relative lack of economic power is the strongest determinant of gender inequalities, especially in such areas as marriage, parenthood, and sexuality.[91] As Valentine Moghadam has shown, Middle Eastern women have played increasingly active roles in their national economies, especially in manufacturing, though their importance in this area still lags behind that of women in Latin America, East Asia, and Southeast Asia.[92] Within the labor force, Middle Eastern women tend to be concentrated in such professions as teaching and nursing, reflecting an occupational gender stereotyping that, in the larger society, remains consonant with their nurturing image. In recent years women have begun making inroads into some of the traditionally male-dominated professions, notably management and engineering. Even in Iran, which witnessed a decrease in female economic productivity after the 1978–79 revolution, postwar reconstruction has necessitated a gradual reversal of this trend. Nevertheless, despite some significant improvements,

Middle Eastern women's overall presence in the labor force remains out of balance with that of men. As Moghadam concludes:

> In most Middle Eastern countries women remain an underutilized human resource because of limited industrialization, the gender ideology stressing women's family roles, and ambivalence on the part of state managers toward the full participation of women in economic development and policy formulation. (54)

The economic advances of Middle Eastern women have been facilitated and reinforced by changes in the two related areas of state policy and education. Although, as Moghadam states, Middle Eastern policymakers have been largely reticent in tackling the "women's question" head-on, significant gender-related legal and political changes have appeared in many countries (excluding the majority of the Gulf countries except Kuwait). Most of these legal and political changes have been piecemeal and gradual—few leaders have had the clout or the wherewithal to proclaim the era of a "new woman," as Atatürk did in Turkey[93]—and many have been instituted in response not so much to coordinated feminist movements as to evolving circumstances and emerging demands. Virtually all Middle Eastern states outside the Arabian peninsula have passed some kind of personal status law guaranteeing the rights of women, although the extent of this legal protection varies widely within the region. To one extent or another, the legal status of women continues to be influenced predominantly by Islamic law, the *shari'a*. Even in Iran and Algeria, where women once enjoyed extensive rights and equality before the law, recent moves toward the Islamization of the legal code have resulted in an official sanctioning of traditional norms, including the prejudicial treatment of women.[94] In the former People's Democratic Republic of Yemen (PDRY), Turkey, and Tunisia, however, far-reaching legal changes in personal status law have been instituted.[95] But even in the Middle Eastern countries where women do not enjoy equal status before the law, their increasing numbers within the workforce have encouraged the passage of numerous labor laws and regulations designed to ensure their protection within the workplace. There are comprehensive social security systems for workers, women included, in the Sudan, Kuwait, and Jordan, and there are generous maternity leave laws for expectant mothers in Iran, Libya, Syria, Jordan, and Iraq.[96]

The third catalyst for change in women's status has been the role of education, the dissemination of which leads to fundamental changes in both the norms and institutions of society. According to Moghadam, recent decades have seen significant improvements in female literacy rates throughout the Middle East, although in a number of countries female illiteracy remains staggeringly high: 88 percent in Oman, 81 percent in Yemen, and 75 percent in the Sudan (122). With the spread of education come the questioning of old social norms and the adoption of new ones, coupled with significant changes to the institution of the family, particularly regarding the age for marriage. Moghadam seems to agree with the assertion made by Fatima Mernissi that state-sponsored education has led to the birth of a generation of mostly unveiled and independent women (125). This argument needs to be qualified, however. The wider availability of educational opportunities to women has, to a great extent, weakened the hold of traditional, specifically Islamic, values over Middle Eastern societies. Since the mid-1980s, however, increasing numbers of female university students and other highly educated women in such ostensibly "nontraditional" countries as Turkey and Egypt have voluntarily adopted the veil and other traditional values and practices.[97] In response to the bewildering effects of social change, a number of women have in recent years rediscovered tradition, or some new interpretation of it, and the veil is a particularly apparent manifestation of it. But there is no denying that higher education for women has had profound effects on the Middle East. Better-educated women tend to marry later in life, and although custom and religion sanction early marriages in the Middle East, the average age at which Middle Eastern women marry has steadily risen. The average marrying age for women is twenty-two in Egypt, Jordan, and Morocco; twenty-four in Tunisia; twenty-one in Algeria; and twenty in Iran. Most men in these countries marry around the age of twenty-five. Even in the conservative oil monarchies, Moghadam reports, the average age of new brides has risen to twenty, while men marry at about twenty-seven (111).

The fourth catalyst for change in women's status has been the prolonged periods of social and political turmoil, especially revolutions and civil wars, which have upset the traditional balance of society, bringing old norms and institutions into question and upholding alternatives in their stead. Consequently, the revolutions in Algeria and Iran, the civil war in Lebanon, and the Palestinian *intifada* have catapulted the issue of women to the forefront and have, in most instances, resulted in altered gender perceptions and roles. During and after Algeria's struggle for independence, several women became national heroines by playing indispensable roles in the movement.[98] Iranian women were similarly instrumental in their revolution's success, actively participating in mass demonstrations, guerrilla activities, and strategic planning.[99] In Lebanon women fought alongside men in a bloody civil war, and women's committees and activities in the Israeli-occupied territories have been a significant component of the Palestinian uprising.[100] Such "emancipatory" activities are bound to influence the social position of women and the values that relate to gender issues. The reflections of a Lebanese Shia woman are telling:

> What is interesting is that my father, who used to be the only supreme authority in the house, never takes any decisions now concerning the family without consulting me first. Sometimes I stay out till eleven o'clock at night and when I come back they give me dinner without ever asking where I have been. For they know that I must have been working somewhere. I feel that they have an utter and complete confidence in me now. Women in the Amal movement have proved their ability to play a responsible role in their country's affairs and most people acknowledge that.[101]

It is unclear just how lasting and permanent—and in what specific direction—these cultural changes concerning women will turn out to be. Historical experience shows that once the period of upheaval is over and new institutions have assumed the place of old ones, traditional habits and customs slowly reemerge, changed in some respects but not substantially. At best, such deeply ingrained traditional values as those related to women are modified only partially and not without significant encouragement from the new political leaders. In Algeria and Iran the very revolutions that promised "liberation" for women have turned out to be quite restrictive of their rights, and Lebanese women enjoy few of the social and political rights they had hoped to gain when their country was on the verge of disintegration. One of the Palestinian women's slogans reveals their keen awareness of the possibility of old, male-dominated values reappearing once the struggle for liberation is over: "The women of Palestine will not be like the women of Algeria!"[102]

The confusing predicament in which Middle Eastern women find themselves today reflects a larger societal ambivalence about values, customs and habits, institutions and classes—an ambivalence about the society as a whole. Because of women's peculiar status, the values attached to gender serve as fairly accurate barometers through which the status of other values can be studied. Cherished values of honor, motherhood, modesty, decency, and femininity have long governed the societies' perceptions and treatment of women. But the forces of change have undermined some of the traditional principles on which gender relations have long been based, while at the same time strengthening others. Political players have not hesitated to manipulate the situation to their own advantage. Thus contemporary Middle Eastern women marry at a later age and are better educated, but they are also increasingly attracted to such outward manifestations of tradition as the headcover and the veil. Many are economically active and politically aware, but rarely can they flex their economic muscles or freely pursue their political agendas. Most seek "liberation," but few are willing to question openly the merits of tradition or to adopt foreign alternatives without question. Like their male counterparts, Middle Eastern women are confronted with a confusing array of choices, and the alternatives they face are not always appealing. For women, however, the necessity of choosing—the deliberate, considered adoption of values and customs—is all the more palpable because it involves their immediate behavior, the way they are perceived and treated by others, and their place within the larger society. Social change has indeed thrown Middle Eastern societies into confusion, but it has affected the lives of women even more deeply than the rest of society.

Conclusion

Middle Eastern societies have in recent decades experienced far-reaching changes in their social institutions, practices, and norms. Change, of course, has always been a part of the region's history and has characterized these societies before, but its most recent incarnation has thrown much of the Middle East into social chaos and cultural confusion. The old has been questioned but not completely negated; the new has been introduced but not fully adopted. Middle Eastern societies thus suffer from an endemic schism that knows no economic or class bounds, affecting all strata and institutions of society with almost equal ferocity. Even such sacred institutions as the family and religion and such jealously guarded norms as those governing gender relations have been subject to change, both deliberately and inadvertently. Some changes have come naturally as a result of systemic transformations of the economy, demographics, and geographic location, while others have been part of deliberate and comprehensive campaigns for change, involving specific policy initiatives, or, on occasion, revolutions from above.

Social change is not without potentially negative ramifications, and under certain circumstances it can lead to social malaise. Profound generation gaps and alienation of large segments of society, usually the lumpen proletariat, are some of the more readily observable manifestations of social change. The crucial variable depends on how the individual and the larger society cope with the emerging side effects of change and transformation. How complete or partial will the processes of change be? How skewed will norms and values become? How assimilated or alienated will the old and new social classes be? How cohesive or disjointed will society become? These unknown outcomes determine the direction of social change and the overall nature of the society that experiences it. As the preceding pages have demonstrated, the more conservative states of the Gulf have been better able to keep the less desirable (politically at least) consequences of social change to a minimum. These oil monarchies have managed to be *active* in relation to social change—controlling, directing, and containing it—rather than *reactive,* as the other states of the region have been forced to be. But, as should be clear from the arguments of this chapter, social change influences not only society but also culture. It is a phenomenon that traverses the two domains, affecting both through its alteration of norms as well as institutions. Indeed, social change affects culture as much as it does society. Thus the precise nuances involved in social change cannot be accurately assessed without reference to the cultural milieu in which it takes place. But understanding cultures, and Middle Eastern ones in particular, requires more than just grasping the dynamics of social change. Culture encapsulates and conveys how and why societies and their institutions think and behave. The next two chapters examine the cultural paradoxes that govern the overall lives of these societies.

5. Popular Culture

SIGNIFICANT ELEMENT in determining the viability and resilience of democracy is the kind of cultural setting in which various political ideals and values—democratic ones included—evolve and gain popular hold. As mentioned in chapter 1, culture is·the third necessary condition (the other two being society and the state) for democracy to exist, and it must have specific characteristics.

Because most modern societies are composed of disparate social groups, discerning the culture of any one society by itself is not easy, and examining the culture of an entire region, especially one as varied as the Middle East, becomes a particularly arduous venture. The changing societies themselves contain contradictory and countervailing elements, each of which may have its own specific cultural orientations. It is easy to detect cultural similarities at the elite/intellectual levels, where the awareness of historical continuities, literature, and language serve as powerful unifying forces among the learned strata.[1] But what of the masses, for whom the grand expositions of scholars mean little or nothing? The ideal of unity, for instance, whether Islamic or Arab, has been a consistent theme in almost all manifestations of high culture.[2] But Middle Easterners as a whole and Arabs in particular can be as prejudiced against one another as any members of different racial or ethnic backgrounds. According to popular wisdom, for example, Egyptians consider themselves superior to all other Arabs; Arabs consider Iranian Shias heathens; Turks perceive themselves to be more sophisticated than other Middle Easterners; Iranians view Arabs as backward and Turks and Azeris as naive; and nobody accords much respect to ethnic minorities such as the Kurds or the Berbers, except perhaps themselves. For all the Islamic exaltations of tolerance and egalitarianism, most Middle Easterners have demonstrated in the recent past a remarkable degree of anti-Jewish sentiments, although that may have begun to change now that peace agreements have been signed by Israeli, Palestinian, and Jordanian leaders. Yet the gap between the ideals of high culture and the realities of popular culture remains as unbridgeable as ever.

The popular cultures themselves are highly fractured and discontinuous. These anomies permeate most of the routine aspects of daily life, and some of their larger effects are more pronounced than others. In Turkey, for example, the sounds of Arabesque and heavy metal rock music appeal to the ears of completely different cultural strata of society; religion is the sole source of identity for some Lebanese, while it is a private matter to many of their compatriots; Morocco's cultural tradition is fractured along Francophone, Berber, and Arab lines; and the list of cultural dissimilarities goes on. Added to these intranational diversities are profound international differences. The eastern and western halves of Turkey are as distinct from one another as Turkey is from Saudi Arabia; Iran's Islamic zealots differ as much from other Iranians as they do from Tunisians; and, from a cultural standpoint, the people of Upper and Lower Egypt tend to have as little in common with each other as all Egyptians have with such close and ostensibly similar neighbors as Libyans and Algerians. It is, therefore, not entirely without merit to question the very existence of a coherent and singularly identifiable "popular culture" in the Middle East. When the cultural milieus of individual countries, especially developing ones, tend to be so torn and disjointed, how could there be any cultural commonalities within a region or a continent?

In looking at a region of such profound cultural diversity as the Middle East, cultural analysis needs to be made on a micro as well as a macro level. Exactly where to draw the line between these levels of analysis is open to interpretation. One would soon conclude, however, that while specific cultural differences exist at the micro level within each nation and between the different nations, there are also some pronounced similarities at the macro level. These common denominators bring some kind of valuative uniformity to the region, while at the same time culturally separating it from other regions. To elaborate on the underlying causes of such cultural similarities would require mapping out a detailed cultural history of the region, a task greater than the one at hand. But a quick survey can be made of such historically unifying forces as language (Arabic in the west, Farsi in the east, and Turkish in the north-central area), religion (Islam), political rule (e.g., colonialism of the Ottomans and later the Europeans, nationalism, personality cults), diplomacy (the Palestinian issue, among others), and a series of historical events (including the Arab-Israeli wars, the Iranian revolution, and the Iran-Iraq war) —all have in their own way cemented regionwide bonds of identity, common experiences, shared values, and ties of fraternal comradeship, as diffuse and rhetorical as they are.[3] What has resulted is the appearance at the popular level of a number of prominent, similar cultural traits and characteristics, or subcultures: Islam, a culture of confusion, a culture of wasted energies, a culture of virility, and a rural culture. The first four largely depend on a person's frame of reference, regardless of whether he or she is a rural or urban inhabitant, while the last subculture is mostly (but not exclusively) limited to those with rural values.

Islam
Islam and Daily Life

An appropriate starting point for examining the role of Islam in Middle Eastern popular culture is to highlight its social and cultural totality. Unlike perhaps any other ideological system, with the possible exception of communism,[4] Islam has meticulously constructed a social and cultural, as well as a political, universe of its own. It is, therefore, above all a cultural system[5] and "a blueprint of a social order,"[6] to borrow from Ernest Gellner. In his thoughtful work on Islam and culture, Bassam Tibi argues that "religions, as cultural systems, are in fact symbolic systems offering a way to perceive reality."[7] One may add that in the Muslim Middle East, Islam by and large *is* reality, offering practical guidelines for daily conduct, language, diet, clothing, value orientations, ritualized practices, and conscious decisions. Historians and sociologists have offered different explanations for Islam's all-encompassing nature. Writing in the 1960s Max Thornburg argued, though not quite in so many words, that the absence of widespread industrial development and its concomitant social and cultural ramifications are largely responsible for the ubiquity of Islamic social and cultural tenets. "The influence of religion among the Middle East masses," he maintained, "has been heightened by the sparsity of other interests, which in more sophisticated societies tend to crowd religion into the background except at times habitually set aside for thinking about it."[8] Ernest Gellner, however, takes a broader view of Islam and cites two reasons for its sociocultural dominance: Islam's proposition that it is definitive and final, and its rapid and early political success. The former reason, Gellner maintains, made it difficult for other blueprints to compete, while the latter inhibited the handing over of some spheres of life to nonreligious authority.[9] Along similar lines, Tibi points to Islam's persistent lack of secularization and remarkable retention of its original essence in comparison to other religions for its overwhelming social, cultural, and political power.[10]

It is important to realize that Islam's pervasiveness would not have continued up until today, especially in light of its territorial expansion, had it not absorbed and in turn been influenced by some of the indigenous cultural forces from the areas in which it grew. Islam's expansion into regions of the *Dar al-Harb*[11] (present-day Iran, Turkey, and North Africa) has necessitated certain basic changes to its central tenets in order to make it consonant with local material and cultural circumstances. The Iranians, in fact, came up with a version of Islam that is radically different (both ideologically and theologically) from the Sunni orthodoxy.[12]

Another characteristic of Islam is that it naturally lends itself to political expression. Because Islam is reality, or at least accounts for much of it, it is at one and the same time a guideline for cultural thought as well as for political order, a blueprint as much for personal hygiene as for political justice. Thus given the right circumstances, it could become as easily politicized as it is ritualized, as much a conscious tool for political expression as it is a subconscious guide for daily life. (This argument is more fully developed in chapter 6.) Suffice it to say that the historically recurrent politicization of Islam, with its latest phase having lasted since the mid-1970s, is greatly facilitated at the mass level by its permeation, consciously and subconsciously, of nearly all aspects of a Muslim's life.

The pervasiveness of Islam in daily life is best illustrated by its influence over numerous routine activities on two levels. The more predominant level is ritualized and subconscious, in which the average Middle Easterner performs religious customs that are heavily imbued with symbolism while having at best a scant understanding of their broader religious significance or even connotation. Prayer, fasting, regularized socioreligious gatherings, and the frequent usage of Islamic phrases and idioms in everyday conversation are a part of one's daily action. An observant Muslim would likely take offense at this assertion, yet it is true that many Middle Easterners embark on various forms of religiously inspired or influenced activity without fully realizing it. Most but not all recurrent manifestations of religious behavior in the Middle East are automatic responses to the prevailing social and cultural setting. Praying, which most Muslims do at least once a week on the Friday sabbath, if not five times a day, as Islam directs them to, and fasting, which takes place during the month of Ramadan, are among the most ritualized aspects of life. Muslims, especially nominal ones, engage in them not so much with the conscious goal of enhancing their religious or spiritual purity but because these rituals *should be observed*. Rituals they may be, but they are simply facets of the prevailing social reality. A more instructive example of ritualized Islam is found in Arabic as well as the other languages of the region—Turkish, Farsi, and various dialects—in the frequent usage of such phrases as *in sha allah* (God willing) and *ma sha' allah* (what God intended) in daily discourse, and the customary exchange of greetings with *Salam aleykum* (Peace be with you) and its response, *Aleykum as-salam* (Peace be with you).

A less pervasive though equally powerful manifestation of Islam as reality is in an individual's appearance. Whereas religiously influenced behavior often tends to be ritualized and subconscious, some Muslims may deliberately reinforce the Islamic reality by bringing their worldly conduct and appearance into closer synchrony with the ideals that their faith upholds. Specifically, women reaffirm the Islamic reality around them by adopting the veil, while men do so by growing beards—two trends that have become increasingly noticeable—and their reasons are varied and numerous, not all of them having to do with religion. An observer of Egyptian families, for example, reports that wearing the veil tends to make a young woman seem morally upright and thus increases her chances of finding a suitable husband.[13] Furthermore, there has been a definite re-Islamization of public and private life in the Middle East in recent decades, a phenomenon whose manifestations go beyond the way people dress and behave in public. But for many believers, Islam's ideal role in daily life, on the one hand, and its social and cultural realities, on the other, have become too different, and so the rituals attached to religious observance (prayer, fasting, and so forth) no longer suffice. Therefore these adherents go above and beyond those rituals, turning Islam into an even more tangible reality: for them the Koran is no longer just a holy book but rather a living source of reference for thought and conduct; the mosque ceases to be a gathering place for Friday prayers and instead becomes a viable social institution; religious idioms are used with deliberate care rather than simply out of habit; and the veil and the beard become symbols of one's faith rather than fashion or morality statements. The inherently political nature of Islam, meanwhile, adds to its potency as a language of political discourse.

Islam and Change

Reinforcing all of these religious characteristics is Islam's stubborn historical refusal to permit to criticism, thereby insulating itself from change and innovation. Tibi's explanation for this is compelling. Unlike Christianity, whose fundamental premises were radically questioned and changed during the Reformation, Islam never underwent a similar sustained reformulation of its core principles, except in an incomplete manner during the rule of the Abbasis from 750 to 1258, which Tibi calls the "epoch of High Islam."[14] Today's Islamic culture continues to be defined in "preindustrial, religious terms."[15] Two primary explanations for Islam's sharp aversion to critical thinking are political and functional in nature. The functional explanation has to do with Islam's dichotomy, as repeatedly highlighted by Gellner, into "folk" and "high" varieties.[16] As Gellner argues, whenever conservative Muslims saw themselves threatened by the onslaught of the West or indigenous drives for change, they would resort to religious populism by replacing high Islam with the folk variety to make it more palatable to the masses.[17] Thus Islamic reformism and Islamic populism have often been used interchangeably to maintain the religion's inviolability. Ruhollah Khomeini's incredible odyssey from the ranks of Iranian ayatollahs to the leadership of a populist, revolutionary movement is a prime example. Such recurrent cycles in the high versus folk dichotomy have blocked any meaningful change to the essential sociocultural functions of Islam or its valuative premises. These functions and premises have been reinforced by the power of political patronage, which has effectively assured that neither the specialized scholars of Islam (the *ulema*) nor the secular holders of power have sought to implement substantive alterations in the faith. Consequently, at least on a social and cultural level, Islam has retained a remarkable completeness, and it continues to assume a whole of range of sociocultural functions that might otherwise have been relegated to other institutions. By and large, therefore, Islam has been neither secularized nor rationalized. Tibi uses the example of the *shari'a*, or Islamic law, to illustrate his point.

> [It] is divine law revealed by God and not to be conceived of in historical terms; according to Islamic cognizance of values it is immutable and eternally valid; in terms of the Islamic notion of law, *shari'a* does not serve to help people shape their social life according to law, since its function is to govern human behavior as regards divine will. The purpose of the Islamic *fiqh* (sacred jurisprudence) scholar consists exclusively in interpreting this will.[18]

All of this underlies Islam's lack of receptivity to change, whether from without or from within.[19] Particularly in the modern era, Islam has faced three sources of pressure that have challenged it to change, at least two of which have at times acted in concert with one another. They include technological innovations and other changes in the material culture of society; political and administrative changes initiated by the state; and doctrinal and valuative changes called for by reformist thinkers and intellectuals. But both the Islamic establishment and the laity have, almost invariably, viewed these modernizing influences with suspicion and even outright hostility, thus either nullifying them outright or gradually diminishing their long-term significance. The introduction of technological and other material innovations was often accompanied by, and in most instances a direct result of, the concomitant penetration of Middle Eastern societies by European industrial and economic interests. Not only were most industrial changes a product of Western intrusion, but also the harsh and exploitative manner in which many changes were brought about —frequently through lucrative government concessions to foreign entrepreneurs[20] and with little regard to local sensibilities—often aroused considerable anger at the popular level. Refuge was thus sought in the confines of the familiar, the indigenous, and the divine. How to come to terms with the onslaught of modern technology and even how to revise the Arabic language in order to make it compatible with Western terminology are troubling preoccupations to many Middle Eastern clerical and secular thinkers.[21]

The state's ostensibly secularizing attempts were equally suspect, even when launched under the banner of improving religion's lot. In the Ottoman Empire, the tension between the religious and political centers of its provinces was kept at manageable levels because the sultan declared his unyielding support and protection for Islam, even if he privately broke its most basic rules and regulations.[22] Later kings and sultans (Egypt's Farouk, Morocco's Hassan, Jordan's Hussein, the kings of Saudi Arabia, and the emirs of its smaller neighbors) have all, in one way or another, presented themselves as "commander of the faithful" and protector of the faith in their domains.[23] Even the virulently secular Mohammad Reza Shah of Iran once claimed to have been visited in a dream by angels who gave him divine instructions.[24] But when states with secularizing agendas have sought to limit Islam's social and cultural influence, the tension between them has often spilled over into violence, whether in the form of skirmishes and scattered violence, as committed by the Muslim Brotherhood in Nasserist Egypt and the Islamists in the Sadat and Mubarak eras, or in large-scale confrontations with widespread, deadly consequences, as in Iran in the late 1970s and Algeria in the late 1980s. Today's Islam, as argued in chapter 2, continues to be a viable social institution throughout the region, although most of its traditional domains of social and cultural activity, such as education and welfare, have been assumed by the government. Thus while state-initiated campaigns for religious change have led to tensions and even to violence, they have failed to change the essential functions of Islam or its pervasiveness at the popular level. The margins and parameters of Islam may have changed as a result of state initiatives, but its overall resonance in daily life, as a comforting psychological cushion, if nothing else, has stayed basically the same.

Finally, another source of pressure on Islam has come from within its own ranks. From the classical period to today, various lay and clerical Muslim thinkers have called for changes in what they perceived as an ossified body of religious tenets and for a reevaluation of some of the religion's core principles in order to synthesize them with contemporary concerns. Three of the more notable reformist Muslim thinkers, Ibn Rushd, known in Latin as Averroës (1126–98); Jamaladdin Afghani (1838–97); and Ali Shariati (1933–77), had a desire to revise Islamic thought from within the Islamic ranks. In addition to these nonclerical personalities, there have been reformist clergymen, including Egypt's Shaykh Mohammad Abdu (1894–1905) and Iran's Ayatollah Mahmud Taleghani (1910–79).[25] For his part, Tibi considers himself one of these thinkers, claiming that "the surmounting of underdevelopment will entail reducing the religious system to a partial system, or secularization."[26] But as compelling as the arguments of these reformers may be, they have been invariably drowned in a sea of orthodoxy and doctrinal conservatism. Often they are rejected outright by the "mainstream" Islamic establishment, be it Egypt's al-Azhar or Iran's Qom, as heretical and even *munafiq* (hypocritical). And if they are applauded, as Shariati and Taleghani are in Iran today, it is often out of necessity or from political prudence rather than from conviction, and thus in name and memory only, not in substance and spirit. In the end, it is the traditional Islam of the orthodox majority that reasserts itself, shaping much of the valuative lenses through which Muslims see the world and the framework that they employ in their lives.

The ramifications of Islam's pervasiveness in everyday life and its unchangeability go beyond signifying its resonance as a social and cultural blueprint. There are also countless nonreligious consequences, the cumulative effects of which may be summed up under the rubric of "a culture of confusion." As chapter 4 demonstrated, the forces of social change have been at work at full velocity in the Middle East for nearly a century.

The push of change—that amorphous though very real drive toward modernity—and the pull of tradition—the cornerstone of which is an unbending Islam—exert incredible influences over the lives and psyches of every man and woman in the region. What results is a paralyzing preoccupation with finding a social and cultural niche for one's self, a constant struggle to define one's identity. This is a debilitating feature of Middle Eastern culture, an unhappy and confused mixture of disjointed and often contradictory values.

Culture of Confusion

If only one word were to sum up the popular culture of the Middle East, it would certainly be "contradiction." From the topless beaches of Antalya to the ultraconservative corners of Erzurum in Turkey; from the angry rampages of Islamic militants to the café-society boulevards of Francophile Algiers; from the opulent Italianate mansions of Jedda, Mecca, and Medina to the not-too-distant bedouin tents encircling each city, the Middle East is a marvel of cultural and sociological contradictions. It is a region where the rich and the poor, the "Westoxicated" and the cultural purist, the ultranationalist and the internationalist, the religious and the secular all live side by side and make up the mosaic of society. In this respect alone, the Middle East is not unique. All societies, especially those in the developing world, contain anomalies in their social makeup and cultural orientations. What distinguishes Middle Eastern societies from others is the rigidity of such contradictions and the inherently uncompromising predicaments in which they place the various strata of the same society. Religion, as noted earlier, is the blueprint for most of the social interaction. But because of Islam's pervasiveness and because its social dictums are, for the most part, relics from the past, the other competing blueprints for social interaction—modernism, Westernism, secularism, consumerism, and various other "isms" such as communism and socialism—also assume a quasi religious fervor. What follows is a clash of cultures whose full magnitude is rarely seen in other parts of the Third World, a battle not only of abstract values but also of contending religious guidelines for sociocultural order. The psychological and cultural anomalies are at worst devastating and at best bewildering. What suffers in the process is the very essence of the self—one's identity—because the entire spectrum of values that define a person are thrown into chaos and confusion.

Identity

Commenting on his own dilemma and the predicament of the larger society he lives in, an Arab character in one of Halim Barakat's novels, *Return of the Flying Dutchman to the Sea,* makes the following statement:

> We are a people who have lost their identity and their sense of manhood. Each of us is suffering from a split personality, especially in Lebanon. We are Arab and yet our education is in some cases French, in some cases Anglo-Saxon and in others Eastern-Mystic. A very strange mixture. We need to go back and search our roots. We're all schizophrenic.[27]

Barakat, a respected sociologist, has his character articulate the daily psychological dilemmas that most Middle Easterners face, especially those who are more educated or are somehow more aware of the nuances of their cultural environment. Identity—the question of what am I?—becomes more than a subject of passing interest and assumes the form of a persistent, debilitating preoccupation. Tibi's insightful comments on changing identity are worth quoting here:

> In a changing world, people have to protect their identity. Their environment no longer seems *determinable;* they need to define it if they are to safeguard their identity. In such a context, religion acquires a crucial function. This social process, which is empirically observable in many non-Western societies, is manifest with particular intensity in societies with a Muslim culture. *The more rapid the social change, the more indeterminable the environment becomes for individuals as personal systems living in a state of transition, and the more marked the need for religion to maintain identity in the process of change.* Change is perceived as an out-and-out threat, and a longing for the past is cultivated as a result. The restoration of what has been repressed by the alien, a return of overlaid indigenous elements, and a parallel reorientation of thought is raised to the level of a program of political action.[28]

The resulting contradictions leave few aspects of life unscathed. Barakat, in fact, goes so far as to define Arab society by virtue of its very contradictions. "Arab society today," he maintains, "is neither traditional nor modern, old or new, capitalist or socialist or feudal, Eastern or Western, religious or secular, pluralistic or universalistic in cultural orientation. It is this very complexity that led to my definition of Arab society as an association of all of these contradictions and several others in a contradictory world."[29]

The peculiarities of the region, moreover, have added potency and force to the generational schism of values. The urban young, especially in the middle and upper classes, sound the trumpets of change through their taste in music and dress, their choice of eateries, diet, idols, habits, and whatever else that defines them—distancing themselves farther from the world of their elders, a world whose appeal they cannot see or appreciate. They prefer instant Nescafé to tea or coffee, American football or basketball to backgammon, Michel Foucault to Naguib Mahfouz, Madonna to Umm Kulthoum. The desires of the modern young and the values of the old have led to a clash of generational values: the young speak the language of rock music, broken hearts, melancholy, alienation, and injustice; the old romanticize "the good old days," chide the young for taking so much of what they have for granted, mourn the moral decay of society, and do not hesitate to preach their often black-and-white image of the world to whoever listens. In the meantime, those in the middle, that is, the thirty-something and middle-aged crowd, oscillate in between, displaying neither the preachy tendencies of their elders nor the plaintiveness of the younger generation. Instead, but not surprisingly, they embody the contradictions of the larger society: their outfits and neckties, music, glossy weeklies, food, and values all suggest the social and cultural schism that has scattered their cultural dispositions, leaving them at once nontraditional and unmodern, inauthentic and unliberated, buttressed by no conviction but hanging by shifting threads of the time. It is, incidentally, from this group that most political leaders and social trend-setters come.

It is my contention that the cultural contradiction so rampant in Middle Eastern societies results in a dichotomy along the lines of "authenticity" versus "liberation." Chapter 4 highlighted the division of Middle Eastern societies into traditional, nontraditional, and in-between social groups, which seek to bridge the gap between tradition and modernity but do not always succeed. Each group yearns for distinct cultural values and uses different frames of valuative reference in daily life. We can now juxtapose those social divisions and cultural orientations, arriving at a three-part stratification of society: those segments of society that are considered socially and culturally "traditional," who seek authenticity in cultural values and ways of life as they know it; those who are "nontraditional" and consciously attempt to liberate themselves from the bonds of tradition; and the hybrid groups who are caught in between, neither pure nor liberated. The legitimizing functions of authentication and liberation for those who engage in them should not be underestimated. At a time when cultures clash, when one's social and cultural environments change with bewildering rapidity, one searches for validation and legitimation. And when a source of validity is found, one tends to cling to it with uncompromising conviction. Such convictions make up the cultural landscape of Middle Eastern societies today. Thus confusion reigns supreme. In everyday life, the confusion over which cultural norms to adopt and which to reject conditions such mundane aspects as the kind of music one listens to, choice of clothing, the color of hair dye, engaging in or abstaining from premarital sex, viewing religion as personal and private or public and communal, and so forth. Every time the Middle Easterner make such choices, he or she is either authenticating a set of cultural values or seeking liberation from them.

Authenticity

Few people would disagree that recent decades have witnessed a steady erosion of traditional culture in the Middle East under the catchall rubric of "modernization." Whether viewed as "cultural erosion"[30] or "a wave of cultural escape plaguing the Arab world,"[31] the valuative as well as the material and economic bases of popular culture are experiencing fundamental transformations. We already know that many social strata not only welcome this process of erosion but also view it as natural, progressive, and evolutionary. But to many this is a threat more frightening than any hostile government or leader could ever pose: it is a threat to the core of one's beliefs, a negation of everything one has come to believe in and cherish. It invades the most sacred domains of life, from the family and religion to physical appearance and entertainment, and it must therefore be countered with full vengeance. It is alien, unfamiliar, and mimetic; it is inauthentic, baseless in tradition, and out of sync with the larger rhythm of life. It must be replaced by a "return to the self,"[32] a rediscovery of the indigenous, an embracement of the past. Traditional culture, in short, must be authenticated.

The search for cultural authenticity has assumed three complementary forms. At a most fundamental level, it has introduced the current re-Islamization of life that has spilled over into politics and other domains. Much about the reemergence of Islam has already been discussed in this chapter and other parts of the book. Suffice it to say that the moral certainty offered by Islam, like that offered by all other religions, serves as a powerful source of validation to those who are uncertain about the righteousness of their own values. Islam's authenticating ability becomes all the more compelling given its pervasiveness in everyday life. Thus by relying on Islam, one settles much of the disillusionment over the bewildering question of who am I? Labeling oneself "Islamic" eliminates a slew of question marks by defining what set of values to adopt, what to wear, how to behave, what television programs to watch and what music to listen to, where to stand on gender and sexual matters, and what political positions to take. A confusing array of difficult choices is now answered by the certainties of religion. An identity once fraught with disillusionment and confusion is now legitimated and authentic.

A second method of authenticating culture is through nostalgic remembrances of past glory, much of which involves a rich Islamic heritage. Many Middle Easterners perceive themselves to be the "pure" offspring of specific ethnic groups and take solace in the grand offerings of a national heritage. Thus many citizens of Turkey may boast about their "Turkishness," Iranians take pride in the grandeur of the ancient Persians, Egyptians consider themselves in historical concert with the majesty of the pharaohs, Bahrainis are proud of their seafaring ancestors, and Saudi Arabians and Kuwaitis view themselves as the rightful heirs of an Arab and bedouin patrimony. The more dire the predicaments of the present, the stronger the resonance of the past. Thus Middle Eastern scholars and laity alike still revel in the Muslims' military victories during the Crusades, brag about the contributions their countrymen made to the worlds of science and knowledge over the centuries, are saddened by the unkindness of history, and damn those whom they hold responsible for past injustices. But historical abstractions can be stretched only so far; a glory once experienced cannot be easily translated into the reality of today.

There is, however, one cultural relic that can still be salvaged, purified of its foreign pollutants, and glorified: it is language, that historical constant from time immemorial, the pride of both ancient and contemporary Persians, Turks, and especially Arabs. Thus the integrity of Arabic has been jealously guarded by Arab cultural purists to the extent that, according to one scholar, it has been reduced to a "sacral, post-fourteenth-century Koranic language."[33] There have also been recurrent attempts to purify Farsi and Turkish of borrowings from Arabic as well as from each other. The classic Persian epic *Shah Nameh* was a product of Firdawsi's (c. 935–1026) monumental endeavor, under royal patronage, to purify Farsi of all Arabic influences, a task that was later taken up in the twentieth century, this time with considerably less success, by Ahmad Kasravi (1890–1946) and others.[34] The Turkish language has also seen bursts of literary activity aimed at purifying it of foreign words. But the efforts of such nineteenth-century Turkish political and literary figures as Ziya Gökalp (c. 1875–1924), like those of their Iranian counterparts, seem to have had little effect on maintaining the purity of the Turkish language.[35] Today, foreign words, both Western and Arabic, form an important part of the lexicons of both Farsi and Turkish.

Anti-Westernism is the third manifestation of the search for cultural authenticity. The West is often seen as the primary cause of the recent political, economic, and sociocultural malaise with which Middle Eastern societies have to contend, and it is therefore deeply resented for what are seen as its ever-present conspiracies against the region and Islam.[36] The political consequences of anti-Westernism are abundant, as represented by the recent spate of kidnappings, assassinations, hijackings, car bombs, and so forth, and their examination is beyond the scope of this book.[37] There is, nevertheless, a deeper psychological element that underlies the vociferous military and diplomatic hostility toward the West in general and the United States in particular. Middle Eastern politicians and other populist demagogues are savvy enough to know that calling the United States "the Great Satan" and chanting "Death to America!" will find receptive ears among their domestic and international audiences. Mention has already been made of the love-hate relationship that most Middle Easterners have with Europe and America, coveting the comfort and luxury of material goods that the West has to offer while deeply resenting the need and longing for them. Raphael Patai's observations are as applicable today as they were when he wrote them more than two decades ago:

> What is particularly resented is the rich array of external manifestations of Western superiority in all the material, economic, technological, and organizational fields. These attainments, which are constantly exhibited or, as the Arabs see it, flaunted by the West, endow it with superior powers. This is especially annoying to the Arab mind because it has been conditioned to regard all such shows as secondary to the true value of morality and religion, in which, they sincerely believe, the West is emphatically wanting and thus very much inferior to the Muslim Arabs. When they nevertheless find that they are unable to resist imitating the West in all the things the West considers important, and that in doing so they involuntarily adopt the scale of values which they think is upheld by the West, their resentment easily escalates into hatred.[38]

The success of the cultural authentication that certain strata of Middle Eastern societies have embarked on, be it through religion, resurrection of a golden age, or anti-Westernism, is open to debate, for it has failed even to slow down the metamorphosis of the norms that govern people's lives. What has resulted instead has been a sharpening of cultural contradictions, with the purists reverting to previous incarnations of cultural forms in the name of authenticity, and those opposed reacting against them in the extreme. The search for authenticity is a call for simplicity of life and a rejection of what are seen as needless complexities. For instance, the necktie, which many bureaucrats and professionals in the Middle East and elsewhere would not consider showing up for work without, is considered the "harness of civilization" by Iranian and other purists. But this defiance of modernism takes little away from the resolve of the many others who thrive not on purity but on change, those who see closer cultural proximity to the West not as mimicry of the infidels but as natural assimilation. For them tradition is something not to uphold but to cast away, not to use to authenticate the present but to set aside in order to move ahead. These Middle Easterners, in fact, are interested not in authentication of their culture but in liberation from it.

Liberation

Given the pervasiveness of religion in the Middle East, cultural liberation for those seeking it is often synonymous with liberation from the restrictive bonds of Islam. To them Islam has been the single most powerful cause of social and cultural stagnation in the modern world, even if it was once a source of great pride and glory. They thus tend to view Islam, at least in its current form, with extreme negativism and to be repulsed by what they perceive as blind and fanatical devotion to it. The purists' cries for authenticity, they argue, are only calls for regression to an era whose time has long passed. What is needed is to cast away the shackles of tradition and come into sync with the modernity of the twentieth century. The primary target of change must be Islam and the limitless range of norms and values that it shapes and influences. But most liberationists are aware that complete liberation from Islam is neither always feasible nor, even for them, completely palatable. One would be hard pressed to find a Middle Easterner today who has absolutely no need for religion to explain the world around him or her. Some Middle Eastern societies may be somewhat less religious than others. For instance, Islam clearly does not play an important role in western Turkey, where Western diffusion has been extensive, or in parts of Iran, where the excesses of the religious regime have turned many against the faith. Yet complete aversion to Islam is not something that a researcher may readily run into, and if there are people who assign negative values to Islam they are not likely to voice their opinions in public. Instead, one is more likely to encounter people seeking an Islam that is secularized, personal, and private. Therefore, considering its inescapability in daily life, adherence to Islam and its adoption as a worldview is a matter of degree, one in which most liberationists take a minimalist view. At most they pay lip service to Islam by engaging in some of its rituals, and they do not hesitate to relinquish piety whenever necessary to pursue other goals.

One's minimalist views of religion and binding tradition are most likely to manifest themselves in one's appearance, behavior, and thoughts. An additional indicator is the material culture one adopts, made especially apparent by flaunting Western consumer goods and even the particular style of one's home decoration. Whereas religious and other private values may be difficult to detect without probing into one's inner life, many liberationists use their looks, homes, and consumption patterns to renounce the sociocultural status quo of the rest of society. Dress is by far the best indicator of one's place in the cultural spectrum, even if women must disguise it from public view by wearing the veil. Even more indicative is dyeing the color of one's hair, done primarily by women, to attain a fairer, lighter, and thus more Europeanized appearance. Millions of makeovers have been done, with many women abandoning the traditional Middle Eastern look for a supposedly more pleasing Western one. Whether or not they realize it, these Middle Eastern blondes are rejecting the position of women in traditional society, through not only their appearance but also their perceptions of themselves.[39]

There have, nonetheless, been changes in women's circumstances that go beyond superficial appearances. Within limits, of course, women's actual positions are in fact changing, and many have begun to exert greater autonomy and power in both the domestic and work arenas. Liberationist women have yet to free themselves from all the bonds imposed by Middle Eastern tradition because the threat of social stigma keeps the strength of most gender values intact.[40] Nevertheless, there are numerous Middle Eastern women who actively seek to defy what they perceive as an oppressive tradition in order to change their status in society.[41]

Mention must be made of rampant escapism among Middle Eastern youth. Although this is a phenomenon that has not traveled beyond the walls of well-to-do neighborhoods in major cities, it is nevertheless symptomatic of attempts to rebel against the prevailing social and cultural atmosphere. With the possible exception of Istanbul, no Middle Eastern city is likely to see a hippie movement appearing. But the increasing appeal of

Western hard rock music to Middle Eastern youths allows them to escape as far from their immediate environment as possible. Western rock music, as performed by the more popular bands Guns N' Roses and Metallica, serves the same liberating function for Middle Eastern youths as it did for East Europeans in the 1980s—it provides a kind of personal statement in a context where most cultural expressions are either officially packaged or deeply immersed in unchanging tradition.[42]

How do the push of liberation and the pull of authenticity translate into the sum total of popular culture in the Middle East? What kind of a consumer of culture is the average Middle Easterner? There are no clear-cut, ready answers to these questions because today's Middle Easterner is consumed by an emotional and psychological struggle over the very essence of his or her identity. To be modern may seem compellingly rational or pleasing, but it often goes against the deeply sown seeds of tradition; to seek comfort in the familiarity of tradition is to ignore the tide of modernity sweeping across the rest of the globe. Compatibility between them is exceedingly difficult if not impossible to achieve and often beyond the understanding of the average person. One has to deal constantly with the uncertainty of what or who one is, an uncertainty that magnifies feelings of vulnerability, inferiority, weakness, extremism, and confusion. With the question of "the self" (identity) under tremendous pressure, there is little time to devote to so abstract and alien a concept as democracy, even if it were vociferously propounded by the popular intellectuals of the day, which it is not. The chaotic character of popular culture, which has legitimate and tangible ramifications for those experiencing it, is thus among the greatest hindrances to the spread of democratic norms in the region. There are, however, other cultural traits that may or may not have any bearing on democracy. One such characteristic may be cynically called a "culture of wasted energies," which means a Middle Eastern propensity to expend considerable energy on matters that may, in the long run, have little effect of any sort on the big picture. While it by no means is an exclusively Middle Eastern phenomenon, some aspects of this cultural feature are worth examining.

Culture of Wasted Energies

Some readers will pause in dismay at my contention that there is such a thing as a "culture of wasted energies" in the Middle East. It is admittedly an imperfect description, but I am at a loss to describe the concept in any other way. In fact, the social scientist in me is troubled by the judgmental connotation of the term. Alas, I maintain, as things now stand, such a culture does indeed exist. Even more disconcerting, to me and surely to others, is the inescapable though value-laden conclusion that, in its present stale form, this cultural phenomenon is both stagnant and stagnating, although to those who endorse it, there may be no higher ideals or sources of fulfillment. I speak of those striking cultural traits that, within the current larger context of the region's politics and society, impel Middle Easterners to adopt values or to take actions that contribute little to the general welfare of society. In a different historical context, these values could be liberating and progressive. At present, however, a peculiar combination of historical, political, and economic factors has reinforced the stagnating, largely antidemocratic effects of such cultural values.

While it is perhaps not obvious to the average Middle Eastern mind, these traits have perpetuated other endemic cultural phenomena, namely Islam, valuative contradictions, machismo, and rural values. But the specific traits to be considered here include honor, "face," and an inability to compromise. Honor and face, in particular, are high ideals in the Middle East, although many perceive and regret a decline in their observance. Overall, these traits continue to govern much of the day-to-day thoughts and actions of Middle Easterners from all sociocultural backgrounds. They form, however, some of the most stubborn obstacles to secularization, to rationalization, and ultimately to democracy. Each of these cultural characteristics reinforces the other, thereby accentuating the overall flavor of the Middle East's popular culture. By the same token, they serve to impede the transformation of cultural norms in a way that would make them more amenable to democracy.

Honor and Face

Of all the cultural forces in the Middle East, notions of honor and integrity are among the strongest. Islam has reinforced Middle Easterners' preoccupation with the protection and preservation of their honor, although the concept itself is not Islamic in origin. By most accounts, the ideal of honor was pervasive enough before the dissemination of Islam, at least in the Arabian peninsula, to have been a cult of its own that developed into a social bond regulating behavior and action.[43] Clearly, personal honor was and continues to be a definite sign of strength, a manifestation of one's integrity in a culture that places great emphasis on matters of face and perception. Within the larger climate in which it grew—first in the harsh conditions of the desert and among warring tribes, then later in the politically hostile atmosphere of the cities—the defense of one's honor assumed profound importance. Its preservation was seen as crucial to the protection of such sacred institutions as the family and religion, and gradually outweighed them in its sway. A logic gradually developed by which the essence of Islam or the family could be sacrificed if that sacrifice kept one's honor intact. This logic continues to influence the minds and behavior of countless Middle Easterners today; in fact, it was common only a few decades ago, and in some instances occurs even today, that a girl who brought shame on the family was killed by a male family member in an effort to salvage what was left of the family's honor and integrity.[44]

Different notions of honor apply to men and to women. On a general level, honor mostly attaches to values associated with sex, honesty and strength of character, chivalry, courage, and posterity. Of these values, the ones that apply overwhelmingly to women are those related to sex, while the rest are predominantly the preserves of men. A woman brings dishonor to the family if she commits adultery, and conventionally her offense is punishable by death, especially as observed among the rural and other tradition-minded strata. Only death can restore the family's honor. But the same standards of honor do not apply to men, whose sexual forays, while supposedly punishable by law, are commonly seen as signs of virility and manhood. A man does not dishonor himself through sexual exploits; he would do so if he broke a promise, became timid, sired no male children, or acted miserly. Social change and the flux of values have done little to alter this; in fact, social change has made the whole issue of honor far more troubling and contentious for many. Abstinence from premarital sex is still required of women, and it is believed that a man's legacy is secured by the birth of male offspring. But sexual matters constitute only one of the issues concerning honor. In countless everyday situations one may have to bear great costs in order to protect his or her honor: the underpaid bureaucrat who must invite colleagues to dinner out of obligation; the errant driver who must shout louder than others to avoid looking effete; the lower-class parents of many girls who feel compelled to produce more children in the hope of having a boy. All such efforts are dictated by concern about how one is perceived by the rest of society. Honor, in the final analysis, is a matter of face.

"Slap your cheeks red if you have to," goes an Iranian proverb, if that is what it takes to make people think you are doing well. Middle Easterners often go to great lengths to save face and prevent the stigma of shame, even if it means incurring unnecessary hardship or physical danger.[45] For women the presentation of a "proper" and "modest" public image is equally important. As one observer noticed among Egyptian women, what is often important is not necessarily a woman's satisfaction with personal moral standards but how she presents herself to the outside world.[46] By men and women alike, troubles must be hidden from even the closest of friends, let alone enemies, for any loss of face is a sign of dishonor and weakness. Particularly for the dispossessed and downtrodden, protection of one's honor has a validating effect. The poor may not have many material possessions, but, as they reason to themselves, they have their honor and dignity. Yet each social class uses the same logic to validate its status in relation to the class above it, and, in turn, the entire society rationalizes its material and technological inferiority to the West with the attitude that "they may have rich pockets, but we have richer souls." The net result is an incredible waste of social energy. People of the same social and cultural group expend much effort in projecting a certain image to one another, even if it means resorting to deceit or suffering extreme hardship.[47] At the same time, however, these very people contrast their own honor with the shamelessness of others in order to justify their own station in life. At the national level, the same logic is applied to explain the international order.

Selfish Individualism

Three interlocking cultural traits in the Middle East may be best summed up under the rubric of selfish individualism. The first is a marked inability to compromise, especially by politicians and leaders. Second, the region's pattern of political evolution and history have given rise to self-righteousness, demagoguery, and lack of consensus, all of which in turn have undermined the potential for compromise and concession. Third, there is a strong cultural component at work as well, especially insofar as the values attached to Islam are concerned. One result of Islam's current refusal to adapt to changing social and economic circumstances—in Tibi's words, its lack of "cultural accommodation [to] social change,"—has been a "defensive cultural chauvinism."[48] Another equally pervasive result has been a stubborn defensiveness within the culture, eroding the chances for compromise and rational consensus. Ironically, a number of Muslim thinkers have considered the *ijma'* (the consensus of the community) as one of the very foundations of the Islamic faith.[49] Theory and practice, however, have not always been in tune in the Middle East.

Difficulty in reaching compromise has been observable at the elite, scholarly level as well as at the level of the masses, but I am focusing specifically on compromise that is cultural and/or political. Trade and commerce have a rich and deeply ingrained tradition in the Middle East, and people have been accustomed to economic and commercial deals and compromises from time immemorial. But politics and culture have been decidedly different matters; political resources have been coveted and jealously guarded by a minority and the culture has been mostly unchanging and unaccommodating. Furthermore, the uncompromising natures of culture and politics have heavily reinforced one another. Islamic societies have developed little or no tradition of rational debate, except during the thirteenth century C.E., and thus to this day scholarly debate is often likely to degenerate into name-calling and the hurling of dogmas. Even Middle Eastern intellectuals who live and write abroad do not seem to be above insulting one another.[50] Although among the elite scholarly and literary circles in Iran and elsewhere in the Middle East one may encounter a genuine thirst for rational debate and scholarly consensus, this is neither the norm nor established tradition. On a more practical level, insofar as the more tangible life of society is concerned, debate, consensus, and compromise are not commonplace occurrences either for scholars or for the masses. For their part, average Middle Easterners consider compromise, even when dictated by the circumstances, a sign of weakness and a potential cause for loss of face. In a value system where issues are viewed in black and white, people tend to arm themselves with norms that are seldom retractable or amenable to compromise. As a cultural phenomenon, then, and especially as a political phenomenon, compromise is not a practice to which Middle Easterners are accustomed.

Reinforcing this aversion to compromise is a consistent refusal to accept blame. A person who is as convinced of the rightness of his or her overall frame of reference as Middle Easterners tend to be is likely to find excuses for his or her shortcomings. It should be noted, however, that many Middle Eastern thinkers, both classic and contemporary, have tried to convince their followers to look within themselves for their failures and miseries.[51] Recent military and technological setbacks have given credence to these writers' arguments.[52] But the popular tendency to blame others for one's own shortcomings continues unabated in the Middle East, and, in fact, gains strength as the region's disparities and inequities become more glaring. Conspiracy theories of all kinds abound, with even the most outlandish assertions gaining popular and at times even intellectual currency—for example, the Americans installed Khomeini in Iran; the Sudanese are the real troublemakers in Egypt; terrorist attacks in Bahrain and Saudi Arabia are the works of Iranian agents; and so forth.[53] Affixing blame to others is prevalent in the political domain, but its cultural ramifications are equally pervasive. Each social group considers another group parasitic and indolent, intellectuals point fingers at one another, and individuals talk of mitigating circumstances, or even unseen forces, as the real causes of their misfortunes.

The third and final manifestation of Middle Easterners' inability to compromise is their seemingly genuine aversion to procedures and rules. The only arena in which Middle Easterners willingly and meticulously follow procedures seems to be in the observance of religious rituals, which often involve elaborate guidelines. Otherwise, looking for shortcuts or ways to circumvent established procedures is not only a norm but also a sign of one's cleverness and, ultimately, ability to survive. Naturally, beating the political system is an even more prized skill and often a source of much pride and boasting. There is, after all, little in the political system with which the average Middle Easterner can identify, and thus its circumvention or even pillage is generally looked on approvingly.

The same mentality applies also to daily life. Even the most casual visitor to the Middle East cannot help but observe how most Middle Easterners loathe standing in lines. Similarly, one cannot avoid the impression that the only rule that governs driving calls for violating as many traffic regulations as possible. Few experiences in life come close to the wildly adventurous chaos that Middle Easterners call driving. An oppressive political heritage, combined with such cultural traits as the belief in one's infallibility and sharply contradicting valuative schisms, seem to have given rise to a peculiar logic of survival: if playing by the (official) rules of the game is not conducive to advancement, then make your own rules. Thus in lieu of the de jure rules that are meant to govern society, a de facto set has evolved, in which bending the rules and procedures *is* the norm.

This Hobbesian picture of Middle Eastern societies as brutish and lawless is not entirely accurate, however. There are laws; they simply are not always the ones set by legal authorities. Every activity in life has a procedure and a logic of its own, such as dealing with a bank clerk, buying bread, or hoping for a promotion at work, but the actual ways in which people go about them are seldom in accordance with the legal procedures established for them. Life in general and daily activities in particular have evolved a logic of their own, one in which bending official rules and regulations is the norm and often a source of pride.

Culture of Virility

Complementing and reinforcing the other traits of Middle Eastern culture (i.e., Islam, cultural schisms, and notions of honor, face, and the self) is the equally powerful ideal of "manhood." In fact, the values attached to the concept of virility are among the most important social and cultural centerpieces of Middle Eastern societies, governing the lives, thoughts, and behavior of virtually all strata of society. Naturally, each of the various social classes has its own perception of the proper place and role of "manhood." As a general rule, the traditional classes of urban society and most of the classes in rural areas tend to perceive gender roles in ways that are not entirely compatible with modern sociocultural and economic realities. Within this cultural worldview, a woman's sexuality is the most important factor defining her as an individual. More important, however, this sexuality is to be safeguarded at all times *by men*, because women are perceived as being too emotional to govern their behavior and incapable of controlling their own desires. Within the sacred institution of the family, ensuring control over a woman's sexuality becomes a matter of honor and dignity. This is a task that many traditionally minded fathers, brothers, and even uncles and male cousins assume for their female relatives. Preserving the family's honor is every member's most essential obligation; the loss of that honor is most likely caused by a female member's indiscretion. Watchful eyes must be kept on the women at all times.

For the most part, the nontraditional strata of society have the same overall attitude toward the proper roles of the sexes, although the extent and rigidity of their views differ. Clearly, the priorities of the nontraditional social classes have resulted in a number of significant changes in their notions of gender, but their overall cultural frame of reference concerning women and the broader ideal of manhood remains the same. Like the more conservative elements of society, nontraditional Middle Easterners define women primarily by their gender, seeing them as rationally less capable than men to act on their valuative beliefs in the larger world. Nontraditional Middle Easterners are of course concerned that a female relative may bring dishonor to the family. But, given today's circumstances, how can a woman not have social and/or economic interactions with others in society, especially with men? After all, only the oil-rich societies of the Arabian peninsula, excluding Kuwait, have the economic wealth to keep women in near isolation.[54] The upshot of all this has been sharp clashes between social and economic realities and cultural ideals, thus further intensifying the psychological dilemmas and search for cultural absolutes by nontraditional Middle Easterners.

There are two underlying causes for the prevalence of the ideal of manhood: the heavy weight of tradition and the reinforcing division of labor that has revolved around gender.[55] As discussed in chapters 2 and 4, the bedouin, tribal heritage remains not only a living memory but also a social and cultural constant for most Middle Easterners, despite the nuances of social change. Anthropological research has shown that in rural and tribal areas, women are more integrated into the economy of the community and are less socially and economically isolated than women tend to be in the cities.[56] But the defense of the tribal community, especially during the many wars and sporadic outbreaks of violence that have occurred, was, for various reasons, entrusted only to men. Islamic mythology provides stories, most of which seem to have historical validity, of women fighting alongside men in defense of the faith.[57] But they were exceptions, not the rule, and warfare and military matters quickly became the preserves of men. By the time tribes grew into dynasties and modern states put an end to tribal warfare, an elaborate culture had evolved in which male masculinity and strength were seen as ultimate signs of survival and were, as a result, highly coveted by both men and women. Simultaneously, gender-specific division of labor also developed. Consonant with their popular image as better administrators and rulers, men became more active within the public sphere at the expense of women, whose domain became increasingly limited to the private spheres of the home and family. A whole host of complementary norms and values, ranging from notions of honor (reinforced by the veil) to stereotypes of women's gullibility, magnified the different social roles and stations assigned to both sexes. Manliness and femininity became two cultural standards in Middle Eastern societies, the former a source of public pride and societal advantage, the latter publicly concealed and only privately valued. Within this context, virility has emerged as a compelling force among all social strata in the Middle East.

The Manly Society

Virility is exhibited in countless ways in everyday life in the Middle East and is reinforced by a variety of seemingly insignificant traits such as smoking, wearing mustaches, and watching imported karate movies—all of which have been adopted by the region's youth culture. Again, the precise manifestations of virility are likely to be based on one's social status, but the flaunting of and respect for manliness are seldom absent from any of the daily rituals of life. The men in the traditional strata are likely to show their manliness by habitually leaving their shirts unbuttoned, spending more time and energy protecting their honor, and being less receptive to greater public roles for women. Traditional women are likely to show equally high regard for virility and modulate their values and behavior accordingly. Most view themselves as sex objects who tempt men, believe in the notion of a "feminine temperament," and are willing to wear the veil in order to safeguard their own as well as their family's honor.[58] The gender-related values of nontraditional Middle Easterners differ mostly in degree rather than in substance. In their eyes, men are better at controlling their sexual urges, are smarter and shrewder, and make better rulers, bosses, and even drivers. A quotation from a female journalist's interview with the late shah of Iran, who was hailed in the Middle East and especially the West as an exemplary defender of modernity, is quite revealing. "Women," he said, "are important in a man's life only if they are beautiful and charming and keep their femininity.... You've never produced a Michelangelo or a Bach. You've never even produced a great chef.... You've produced nothing great, nothing.... You're schemers, you're evil. All of you."[59]

The picture painted thus far of women's predicament in the Middle East is a bleak one. This is not to suggest, however, that Middle Eastern women are necessarily "inferior," "repressed," or "exploited" because of their gender and the stereotypes attributed to them. There are, of course, vast inequalities in access to power and in the levels of economic and psychological dependence between the sexes. Nevertheless, women do not necessarily see their position as inferior, and at times they may even revel in the differential treatment that society gives them. Although women's rights movements have had long histories in most Middle Eastern countries,[60] few women would fundamentally change their social and cultural roles. What may be perceived as restrictive in one cultural context could be seen as liberating or honorable in another. A Lebanese woman summed up her perceptions of women's situations in her country as follows:

> The Lebanese woman has no reason to envy any woman in the world. I have lived in North and South America and experienced different attitudes to women. I still like women to have their pride, honor, and dignity. We have beautiful traditions and we should keep them. Cleanliness in mind as well as in body is lovely. Women's honor is priceless; if she wins the whole world and loses her honor she won't be in an enviable position. The Western woman has lost her family. I love my family. I would not exchange my family's happiness with anything, absolutely anything, in the world. When we sit together around the table to eat, I feel I am the happiest person on earth. Western women miss this precious feeling.[61]

In fact, many women in the Middle East, especially those past their teens and twenties, are satisfied with the way things are, as long as the situation is not taken to the extreme. Many Iranian women, for example, resent wearing the veil because it is a government mandate. For those who do not have to wear it, however, it remains an option that may be used to one's advantage. Traditional women and even those among the nontraditional strata are likely to have developed a set of philosophical and cultural justifications through which they not only explain their circumscribed position but also take advantage of it; for example, while men may use their ability to coerce or exert force (manliness) in order to get what they want, women may resort to more subtle means of persuasion (femininity).

Men in Control

With such cultural values deeply ingrained in the popular psyche of most Middle Easterners, it is little wonder that men are in full control, in the public as well as private domains. On the most general level, this control manifests itself in the realms of politics, economics, and society. Socially, men's control is sanctioned through the elaborate cultural norms previously mentioned and is exercised within the institution of the family. The powers of fathers and husbands go beyond simply those of the head of the family because they are in full control of the family's fortunes and well-being. More important, few changes to the family's situation are ever possible without the husband's or father's full blessing (e.g., a wife's decision to seek employment, the marriage of sons and especially daughters). Social change has, nevertheless, necessitated certain transformations in even the most conservative strata of society, affecting the familial role and position of women in the process. The age difference between marriage partners, for example, has been narrowing as women tend to marry somewhat later in life than they once did. Similarly, the practice of polygamy, while still prevalent in the Arabian peninsula, is on the decline in most major metropolitan centers.[62] A series of legal changes have also enhanced women's positions both inside and outside the family institution. A significant number of norms pertaining to women's roles within the family and the larger society, however, have proven impervious to change. "Love marriages" are still considered largely suspect; most parents have criteria that their child's potential spouse must meet;[63] virginity is still expected of most women if they hope to find suitable husbands (some who lost their virginity have resorted to the surgical mending of their hymens);[64] men still have a decided advantage in divorce cases, and most women refrain from filing for divorce because of the accompanying social stigma; and even if the practices are less prevalent, husbands' threats of polygamy and summary divorce still exist.

A number of legal and economic mechanisms have further reinforced women's inequality. It was previously mentioned that some legal transformations aimed at enhancing women's positions have occurred in various Middle Eastern countries. The extent and significance of these changes vary significantly within the region. In the former People's Democratic Republic of Yemen, for example, far-reaching legal reforms were implemented in order to establish free-choice unions and abolish the customary practices of bride price and child marriage.[65] Yet the only country in the Arabian peninsula to have enacted laws remotely pertaining to the status of women is Kuwait, and tradition and custom continue to be strong determinants of a woman's place in society.[66] Elsewhere in the region, with the exceptions of Israel, Turkey, and Tunisia, legal reforms in the most important domain of women's activities, namely, the family, have at best been halting.[67] Within the Islamic world, only Tunisia and Turkey have banned polygamy altogether, and in other countries most of the legal mechanisms for the control of women in the family remain the same.[68]

Economically, women are similarly disadvantaged, although, again, the extent and nature of women's involvement in the labor force must be viewed in cultural context. In a social setting that upholds informality, honor and dignity, face, and the stability of the family, most women prefer not to work unless it is an absolute economic necessity. Middle Eastern societies, in sum, reward women more for their roles as wives and mothers than as workers and contributors to families' incomes.[69] A man derives respect from being a good provider; a woman does so by being a good mother and wife. Thus Middle Eastern women, especially those in the middle classes and above, consider it below their station to hold formal jobs outside the home. But attitudes are beginning to change, largely because of diffusionary social change and economic pressure. In a survey conducted in Egypt in the late 1980s, an overwhelming number of young women mentioned employment as a means for self-actualization, equality, participation in society, and responsible enfranchisement.[70] The young and the less traditional members of society are especially likely to view female employment as a remedy to women's sociocultural and economic isolation, which many are beginning to consider indefensible. In fact, in Turkey many young men and women respect former Prime Minister Tansu Çiller, not because of her political and economic policies, which have by and large been ruinous for the country, but because she is blazing a path for other women in the region.

The result of all this cultural machismo is a built-in inequality of the sexes, an inequality that does not matter to everyone. Insofar as gender roles and positions are concerned, the prevailing cultural norms of society seem to have evolved directly from the "separate and unequal" premise. Yet despite the legal and larger social restrictions placed on them, women are not socially and culturally powerless; in fact, some of the very tools that are used to ensure women's inequality and separateness can also have beneficial results. Such concepts as honor, dignity, and "ladies first" are sometimes used as effectively to buttress a woman's advantage as to justify her seclusion and isolation. The veil is as much a source of anonymity and cover to facilitate mobility in public as it is a tool for robbing women of their individuality. Most important, the powerful role that women play as mothers must not be overlooked or underestimated, especially in light of the centrality of the family in the Middle East. As Andrea Rugh has noted, mothers

> are the central figures in the central institution of the society; they control the organization of the domestic domain and financial dispersals a good part if not all of the day; they are potent forces in the communications between the households; they control those things that are most valued by the men—sex, honor, children, a happy, well-organized household.[71]

In a cultural milieu where respect for elders is constantly emphasized, adult sons and daughters treat their mothers with more deference than they do their fathers. In sum, the public image of the Middle Eastern woman as powerless, meek, and disenfranchised is not always consistent with her actual position in the private domain. But the inequality of women is still an inescapable fact of life, and, especially in the conservative Gulf countries and Iran, women suffer countless petty restrictions and limitations that often have little rational basis. Iran's law of *qisas* (retribution), according to which the testimony of a woman is worth half a man's, is an example.[72] Whether in the name of religion or tradition, "public morality" is often invoked to defend the many inequities that Middle Eastern women face. Misguided perceptions of modernity and liberation—miniskirts and other revealing clothes, dyed hair, premarital sex, and so forth—add further fuel to more baseless dogmas from the opposite extreme. The society's imbalance, in the meantime, continues largely unabated. And when there is a genuine, mass-based effort to improve the conditions of women, as emerged in most Middle Eastern countries in the first few decades of this century, it is quickly seized by the greater powers of the government and made part of an officially tailored, innocuous state feminism.[73] Although some significant changes have been made in the past few decades, there still remain insurmountable legal and cultural barriers to women's equality.

Rural Culture

This chapter's focus has so far been on the urban cultural landscape, but rural culture cannot be ignored, both for its contribution to the overall cultural makeup of society and for its parallels with the culture of the city. The built-in assumption of the political primacy of urban culture in the preceding sentence is intentional. In the conduct of national politics, rural culture has been either not a factor or at best a tool to be manipulated and has contributed little of its own essence and spirit. As much as anthropologists and other social scientists may find fault with this argument, the overall cultural significance of the countryside to the average Middle Eastern country has been marginal. Despite the most concerted efforts, the long arm of the modern state has only slightly altered rural culture, and then only in form, not in substance. Even in Israel, where the birth of an entirely new country has brought about significant changes to the material culture of the rural Arab population, the adaptive cultures of most villagers and bedouins have retained much of their original character.[74] Similarly, the possibilities of cultural diffusion from the countryside to the city have been increasingly curtailed by the growing economic, political, and societal distance between them. The influx of rural immigrants into the cities has not reduced the rural-urban cultural gap either, creating instead a group of "urban villagers" with their own distinct values and norms.[75] There are, therefore, separate dynamics governing the cultures of the city and the village and operating in seemingly separate realms.

But to isolate rural and urban cultures completely from one another is not altogether accurate either, for there are underlying currents of similarity between them. After all, as different as they may be, the two cultural domains form the same loosely bound cluster of national identity, and on the most abstract, general level, they indeed share certain common bonds arising from professing the same religion, speaking the same language, belonging to the same ethnonational group, and being subject to the same political authority. But even at these general levels, the differences separating them can be astounding. The rituals and beliefs attached to the same religion are often markedly different in the city than in the country; distinctive accents and dialects separate members of the same linguistic group; most of the region's ethnic minorities tend to be concentrated in the rural areas; and the extent and nature of state authority in the cities versus the countryside are incomparable. It is, therefore, important to bear in mind that the popular cultures of the cities and the villages operate in distinctly separate contexts and are governed by dynamics that have little in common. Thus the rural cultural milieu is best examined *within* itself.

Tradition

In a basic, oversimplified way, rural culture may be viewed as a traditional version of urban culture, unspoiled by the ravages of social change and largely free of the skewed, valuative dichotomies found in the cities. This is not to imply that change has not occurred in the countryside, for there have indeed been important forces of change, both from within and without, at work for some time. But the net result has failed to alter fundamentally the prevailing rural cultural tradition or to instill into the culture a built-in sense of dynamism or receptivity to change. If anything, as it will be shown, most external influences have been regarded as suspect and unwelcome, thereby strengthening the resonance of tradition and a general unease with change. Also, because of its economic and political situation within the larger national context, the village has not been able to define itself without reference to the city. This relationship has not always been a positive one: the village is what the city is not and vice versa. Thus while the culture of the city may thrive on change and struggle to authenticate or liberate itself, the culture of the village, at least to the minds and hearts of the inhabitants experiencing it, needs little or no change. The city may be richer in its economy and more advanced in its industry, but the village is valuatively and culturally pure. This justification, to which most villagers resort in explaining their *national* position, bears an uncanny resemblance to the one that urban residents use to explain their *international* position.

Within the generally conservative rubric of rural culture, several reinforcing features can be discerned. Most significant is a rich folklore that gives rural inhabitants a sense of identity and place. An important and integral part of this folklore is religion, reinforced and disseminated by local clerics. Last, there is a notable (though waning) attachment to the land and its products, a sense of pride in the agrarian life that has been affected by the steady decline of agriculture and the growing lure of industry.

Folklore is by far the most indispensable component of rural culture.

It is based on the lives of the village functionaries—the cleric, butcher, village head, washer of the dead, barber, midwife, *hajji* (one who has made pilgrimage to Mecca), teacher in the local school, and so on—and an oral tradition that gives the village a sense of history and place.[76] Much of this folklore is steeped in aspects of a tradition that the village considers uniquely its own: a dialect or accent that is different from those found elsewhere; local myths concerning *jinns* and other supernatural beings; the inflated story of a hometown hero; a local shrine and the history of the religious dignitary buried in it; and particular rituals observed in such communal gatherings as weddings, circumcision ceremonies, and funerals. Entwined with these aspects is a religious tradition, often a victim of the local clergy's poor training, that does not always accurately reflect the principles and premises of the faith.

Another aspect of rural culture that merits discussion is its general distrust of secular state authority. The village believes in its own wisdom and in the strength of those traditions that have for centuries defined its life. Urbanites are often considered misinformed, intrusive, corruptible, opportunistic, and deceitful. Those who represent the government are especially viewed with suspicion, for their claims to improve the life of the village are often seen as a pretext for less noble goals. Governments often send officials to the villages to improve farming methods, introduce hygiene and vaccination, and serve as teachers in the local school. But most villagers do not want to be told how to farm more effectively or to wash themselves, for not it is only an insult to their pride but also they do not trust the officials' motives. Even government-sanctioned glorification of the peasantry by virtually all Middle Eastern states has failed to assuage rural inhabitants' suspicions and fears. Villagers want nothing from the city except its material riches and goods. They certainly would rather not have anything to do with the government or its local agents, who are in turn suspected of wanting to exploit the village for their own good. Young rural adults are attracted to the city and thus villagers further resent the city because they tend to see the state as an extension of the same sinister forces that make up and govern urbanites.

Conclusion

Popular culture in the Middle East is highly disjointed, fractured, and constantly challenged to define itself. Its cornerstone is Islam, which is substantially different in every country. Islam permeates most aspects of life, from linguistic idioms to popular rituals and activities, but its core principles and premises have not changed over the centuries. Steeped in tradition, Islam has yet to be open to routine critical discourse by its adherents. It continues to govern the minds and hearts of millions of devotees, but its old-fashioned prescriptions bear little resemblance to the prevailing realities of modern life. Thus the believer is torn, divided in the psychic self about what to believe and how to observe those beliefs. This division is found in the larger society as well, where it shatters the common bonds of identity and valuative cohesion. Thus the Middle Easterner is lost and confused, not only by whether or not to believe but also by the very definition of the self. Some find shelter in the comfort of tradition and seek the authenticity that they consider threatened by the intrusion of foreign and alienating norms. Others go in the opposite direction by embracing the new, the different, the foreign—all in the name of becoming modern. And still others, who in fact make up the society's majority, are caught in between the worlds of tradition and modernity. Such deeply ingrained notions as honor and individualism add flavor to this cultural schism, which is widened by the ethos of virility and male superiority. Somewhere in the distance, isolated and only loosely connected with this bigger drama, is the culture of the countryside, proud of itself and disdainful of the norms of the city.

Covering all the social and cultural systems, meanwhile, is an umbrella of tension, a friction-ridden mentality not unlike the workings of a broken bureaucracy. Similar to the mammoth and ever-expanding bureaucracies that symbolize the edifice of the state, the cultural and structural contradictions of society make for a volatile, or at best emotionally expressive, social setting. There is, on the one hand, a bureaucratic mentality that permeates the behavior and thoughts of many people: fears of taking initiatives and crisis eruption, preoccupation with authorization from a higher authority, and a penchant for paperwork. Of all the things that Middle Eastern bureaucracies may be famous for, efficiency is not one of them. On the other hand, the desire to circumvent procedures and beat the system is equally pervasive. The resultant frustrations are troubling; temper tantrums and quick bursts of anger sometimes erupt into quarrels and arguments. This tendency to argue, to show gestures of disgust, to blow one's car horn with menace is not, contrary to what some have suggested, a result of some innate psychological disposition.[77] It is, rather, an extension and by-product of a hassled and hassling mentality, a result of the Middle Easterners' endless preoccupation with the protection or upgrading of status, be it social, cultural, economic, or political. This mentality derives from a sense of insecurity in a sociopolitical domain filled with real or imagined threats, and it reveals a deeply troubled psyche. In many respects, what I have called the "culture of wasted energies," apart from its component of honor, is most accurately a politically anchored and conditioned phenomenon.

Popular culture only tangentially affects the overall political life of a nation. Of far more direct significance is political culture, which is a derivative of popular culture. If popular culture, in the broadest of terms, is the way society thinks and behaves, then political culture is the way that society thinks and behaves in relation to the state. There is thus a direct and significant relationship between these two forms of culture, and the dynamics of one directly affect those of the other. With this general understanding of popular culture in the Middle East, we can now proceed to examine the region's political culture.

6. Political Culture

Y ITS VERY nature, Middle Eastern culture is inherently political. No state, whether virulently secular, such as Turkey's and Tunisia's, or powerful and overarching, such as Egypt's and prerevolutionary Iran's, has ever been able to divorce itself completely from the powerful social currents gripping its societies. Much to the chagrin of some politicians, Middle Eastern culture has long influenced, if not directly shaped, whatever "the political" has stood for. The marriage of politics and culture has been intimate, inseparable, and mutually reinforcing. There is, furthermore, in the Middle East a specific aspect of culture that is particularly directed toward politics. Of course, not every social or cultural value is inherently political, but even apolitical thoughts and values may be politically manipulable. The combination of culture and politics may be more pervasive than in other contexts, but there are still discernible differences between culture per se and those facets of it that are specifically political. It is here that the concept of political culture becomes useful, where we can point to politically specific elements of culture and examine their direct political relevance.

Understanding the political priorities and beliefs of a population is impossible without knowledge of its political culture. It is through political culture that a society formulates and expresses—both overtly, through open manifestations of political expression, and covertly, through subtle sociopolitical nuances and personally held beliefs—its general sentiments toward the body politic. In its broadest sense, political culture denotes the overall perspective in which the larger society views everyone and anything that may somehow be related to politics. While many different definitions of political culture have been offered,[1] all have a common theme—simply, political culture is that facet of popular culture that deals specifically with politics. It is, in sum, all the commonly held perceptions that relate to whatever is or may be construed as political. Thus by its very nature, political culture has different forms and gradations. Much has been written on the differences between "mass" and "elite" political cultures and on what may be predominantly "parochial," "subject," or "participant" political cultures.[2] Equally important, though less widely recognized, is that one's actual political views are not always openly expressed. Particularly in repressive, nondemocratic polities, there is a stark difference between one's "regime orientations," or perceptions of the specific political personalities and establishments in power, and one's "political orientations," or broader feelings about politics.[3] Given the nature of politics in the Middle East and the ways in which states and societies have interacted, this distinction is especially significant.

There are four predominant aspects of political culture in the Middle East, with various degrees of intensity in one country or another: Islam; the cult of personality; nationalism, which has long been one of the region's most powerful forces; and the Palestinian issue, which may finally be heading toward resolution if tangible progress continues on the Palestinian-Israeli front. In one way or another, each of these features reinforces the other and, in turn, may give rise to other features that are unique to particular national contexts. Omitted from this list, however, are some politically relevant cultural traits that may be quite significant in a particular Middle Eastern country but unimportant in others. Regional and linguistically based ethnocentrism, for example, has been a prominent feature of politics in Morocco, Turkey, and Iran, with the Berbers, Kurds, and Azeris being largely left out of the political process of each country. But ethnocentrism is rather insignificant in the politics of such relatively homogeneous countries as Egypt, Libya, Tunisia, and Algeria. Confessionalism goes a long way in shaping and influencing Lebanese political culture, but not those in most other Middle Eastern countries.[4] And while tribalism accounts for much of the popular social and cultural views toward politics in the Arabian peninsula, it is hardly a political force elsewhere in the region. But one can find such ubiquitous, culturally based political features as Islam, personalities striving to become deities, nationalism, and an amorphous, loosely articulated (though changeable) affinity to the Palestinians. Together these cultural forces have come to shape much of the way most Middle Easterners look at politics.

Emphasis in this chapter is on Islam and the cult of personality, each of which has reinforced the other as well as affecting other political and cultural forces in the region. While Middle Eastern nationalism and the

Palestinian question have been widely discussed,[5] Islam and the cult of personality have not received the attention they deserve. Nationalism and the ramifications of what may be best described as the "Palestine syndrome"—at least up until recent events—have been equally important in formulating popular values and perceptions toward political issues almost everywhere in the Middle East. Most leaders have in one way or another sought to claim the mantle of the Palestinian cause, on the one hand, and to manipulate the nationalist sentiments of their subjects, on the other. The legitimacy of the leader has been intrinsically tied to these two factors almost everywhere in the Middle East, although a number of political and diplomatic dynamics have made the Palestinian issue more relevant and pressing in those countries closer to Israel, namely, Egypt, Jordan, Syria, and Lebanon. The more geographically distant countries of Iran, Iraq, and Libya have nevertheless voiced their share of rhetoric for liberation, driven almost entirely by domestic political agendas rather than fraternal obligations to or sympathies with the Palestinians. Nationalism has played an even more compelling role and, especially since the 1920s and 1930s, has been an inherent feature of popular sentiments as well as almost every Middle Eastern political ideology, official and nonofficial.

Nationalism and the Palestinian issue have, as a result, functioned as a double-edged sword. Political leaders have manipulated them in order to enhance their own legitimacy, cognizant that ignoring either runs the risk of incurring popular anger. Every leader, therefore, has gone to great pains to embody popular nationalist sentiments and aspirations, and these efforts have been helped by the region's vulnerability to personality cults. These leaders have not only called for the liberation of Palestine but also at times aspired to be its liberator. Much of what Nasser, Qaddafi, and later Saddam Hussein did, as well as Arafat and other Palestinian activists, could be explained in reference to their actual and rhetorical efforts in support of the Palestinian cause and their image as popular heroes. In this sense, the Palestinian issue and nationalism have been tools for furthering personality cults of one variety or another. But the Palestinian cause seems to be moving out of the hands of non-Palestinian would-be liberators, as its usage in the service of enhancing or questioning political legitimacy is steadily diminishing. Nationalism lives on, however, and its strength is often reinforced by the region's seemingly chronic geopolitical and domestic instability. Neither leaders nor political activists can afford to ignore or even sidestep it, since they are often a direct product of its currents and nuances.

Islam

Just as instrumental as nationalism and the Palestinian issue in formulating political values and sentiments, Islam is a phenomenon that started as a predominantly political movement. As discussed in the previous chapter, Islam is one of the most powerful forces in the popular culture of literally every Middle Eastern country, influencing, if not directly governing, popular beliefs, customs, practices, and traditions. This is not, of course, where Islam's influence ends. From the very beginning, Islam's struggle to establish a new religious and ethical universe necessarily assumed considerable political dimensions, and the community of the faithful (*umma*) that was eventually established was as much a religious phenomenon as it was a political one.[6] This intrinsically political element has never left Islam, and although at times it may have been subsumed under the greater weight of nonreligious and other historical forces, it has remained an inherent part of the religion. "Political Islam," therefore, is a subject rich enough to merit numerous volumes, and its reemergence as a compelling political force in recent decades has especially heightened scholarly, as well as journalistic, interest.[7] The focus here is of necessity both narrow and specific. How and why has Islam come to be such a dominant forum for popular political expression in the Middle East in recent years? What exactly are the dominant features and the nature of this political rediscovery of Islam? How much of this repoliticization is state-directed and how much is a product of social and cultural developments? How permanent or transient is this political radicalization of Islam likely to be?

Political Islam

An important facet of the current repoliticization of Islam is that it has been taking place along three clearly separate yet reinforcing axes: at the official state level, at the level of the more learned elite culture, and at the populist level of the masses. In a few countries, notably Iran and to a lesser extent Saudi Arabia in the early 1980s, Islamic repoliticization occurred simultaneously on all three levels, with the people's and the elite's rediscovery of Islam being complemented and reinforced by the religious agendas of the state. What resulted in each case was the emergence of a powerful theocratic state, which demanded and received unbridled mass following even under the most taxing circumstances.[8] As much as it was said to have tried, the Islamic Republic of Iran never successfully "exported" its revolution, but it did make Islam the overall framework on which its own foundations and subsequent policies were based.[9] In most other Middle Eastern countries, however, the policies of the state remained largely secular and thus hopelessly out of sync with the increasingly religious sensibilities of the populace. Attempts by various leaders to stress their personal piety to their people have largely failed to placate religiously inspired pressure from below.[10] From Morocco, Algeria, Tunisia, and Egypt to Syria, Jordan, and Iraq, and down to the Gulf countries of Kuwait and Bahrain, to name only a sample, the cultural wave of Islamic politicization has not been accompanied by a similar trend at the state level. While society has rediscovered Islam as the idiom through which it can express itself politically, the state has neither welcomed this form of expression nor has it necessarily modulated itself accordingly. Only in Jordan did the regime open the safety valve of the parliament to allow for the election of the practitioners of political Islam to official positions.[11] The Moroccan state did not go as far. Its response has been relatively measured, unlike the violent reactions of most other regimes.[12] There have been waves of arrests of actual and alleged "Islamic fundamentalists" in nearly every country and occasional assassinations and executions, with the backlash in Algeria and Egypt being particularly violent.[13] Except in postrevolutionary Iran, Middle Eastern societies' quest for the Islamization of their polities has often left a messy trail of blood and violence.

These violent reactions by a majority of states only underscore the social and cultural pervasiveness of Islam's repoliticization. Whether it is called "Islamic fundamentalism," "political Islam," "radical Islam," or Islamic "fanaticism,"[14] there is little doubt that Islam has emerged as a potent populist phenomenon through which the average person, long politically alienated, has found a powerful and accessible means of expressing himself or herself politically. The current politicization of religion is, in other words, an overwhelmingly mass-based, grassroots movement that provides a medium for political expression that was previously unavailable to many. Populist Islam affords the average Middle Easterner what for so long had been beyond his or her grasp and even imagination—a sense of political relevance. It has everything that a mass-based, populist movement could ever hope for:

- An ideology that is both deeply held and intrinsically political (Islam)
- Forums and meeting halls that are numerous, sacred, and often politically autonomous (mosques)[15]

- Ideologues who are often venerable and sometimes spellbinding in their oratorical skills (the *ulema*)[16]
- Sympathizers and adherents with considerable clout and prestige in society (students and the middle classes)[17]
- Foot soldiers with little to lose who are often eager to make extreme sacrifices for the cause (the poor and the disinherited)

Most important, political Islam offers an immediate plan of action, a call that the restive and disillusioned masses are only too eager to answer.[18]

All of this has taken place within an overwhelmingly supportive cultural and intellectual environment. Long before the masses and their populist leaders discovered Islam's political usefulness, it was heralded by a number of Middle Eastern intellectuals as the most promising remedy for salvation, not only for the afterlife but also for seemingly hopeless contemporary political predicaments. In some respects, this intellectual rediscovery of Islam predates its rebirth at the popular, mass level, thus laying a theoretical framework within which Islam and political action were later synthesized. While political theoreticians are found in all eras of Islamic history, their latest incarnation can be traced back to the period ranging from the 1950s through the 1970s. Egypt's Muhammad Hussein Heykal (1888–1956) and Iran's Ali Shariati (1933–77) were two of the more renowned figures who personified this trend.[19] These men—women were conspicuously absent from the movement to link theoretically Islam with politics—and their like-minded colleagues were far from the current, conventional notion of "fundamentalist." They were, if anything, radically progressive, seeking to synthesize a reinterpreted, reinvigorated Islam with contemporary social and political conditions. They were as faithful to modern sociological ideas—those that were prevalent in Europe and particularly those advanced by German sociologists and French existentialists—as to teachings of Islam and the Koran. Thus their aim was not simply to change society but to advance it as well, and for that purpose, they reasoned, Islam was the best tool. These were "the new partisans of the cultural heritage" (*turathiyyun judud*), who sought to bring about a new, nationalist, and progressive variety of "cultural Islam" (*Islam hadari*).[20] Muslim societies needed to look no further than the cornerstone of their own tradition, for Islam was itself a most progressive phenomenon. What was first needed, therefore, was a "return to the self," to borrow Shariati's celebrated phrase,[21] and a rediscovery of one's own "authenticity" (*asala*).[22]

Coming on the heels of repeated military defeats, increasingly corrupt and incompetent regimes, and the growing failure of such secular alternatives as Marxism, Pan-Arabism, and Arab socialism, the political Islam of the intelligentsia had a powerful resonance throughout the region. Not only was it being advanced by men who were respected by many youths but also the constant reference to Islam made it more appealing and understandable than the largely alien and abstract babblings of Marxists, Maoists, and socialists. The message of the political Islamists had a familiar ring to it, and their call to reconstruct the polity along progressive Islamic lines found appeal among most strata of society. Young people, who were restlessly in search of a new blueprint for action, were the most impressed, finding the call to authenticity both reassuring and compelling. Ali Merad has noted that

> the various literature and political writings [on Islam] appeal to religious feelings, to the nostalgia of the past golden age of Islam when the community had presumably lived the Qur'anic message in its completeness and truth. But this kind of literature is likely to also excite the imagination of the impatient youth and to create enthusiasm and deep sentiments for the old times, closely associated with the ideal image of their roots and great ancestors.... The ideological implications of *asala* are considerable. Authenticity could not only legitimise the rejection of Western moral and cultural values, but also construct a moral and social order which influences young Muslims or inspires in them critical tendencies toward the established order.[23]

Islam and the State

Islam, of course, achieved its ultimate political synthesis in Iran in 1979, when an initially secular revolution turned into an Islamic one. The birth and establishment of the Islamic Republic of Iran was not so much the product of a sustained drive by Islam to capture political power as it was the result of larger forces interacting and gradually making room for a politicized Islam to emerge.[24] Despite what much of the literature coming out of Iran would have us believe, the 1978–79 revolution did not initially begin as "Islamic," though it surely became one.[25] What made the Iranian revolution ultimately Islamic was not too different from what had helped politicize Islam elsewhere: the intellectual groundwork had already been laid by the likes of Shariati and others; Marxists and other non-Islamic activists were in disarray and socioculturally alienated; the regime made a point of persecuting religious activists; and the clergy steadily emerged as the one social group with the most resonant message (Islam) and the best platform from which to mobilize the masses (the pulpit).[26]

The largely inadvertent rise of Islam to political prominence signified an astonishing development for both Iran and the rest of the region. For Islam had now proven itself to be a viable and very real political force, and, once in the hands of Iran's emboldened clerics, it blazed a trail few had dared tread before. Armed with the dogma of religion and the zeal of their revolution, the self-righteous Iranian clergy picked on successive "enemies of the people" and the "corrupt on Earth": Saddam Hussein, Anwar Sadat, the House of Saud, the United States, the "Jews in Palestine," Salman Rushdie—all were fair game, each the enemy not only of Iran but also of Islam, the people, and the Middle East as a whole. Although the Iranians failed in large measure to export their revolution, this did not reduce the appeal and power of their message or, for that matter, the fears of those still in power. Islam was now a force to be reckoned with—indeed, the *only* force. For most of the Middle Eastern masses, the Iranian example signified hope and aspiration, the successful merging of familiar theory and pious practice. For most states, however, Iran was nothing but a cancer, its infectious virus deadly and threatening. Islam of the Iranian variety, they reasoned, must be contained and eradicated. Thus when Saddam Hussein attacked Iran in September 1980, there was much more at stake than simple territorial geography. Under threat was the legitimacy of the whole Middle Eastern political order and the underlying logic of the region's official politics. It is no wonder that most Arab states rushed to Iraq's financial and military rescue when Saddam Hussein took on the ayatollahs of Tehran.[27]

The Iranian revolution and the Iran-Iraq war were only two of the unfolding dramas that fanned the flames of Islamic radicalism throughout the Middle East. There were two other events, one already in the making and the other soon to follow, that further crystallized the merging of Islam and politics. The disintegration of Lebanon, begun as a civil war in 1975, had reached its bloodiest and most brutal proportions in the 1980s. The second event was a more intense postscript to the Iran-Iraq war, namely, Iraq's invasion of Kuwait and the ensuing Gulf War. Each of these wars advanced the cause and call of political Islam, transforming it into a more relevant, resonant, and powerful source of identity, an expression of the self, and a language of politics.

Lebanon's destruction was particularly wrenching, and the emotional response it elicited was proportionally more intense and violent. The Lebanese quagmire represented more than the death of an artificial state or the upset of a confessional order: it brought to the fore and highlighted the wretchedness of the Muslims, especially the Shias, and impressed on both the Lebanese and others that the predicaments of the country's different confessions were far from just and equitable.[28] What was all the more troubling, especially to Lebanese Muslims, was that no one seemed to care—not the Western powers nor even their Muslim brethren elsewhere in the Middle East. In 1982 Israeli tanks rolled into Lebanon and occupied much of the country; in 1983 Christian Phalangist forces massacred thousands of Palestinians in the Sabra and Shatila refugee camps, and Israeli air attacks became a regular feature of daily life[29]—throughout this whole time, Lebanese Muslims felt abandoned and on their own. Only Iran's irregular Revolutionary Guards provided some comfort, but the gesture was more symbolic than substantive, and even Syria's mighty army seemed incompetent and irrelevant. Thus Lebanese Muslims clung to the one thing they had—their religion as a source of identity. The Muslims became more zealous and determined, and they eventually raised their religion's banner and proclaimed its glory whenever and however they could. Throughout the 1980s, the Islam that was beamed out of Iran for the rest of the world to witness found an equally powerful and fanatical partner in Lebanon.

The 1980s came to a close with yet another stimulus for Islam's politicization, namely, the Gulf War. Besides making a hero out of Saddam Hussein to many Middle Easterners, the Gulf War enhanced the popular Middle Eastern belief that the West had never forgiven the Arabs for the Crusades and that Kuwait's liberation was a poor excuse for punishing Iraq and, by inference, innocent Muslims. Few bought the West's argument that the war was over matters of principle, national sovereignty, and personal freedom—none of which the West had done anything to uphold for the Palestinians. Moreover, although the addition of Arab armies to the Allied forces was meant to add legitimacy to the campaign against Iraq, it further delegitimized the authority of the Middle Eastern leaders who had jumped on the anti-Iraqi bandwagon. Tempted by the allure of Saudi largesse and currency, these leaders were seen to be engaging in "*riyal*politiks"[30] rather than a morally driven imperative to liberate Kuwait. To the average Middle Easterner, the entire affair seemed like a poorly disguised attack on the integrity of the Middle East in general and on Islam in particular. In his study of Islamic responses to the Gulf War, James Piscatori reports the words of a preacher in Jerusalem's al-Aqsa mosque at the time: "Arab leaders are giving Muslim lands to the Americans."[31] In Jordan the Muslim Brotherhood called on all Muslims to "purge the Holy Land of Palestine and Najd and Hijaz (in Saudi Arabia) from the Zionists and Imperialists" (6–7). Even in tightly controlled Saudi Arabia, a well-known Muslim scholar admonished his coreligionists for having turned the United States into their God (9). In literally every Middle Eastern country, there was some form of popular sympathy for Iraq and animosity for the Allied campaign. Piscatori quotes the militant words of a progovernment newspaper in Algeria that summed up the popular sentiments prevailing in virtually all corners of the region: "The battle that has begun in the Gulf is not Iraq's but that of the Arab and Muslim countries against the great Western powers—the United States, Britain, France, and the West's creature, Israel" (16). Whatever the logic of the diplomacy behind it, the war, in many Middle Eastern eyes, was in essence against Islam. In turn, the sheer scope of the campaign, and the subsequent choking of Iraq with economic sanctions designed to starve Saddam out of office, only strengthened the appeal and powers of Islam.

By the time the Gulf War drew to a close, Islam's merger with politics had taken a peculiar turn in the Middle East. The state's preexisting relationship with political Islam became a crucial determinant. In countries where political Islam had been co-opted by the state or had become an actual force in shaping official state policies and agendas, namely, in Iran and, at least semiofficially, Lebanon, political Islam began to die off as a viable, autonomous means for self-expression and political participation. As elsewhere in the region, political Islam had grown in popularity in Iran and Lebanon because of the dismal failures of other alternatives. It was thus with much fanfare and anticipation that political Islam was embraced and catapulted into the status of an official religion. But once in power—or its near approach to power in Lebanon—it proved as ruinous and disappointing as what it had replaced. Political Islam had raised Iranian and Lebanese hopes to a high pitch. Its message was one of unparalleled salvation, progress, and authenticity, *the* answer to the multitudes of social, cultural, and political ills that plagued society. And it had attracted the masses by the millions, thousands of whom had sacrificed and lost their lives for it. But only a minority reaped its benefits, and most of them only temporarily. Political Islam did give hope and in fact benefited Iran's disinherited (*mustazafan*) and Lebanon's Shias. But its very penchant for radical and often violent action increasingly undermined its purchase among the rest of the population. The Iranian and Lebanese middle and upper classes, especially those in the nontraditional strata, have become especially disenchanted with the excesses committed under the banner of

Islam. The bloodbath of Lebanon and the unfathomable repression of the Islamic Republic did much to stain the image and popularity of Islam. The discrepancy between what religion had promised and what it was producing was quite unsettling. Even for the most disillusioned and vulnerable, there is a point at which violence and propaganda cease to have any redeeming value.

What has resulted is a growing marginalization, in fact deradicalization, of political Islam in the two countries where it achieved official or quasi-official status. It is by no means dead in either Iran or Lebanon, and there are still occasional manifestations of "Islamic fundamentalism"— car bombs and other acts of state-sponsored terrorism—in which groups from one or the other country are implicated.[32] Nevertheless, at the mass, popular level, there is now disenchantment and disillusionment with political Islam, especially the kind that we saw in the 1980s. Few Iranians or Lebanese are still taken with the idea that Islam can provide social and political salvation, especially if its price is the death and destruction that took place in the 1980s. The diminishment of popular religious fervor has not escaped the attention of those in power, with both the Iranian and the Lebanese states trying, not always successfully, to modulate themselves to the changing priorities of their populace. In Lebanon the dominant mood of the 1990s is one of construction and conciliation, though the confessional mentality still abounds and intrasocietal resentment, especially by the Shias, still prevails.[33] The mood of most Iranians has similarly changed, though the populist mechanisms of the state have made this change somewhat more halting and its precise trajectory more difficult to pinpoint. Nevertheless, gone are the days when countless Iranians gladly sacrificed their lives for religion and took unbridled pride in being citizens of the *Islamic* Republic. After years of war, inflated government rhetoric, and political repression, what many Iranians seem to be most interested in is a normalization of life. The wounds of the 1978–79 revolution and its traumatic aftermath are deep enough not to bring a total separation of Islam and politics in Iranian history or the popular psyche anytime soon; in fact, perhaps never. But Islam is now more likely to be perceived as yet another social and political force instead of a means of salvation. This trend seems to be confirmed by the increasingly pragmatic, nonideological turn of the Iranian government in recent years.[34]

But Iran and Lebanon are not representative of the rest of the Middle East, and nowhere else has Islam had a chance to transcend the popular, societal level to reach that of the state. In fact, the very reaction of other states to the growing strength of political Islam, which, with the exception of Jordan, has tended to be repressive and outright violent, has helped to enhance the legitimacy of the new trend. In nations other than Iran and Lebanon, political Islam has not yet become the "official Islam" (*Islam rasmi*) of the state and has thus retained much of its popular legitimacy and sociocultural resonance. In the meantime, the newfound piety of the region's political actors has failed to stem the tide of religious politicization among the masses.[35] Given their history of corruption, their reputations, and the extent of popular resentment against them, most of the current crop of leaders will need to offer much more than well-publicized pilgrimages to Mecca or prayers in public in order to dispel the negative impressions that their people have of them. Whatever alternative currently exists to political Islam will be perceived as corrupt and thus devoid of any legitimacy. And, as the subconscious reasoning goes, that political Islam may not have triumphed in Iran does not mean that it could not succeed elsewhere. Besides, what most Middle Easterners know or choose to remember of the Iranian revolution is its larger accomplishments—the overthrow of the shah, its stand against the United States and Israel, its seeming devotion to the high ideals of Islam—and not its more unpleasant side effects. Most Islamic aspirants were too far from Iran to comprehend the repression of the ayatollahs, their petty restrictions on life, the corruption of their system, the compulsory and choreographed shows of popular devotion to the "leader," and the largely failed promises of the revolution. Political Islam for them is still untested and untried, and they have no reason to expect anything other than its complete success if it should win official power. From Turkey in the east all the way to the Maghreb, political Islam continues to grow ever more powerful, its strength reinforced by deteriorating economic and political realities, on the one hand, and popular longing and disillusionment, on the other.

Islam has, therefore, come to shape much of the political culture of the Middle East, becoming an integral facet of people's perception of politics. It is for many the blueprint for escape from the corruption and drudgery of contemporary politics. It provides clear and ready answers for the debilitating dilemmas that plague society, answers that are both resonant and compelling. Its resonance and extreme devotional features account for Islam's political success. Other ideologies resort to abstractions to get their message across, rely on elite ideologues to articulate their platforms, and use clandestine or at best socially vacuous forums to propagate their cause. But Islam is both real and familiar, its ideologues and articulators are none other than the clergy or other "men of the people," and its forum is as accessible and widespread as neighborhood mosques and other religious gathering places. This is not to imply that Islamic revolutions of the Iranian kind are likely to occur elsewhere in the region. On the contrary, the Iranian revolution emerged in a uniquely Shia context, and it is hard to imagine replicating its intricacies elsewhere in the Middle East. The leaders of other states have also taken precautionary measures, ranging from emphasizing their own religiosity to unleashing reigns of terror, in an attempt to preempt upheavals akin to those that engulfed the Iranian monarchy. There is, however, likely to be continued friction between society-based, populist political Islam and skeptical, defensive states, manifested in such acts of violence as assassination attempts and bombings, which have become regular features of Middle Eastern politics. But this friction is unlikely to spill over into Iranian-style revolution. The best the Islamists can hope for may be a protracted and bloody civil war with government forces, as in Algeria, where it is being fought without the support of most Algerians.[36] Middle Eastern political cultures may have become Islamicized to a large extent, but they have not yet become sufficiently revolutionized.

The Cult of Personality

Another feature of Middle Eastern political cultures is their pronounced tendency to worship personalities. It is not only a region of kings and prophets, but also of would-be kings and prophets, of men aspiring to be larger than life and of people in a seemingly eternal search for heroes, warriors, and saviors.[37] It is a region where the illusion of grandeur often becomes historical reality, where the force of personality strives and frequently becomes the dominant dynamic of historical progression. This is not akin to the laughable, tin-pot dictator, claiming to be president for life and the embodiment of whatever his nation has to offer, such as the childish despots that Africa has so frequently produced and who have been the butt of jokes both outside their countries and, most tellingly, among their own people.[38] The Middle East has, of course, seen its fair share of such buffoons, its political history replete with numerous kings and sultans of the past and colonels and generals of the present for whom greatness has remained largely elusive. But equally pervasive and far more influential have been genuine Leaders, Fathers, and *Imams,* men who became history's movers and shakers and who did move and shake entire nations and beyond. The pharaonic syndrome may have started in Egypt, but variations of it are found elsewhere in the Middle East. Hence such twentieth-century figures as Atatürk, Nasser, and Khomeini, individuals endowed with tremendous charisma who whipped their nations and others into popular frenzies with seemingly little effort. These were truly powerful leaders—genuinely popular and charismatic, regardless of the disasters they later brought on their people.

Prophets and Leaders

Giant personalities were, of course, a recurrent theme in Middle Eastern history long before its Islamic phase, when, in the Iranian Empire, for example, the notion of divine kingship was an established tradition.[39] The tremendous personality of Muhammad, with all the extraordinary attributes accorded to a prophet, further strengthened the overwhelmingly important role that individual personalities were to play later in Middle Eastern history. As a divine messenger, founder of the Islamic community (the *umma*), soldier-politician, and savior, the Prophet has long served as the exemplar whom countless Middle Eastern leaders have sought to emulate. Personal and patrimonial networks similar to the ones through which he secured alliances and administered the *umma* have now become an inseparable feature of Middle Eastern political systems of all kinds.[40] But equally resonant have been leaders' attempts to appeal to the populace through charismatic authority, to build and rebuild political and national communities anew, and to be soldier, politician, and "leader" simultaneously. However one may define them, "great men" have indeed existed in the contemporary history of the Middle East, and it would be unfair to marginalize the efforts of the likes of Atatürk and Nasser. While only a handful of men have succeeded in such ambitious endeavors, it has not deterred many others from trying to play the role. The result has been a peculiar collection of historical oddities, men of vastly unequal stature, all of whom have tried to etch their names in history in bold letters, although only a few have succeeded. Qaddafi, Sadat, Mubarak, and Saddam Hussein have all tried to fill the giant shoes of Nasser and Atatürk; the shah of Iran fancied himself a modern-day Cyrus the Great; Kings Hassan and Hussein portray themselves as contemporary "commanders of the faithful"; Khomeini's awesome charisma paralleled that of the hidden Imam Mehdi for Iranian revolutionaries; and today's squabbling Turkish politicians still function in the overpowering shadow of Atatürk.

One only needs to be mindful of the implications of the following quotations to grasp the depth and resonance of this phenomenon:

> MUSTAFA KEMAL (ATATÜRK).—Let the people leave politics alone for the present. Let them interest themselves in agriculture and commerce. For

ten or fifteen years more I must rule. After that I may be able to let them speak openly.[41]

KING FAROUK.—My good Pasha, the will of the people emanates from my will.[42]

GAMAL ABDEL NASSER.—I want to lead the nation to self-aware-ness. . . . I wish to conquer no foreign land in the name of the Arab nation. I want to only assemble members of this nation, who, once gathered, will have no need for additional living space.[43]

The pages of history are full of heroes who created for themselves roles of glorious valor which they played at decisive moments. Likewise the pages of history are also full of heroic and glorious roles which never found heroes to perform them. For some reason it seems to me that within the Arab circle there is a role, wandering aimlessly in search of a hero. And I do not know why it seems to me that this role, exhausted by its wandering, has at last settled down, tired and weary, near the borders of our country and is beckoning us to move, to take up its lines, to put on its customs, since no one else is qualified to play it. . . . And now I go back to that wandering mission in search of a hero to play it. Here is the role. Here are the lines, and here is the stage. We alone, by virtue of our place, can perform the role.[44]

ANWAR SADAT.—Although the spirit of challenge in me had always been alive (as a basic constituent of my very character), it had never been so vigorous and intensive as when I took over power. I believe it was my responsibility, when I came over to hand over power eventually, to see that we had overcome all our difficulties and hardships—those of a full-blooded military defeat, a collapsing economic situation, and a stifling po-litical isolation.

There is a long way for me and my people to go before we achieve a life where love, peace, prosperity, and the integrity of man prevail. May God guide our steps and those of our fellow men everywhere.[45]

MOHAMMAD REZA PAHLAVI.—We strengthened Iran's independence and unity in 1945–46; we pulled the country out of chaos in 1953. We next put our economy and finances in order; we wrested our oil resources from foreign ownership; and from 1963 we set our people, with their overwhelming approval, upon the road of common sense and progress, to-ward the Great Civilization.[46]

SADDAM HUSSEIN.—I've always preferred to make my decisions without the involvement of others. My decisions are hard, harsh, just like the desert. Usually it looks so quiet and kind, but suddenly it erupts with rage, mightily fighting the gusts of storm and gales. And this outburst of the desert's rage gave me the feeling that I was on the brink of the end of time.[47]

Grandiose declarations, often invoking the image of past historical figures, are not unique to the Middle East; they occur in even the most institutionally routinized, liberal democratic political settings. Similarly, as cynical as it may sound, one would be hard pressed to find liberal democratic politicians who would not push the limits of power beyond democratic norms had they not been restrained by various constitutional mechanisms.[48] What sets the Middle East apart is the social and cultural resonance of personality cults, the larger society's general receptivity to the appeal of larger-than-life personalities. The cult of personality that has become such an overriding force in Middle Eastern politics, especially in the post-Ottoman and postcolonial periods, is as much a result of social and cultural vulnerability to charismatic movements as it is of the charisma of particular ambitious individuals. Few societies—even those displaying social and cultural characteristics that facilitate the emergence of charismatic personalities (e.g., *personalismo* and *caudilloismo* in Latin America)[49]—are as easily spellbound by the aura of populist leaders as are those of the Middle East.

The aspiration to be larger than life is not limited to official state actors. Revolutionaries, political activists, and even the intelligentsia are caught up in a perpetual cycle of hero-making and hero-worshipping. In the Middle East, the cult of personality goes well beyond the confines of official power. Not only does it trickle down and resonate throughout the political system, thereby inflating each state operative with a disproportionate sense of self-importance, but also it grips the nonofficial, nonstate political activist as well, in turn bestowing on him or her a similarly egotistical sense of mission. Clearly, forces greater than a large concentration of populist aspirants must account for the phenomenon's historic prevalence. The Middle Eastern love for modern-day saviors of all kinds is more than coincidental; it is at once social, cultural, and political.

Two general types of forces are responsible for the recurrence of personality cults, one pertaining to Islam and the other to the pattern of political development. These factors are interrelated, and they have greatly reinforced each other. Islam established religious and political precedents, but at the same time its message and the political system it established also glorified the role of the individual and the importance of personal leadership.[50] In this respect, Islam demands considerable responsibility from its adherents, calling on the faithful to be actively engaged in the trusteeship of the Prophet's tradition (*vesayat*) in leadership (*imamat*), preparedness (*intizar*), exegesis (*ijtihad*), and imitation (*taqlid*).[51] The significance of personal initiative has been validated in Islamic thinking and in the political evolution and geopolitical and military expansion of the *umma*.[52] Islam's stern warnings against arrogance and haughtiness (*istikbar*) notwithstanding, the dominant intellectual trend in Islam has viewed man in an activist mold.[53] With the Prophet as the ultimate model of religious and political leadership, all subsequent leaders of the *umma* have strived to be at one and the same time religious leaders, statesmen, and military commanders. The institution of the caliph was meant to epitomize such a praxis.[54]

This in turn led to the second group of factors that aggrandized the leader's personal powers: as the state's authority became concentrated within the individual ruler, political institutions were not allowed to grow autonomously. Power became increasingly personalized, legitimated not so much institutionally or culturally as by reliance on patronage and charisma. In the absence of established institutions or principles, boastfulness and self-aggrandizement became a matter of political necessity, tricking down through the system as a safeguard against the arbitrariness and absolutism at the top. The cult of personality, therefore, was often the most apparent manifestation of the leader's might, in essence representing the fragility of the institutions through which he ruled. In response, opposition movements assumed a similar personal flavor, turning politics into a contest between personalities rather than a struggle over principles.

To point to the pervasive role of personalities in Middle Eastern politics does not minimize the extent of their individual variations and political differences. Iliya Harik, for example, has classified five different kinds of states in the Middle East: (1) the *imam*-chief type (Oman); (2) the alliance system of chiefs and *imams* (Saudi Arabia); (3) the traditional secular system (Kuwait, Qatar, Bahrain, the United Arab Emirates, Yemen, and Lebanon); (4) the bureaucratic-military oligarchy type (Algeria, Tunisia, Libya, and Egypt); and (5) the colonially created state systems (Iraq, Syria, Jordan, Palestine-Israel).[55] Using political economy as their matrix, Richards and Waterbury have also come up with classifications of Middle Eastern states, categorizing them as "socialist republics" (Algeria, Tunisia, Libya, Egypt, the Sudan, Yemen, and Iraq), liberal monarchies (Jordan and Morocco), nonmonarchical pluralist states (Turkey, Israel, and Lebanon), and "curiosities" that thrive on their uniqueness (Iran and Libya).[56]

Yet regardless of their vastly different economic and/or political systems and their specific policies and agendas, every Middle Eastern regime has at the core a strong element of personality. With varying degrees of success, in literally every country the central institution of the state consists of the leader himself. His powers may be supported by an authoritarian, bureaucratized state apparatus, as in Algeria, Egypt, Syria, and Iraq, or by a real or concocted tribal tradition, as in Jordan, Saudi Arabia, and the rest of the Arabian peninsula. He may rule through sheer coercion, as did Iran's Reza Shah, through coercion combined with charisma, as did Atatürk and Khomeini, or by counting on the political passivity of the masses because of their economic preoccupation, as did the shah of Iran and Egypt's Sadat. Nevertheless, in all cases the leader is at the apex of political power, his powers are absolute, and he is answerable to no one other than himself and God. Not only does the leader head the state but also, in most cases, he *is* the state.[57]

There are several mechanisms through which the leader propagates his cult of personality and seeks to instill it within the popular psyche; they range from manipulating history books to commissioning works of art in his honor.[58] The variety of ways in which today's prophet-leaders and soldier-politicians inculcate the masses with the religion of their personality differs from one country to another. On succeeding Sadat, who perceived himself to be a noble servant of his people,[59] President Mubarak went to great pains not to be seen as another megalomaniac and significantly changed the style—but not the substance—of leadership.[60] In contrast, Saddam Hussein's penchant for self-glorification seems to have no limits, going so far as to name a missile after himself (the al-Hussein).[61] In western Turkey it is tradition that when a young child begins to talk, he or she learns to identify father, mother, siblings, and Atatürk. The most common form of propaganda are portraits and statues, almost always larger than life, which dot major squares and plaster all suitable walls where the leader's image has maximum exposure. The particular image of the leader conveyed through the visual arts depends on the national priorities at work within the specific country. Atatürk is seen everywhere in Turkey as the smartly dressed modern founder, teacher, builder, and father the Turks believe him to have been. Iranian portraits emphasize Khomeini's humanity and humility, while in Jordan the King is often seen wearing the *kaffiyeh,* the traditional Arab headcover for men. In Damascus and other Syrian cities, a smiling Hafez Assad, pictured much younger than he actually is, appears everywhere, his photograph often accompanied by the Ba'ath Party's colors or slogans. In Morocco every establishment that houses five or more people must display, by law, a portrait of King Hassan, and every city has a store that specializes in the sale of the king's photographs. In Tunisia street portraits of President Zein Alabedin Ben Ali are only slightly less numerous. In one of the more popular photographs, the president is shown clasping his hands in a symbolic display of determination.

Other popular propagandistic displays include having the leader's picture on coins and stamps, or, in extreme cases, composing popular songs in praise of the king or the president. While in Iraq there are approximately 200 songs in Saddam Hussein's honor, a rather more modest number have been composed for Khomeini and King Fahd. Equally prevalent are monuments named after the leader or his family members, suggesting that the region has succumbed to a severe "edifice complex."[62] Most sports stadiums, hotels, hospitals, bridges, highways, ports, dams, and other massive public works are named after the head of state or someone closely affiliated with him. In Jordan, for example, the national airline, *Alia,* is named for the country's former queen. Finally, almost all Middle Eastern politicians, with the exception of the Israeli, Lebanese, and secular Turk leaders, have tried to trace their lineage directly to the prophet Muhammad, even if it meant rewriting their family's genealogy. The stature of today's prophet-leader is enhanced if he is actually somehow linked with the Prophet.

History, of course, is replete with strong personalities who have sought to personify the state. The famous phrase attributed to Louis XIV, "L'état, c'est moi," has served as the motto for dictators and charismatic leaders the world over.[63] Most of the world's political systems, with the exception of those in several African countries, have evolved to the point of checking the powers of individual personalities, but the evolution of those in the Middle East has remained skewed and stunted. Table 6.1 (p. 220) shows the general historical trends that have marked the politics of each region of the globe, specific national variations notwithstanding. In each instance (except for Africa and the Middle East), political systems and principles eventually emerged from the shadow of the leaders (especially monarchs) who embodied or perpetuated them—at times gradually (Britain), but more often abruptly (Germany, Italy, and Spain, among others). Thus the body politic became increasingly less reliant on specific personalities and acquired an institutional resonance of its own. But in the Middle East, "sultanism" and its modern variation of presidents for life have remained constant features of the political landscape. Modern state builders such as Atatürk, Bourguiba, Nasser, Qaddafi, the al-Sauds, the

TABLE 6.1

REGIME TYPES IN DIFFERENT REGIONS OF THE GLOBE

Historical period	Middle East	Western Europe	East Asia	Latin America	Africa	Eastern Europe
1700s–1920s	Sultans/kings	Monarchy	Emperors	Caudillos/ republicanism	Chiefs	Monarchy
1920s–1940s	Mandatory rule	Institutional experimentation	Emperors	Republican populism (1930s–1960s)	Colonialism	Monarchy
1940s–1980s	Sultans/kings	Democratic consolidation	Institutional rupture/ consolidation	Populism/ bureaucratic authoritarianism	Colonialism (1940–1960)/ institution building (1960–1980)	Communism
1980s–present	Sultans/kings	Postmaterialism/ emancipation politics	Institutional consolidation	Democratization	Political insti- tutionalization	Democratization

al-Sabahs, the Pahlavis, and the Hashemites not only became the state but also remained the state.

This condition of arrested development has been largely attributed to the British mandatory rule (lasting from the 1920s to the mid- and late 1940s) that interrupted the evolution of political principles while enhancing the powers and, eventually, the legitimacy of specific leaders and ruling families. But this is at best simplistic, for it ignores the importance of a number of other dynamics and does not account for the perseverance of personality cults in countries that were not subject to British mandatory rule (Turkey, Iran, Syria, and much of North Africa). Instead of blaming only European colonialism for the prevalence of Middle Eastern personality cults, attention needs to be paid to the combined effects of a series of historical, political, and sociocultural factors, of which colonialism was only a part. Clearly, the importance that Islam places on the role of the individual and the high esteem in which personal initiative is held account for the continued rise of personalist, charismatic leaders in the Middle East. Combined with this has been the state's inability, often its unwillingness, to break away completely from the forces of society, frequently having to abide by or at least to manipulate society's cultural predispositions in order to attain or simply stay in power. Even the most radical political departures from one system to another, as occurred in Turkey, for example, failed to alter fundamentally the social foundations of political power or the cultural premises according to which it was exercised.[64] In order to compensate for their weakness in relation to society, states devised a variety of methods aimed at enhancing their political legitimacy, social clout, and cultural resonance. The natural system that emerged in response to this need to gain a foothold in society was a patrimonial one based on patronage and the fostering of clientalist ties with successive social strata.[65] Throughout the Middle East today, political systems as diverse as the republics of Turkey and Egypt, the populist states of Iran and Libya, and the sultanist regimes of the Arabian peninsula rely on patrimonial and clientalist control mechanisms of one form or another. The leader, whose paramount powers are unsurpassed, is placed at the apex of the system and is assisted by deputies who are the lesser leaders in their own respective spheres of influence, and the pattern is repeated down to the lowest echelons of the state.

But the personality cult found in the Middle East is not a political phenomenon alone but, instead, an equal opportunity plague. Also afflicted, along with the state, are successive strata of society—from the highest-ranking government bureaucrats to intellectuals, university students, civil servants, other members of the middle classes, and so forth —all of whom consider either themselves or a superior the primary authority among the reference groups with whom they interact. This inflated sense of personal importance is particularly pronounced among politicians and political activists; in fact, it is a direct result of the ways in which the political process has evolved and currently operates. But it trickles down through to the rest of society as well. Politicians perpetuate godlike images of themselves in order to compensate for the legitimacy that so often eludes them. For their part, intellectuals and opposition activists create contending divine images of their own in order to counter the overarching personality of the official leader. In addition, the very act of political opposition valorizes them in their own and the public's eyes and, by making instant heroes out of them, turns their activities into a contest between personalities rather than political principles. But this is not where the cult of personality ends, because the rest of society cannot escape its full effects. As a whole, Middle Eastern societies may indeed have a pronounced inferiority complex vis-à-vis the West. But when it comes to each society with the region, an equally pervasive culture of self-importance characterizes the different social groups' perceptions of themselves in relation to the groups below them. Just as the leader projects an all-important, often messianic image of himself to the rest of society, so do successive social groups to those below their station, and, from the top down, the whole society thus becomes inundated by diminishing cults of lesser personalities.

Conclusion

Two of the strongest elements of Middle Eastern political culture are Islam and the cult of personality, although nationalism and the Palestinian syndrome, so far at least, have been powerful as well. These forces combined have given a particular flavor to Middle Eastern politics both at the official and popular levels. Insofar as Islam is concerned, no regime, no matter how secular, has been able to escape completely from its overarching reach; in fact, many of the political establishments in the region have come to rely on it as the primary source of their legitimacy. At the same time, however, Islam has served as a powerful, often militant idiom of political discourse by opposition activists, providing them with theoretical blueprints for the ideal state and practical guidelines for immediate action. The pulpit has been as much of a vehicle for political opposition as it has been a tool for fostering complacence and conformity. In the process, religion has added considerable strength to the role of individual person-alities, with both leaders and opposition activists striving to attain posi-tions akin to divinity. The image projected by Middle Eastern politicians and other political aspirants is often larger than life, and seldom does it reflect the true merits of the person being glorified. Middle Eastern politi-cal culture is in many ways ideally suited to hero worship. Atatürk, ruth-less and despotic, died decades ago but most Turkish citizens still adore him; Nasser ruined Egypt but most Egyptians still cherish his memory; Khomeini betrayed the hopes of millions but to many Iranians he is still a sacred *imam*. And in their own ways, Qaddafi and Assad, Arafat and King Hassan, Saddam Hussein and King Hussein try to immortalize themselves before their own people. Opposing each of them are lesser di-vinities who, often robbed of ideological legitimacy and popular regard, resort to the same form of self-glorification in order to get their message across and win mass support.

Sacrificed in the process is civil discourse, ideological give-and-take, and political bargaining. Instead, demagoguery becomes the overriding political language. Standard clichés praising the Great Leader or denounc-ing his dastardliness form the essence and extent of official and nonofficial politics. The state and society are more adept at hurling insults and slo-gans at one another than at genuinely trying to complement, reinforce, and refine their functions. They share nothing except mutual distrust, ma-nipulation, rhetoric, and resentment. The gap between the regime orienta-tions of people—what the government wants them to think and what they in turn tell the government that they think—and their actual political orientations—what they really think—remains as wide as ever. As the crucial cultural link between state and society, political culture in the Middle East has not brought either side closer to the other. If anything, it has magnified the state-society antagonism so that the relationship re-mains conflictual or, at best, marked by a lack of consensus and trust. Middle Eastern political cultures may be susceptible to many things—per-sonality cults, demagoguery, self-importance, manipulation, opposition, and so forth—but democracy is not one of them.

7. Conclusion

OCIETIES CHANGE. The "natural" order according to which cultures and communities of people operate are periodically revised and rearranged, sometimes violently and fundamentally; political ideologies, forces, and obstacles rise and fall; and social forces, institutions, and classes at different times serve as vehicles for different social and political cosmologies. Age-old beliefs and customs eventually become outdated no matter how vivid and real they may be in the memory of the living. The luster of cherished values fades with time irrespective of how devout and persistent their adherents. Those aspects of life that are resilient can survive only by adapting to change. If civilizations do clash, to borrow Samuel Huntington's metaphor, they do so with their own past and future, often quietly and over time, but occasionally with force and rapidity. If there is indeed a "natural order" to the inner workings of societies and cultures, it is, in one form or another, one of changeability and transformation.

Middle Eastern cultures and societies, of course, are no exception. They change, have changed, and will continue to do so. Social classes and institutions, movements and ideologies, social patterns and cultural blueprints, all have been subject to the ravages of time and the forces of change. Striking continuities notwithstanding, today's Middle Eastern cultures and societies can hardly be compared to what they were twenty years ago, or those of twenty years before that time. There is, therefore, no longer a "Middle Eastern exceptionalism"[1] that sets the region in a social and cultural class of its own, separate from other comparable areas of the Third World. But just as there are conditions that are largely specific to, say, Africa or Latin America, there are those that are particularly strong or pervasive in the Middle East. What sets this region apart from the rest of the globe or, more specifically, the Third World, is not so much the nature of the social and cultural changes that have taken place there as the larger ramifications in the various domains of life. The institutional cornerstones of society continue to be the family, tribes and/or ethnic groups, religion, the educational establishment and its products, and various informal gathering places, all of which have to contend with the pushes and pulls exerted on them by such forces as primordial loyalties, economic development, and political autocracy. These forces have had profound impacts on the lives of both the rural and urban classes, who have simultaneously been subjected to radical cultural and structural transformations courtesy of the social change that has gathered increasing steam since the 1950s and 1960s. The resultant cultures of the region have become marked by confusion, a fetish for the inconsequential, mimicry, and distorted change. This mélange has given birth to a set of extraordinary paradoxes that the insider readily accepts: antiquated Islam no longer seems outdated but has become quite contemporary and indeed liberating; virility and manhood form not only the man's view of his world but also the broader prism through which the larger society, both male and female, looks at the surrounding universe; the cult of personality promises not despotism in its embryonic and mature stages but rather virtue, aspirations, hopes, valiance, and liberation; intolerant dogmas become banners of democracy, and undemocratic slogans become democratic ABCs.

How can democracy possibly fare well under these circumstances? For a democracy to be viable, three key ingredients are necessary, one specifically political and the other two largely sociocultural. They include the political institutions and mechanisms of the state; a well entrenched, democratically committed elite; and, most important, a civil society. The effects of one without the others are invariably vacuous and incomplete. Democratic political institutions are necessary but insufficient on their own. They must be buttressed by a democratic—or at least democratizing—civil society, at the tip of which are a set of democratically committed elites whose adherence to democracy goes beyond mere rhetoric to a belief in its principles that permeates conscious actions as well as the subconscious.

This book has focused on the prerequisites for democracy in the Middle East and on the more general social and cultural contexts of the region, demonstrating that the necessary sociocultural dynamics conducive to viable and genuine processes of democratization have been largely absent. Without this firm social and cultural grounding, the supposed democratic openings that have taken place in the region have resulted in either quasi democracies—as in Turkey, Lebanon, and Israel—or in premature deaths before embryonic ones have had a chance to blossom—most violently in Algeria and with less bloodshed in Tunisia and Egypt. "Controlled" or "guided" democracies have also sprung up in a few countries, most notably in Jordan and Egypt and to some extent in Kuwait, although, once again, these are state-sponsored democracies imposed from above with little meaning or resonance throughout society. The collapse of Yemen's brief experiment with democracy following the unification of its two halves in 1990 came to a head in 1994, when a full-scale civil war erupted along preunification lines. Elsewhere in the Arabian peninsula—from Saudi Arabia in the west to Qatar, Bahrain, the United Arab Emirates, and Oman in the east—societal pressures for democracy have been placated by the massive infusion of petrodollars into the economy, on the one hand, and the deliberate political and cultural marginalization of disenfranchised groups, namely, expatriate workers, on the other. In Morocco, Libya, Syria, Iran, and Iraq, politically significant social groups have been either incorporated into the regime under various populist pretexts or effectively neutralized by the state's coercive arms, or, as is often the case, they have simply abandoned the political cause and instead pursued quiet lives of despair and disillusion. Simply put, however vital democratic ideals may be in the Middle East, they are far from attaining any kind of reality now or in the foreseeable future. The characteristics required by the social and cultural imperatives of democracy simply do not exist there.

For these characteristics to appear and then thrive, three particular transformations of Middle Eastern culture and society are necessary. First and foremost, a democratic political culture needs to evolve. Without it there can be no democratic self-organization on the part of various social segments, especially intellectuals, who set the broad parameters of high culture in general and political thought in particular. Related to the larger phenomena of political culture and civil society is Islam, which, again, in its current militant form poses an immovable obstacle to social and cultural democratization. If the basic principles of democracy are to develop and gain resonance in the Middle East's society and culture, Islam's uncompromising self-righteousness and its adherents' tendency to see the world in black and white must begin to admit criticism and the possibility of compromise. Finally, the very political economy must change. The Middle East is home to perhaps the largest collection of rentier states, most of which have been able to exercise a remarkable degree of political and economic autonomy from their societies. The resultant state-society gap and society's general sense that it has little at stake politically impede the possibilities for democratizing pressures from below. These are not, of course, the only impediments to social and cultural democratization. Particular national idiosyncracies, unique cultural and historical experiences, and specific political and economic forces all determine the likelihood of democratic openings within a specific country. Nevertheless, on a regional and transnational scale, the factors mentioned above have combined to make democracy socially and culturally alien to the Middle East.

There can be no "democracy without democrats,"[2] genuine ones who both profess and internalize the political and psychological values encapsulated in the concept of democracy. But therein lie two of the impediments to democracy: the region has few *democrats,* and those who boast about being democratic have little or no understanding of what *democracy* truly is. Demagogues and believers in a cause may call themselves democrats no matter how actually undemocratic their mission or how insincere their protests about the exclusion of other voices. This is precisely what has happened in Algeria with the Islamic Salvation Front, a most demagogic and antiliberal group now waging war against an Algerian state it considers intolerably illiberal. Egypt's Jamaat Islami is hardly any more democratically enlightened, and it is doubtful that the Tunisian al-Nahda's democratic vows spring from genuine conviction rather than from political expedience.[3]

Who is to blame for this absence of democrats is itself a matter of conjecture. Insofar as the activist or the intellectual is concerned, how can he or she engage in democratic discourse with a state that responds to dissidents with guns and prison sentences? Democracy may be a cultural phenomenon in its inception, but ultimately it needs political space in which to emerge, grow, and thrive. But shifting blame, itself a prevalent Middle Eastern trait, is hardly the answer. It is true that Middle Eastern states are frequently run by unenlightened and often corrupt, antidemocratic, and at times outright barbaric despots. But the archaic nature of the state does not absolve society for its antidemocratic tendencies. What the Middle East needs are *democrats,* voices not so much of conscience but of reason, not so much of passion but of coldly dispassionate dialogue and discourse. Every Middle Eastern country has had its own celebrated version of Naguib Mahfouz or Che Guevara; each now needs its own Václav Havel or Lech Walesa. If intellectuals are to have genuinely democratic commitments, they must preach and practice tolerance—tolerance of the different, the other—and their point of reference must be laws other than those divinely revealed or based on religious faith. The power of religious principles and practices may be effective when confronting authoritarian states, but it is inadequate for the establishment of democracies. Democracy requires that the very notion of power be separated from what is considered sacrosanct. Middle Eastern intellectuals have so far been unable to resolve these core philosophical contradictions or to give them greater popular currency.

This is not to assert that there are no truly democratic aspirants or activists in the Middle East; indeed there are. Many of them are lecturing in universities, reading in libraries under mounds of books, participating in spirited debates and arguments, or working quietly in their government or private offices. But their voices are few and faint, easily drowned out by the desperate cries of the disillusioned and disenchanted masses in search of easy, quick answers and who are impatient and intolerant. There are few democrats in the Middle East and an even smaller audience with whom they can communicate. The problem is not an easy one to tackle: on one level, Middle Eastern intellectuals need to become democratic, while on another level, Middle Eastern masses need to become receptive to what they have to say. Nothing short of massive social engineering will suffice.

Of all the social and cultural impediments to democracy that must be targeted for change, Islam and education are of particular significance for their pervasiveness. Throughout the Middle East, formal education is widely available and readily accessible even in remote areas. Both elementary and higher education have now become the norm, especially in the larger metropolitan areas, and although access to and levels of education remain highly uneven among the various social classes and between the sexes, a sizable portion of Middle Easterners have received some formal education. The problem, however, lies in the kind of skills that educational establishments, both schools and universities, bestow on their pupils. Primary and secondary schools invariably emphasize rote memorization and mechanical math skills at the expense of critical thinking, individual initiative, and independent analysis. Instruction in a typical school week consists of the inculcation of mathematical formulas and a familiarity with officially approved personalities and historical events.[4] Little time is left for the student to become acquainted with the social sciences or, for that matter, with anything else that falls outside the rigidly devised curriculum. The same pattern continues at the university level, though with somewhat more subtlety. Apart from the societal and family pressures on students to study the "real" sciences and not waste time on fanciful abstracts, the state-controlled social science education is seldom conducive to acquiring skills with which one's social and political universe can be critically examined. Political and social theory, for example, are infrequent offerings, whereas such innocuous subjects as law, economics, and anthropology—all critically diluted—are widely taught.

For democracy to evolve in the Middle East, a fundamental and thorough overhaul of educational establishments and practices is needed: in fact, the basic premises on which Middle Eastern education are commonly based must change. The problem at the university level seems somewhat easier to rectify: in simplest terms, the state's overt as well as its covert political control mechanisms over instruction must be removed. But at the primary and secondary levels, with traditions in the Middle East dating back centuries, the problem is not so much one of political control as it is overall pedagogy. Basic education has always featured, both traditionally and in recent years, rote memorization, regurgitation, repetition, and uncritical recitation. Whatever merits these educational practices may have, the teaching of tolerance and the acceptance of debate are not among them. If democracy is to acquire any meaningful measure of popular resonance, the critical and analytical skills of the masses must be nurtured from a young age. At present, however, the skills that graduates have at best prepare them for patriarchal obedience and unquestioning acceptance. No wonder the region's political nonconformists are often as dogmatic as the despots they seek to overthrow.

Islam's influence as a social force must also be targeted for change. The question of whether Islam is inherently antiliberal and nondemocratic is both highly controversial and subjective. Much has been written recently on Islam's inherent democratic possibilities or its authoritarian tendencies.[5] This debate, while of great theoretical and theological significance, is largely irrelevant to the discussion of democratic potential in the region. The reason is simple: regardless of the theoretical underpinnings of its cosmology, the social, cultural, and political manifestations of Islam in the Middle East, especially in the contemporary era, have turned it into a decidedly antidemocratic phenomenon. Contemporary interpretations of Islam have not helped to free women from the spatial isolation and political seclusion of the male-dominated society. Although Islam itself may not be inherently misogynistic, its interpreters and implementers almost without exception have been.[6] Democracy cannot exist when half the population is viewed as unequal in rank and status, and the sanctioning of this inequality, whether or not it is justifiably based on religion, must end. Nor can democracy gain adherents from among people for whom the profane is often the sacred and the sacred always beyond reproach.

For a religion priding itself on the feasibility of a direct connection between the person and the Creator, Islam has a remarkably high number of *imams, muftis,* and other religious functionaries who, wielding social and political powers of varying degrees, have seldom served as proponents of democratic initiative and tolerance. And although there has been no shortage of them engaging in political opposition, these religious leaders have more frequently acted in silent or active complicity with authoritarian states than as the building blocks of democratic civil societies. In short, Islam—or, more specifically, what today's Islam in the Middle East stands for—must undergo a radical and far-reaching process of reformation, whereby its politically machinated doctrines cease to be shelters for undemocratic practices and instead become another means through which society democratically organizes and expresses itself.

The tired cliché that the basic problem with Islam is that it is by nature political and that religion and politics do not mix is without theoretical validity or historical basis. Regardless of its core tenets, any ideology can be interpreted democratically or undemocratically. Students of European history would be hard-pressed to explain the emergence of democracy on the continent in the twentieth century without reference to the sustaining role of religion, just as they would be if they were to discuss the nature and catalysts for absolutism in the seventeenth and eighteenth centuries. Religion in itself, Islam included, is neither democratic nor undemocratic. What makes it one or the other is its particular and actual manifestation, its role as one of the conduits through which the masses express their changing emotional and political needs, and the interpretations and priorities of those entrusted with interpreting and propagating it to the larger society. The best contemporary Islam has done so far is to serve as a language of political protest, having yet to become a bastion of democracy or a catalyst for democratization. Given that Islam is *the* prism through which most Middle Easterners view their universe, democratization in the region will not be possible without Islam's own democratization. For Islam to have become simply "politicized" is insufficient; it must now become democratized as well.

*   *
*

What are the prospects for democracy in the Middle East? The road ahead looks neither smooth nor promising. This is not the conclusion I had hoped for, but the current manifestations of Middle Eastern culture and society, as well as the region's political realities, make any other conclusion only wishful thinking. The situation is not, of course, hopeless.

Within the span of only four or five decades, the Middle East has come a very long way. With few exceptions (Egypt, Oman, Iran, and Turkey), most Middle Eastern states did not even come into existence until after the British lost their hegemony in the region between 1945 and 1970. The Gulf countries have gone from little more than small city-states, many no more developed than large encampments, to vibrant, modern nation-states in many respects. All of this has been compressed into only a few decades, during which state-building and political institutionalization have had to occur in order for democratization to appear later. Democracy, in the meantime, does not appear overnight; even in its birthplace it had to overcome centuries of obstacles and difficulties. There have been more than a few attempts in the Middle East, most of them prior to the 1960s and 1970s, to raise people's democratic consciousness, to set up representative and parliamentary institutions, and to reinvigorate the progressive dynamism found within Islam. But, as argued in the preceding chapters, much remains to be done.

The lessons drawn from other democratization processes, in the recent as well as the distant past, offer us much to apply to the Middle East. Pacts and negotiations must replace rigged ballot boxes, repressive police forces, shouting, and communicating with bullets. Dogma, religious or secular, must give way to reason and a spirit of compromise. Discourse needs to replace accusations and convenient labels of treachery and treason that often are so readily attached to those who differ or dare to criticize.[7] Middle Eastern political cultures, in other words, must stop being zero-sum games. Democratic elites do not emerge spontaneously, but they are what the Middle East needs; civil society does not evolve under just any conditions but requires care, nurturing, and, more than anything else, a willingness to tolerate debate. The will to democratize, which the Middle East sorely lacks, is what it needs most.

Notes

Preface

1. An insightful survey of various methodologies within the discipline of comparative politics can be found in Gabriel Almond, *A Discipline Divided: Schools and Sects in Political Science* (Newbury Park, Calif.: Sage, 1990).

2. Elie Kedourie, *Democracy and Arab Political Culture* (Washington, D.C.: Washington Institute for Near East Policy, 1992), 104; see also idem, *Politics in the Middle East* (Oxford: Oxford University Press, 1992).

3. Bernard Lewis, *The Shaping of the Modern Middle East* (Oxford: Oxford University Press, 1994), 59.

4. See especially Albert Hourani, *A History of the Arab Peoples* (Cambridge, Mass.: Harvard University Press, 1991); also, idem, *The Emergence of the Modern Middle East* (Berkeley: University of California Press, 1981).

5. For a critical indictment of orientalism, see Edward Said, *Orientalism* (New York: Vintage, 1978). For a review of orientalist and anti-orientalist perspectives, see Simon Bromley, *Rethinking Middle East Politics* (Austin: University of Texas Press, 1994), 6–45.

6. Samuel P. Huntington, *The Third Wave: Democratization in the Late Twentieth Century* (Norman: University of Oklahoma Press, 1991), 298.

7. H.A.R. Gibb, *Modern Trends in Islam* (Chicago: University of Chicago Press, 1947); and idem, *Mohammedanism* (Oxford: Oxford University Press, 1962).

8. Samuel P. Huntington, "The Goals of Development," in *Understanding Political Development*, ed. Myron Weiner and Samuel P. Huntington (New York: HarperCollins, 1987), 24.

9. Huntington, *Third Wave*, 298.

10. Saad Eddin Ibrahim, "Civil Society and Prospects for Democratization in the Arab World," in *Civil Society in the Middle East*, ed. Augustus Richard Norton (Leiden: E.J. Brill, 1995), 30.

Chapter 1. The Social Origins of Democracy

1. See, for example, Robert Pinkney, *Democracy in the Third World* (Boulder, Colo.: Lynne Rienner, 1993); Samuel P. Huntington, *The Third Wave: Democratization in the Late Twentieth Century* (Norman: University of Oklahoma Press, 1991); Larry Diamond, Juan Linz, and Seymour Martin Lipset, eds., *Politics in Developing Countries: Comparing Experiences with Democracy* (Boulder, Colo.: Lynne Rienner, 1990); Larry Diamond, ed., *Political Cul-*

ture and Democracy in Developing Countries (Boulder, Colo.: Lynne Rienner, 1993); Anthony Birch, *The Concepts and Theories of Modern Democracy* (London: Routledge, 1993); Giuseppe Di Palma, *To Craft Democracies: An Essay on Democratic Transitions* (Berkeley: University of California Press, 1990); Robert Dahl, *Democracy and Its Critics* (New Haven: Yale University Press, 1988); Geraint Parry and Michael Moran, eds., *Democracy and Democratization* (London: Routledge, 1994); Georg Sorensen, *Democracy and Democratization* (Boulder, Colo.: Westview, 1993); and Ian Budge and David McKay, eds., *Developing Democracy* (London: Sage, 1994).

2. See, for example, Heather Deegan, *The Middle East and Problems of Democracy* (Boulder, Colo.: Lynne Rienner, 1993); Steven R. Dorr, "Democratization in the Middle East," in *Global Transformation and the Third World,* ed. Steven Dorr, Barry Shutz, and Robert Slater (Boulder, Colo.: Lynne Rienner, 1993), 131–57; and Richard Sklar and Mark Strege, "Finding Peace through Democracy in Sahelian Africa," *Current History* 91, no. 565 (May 1992): 224–29.

3. For an insightful survey of the theories of democracy, both classic and contemporary, see Giovanni Sartori, *The Theory of Democracy Revisited,* 2 vols. (Chatham, N.J.: Chatham House, 1987).

4. Huntington, *Third Wave,* 7; Sorensen, *Democracy and Democratization,* 10.

5. Joseph Schumpeter, *Capitalism, Socialism, and Democracy,* 3d ed. (New York: Harper and Brothers, 1947), 269.

6. Sorensen, *Democracy and Democratization,* 10.

7. Robert Dahl, *Polyarchy* (New Haven: Yale University Press, 1971), 8.

8. Huntington, *Third Wave,* 7.

9. David Held, quoted in Sorensen, *Democracy and Democratization,* 10.

10. Sorensen, *Democracy and Democratization,* 12.

11. The scope of this book does not allow for further elaboration of this point, which is, admittedly, somewhat of an oversimplification. For more on varying definitions of democracy and their critiques, see Birch, *Concepts and Theories of Modern Democracy,* 45–68.

12. Mehran Kamrava, "Conceptualizing Third World Politics: The State-Society See-Saw," *Third World Quarterly* 14, no. 4 (1993):703–16.

13. Lyman Tower Sargent, *Contemporary Political Ideologies* (Belmont, Calif.: Wadsworth, 1993), 42. For more on the connection between Greek and modern democracy, see Sartori, *Theory of Democracy Revisited,* 278–97.

14. Sorensen, *Democracy and Democratization,* 19; see also Arend Lijphart, "Democratic Political Systems," in *Contemporary Political Systems,* ed. Anton Bebler and Jim Seroka (Boulder, Colo.: Lynne Rienner, 1990), 71–86.

15. Lijphart, "Democratic Political Systems," 77.

16. Ibid., 78–79.

17. Sorensen, *Democracy and Democratization,* 74.

18. Ibid., 81.

19. Ibid., 83.

20. Mehran Kamrava, *Understanding Comparative Politics: A Framework*

for Analysis (London: Routledge, 1996), especially 31–42.

21. For more on political culture, see ibid., 58–73. See also chap. 6.

22. For an insightful treatment of the concept of civil society, see Ernest Gellner, *Conditions of Liberty: Civil Society and Its Rivals* (New York: Penguin, 1994).

23. There are also widespread violations of the rights of Indians in Guatemala, which, even by the most charitable accounts, cannot be considered a democratic country. Neither can Brazil be categorized as democratic, although the human rights violations there are committed mostly for economic reasons, not political ones.

24. Craig Baxter, "Democracy and Authoritarianism in South Asia," *Journal of International Affairs* 38, no. 2 (Winter 1985):314.

25. *World Press Review* 41, no. 12 (December 1994):20.

26. For more information on female leaders in South Asia, see ibid., 18–20. See also Linda Richter, "Exploring Theories of Female Leadership in South and Southeast Asia," *Pacific Affairs* 63, no. 4 (Winter 1990–91):524–40.

27. From its creation in the 1920s until 1938, the PRI was called the Partido Nacional Revolucionario (PNR); it then became the Partido de la Revolución Mexicana (PRM) from 1938 to 1946, when it acquired its present name.

28. According to one observer, the PRI "has mainly functioned as a kind of ministry of elections, in the sense that its principal function has been to mobilize electoral support for the PRI during presidential, state, and local elections." Susan Kaufman Purcell, "Mexico," in *Latin American Politics and Development,* ed. Howard Wiarda and Harvey Kline (Boulder, Colo.: Westview, 1990), 413.

29. Caroline Knight, "Traditional Influences upon Lebanese Politics," *Journal of Social, Political, and Economic Studies* 17, nos. 3–4 (Fall/Winter 1992):328–29. See also Samir Khalaf, *Lebanon's Predicament* (New York: Columbia University Press, 1987), 136.

30. Serif Mardin, "Religion and Politics in Modern Turkey," in *Islam in the Political Process,* ed. James Piscatori (Cambridge: Cambridge University Press, 1983), 145, 152–53.

31. For a succinct treatment of politics in modern Turkey, see Elie Kedourie, *Politics in the Middle East* (Oxford: Oxford University Press, 1992), 93–154.

32. For more on Turkey's overall policy toward the Kurds, see Philip Robins, "The Overlord State: Turkish Policy and the Kurdish Issue," *Journal of International Affairs* 69, no. 4 (October 1993):657–76.

33. For more on the actual or potential paralysis of quasi-democratic systems, see Charles Anderson, "Toward a Theory of Latin American Politics," in *Politics and Social Change in Latin America: Still a Distinct Tradition?* ed. Howard Wiarda (Boulder, Colo.: Westview, 1992), 239–54.

34. What follows is not meant to be an exhaustive survey of the literature on democratization. Instead, it highlights the arguments of two prominent theorists who take a position contrary to mine by maintaining that political cul-

ture is *not* a determining factor in processes of democratization.

35. Di Palma, *To Craft Democracies,* 145.

36. Huntington, *Third Wave,* 15–16.

37. Samuel P. Huntington, "The Clash of Civilizations?" *Foreign Affairs* 72, 3 (Summer 1993):22–49. For a series of responses to this article, see *Foreign Affairs* 72, no. 4 (September/October 1993): 2–21.

38. Samuel P. Huntington, "The Goals of Development," in *Understanding Political Development,* ed. Myron Weiner and Samuel P. Huntington (New York: HarperCollins, 1987), 3–32.

39. Huntington, "Clash of Civilizations?" 22.

40. Di Palma, *To Craft Democracies,* 8.

41. Huntington, *Third Wave,* 114.

42. Di Palma, *To Craft Democracies,* 27–28.

43. See Guillermo O'Donnell, Philippe Schmitter, and Laurence Whitehead, eds., *Transitions from Authoritarian Rule: Southern Europe* (Baltimore: Johns Hopkins University Press, 1986).

44. Philippe Schmitter, "An Introduction to Southern European Transition from Authoritarian Rule: Italy, Greece, Portugal, Spain, and Turkey," in O'Donnell et al., *Transitions from Authoritarian Rule,* 9.

45. Ilkay Sunar and Sabri Sayari, "Democracy in Turkey: Problems and Prospects," in O'Donnell et al., *Transitions from Authoritarian Rule,* 186.

46. In eastern Europe, Romania and Albania are in the same predicament after their respective democratic transitions. See J.F. Brown, *Surge to Freedom: The End of Communist Rule in Eastern Europe* (Durham, N.C.: Duke University Press, 1991), 199–245.

47. For more on this point, see Rusen Çakir, *Ne Seriat ne demokrasi: Refah Partisini anlamak* (Neither Sharia nor democracy: The Refah Party analyzed) (Istanbul: Siyabeyaz, 1994).

48. See Jean-François Bayart, *The State in Africa: The Politics of the Belly* (London: Longman, 1993), 242–52.

49. J.P. Nettl, "Ideas, Intellectuals, and Structures of Dissent," in *On Intellectuals,* ed. Philip Rieff (Garden City, N.Y.: Anchor Books, 1970), 67–68.

50. For some of Havel's writings, see Václav Havel, ed., *The Power of the Powerless* (Armonk, N.Y.: M.E. Sharpe, 1985); and Havel, "Anti-Political Politics," in *Civil Society and the State,* ed. John Kaene et al. (New York: Verso, 1988), 381–98.

51. Gellner, *Conditions of Liberty,* 5.

52. Ibid., 105.

53. Ibid., 101. Gellner's arguments in this regard are more thorough and complex than can be discussed in the context of this chapter. Briefly, Gellner considers the development of a modern homogeneous culture as a natural by-product of the emergence of "the modular man"—someone who is changeable, not bound to uncompromising, irrational rituals and traditions, and adaptable in outlook and social functions to the changing realities of social desires and political roadblocks. For further reading, see ibid., 97–108, especially 99–101.

54. See especially Huntington, *Third Wave,* 110–74; and Di Palma, *To*

Craft Democracies, 103–4.

55. C. Seddon, "Algerian Civil War," *New Statesman and Society* 6 (3 December 1993): 11.

56. In 1995 Algeria was plunged into a costly civil war, with scores of civilians killed by FIS commandos, as well as FIS supporters by government soldiers.

57. J.F. Brown, "The Military and Society: The Turkish Case," *Middle Eastern Studies* 21 (July 1989): 387–404.

58. Kedourie, *Politics in the Middle East,* 140–42, 147–48.

59. See Mehran Kamrava, *Politics and Society in the Third World* (London: Routledge, 1993), 160–63.

60. See, for example, the special issue of the *Middle East Journal* 47, no. 2 (Spring 1993).

61. Augustus Richard Norton, ed., *Civil Society in the Middle East* (Leiden: E.J. Brill, 1995).

62. Norton, "Introduction," in ibid., 3.

63. Neil Hicks and Ghanim al-Najjar, "The Utility of Tradition: Civil Society in Kuwait," in Norton, *Civil Society,* 212–13.

64. Saad Eddin Ibrahim, "Civil Society and Prospects for Democratization in the Arab World," in Norton, *Civil Society,* 42.

65. Laurie A. Brand, "In the Beginning Was the State . . . : The Quest for Civil Society in Jordan," in Norton, *Civil Society,* 184.

66. Muhammad Muslih, "Palestinian Civil Society," in Norton, *Civil Society,* 249–58, 268.

67. Norton, "Introduction," 25.

68. Ibrahim, "Civil Society and Prospects for Democratization," 30.

69. These contributors use Norton's definition of civil society as their focus of analysis: it is "more than an admixture of various forms of association."

> It also refers to a quality, civility, without which the milieu consists of feuding factions, cliques and cabals. Civility implies tolerance, the willingness of individuals to accept disparate political views and social attitudes; to accept the profoundly important idea that there is no right answer. I would like to emphasize that it is as relevant to look for civility within associations as it is to observe it between them. . . . Civil society is also a cast of mind, a willingness to live and let live. (Norton, "Introduction," 11–12)

70. Raymond A. Hinnebusch, "State, Civil Society, and Political Change in Syria," in Norton, *Civil Society,* 42.

71. Mustapha K. al-Sayyid, "A Civil Society in Egypt?" in Norton, *Civil Society,* 290.

72. Eva Bellin, "Civil Society in Tunisia," in Norton, *Civil Society,* 147.

73. Giacomo Luciani, "The Oil Rent, the Fiscal Crisis of the State, and Democratization," in *Democracy without Democrats? The Renewal of Politics in the Muslim World,* ed. Ghassan Salame (London: I.B. Tauris, 1994), 132–33, 140.

74. Alan Richards and John Waterbury, *A Political Economy of the*

Middle East: State, Class, and Economic Development (Boulder, Colo.: West-view, 1990), 225–26.

Chapter 2. Social Forces and Institutions

1. Some recent works include Khaldoun Hasan al-Naqeeb, *Society and the State in the Gulf and Arab Peninsula: A Different Perspective*, trans. L.M. Kenny (London: Routledge, 1990); Halim Barakat, *The Arab World: Society, Culture, and the State* (Berkeley: University of California Press, 1993); James Bill and Robert Springborg, *Politics in the Middle East*, 4th ed. (New York: HarperCollins, 1994); Edmund Burke III, ed., *Struggle and Survival in the Modern Middle East* (Berkeley: University of California Press, 1993); Guilain Denoeux, *Urban Unrest in the Middle East: A Comparative Study of Informal Networks in Egypt, Iran, and Lebanon* (Albany: SUNY Press, 1993); Elie Kedourie, *Politics in the Middle East* (Oxford: Oxford University Press, 1992); Philip Khoury and Joseph Kostiner, eds., *Tribes and State Formation in the Middle East* (Berkeley: University of California Press, 1990); Alan Richards and John Waterbury, *A Political Economy of the Middle East: State, Class, and Economic Development* (Boulder, Colo.: Westview, 1990); Hisham Sharabi, *Neopatriarchy: A Theory of Distorted Change in Arab Society* (Oxford: Oxford University Press, 1988); and Sami Zubaida, *Islam, the People, and the State: Political Ideas and Movements in the Middle East* (London: I.B. Tauris, 1993).

2. Both Damascus and Allepo claim to be the oldest, continuously inhabited cities in the world, although the earliest cities are known to have been along the great river valleys of the Nile, the Tigris-Euphrates, the Indus, and the Huang Ho in China. See Lewis Mumford, *The City in History: Its Origins, Its Transformation, and Its Prospects* (New York: Harcourt, Brace and World, 1961), 55–61. For an insightful account of the life and evolution of the city in the Middle East, see also Albert Hourani, *A History of the Arab Peoples* (Cambridge, Mass.: Harvard University Press, 1991), chap. 7.

3. Sharabi, *Neopatriarchy*, 4.

4. Bill and Springborg, *Politics in the Middle East*, 151–52.

5. Al-Naqeeb, *Society and the State*, 6.

6. Leonard Binder, *In a Moment of Enthusiasm: Political Power and the Second Stratum in Egypt* (Chicago: University of Chicago Press, 1978), 29.

7. See Richards and Waterbury, *Political Economy*, 186–87.

8. Roger Owen, *State, Power, and Politics in the Making of the Modern Middle East* (London: Routledge, 1992), 37.

9. Richards and Waterbury, *Political Economy*, 193.

10. Ibid., 219–23.

11. Bill and Springborg, *Politics in the Middle East*, 18.

12. Barakat, *Arab World*, 23–24.

13. Bill and Springborg, *Politics in the Middle East*, 66.

14. For a full discussion of this phenomenon, see Hilal Khashan, *Inside the Lebanese Confessional Mind* (Lanham, Md.: University Press of America, 1992).

15. Denoeux, *Urban Unrest*, 1.

16. Bill and Springborg, *Politics in the Middle East*, 94. In Iran, women have socialized in such religious charity events as *dowreh* (literally, cycle) or *sofreh* (literally, tablecloth), in which prayer ceremonies are usually followed by an elaborate meal and, eventually, nonreligious conversation. See William Green Miller, "Political Organization in Iran: From Dowreh to Political Party," *Middle East Journal*, 23, no. 2 (Spring 1968): 163–65.

17. See Mehran Kamrava, *Politics and Society in the Third World* (London: Routledge, 1993), 124–32.

18. Barakat, *Arab World*, 22.

19. For more on cultural ramifications of this phenomenon, see chap. 4.

20. Sharabi, *Neopatriarchy*, 70.

21. Richards and Waterbury, *Political Economy*, 26.

22. Mehran Kamrava, *Understanding Comparative Politics: A Framework for Analysis* (London: Routledge, 1995), 38, 49–55.

23. Barakat, *Arab World*, 23.

24. Raphael Patai, *The Arab Mind* (New York: Charles Scribner's Sons, 1973), 42.

25. Quoted in Andrea Rugh, *Family in Contemporary Egypt* (Syracuse: N.Y.: Syracuse University Press, 1984), 60–61.

26. Republic of Turkey, *Constitution of the Republic of Turkey* (Ankara: Basan Matbaacilik Sanayi, 1982), 26–27. This is almost verbatim from Article 35 of the 1961 constitution. The 1979 Constitution of the Islamic Republic of Iran goes one step further by linking the importance of the family to the esteemed position of women. The protection of the family and the rights of women are both guaranteed in Article 21. The Constitution's Preamble, however, discusses the two issues in greater detail. It states the following:

> The family is the fundamental unit of society and the major center for the growth and advancement of man. Compatibility with respect to belief and ideal is the main consideration in the establishment of a family, for the family provides the primary basis for man's development and growth. It is the duty of the Islamic government to provide the necessary facilities for the attainment of this goal. This view of the family unit delivers women from being regarded as an object or as an instrument in the service of consumerism and exploitation. Not only does woman recover thereby her momentous and precious function of motherhood, rearing alert and active human beings, she also becomes the fellow struggler of man in all the different areas of life. Given the weighty responsibilities that woman thus assumes, she is accorded in Islam great value and nobility. (*Constitution of the Islamic Republic of Iran*, Hamid Algar, trans. [Berkeley: Mizan Press, 1980], 22)

27. See especially Sharabi, *Neopatriarchy*; Bill and Springborg, *Politics in the Middle East*, chap. 3; Barakat, *Arab World*, chap. 6; and Rugh, *Family in Contemporary Egypt*.

28. Barakat, *Arab World*, 23.

29. Iliya Harik, "Privatization and Development in Tunisia," in *Privatization and Liberalization in the Middle East,* ed. Iliya Harik and Denis Sullivan (Bloomington: Indiana University Press, 1992), 215.

30. Richards and Waterbury, *Political Economy,* 270.

31. Barakat, *Arab World,* 55–56.

32. Bill and Springborg, *Politics in the Middle East,* 121.

33. Barakat, *Arab World,* 23.

34. For a comprehensive examination of the literature on tribalism in the Middle East, see Richard Tapper, "Anthropologists, Historians, and Tribespeople," and Steven Caton, "Anthropological Theories of Tribe and State Formation in the Middle East: Ideology and the Semiotics of Power," both in Khoury and Kostiner, *Tribes and State Formation.*

35. In "Anthropologists, Historians, and Tribespeople," Tapper maintains that there is a subtle difference between a tribal chieftaincy and a confederacy in terms of their political organization and cohesiveness (p. 69). A chieftaincy, he states, "is a territorially bound collectivity of groups (usually tribal groups) with coordinated and possibly dynastic leadership but with little elaboration of government or stratification of society." However, he defines a confederacy as "a union of tribal groups for political purposes, sometimes an alliance on the basis of imputed common descent (like the Bakhtiyari), usually with central leadership but sometimes without (as among the Yamut Turkmen)—though some would term such uncentralized alliance a coalition."

36. Patai, *Arab Mind,* 77.

37. Sharabi, *Neopatriarchy,* 28.

38. Bassam Tibi, "The Simultaneity of the Unsimultaneous: Old Tribes and Imposed Nation-States in the Modern Middle East," in Khoury and Kostiner, *Tribes and State Formation,* 127.

39. Khoury and Kostiner, "Introduction: Tribes and the Complexities of State Formation in the Middle East," in Khoury and Kostiner, *Tribes and State Formation,* 4.

40. Barakat, *Arab World,* 50–51.

41. Khoury and Kostiner, "Introduction," 5.

42. Ibid., 9.

43. Lois Beck, "Tribes and State in Nineteenth- and Twentieth-Century Iran," in Khoury and Kostiner, *Tribes and State Formation,* 194–95.

44. Barakat, *Arab World,* 52.

45. Patai, *Arab Mind,* 84.

46. Ernest Gellner, "Tribalism and the State in the Middle East," in Khoury and Kostiner, *Tribes and State Formation,* 112.

47. Beck, "Tribes and State," 187.

48. Ibid., 196.

49. Milton Esman and Itamar Rabinovich, "The Study of Ethnic Politics in the Middle East," in *Ethnicity, Pluralism, and the State in the Middle East,* ed. Milton Esman and Itamar Rabinovich (Ithaca, N.Y.: Cornell University Press, 1988), 3.

50. Ibid., 3–4.

51. Rabinovich, "Arab Political Parties: Ideology and Ethnicity," in Esman and Rabinovich, *Ethnicity, Pluralism, and the State,* 156.

52. Hanna Herzog, "Political Ethnicity as a Case of Socially Constructed Reality: The Case of Jews in Israel," in Esman and Rabinovich, *Ethnicity, Pluralism, and the State,* 145.

53. See Thomas L. Friedman, *From Beirut to Jerusalem* (New York: Farrar, Straus and Giroux, 1989), 76–105, for more on this incident and other effects of tribalism and ethnicity on Middle Eastern politics.

54. The suppression of the Shias in Kuwait was the least bloody of all three examples cited here. See, for example, *New York Times,* 9 November 1986, 10. For Iran, see Lois Beck, "Revolutionary Iran and Its Tribal Peoples," *Merip Reports,* May 1980, 14–20. Kanan Makiya, *Cruelty and Silence: War, Tyranny, Uprising, and the Arab World* (New York: Norton, 1993), 135–40 and 159–99, offers firsthand and dramatic evidence of the Iraqi government's various campaigns against the Kurds, Shias, and Iraqi people in general.

55. Esman and Rabinovich, "Study of Ethnic Politics," 22.

56. Patai, *Arab Mind,* 75.

57. Daniel Levine, "Assessing the Impact of Liberation Theology in Latin America," *Review of Politics* 50, no. 2 (Spring 1988): 241–63.

58. See, for example, G.H. Jansen, *Militant Islam* (New York: Harper and Row, 1979).

59. For a concise discussion of the birth of Islam, see Alfred Guillaume, *Islam* (New York: Penguin, 1956), chaps. 1, 2, and 3.

60. Ernest Gellner, *Muslim Society* (Cambridge: Cambridge University Press, 1981), 1.

61. John Esposito, *Islam: The Straight Path* (Oxford: Oxford University Press, 1991), 156–57.

62. Except in Lebanon and Israel, all regimes in the region have declared Islam to be the state religion, and leaders have paid dearly for conduct considered offensive to the faith.

63. Fouad Ajami, *The Arab Predicament: Arab Political Thought and Practice since 1967* (Cambridge: Cambridge University Press, 1981), 176.

64. Sharabi, *Neopatriarchy,* 141.

65. Alexander Cudsi and Ali Dessouki, "Introduction," in *Islam and Power,* ed. Alexander Cudsi and Ali Dessouki (London: Croom Helm, 1981), 7.

66. Gellner, *Muslim Society,* 67–68.

67. In recent years, for example, female university students wearing Islamic dress have been harassed by authorities in Egypt and Turkey.

68. Egypt, of course, is by no means the only Middle Eastern country to have undergone this experience, although it provides a significant case in point. For an account of Egypt since the 1980s, see Hamied Ansari, *Egypt: The Stalled Society* (Albany: SUNY Press, 1986), especially chaps. 8–10.

69. Lawrence A. Hoffman, "Introduction: Land of Blessing and 'Blessings of the Land,'" in *The Land of Israel: Jewish Perspectives,* ed. Lawrence Hoffman (Notre Dame, Ind.: University of Notre Dame Press, 1986), 20. Emphasis added.

70. The political, ideological, and historical contexts within which Jewish and Israeli identities are formulated and expressed can easily lead to their radicalization. See, for example, Ian Lustick, *For the Land and the Lord: Jewish Fundamentalism in Israel* (New York: Council on Foreign Relations, 1988).

71. For a discussion of education in developing countries, see Kamrava, *Politics and Society,* 157–61.

72. Muhammad Hussein Heykal, *Oktobr 1973: Selah wa siyasa* (October 1973: Guns and politics) (Cairo: Al Ahram, 1994).

73. J.P. Nettl, "Ideas, Intellectuals, and Structure of Dissent," in *On Intellectuals,* ed. Philip Rieff (Garden City, N.Y.: Anchor Books, 1970), 89–90.

74. Kamrava, *Politics and Society,* 160–64.

75. Although the purpose here is not to examine those Middle Eastern intellectuals residing in the West, recent polemics make their mention necessary. At the center of the raging debate are those who point to larger historical phenomena as the cause for the "malaise" of the Arabs, and those who place the blame more on the Arabs themselves. Most notable of the first group is Edward Said, whose books *Orientalism* and *Culture and Imperialism* have become leading texts on prejudicial misinterpretations by Western scholars in their studies of the Middle East. On the other side are such scholars as Fouad Ajami and, more recently, Kanan Makiya and Mansour Farhang (each, of course, differing slightly in his arguments). In a bitter critique of Arab intellectuals' silence about the atrocities committed by the Iraqi regime in recent years, Makiya points to "the glaring collective failure of an intelligentsia to evolve a language of rights and democracy to supplement the language of nationalism" (*Cruelty and Silence,* 316). "Often," he writes,

> those very Arab intellectuals who studied in the West turn out to be the worst offenders; they are, therefore the most responsible. They churn out intelligent nationalist ideology inimical to a genuine concern for the human rights of others far better than the Saddam Husseins of this world. Everyone expects propaganda to issue from Ba'athi spokespersons. But, the intellectuals I have been quoting—by virtue of the positions that they occupy—are deemed to be rational and responsible interpreters of the Arab world both to Westerners and to the Arabs themselves, who unfortunately will still look up to an Egyptian teaching at the University of London more than they will to someone teaching at 'Ain Shams University in Cairo. (p. 32)

Makiya's sharp critique has elicited equally pointed, at times personal, responses. Eqbal Ahmad, a Pakistani scholar residing in England, had this to say about Makiya and his latest book:

> Cut off from traditional Muslim values and also having lost his acquired Marxist moorings, he is a man adrift, afflicted by a terminal case of self-love.... With his realizations, dual lives, pseudonymous pretensions, ill-founded hates and self-absorptions, Makiya is a mess, just the type the

media would find suited to personify the good Arab.... (Ahmad, "The Question of Iraq," *Nation,* 9 August 1993, 182)

For more on this debate and replies from Makiya and Ahmad, see the *Nation,* 8 November 1993, 518, 544–48. See also Mouin Rabbani, "Unmasking Makiya: Iraq and Arab Intellectuals," *Third World Quarterly* 15, no. 2 (1994):342–50; and As'ad AbuKhalil, "Arab Intellectuals on Trial," *Middle East Journal* 47, no. 4 (Autumn 1993):695–706.

76. AbuKhalil, "Arab Intellectuals," 706. This quotation should not be taken out of the larger context of the article, which is a critical review of Makiya's book cited above. For a brief account of two noted Iranian intellectuals, see Asghar Fathi, "Communication Strategies for Social Change in Iran: Kasravi and Shariati," paper presented at the annual meeting of the Middle East Studies Association of North America, Phoenix, Ariz., 19–22 November 1994.

77. For an insightful account of the intellectual mood of the Middle East after 1967, see Ajami, *Arab Predicament.*

78. Kamrava, *Revolution in Iran,* 67.

79. For a discussion of the writings of Egypt's Heykal and Iran's Shariati, see Charles Smith, "The Intellectual, Islam, and Modernization: Heykal and Shariati," in *Comparing Muslim Societies,* ed. Juan R.I. Cole (Ann Arbor: University of Michigan Press, 1992), 163–92.

80. See Hourani, *History of the Arab Peoples,* 302–9.

81. The idea of a contemporary *nahda* is especially expounded on in the writings of Hasan Hanfi. See Issa Boullata, *Trends and Issues in Contemporary Arab Thought* (Albany: SUNY Press, 1990), 40–45.

82. For an analysis of the writings of such Arab intellectuals as Sharabi, Anwar Abu Malik, Jalal Amin, and Samir Amin, see ibid., chap. 4. For a thorough study of the life and writings of Naguib Mahfouz, see Rasheed el-Enany, *Naguib Mahfouz: The Pursuit of Meaning* (London: Routledge, 1993). See also Matti Moosa, *The Early Novels of Naguib Mahfouz: Images of Modern Egypt* (Gainesville: University Press of Florida, 1994). For a personal account of Mahfouz's life, see Milton Viorst, *Sandcastles: The Arabs in Search of the Modern World* (New York: Knopf, 1994).

83. In March 1995, the Turkish government accused Kemal of violating the Anti-Terror Law through his writings and, as of this writing, was seeking to imprison him for his pro-Kurdish sentiments. *New York Times,* 14 March 1995, A4.

84. Most of these books deal with abstract philosophy, Islamic history, and other nonpolitical topics. Among the plethora of published literature are those that touch on sensitive social and cultural issues, and at times even political ones, although they are disguised through the use of allegory and allusion. See, for example, Soraya Sullivan, trans., *Stories by Iranian Women since the Revolution* (Austin: Center for Middle Eastern Studies, University of Texas, 1991).

85. See Boullata, *Trends and Issues,* 150–51.

86. Eric Davis, "Theorizing Statecraft and Social Change in Arab Oil-Producing Countries," in *Statecraft in the Middle East: Oil, Historical Memory, and Popular Culture,* ed. Eric Davis and Nicolas Gavrielides (Miami: Florida International University Press, 1991), 29–30.

87. Masoud Kheirabadi, *Iranian Cities: Formation and Development* (Austin: University of Texas Press, 1991), 78–79.

88. W.G. Miller, "Political Organization in Iran," 163–65.

89. It is no coincidence that most of these institutions are segregated along gender lines, with *dowrehs* and *hammams* being largely the domains of activity for women and the rest dominated by men. For more on this social segregation, see chap. 5.

90. Kheirabadi, *Iranian Cities,* 65.

91. For an in-depth look at the role and functions of mosques, and of preachers specifically, in Jordan, see Richard Antoun, *Muslim Preachers in the Modern World: A Jordanian Case Study in Comparative Perspective* (Princeton: Princeton University Press, 1989).

92. Ibid., 227.

Chapter 3. Social Classes

1. Quoted in Tom Bottomore, ed., *A Dictionary of Marxist Thought* (London: Blackwell, 1983), 209.

2. Karl Marx, *The Communist Manifesto* (Chicago: Gateway Editions, 1987), 13.

3. Berch Berberouglu, *Political Sociology: A Comparative/Historical Approach* (Dix Hills, N.Y.: General Hall, 1990), 2–3.

4. Roger Owen, *State, Power, and Politics in the Making of the Modern Middle East* (London: Routledge, 1992), 43.

5. James Bill and Robert Springborg, *Politics in the Middle East,* 4th ed. (New York: HarperCollins, 1994), 132. For a concise analysis of the role of class, especially of the working classes, in the Middle East, see Zachary Lockman, "Introduction," in *Workers and Working Classes in the Middle East: Struggles, Histories, Historiographies,* ed. Zachary Lockman (Albany: SUNY Press, 1994), xi–xxxi. See also John Waterbury, "Twilight of the State Bourgeoisie?" *International Journal of Middle East Studies* 23, no. 1 (February 1991):1–17.

6. Halim Barakat, *The Arab World: Society, Culture, and State* (Berkeley: University of California Press, 1993), 20–21.

7. See, for example, Jacqueline Ismael, *Kuwait: Dependency and Class in a Rentier State* (Gainesville: University Press of Florida, 1993), chap. 5, especially 102–11.

8. Alan Richards and John Waterbury, *A Political Economy of the Middle East: State, Class, and Economic Development* (Boulder, Colo.: Westview, 1990), 401.

9. Sami Zubaida, *Islam, the People, and the State: Political Ideas and Movements in the Middle East* (London: I.B. Tauris, 1993), 87. John Waterbury, one of the most astute scholars of Middle Eastern economies, also makes

the following observation regarding a social class he calls the "state bourgeoisie": "One finds a class defined by formal position, not by collective action. It is a class without observable solidarity but one whose members have many options, including self-liquidation. It has not collectively opposed policies...." (Waterbury, "Twilight of the State Bourgeoisie?" 14)

10. Hisham Sharabi, *Neopatriarchy: A Theory of Distorted Change in Arab Society* (Oxford: Oxford University Press, 1988), 75.

11. Admittedly, this is a poor typology because it includes a number of in-between cases. Broadly speaking, however, the economies of Iran, Turkey, Iraq, Syria, Lebanon, Jordan, Egypt, Tunisia, Morocco, and Algeria are more integrated and less overtly dependent on oil as the sole source of revenue, although Iran, Iraq, and Algeria would face economic paralysis without oil revenues. In contrast, Saudi Arabia, Kuwait, Bahrain, Qatar, the UAE, Oman, and Libya rely almost entirely on petroleum as their economic mainstay. Some of these countries have in recent decades made attempts at economic diversification, with sizable agricultural projects in Libya and Saudi Arabia as examples. Nevertheless, for the time being at least, their class structures reflect the economies' long dependence on the export of petroleum.

12. I have deliberately not used such terms as "bourgeoisie" and "petite bourgeoisie" in order to avoid possible confusion over meaning and exact definition. For an analysis similar to the one here, see Barakat, *Arab World,* 63–96.

13. For an examination of urban bias, see Mehran Kamrava, *Politics and Society in the Third World* (London: Routledge, 1993), 80–81.

14. Barakat, *Arab World,* 87.

15. Bill and Springborg, *Politics in the Middle East,* 121. Waterbury discusses at great length the position and attributes of the "state bourgeoisie," which, he argues, is "merely the proxy for a dominant or would-be dominant class. It helps consolidate the interests of that class, and eventually merges with it through the privatization or plunder of the state sector" (Waterbury, "Twilight of the State Bourgeoisie?" 6).

16. Until recently, physicians and engineers in a number of Middle Eastern societies were also considered part of the upper-middle class, and in many cases they still are. In countries with ever-increasing numbers of university graduates entering the workforce and competing for jobs, and in those with mounting economic difficulties, such as Egypt, Iran, and Algeria, many of the younger physicians and especially engineers have had difficulty bringing their expectations in tune with reality. And despite the social prestige accorded them by the rest of society, their purchasing power places most doctors and engineers closer to the middle, rather than the upper-middle, class.

17. Bill and Springborg, *Politics in the Middle East,* 124.

18. For an account of the role of *bazaari* merchants in the Iranian revolution, see Mehran Kamrava, *Revolution in Iran: The Roots of Turmoil* (London: Routledge, 1990), 111–13, 121–22.

19. See, for example, Tim Niblock, "International and Domestic Factors in the Economic Liberalization Process in Arab Countries," in *Economic and*

Political Liberalization in the Middle East, ed. Tim Niblock and Emma Murphy (London: British Academic Press, 1993), 55–87.

20. Raphael Patai, *The Arab Mind* (New York: Charles Scribner's Sons, 1973), 105.

21. Andrea Rugh, *Family in Contemporary Egypt* (Syracuse, N.Y.: Syracuse University Press, 1984), 50.

22. See, for example, Barakat, *Arab World,* 91–94; and Richards and Waterbury, *Political Economy,* 288.

23. Valentine Moghadam, "Industrial Development, Culture, and Working Class Politics: A Case Study of Tabrizi Industrial Workers in the Iranian Revolution," *International Sociology* 2, no. 2 (June 1987):165.

24. Economic activities in the urban areas of the Third World are found in the formal and informal sectors. Formal economic activities (e.g., bureaucratic, factory, or industrial jobs) involve formal procedures and institutions, and therefore a higher level of technical or administrative know-how is needed. Conversely, there are kinds of economic activity that are minimally or completely informal, ranging from running a family-owned store to street vending and working as servants and maids; it is often the lumpen proletariat that is employed in the informal economic sector. For a more detailed discussion, see Kamrava, *Politics and Society in the Third World,* 50–57.

25. See, for example, the various chapters in Lockman, *Workers and Working Classes.*

26. Lockman, "Introduction," xxix.

27. See Feroz Ahmad, "The Development of Working Class Consciousness in Turkey," in Lockman, *Workers and Working Classes,* 158–59.

28. Mansoor Moaddel, "Class Struggle in Postrevolutionary Iran," *International Journal of Middle East Studies* 23, no. 3 (August 1991):326.

29. David Seddon, "Austerity Protests in Response to Economic Liberalization in the Middle East," in Niblock and Murphy, eds., *Economic and Political Liberalization,* 88–100.

30. Algeria's deviation is caused by the steady departure of much of the urban-based French community during the years following the country's 1954–62 revolution.

31. An interesting account of the life of the underclass in the Middle East can be found in Unni Wikan, *Life among the Poor in Cairo,* trans. Ann Henning (London: Tavistock, 1980).

32. Sharabi, *Neopatriarchy,* 23.

33. Richards and Waterbury, *Political Economy,* 414.

34. For more on the economic slowdown during the 1980s and its effect on the various social classes in the Middle East, see Seddon, "Austerity Protests," 88–113.

35. A look at the population sizes of other Middle Eastern countries is quite revealing: Iran, 56 million; Iraq, 19 million; Egypt, 55 million; Algeria, 26 million; and Morocco, 25 million; Syria and Jordan, with populations of 12 million and 3 million respectively, have relatively few natural resources and insufficiently developed industrial infrastructures. All statistics are from Gregory

Thomas Kurian, ed., *Encyclopedia of the Third World,* vols. 1–3, 4th ed. (New York: Facts on File, 1992).

36. For more on the rentier state, see Hootan Shambayati, "The Rentier State, Interest Groups, and the Paradox of Autonomy: State and Business in Turkey and Iran," *Comparative Politics* 26, no. 3 (April 1994): 307–31.

37. See Rosemarie Said Zahlan, *The Making of the Modern Gulf States: Kuwait, Bahrain, Qatar, the United Arab Emirates, and Oman* (London: Unwin Hyman, 1989), chaps. 1 and 3.

38. Ibid., 88.

39. Ibid., 79. It is telling that after the Gulf War, many Kuwaitis equated the regaining of national sovereignty with the reestablishment of the al-Sabahs to power as well as the military defeat of the invaders.

40. For more on the *majles,* see F. Gregory Gause III, *Oil Monarchies: Domestic and Security Challenges in the Arab Gulf States* (New York: Council on Foreign Relations, 1994), 25–27.

41. Michael Fields, *The Merchants: The Big Business Families of Saudi Arabia and the Gulf States* (Woodstock, N.Y.: Overlook Press, 1985), 105.

42. Ibid., 109–11.

43. Ibid., 101–2.

44. Khaldoun Hasan al-Naqeeb, *Society and State in the Gulf and the Arab Peninsula: A Different Perspective,* trans. L.M. Kenny (London: Routledge, 1990), 103.

45. Fields, *Merchants,* 103.

46. Ismael, *Kuwait,* 129–30.

47. Zahlan, *Making of the Modern Gulf States,* 83.

48. Fields, *Merchants,* 101.

49. Ismael, *Kuwait,* 103–4.

50. Fields, *Merchants,* 102.

51. Zahlan, *Making of the Modern Gulf States,* 96. For an account of some of the businesses in which Saudi princes engage, see Fields, *Merchants,* 112–15.

52. See, for example, "The Merchant of Debt," *The Economist* 302 (7 February 1987): 77; and "Mr. Fix-it in a Fix," *The Economist* 311 (22 April 1989): 76.

53. Al-Naqeeb, *Society and State,* 9–10.

54. Fields, *Merchants,* 11. This book offers a thorough, insightful, and painstakingly researched account of most merchant houses in the region.

55. Ibid., 7. According to Fields, some of the most noteworthy and wealthy Gulf merchant families are the following: Alireza (Jeddah); Alqhanim (Kuwait); Olayan (Saudi Arabia); Juffali (Saudi Arabia); Sultan (Oman and Kuwait); Alqosaibi (Dammam, Riyadh, and Bahrain); Ahmed Hamad Alqosaibi (Alkhobar); Darwish (Qatar); and Kanoo (Bahrain and Dammam).

56. Saad Eddin Ibrahim, *The New Arab Social Order: A Study of the Social Impact of Oil Wealth* (Boulder, Colo.: Westview, 1982), 8.

57. Ismael, *Kuwait,* 107.

58. Ibrahim, *New Arab Social Order,* 8.

59. Kamrava, *Politics and Society,* 46–47.

60. Ibrahim, *New Arab Social Order,* 8.

61. Ismael, *Kuwait,* 106.

62. Ibid., 105.

63. See al-Naqeeb, *Society and State,* 128–32.

64. See Laurie Brand, *Palestinians in the Arab World: Institution Building and the Search for State* (New York: Columbia University Press, 1988).

65. Aziz Haidar, "The Different Levels of Palestinian Ethnicity," in *Ethnicity, Pluralism, and the State in the Middle East,* ed. Milton Esman and Itamar Rabinovich (Ithaca, N.Y.: Cornell University Press, 1988), 98.

66. Ismael, *Kuwait,* 118.

67. Ibid., 119.

68. Gil Feiler, "Migration and Recession: Arab Labor Mobility in the Middle East, 1982–89," *Population and Development Review* 17, no. 1 (March 1991):135.

69. Gil Feiler, "Palestinian Employment Prospects," *Middle East Journal* 47, no. 4 (Autumn 1993):635–36.

70. Feiler, "Migration and Recession," 138.

71. For a thorough and highly informed analysis of migrant laborers in the Gulf countries, see Roger Owen, *Migrant Workers in the Gulf* (London: Minority Rights Group, 1985). The updated report (1992) examines the aftermath of the Gulf War on the laborers; see Nicholas Van Hear, *Update: Migrant Workers in the Gulf* (London: Minority Rights Group, 1992).

72. Feiler, "Palestinian Employment Prospects," 639–40.

73. Van Hear, *Update,* 3.

74. According to Van Hear, the migrants added 8 percent to Jordan's population and 10 percent to its labor force; Yemen's population swelled by 7 percent and its labor force by 15 percent; Egypt received up to 700,000 returnees and lost an estimated $1 billion in remittances in 1990 and 1991; and some 54,000 Palestinians were believed to have returned to the occupied territories (ibid., 2–3).

75. Brand, *Palestinians in the Arab World,* 108.

76. Feiler, "Migration and Recession," 136.

77. Mostafa Nagi, "Migration of Asian Workers to the Arab Gulf: Policy Determinants and Consequences," *Journal of South Asian and Middle Eastern Studies* 9, no. 3 (Spring 1986):22.

78. Feiler, "Palestinian Employment Prospects," 650. Although the situation in the occupied territories was far from conducive to a wholesale repatriation of Palestinians from the diaspora, in October 1995 Colonel Qaddafi forcibly evicted a number of Palestinians living and working in Libya for return to the West Bank or the Gaza Strip. (Qaddafi's real motive was to complicate the ongoing Palestinian-Israeli negotiations.)

79. Richards and Waterbury, *Political Economy,* 149–51. These campaigns have had varying degrees of success. In one form or another, initiatives toward land reform started in 1945 in Turkey, in 1952 and 1961 in Egypt, in 1958 in Iraq, in 1958 and 1963 in Syria, and in 1962 in Iran.

80. Colbert C. Held, *Middle East Patterns: Places, Peoples, and Politics* (Boulder, Colo.: Westview, 1989), 372.

81. Bill and Springborg make the following observation about Saudi Arabia's advances in agriculture:

> While Saudi Arabia has proven to the world that it can grow wheat, it has done so at tremendous monetary and ecological cost to itself. According to an informed observer, "What it boils down to is the Saudis are exporting their money and exporting their water." He might have added that the massive subsidies further enriched Saudi private investors and the multinational agricultural companies employed by them. (Bill and Springborg, *Politics in the Middle East*, 431)

82. For more on *dhow* construction and the pearl industries, see Ismael, *Kuwait*, 61–66.

83. Ibrahim, *New Arab Social Order*, 6–7.

84. Ibid., 6.

85. Barakat, *Arab World*, 57.

86. Leonard Binder, *In a Moment of Enthusiasm: Political Power and the Second Stratum in Egypt* (Chicago: University of Chicago Press, 1978), 20.

87. Barakat, *Arab World*, 57.

88. Ibid., 56.

89. Kamrava, *Revolution in Iran*, 100.

90. Richards and Waterbury, *Political Economy*, 402.

91. Ibid., 403, 408.

92. Binder, *In a Moment of Enthusiasm*, 28.

93. Nicholas Hopkins, "Clan and Class in Two Arab Villages," in *Peasants and Politics in the Modern Middle East*, ed. Farhad Kazemi and John Waterbury (Miami: University Press of Florida, 1991), 259.

94. Richards and Waterbury, *Political Economy*, 404.

95. Bill and Springborg, *Politics in the Middle East*, 125–26.

96. John Waterbury, "Peasants Defy Categorization (as Well as Landlords and States)," in Kazemi and Waterbury, *Peasants and Politics*, 3.

97. See, for example, Kazemi and Waterbury, *Peasants and Politics*, especially Kazemi, "Peasant Uprisings in Twentieth-Century Iran, Iraq, and Turkey," 101–21.

98. Mehran Kamrava, *Revolutionary Politics* (Westport, Conn.: Praeger, 1992), 29–32.

99. Donald Quataert, "Rural Unrest in the Ottoman Empire, 1830–1914," in Kazemi and Waterbury, *Peasants and Politics*, 40.

100. Kazemi, "Peasant Uprisings," 101.

101. For Oman's Dhofar revolution, see Zahlan, *Making of the Modern Gulf States*, 112–14. For the Polisario movement, see Anthony G. Pazzanita, "Morocco versus Polisario: A Political Interpretation," *Journal of Modern African Studies* 32, no. 2 (June 1994):265–78.

102. Kamrava, *Revolutionary Politics*, 28–29.

103. Waterbury, "Peasants Defy Categorization," 5.

104. Kazemi, "Peasant Uprisings," 104.

105. Waterbury, "Peasants Defy Categorization," 13.

106. The word *bedouin* or "desert dweller" is often used in reference to the nomadic inhabitant of the desert in Arab countries. It is not, however, used to refer to the same group in the non-Arab countries of the Middle East, namely, Iran and Turkey. Thus the terms "tribal nomads" and "bedouins" are used interchangeably in this section and refer to the same social class.

107. Ernest Gellner makes an interesting observation about Somalia:

> Independent Somalia proscribed tribal identification and made it illegal for men to proclaim or inquire after it. Hence men would ask or tell each other about each other's ex, meaning ex-clan, the units themselves being officially held no longer to exist. (Somalia is not unique in this respect.) So a Somali referring to his ex did not mean his ex-wife. This usage became so widespread that authorities also proscribed the use of the term ex, because it had virtually come to mean "clan." When an anthropologist then enquired whether one could ask a man about his "ex-Ex," he was invited to keep his jokes to himself. (Gellner, *Muslim Societies* [Cambridge: Cambridge University Press, 1981], 62)

108. Barakat, *Arab World,* 50.

109. T. Firouzan, "Darbare-ye tarkib va sazman-e eelat va ashayer dar Iran" (Concerning the composition and organization of tribes and clans in Iran), in *Eelat va ashayer* (Tribes and clans) (Tehran: Agah Organization, 1362/1983), 8–9.

Chapter 4. Social Change

1. The study of social change was quite popular among scholars in the 1960s and early 1970s, especially among modernization theorists, but it has fallen out of fashion in recent years. Yet Third World countries continue to experience social change, and its effects still have profound consequences for both their social and political spheres. Understanding Third World societies, particularly those of the Middle East, requires careful attention to this important phenomenon. For some of the more significant earlier works on the subject, see S.N. Eisenstadt, *Modernization: Protest and Change* (Englewood Cliffs, N.J.: Prentice Hall, 1966); S.N. Eisenstadt, ed., *Comparative Perspectives on Social Change* (Boston: Little, Brown, 1968); and Amitai Etzioni and Eva Etzioni, eds., *Social Change: Sources, Patterns, and Consequences* (New York: Basic Books, 1964). For more recent works on the subject, see, for example, Pierre Bourdieu and James Coleman, eds., *Social Theory for a Changing Society* (Boulder, Colo.: Westview, 1991); R. Alan Hedley, *Making a Living: Technology and Change* (New York: HarperCollins, 1992); and Daniel Chirot, *How Societies Change* (Thousand Oaks, Calif.: Pine Forge, 1994).

2. Hermann Strasser and Susan Randall, *An Introduction to the Theories of Social Change* (London: Routledge and Kegan Paul, 1981), 23.

3. For a full discussion of social change, see Mehran Kamrava, *Politics and Society in the Third World* (London: Routledge, 1993), chap. 4.

4. Wilbert Moore, "Social Change," in *International Encyclopedia of the Social Sciences,* ed. David Sills, vol. 14 (New York: Crowell, Collier and Macmillan, 1968), 366.

5. Ibid., 365.

6. For a more historical account of the spread and ramifications of social change, see Daniel Chirot, *Social Change in the Modern Era* (New York: Harcourt Brace Jovanovich, 1986).

7. S.N. Eisenstadt, *Revolutions and the Transformation of Societies: A Comparative Study of Civilizations* (New York: Free Press, 1978), 1.

8. Ibid., 1–2.

9. Mehran Kamrava, *Revolutionary Politics* (Westport, Conn.: Praeger, 1992), 114–17.

10. For some of the more recent works on the subject, see Edmund Burke III, ed., *Struggle and Survival in the Modern Middle East* (Berkeley: University of California Press, 1993); Hisham Sharabi, *Neopatriarchy: A Theory of Distorted Change in Arab Society* (Oxford: Oxford University Press, 1988); Halim Barakat, *The Arab World: Society, Culture, and State* (Berkeley: University of California Press, 1993), esp. chaps. 6, 7, and 8; James Bill and Robert Springborg, *Politics in the Middle East,* 4th ed. (New York: HarperCollins, 1994), chap. 1; and Valentine Moghadam, *Modernizing Women: Gender and Social Change in the Middle East* (Boulder, Colo.: Lynne Reinner, 1993). Two of the classic works on the subject are Daniel Lerner, *The Passing of Traditional Society: Modernizing the Middle East* (London: Free Press, 1956); and Manfred Halpern, *The Politics of Social Change in the Middle East* (Princeton: Princeton University Press, 1964).

11. Roger Owen, "The Arab Oil Economy: Present Structure and Future Prospects," in *Arab Society: Continuity and Change,* ed. Samih Farsoun (London: Croom Helm, 1985), 17.

12. Glen Balfour-Paul, "Kuwait, Qatar, and the United Arab Emirates: Political and Social Evolution," in *Arabia and the Gulf: From Traditional Society to Modern States,* ed. Ian Richard Netton (London: Croom Helm, 1986), 158.

13. Owen, "Arab Oil Economy," 17.

14. Ibid., 19.

15. Alan Richards and John Waterbury, *A Political Economy of the Middle East: State, Class, and Economic Development* (Boulder, Colo.: Westview, 1990), 238.

16. Ibid., 406.

17. Owen, "Arab Oil Economy," 19.

18. Ibid., 18. For a basic survey of Qatar's economic development in the 1970s, see Zuhair Ahmad Nafi, *Economic and Social Development in Qatar* (London: Francis Pinter, 1983).

19. Pradeep Bhargava, *Political Economy of the Gulf States* (New Delhi: South Asia Publishers, 1989), 92–93.

20. John Dixon, "Social Security in the Middle East," in *Social Welfare in the Middle East,* ed. John Dixon (London: Croom Helm, 1987), 174. See other chapters of this book for discussions of social welfare policies in Egypt, Israel,

Jordan, Kuwait, and Turkey.

21. Richards and Waterbury, *Political Economy,* 186.

22. Ibid., 187.

23. For a detailed discussion of the "political economy of structural adjustments," see ibid., 227–37.

24. Paul Jabber, "Forces of Change in the Middle East," *Middle East Journal* 42, no. 1 (Winter 1988):10.

25. Ibid., 9.

26. For more on urbanization in the Third World, see Kamrava, *Politics and Society,* 71–105.

27. For a thorough and insightful (although outdated) account of urbanization in the Persian Gulf countries up to the 1980s, see Michael Bonine, "The Urbanization of the Persian Gulf Nations," in *The Persian Gulf States: A General Survey,* ed. Alvin Cottell (Baltimore: Johns Hopkins University Press, 1980), 225–78.

28. V.F. Costello, *Urbanization in the Middle East* (Cambridge: Cambridge University Press, 1977), 33.

29. Bonine, "Urbanization of Persian Gulf Nations," 275.

30. Barakat, *Arab World,* 62–63.

31. Lerner, *Passing of Traditional Society,* 79.

32. Sharabi, for example, sees imperialism as a direct "contributor" to the phenomenon of neopatriarchy (discussed later in this chapter). He writes: "Strictly speaking, all subsequent modernization unfolded with relations of *subordination* and *dependency;* under *direct* European domination, modernization became a function of the system of colonial rule and imperial domination." See Sharabi, *Neopatriarchy,* 61.

33. On a recent visit to Egypt, an associate of mine asked a villager to name three of his heroes, and the young man replied, "Saddam Hussein, Muammar Qaddafi, and Bob Marley."

34. Walid Kazziha, "Egypt in the Balance," in *Contemporary Egypt: Through Egyptian Eyes,* ed. Charles Tripp (London: Routledge, 1993), 123.

35. Although the first elections since 1967 were held in November 1989, it was not until 1992 that martial law and the ban on political parties were lifted. See Michael Collins Dunn, "Islamist Parties in Democratizing States: A Look at Jordan and Yemen," *Middle East Policy* 2, no. 2 (1993):16–27.

36. For a journalistic account of religiously inspired violence in the Middle East in the 1980s, see Robin Wright, *Sacred Rage: The Wrath of Militant Islam* (New York: Simon and Schuster, 1986). See also Michael Collins Dunn, "Fundamentalism in Egypt," *Middle East Policy* 2, no. 3 (1993):68–77.

37. Trevor Mostyn, "The Media of Communication," in *Cambridge Encyclopedia of the Middle East and North Africa,* ed. Trevor Mostyn (Cambridge: Cambridge University Press, 1988), 149–50.

38. William Rugh, *The Arab Press* (Syracuse, N.Y.: Syracuse University Press, 1987), 7.

39. Ibid., 20.

40. Mostyn, "Media of Communication," 153.

41. The information concerning the popularity of the Michael Jackson interview in Morocco was relayed to the author by Natalya Hicks. As the examples offered here demonstrate, foreign cultural influence has usually meant *American* cultural influence, and the reach of American culture has by no means been limited to the Middle East alone. For more on the globalization of American culture, see *World Press Review* 39, no. 11 (November 1992).

42. Douglas Boyd, *Broadcasting in the Arab World: A Survey of the Electronic Media in the Middle East,* 2d ed. (Ames: Iowa State University Press, 1993), 135. In Saudi Arabia, it must be noted, television and radio programming are quite restricted and heavily censored in order to conform to official and religious guidelines. According to government directives, the following scenes must be censored from all imported programs before they can be shown on Saudi television:

1. Scenes which arouse sexual excitement
2. Women who appear indecently dressed, in dance scenes, or in scenes that show overt acts of love
3. Women who appear in athletic games or sports
4. Alcoholic drinks or anything connected with drinking
5. Derogatory reference to any of the "heavenly Religions"
6. Treatment of other countries with praise, satire, or contempt
7. Reference to Zionism
8. Material meant to expose monarchy
9. All immoral scenes
10. References to betting or gambling
11. Excessive violence

(Quoted in ibid., 158–59. This book contains invaluable information concerning broadcasting in various Arab countries.)

43. Ibid., 5–6.
44. *New York Times,* 13 April 1993, A4; and 23 April 1993, A6.
45. Lerner, *Passing of Traditional Society,* 50.
46. Halpern, *Politics of Social Change,* 70.
47. Hisham Sharabi, "The Dialectics of Patriarchy in Arab Society," in Farsoun, *Arab Society,* 88.
48. Ibid., 89.
49. Sharabi, *Neopatriarchy,* 7.
50. Sharabi, "Dialectics of Patriarchy," 90.
51. Lerner, *Passing of Traditional Society,* 83.
52. Sharabi, *Neopatriarchy,* 6.
53. Ralph Magnus, "Societies and Social Change in the Persian Gulf," in Cottrell, *Persian Gulf States,* 395.
54. Khaldoun Hasan al-Naqeeb, *Society and State in the Gulf and Arab Peninsula: A Different Perspective,* trans. L.M. Kenny (London: Routledge, 1990), 6.
55. Magnus, "Societies and Social Change," 393.
56. See B.R. Pridham, "Oman: Change or Continuity?" in Netton, *Arabia*

and the Gulf, 132–55.

57. Quoted in Balfour-Paul, "Kuwait, Qatar, and the United Arab Emirates," 168.

58. Doreen Hinchcliffe, "Women and the Law in the United Arab Emirates," in Netton, *Arabia and the Gulf,* 241.

59. Ibid., 239.

60. Magnus, "Societies and Social Change," 396.

61. Boyd, *Broadcasting in the Arab World,* 143–44.

62. J.S. Birks and C.A. Sinclair, "Economic and Social Implications of Current Development in the Arab Gulf: The Oriental Connection," in *Social and Economic Development in the Arab Gulf,* ed. Tim Niblock (London: Croom Helm, 1980), 151.

63. Roger Webster, "Human Resources in the Gulf," in Netton, *Arabia and the Gulf,* 194.

64. Birks and Sinclair, "Economic and Social Implications," 151.

65. Magnus, "Societies and Social Change," 391.

66. Balfour-Paul, "Kuwait, Qatar, and the United Arab Emirates," 164–65.

67. Pridham, "Oman," 139. From this total, more than 5,000 teachers were from Egypt.

68. Magnus, "Societies and Social Change," 386.

69. Hinchcliffe, "Women and the Law," 239.

70. Donald Cole, "Pastoral Nomads in a Rapidly Changing Economy: The Case of Saudi Arabia," in Niblock, *Social and Economic Development,* 115–16.

71. Ibid., 118–19.

72. Al-Naqeeb, *Society and State,* 125–26.

73. Ibid., 128.

74. Pridham, "Oman," 132.

75. Joel Migdal, *Strong Societies and Weak States: State-Society Relations and State Capabilities in the Third World* (Princeton: Princeton University Press, 1988).

76. See Bill and Springborg, *Politics in the Middle East,* 187–90.

77. Ibid., 183.

78. Roger Owen, *State, Power, and Politics in the Making of the Modern Middle East* (London: Routledge, 1992), 27. For a concise and lucid account of Atatürk's career and policies, see Elie Kedourie, *Politics in the Middle East* (Oxford: Oxford University Press, 1992), 93–108.

79. Richards and Waterbury, *Political Economy,* 187.

80. Anthony Parsons, "Hashemite Iraq and Pahlavi Iran," in Netton, *Arabia and the Gulf,* 114–15. See also Mehran Kamrava, *The Political History of Modern Iran: From Tribalism to Theocracy* (Westport, Conn.: Praeger, 1992), 55; and idem, *Revolution in Iran: The Roots of Turmoil* (London: Routledge, 1990), 97–100.

81. See Mohammad Reza Pahlavi, *Answer to History* (New York: Stein and Day, 1980), 193–94.

82. Moghadam, *Modernizing Women*, 22.

83. Mehran Kamrava, *Revolutionary Politics* (Westport, Conn.: Praeger, 1992), 8–9, 77–78.

84. In revolutions that have a strong economic and class component, as in the major ones in Russia, China, Vietnam, and to a lesser extent in Cuba, a "cultural revolution" often entails the eradication of all social strata that the government brands "counterrevolutionary."

85. John Ruedy, *Modern Algeria: The Origins and Development of a Nation* (Bloomington: Indiana University Press, 1992), 224.

86. For a brief yet comprehensive statistical account of population growth in the Middle East, see Abdel R. Omran and Farzaneh Roudi, *The Middle East Population Puzzle* (Washington, D.C.: Population Reference Bureau, 1993).

87. Nur Vergin, "Social Change and the Family in Turkey," *Current Anthropology* 26, no. 5 (December 1985):574.

88. See Fahed al-Thakeb, "The Arab Family and Modernity: Evidence from Kuwait," *Current Anthropology* 26, no. 5 (December 1985):567; and Djamchid Behnam, "The Muslim Family and the Modern World: Papers from an International Symposium, The Tunis Conference," *Current Anthropology* 26, no. 5 (December 1985):556.

89. Behnam, "Muslim Family and the Modern World, 555–56.

90. One of the most insightful treatments of women in the Middle East is Moghadam's *Modernizing Women*. Some other publications on the subject include Judith Tucker, ed., *Arab Women: Old Boundaries, New Frontiers* (Bloomington: Indiana University Press, 1993); Nikki Keddie and Beth Baron, eds., *Women in Middle Eastern History: Shifting Boundaries in Sex and Gender* (New Haven: Yale University Press, 1991); and Deniz Kandiyoti, ed., *Women, Islam, and the State* (Philadelphia: Temple University Press, 1991). See also Soraya Altorki, *Women in Saudi Arabia: Ideology and Behavior among the Elite* (New York: Columbia University Press, 1986).

91. Moghadam, *Modernizing Women*, 145.

92. Ibid., 41.

93. Maxine Molyneux, "The Law, the State, and Socialist Policies with Regard to Women: The Case of the People's Democratic Republic of Yemen, 1967–1990," in Kandiyoti, *Women, Islam, and the State*, 41.

94. Moghadam, *Modernizing Women*, 58–59.

95. For more on the position of women in the former PDRY, see Molyneux, "The Law, the State, and Socialist Policies," 237–71.

96. Moghadam, *Modernizing Women*, 33–34.

97. Mervat Hatem, "Egypt's Middle Class in Crisis: The Sexual Division of Labor," *Middle East Journal* 42, no. 3 (Summer 1988):416–17, 419.

98. Moghadam, *Modernizing Women*, 83–84.

99. See, for example, Guity Nashat, ed., *Women and Revolution in Iran* (Boulder, Colo.: Westview, 1983).

100. For an account of women's participation in the Palestinian *intifada* see Philippa Strum, *The Women Are Marching: The Second Sex and the Palestinian Revolution* (Chicago: Lawrence Hill Books, 1992).

101. Quoted in Bouthaina Shaaban, *Both Right and Left Handed: Arab Women Talk about Their Lives* (Bloomington: Indiana University Press, 1988), 92.

102. Strum, *Women Are Marching,* 1.

Chapter 5. Popular Culture

1. Maxine Rodinson, *The Arabs,* trans. Arthur Goldhammer (Chicago: University of Chicago Press, 1979), 12.

2. For a concise account of attempts at fostering Pan-Arab unity, see Roger Owen, *State, Power, and Politics in the Making of the Modern Middle East* (London: Routledge, 1992), 81–107.

3. In an insightful essay on popular culture in the Middle East, Sami Zubaida points to the historical processes of Arabization and Islamization as central unifying elements in the culture of the region. See his *Islam, the People, and the State* (London: I.B. Tauris, 1993), 101. While I agree with the overall premise of Zubaida's thesis, I would argue that the additional elements mentioned here perpetuate, as much as possible, a common, living cultural heritage in the Middle East.

4. See Ernest Gellner, "Islam and Marxism: Some Comparisons," *International Affairs* 67, no. 1 (1991):1–6.

5. Bassam Tibi, *Islam and the Cultural Accommodation of Social Change,* trans. Clare Krojzl (Boulder, Colo.: Westview, 1990), 2.

6. Ernest Gellner, "A Pendulum Swing Theory of Islam," in *Sociology of Religion,* ed. Ronald Robertson (New York: Penguin, 1969), 127.

7. Tibi, *Islam and Cultural Accommodation,* 9.

8. Max Thornburg, *People and Policy in the Middle East* (New York: Norton, 1964), 49.

9. Ernest Gellner, *Muslim Society* (Cambridge: Cambridge University Press, 1981), 2.

10. Tibi, *Islam and Cultural Accommodation,* 51–52.

11. *Dar al-Islam* is the "abode of Islam," while *Dar al-Harb,* where most Muslims do not live, is the "abode of war."

12. See Hamid Enayat, *Modern Islamic Political Thought* (London: Macmillan, 1982), 18–51.

13. Andrea Rugh, *Family in Contemporary Egypt* (Syracuse, N.Y.: Syracuse University Press, 1984), 232.

14. Tibi, *Islam and Cultural Accommodation,* 26.

15. Ibid., 152.

16. Ernest Gellner, *Postmodernism, Reason, and Religion* (London: Routledge, 1992), 10–14.

17. Gellner, "Islam and Marxism," 6.

18. Tibi, *Islam and Cultural Accommodation,* 69.

19. Raphael Patai, whose controversial observations should be taken with a grain of salt, draws larger inferences from Islam's lack of receptivity to critical thinking by arguing that "in general the Arab mind, dominated by Islam, has been bent more on preserving than innovating, on maintaining than im-

proving, on continuing than initiating." As unique as they each may claim to be, Turkish and Iranian minds are not very different from that of the Arabs in this respect. See Patai, *The Arab Mind* (New York: Charles Scribner's Sons, 1973), 154.

20. For a discussion of one such concession, see Nikki Keddie, *Religion and Rebellion in Iran: The Tobacco Protests of 1891–92* (London: Frank Cass, 1966).

21. For insightful elaborations of the dilemmas of the Arabic language in the modern world, see Tibi, *Islam and Cultural Accommodation*, 76–101; and Jacques Berque, *Cultural Expressions in Arab Society Today*, trans. Robert Stookey (Austin: University of Texas Press, 1974), 32–47, 279–301.

22. Serif Mardin, "Religion and Politics in Modern Turkey," in *Islam in the Political Process*, ed. James Piscatori (Cambridge: Cambridge University Press, 1983), 138–42.

23. "Commander of the Faithful" is one of King Hassan's self-proclaimed titles. King Hussein considers himself to be the custodian of the al-Aqsa mosque in Jerusalem, and Saudi kings claim custodianship over the mosques in Mecca and Medina.

24. Mohammad Reza Pahlavi, *Answer to History* (New York: Stein and Day, 1980), 57.

25. For a magnificent collection of essays by a whole range of Muslim thinkers, see John Donohue and John Esposito, eds., *Islam in Transition: Muslim Perspectives* (Oxford: Oxford University Press, 1982).

26. Tibi, *Islam and Cultural Accommodation*, 69.

27. Quoted in Patai, *Arab Mind*, 203.

28. Tibi, *Islam and Cultural Accommodation*, 130. Emphasis in original.

29. Halim Barakat, *The Arab World: Society, Culture, and State* (Berkeley: University of California Press, 1993), 22.

30. Nels Johnson, "Mass Culture and Islamic Populism," in *Mass Culture, Popular Culture, and Social Life in the Middle East*, ed. George Stauth and Sami Zubaida (Boulder, Colo.: Westview, 1987), 167.

31. Fouad Ajami, *The Arab Predicament: Arab Political Thought and Practice since 1967* (Cambridge: Cambridge University Press, 1981), 175.

32. Ali Shariati, *Bazgasht beh khish* (Return to the self) (Tehran: n.p., n.d.).

33. Tibi, *Islam and Cultural Accommodation*, 100.

34. For more on Kasravi, see Ervand Abrahamian, "Kasravi: The Integrative Nationalist of Iran," in *Towards a Modern Iran: Studies in Thoughts, Politics, and Society*, ed. Elie Kedourie and Sylvia Haim (London: Frank Cass, 1980), 96–131.

35. For a general discussion of the transformation of the Turkish language, particularly since the birth of the republic, see Kathleen Burrill, "Modern Turkish Literature," in *The Cambridge Encyclopedia of the Middle East and North Africa*, ed. Trevor Mostyn (Cambridge: Cambridge University Press, 1988), 202–3.

36. Johnson, "Mass Culture," 167.

37. For more on anti-Western (especially anti-American) sentiments in the Middle East, see Richard Parker, "Anti-American Attitudes in the Arab World," *Annals of the American Academy of Social and Political Sciences* 497 (May 1988):46–57.

38. Patai, *Arab Mind,* 299.

39. Young men also grapple with questions of identity, as indicated by their appearance—not cutting their hair and, more commonly, refusing to have a mustache. Mustaches are popular in the Middle East because they signify manliness and are considered by most social classes as aesthetically attractive. Many "modern" young men, however, equate them with traditionalism and therefore make a point of being clean shaven.

Cigarettes serve a similar function among young Middle Eastern women who consider them expressive symbols of liberation. Just as smoking is an extension of the macho image for most Middle Eastern men—there is often a carefully personalized, gender-specific pattern to a smoker's lighting of a cigarette, hand gestures, manner of inhaling and exhaling the smoke, and other related rituals—women frequently use it to signal their modernity. For most smokers in the region, cigarettes represent individuality, self-assertion, and nonconformity. Of course, only the best (i.e., the most prestigious) foreign brands, such as Marlboro and Winston, will do.

40. Bouthaina Shaaban, *Both Right and Left Handed: Arab Women Talk about Their Lives* (Indianapolis: Indiana University Press, 1988), 37.

41. One such figure is the Moroccan Fatima Mernissi, who has authored a number of books on the subject of Middle Eastern women, including *Beyond the Veil: Male-Female Dynamics in Modern Muslim Society* (Bloomington: Indiana University Press, 1987). The Egyptian psychiatrist Nawal al-Saadawi has also published numerous books dealing with the position of Middle Eastern women and has been a prominent figure in the women's rights movement in Egypt; in fact, she was once jailed by Sadat's government for her political activities. Two of al-Saadawi's books that have been translated into English are *God Dies by the Nile* (London: Zed, 1985); and *The Hidden Face of Eve: Women in the Arab World,* trans. Sherif Hatata (Boston: Beacon, 1980).

42. For the role of rock music in the former Soviet bloc, see Sabrina Ramet, *Social Currents in Eastern Europe: The Sources and Meaning of the Great Transformation* (Durham, N.C.: Duke University Press, 1991), 212–39.

43. Rodinson, *Arabs,* 164.

44. See, for example, Shaaban, *Both Right and Left Handed,* 3–5.

45. Patai, *Arab Mind,* 105.

46. Rugh, *Family in Contemporary Egypt,* 159. The author goes on to say that "the normative restrictions that are self-imposed recognize that the world of women consists of appropriate places to go, approved kinds of transportation, legitimate purpose, the right kinds of dress, and appropriate companions, all determined by a person's station in life and her general circumstances. To violate these principles risks social sanctions. To project the image of a respectable 'nice girl' brings society's approval and perhaps, as hoped for, a good husband" (160).

47. For example, for the story of an Iranian worker who, despite pressing financial needs, would not accept a job he considered socially demeaning and unsuited to his skills, see Fakhreddin Azimi, "Amir Agha: An Iranian Worker," in *Struggle and Survival in the Modern Middle East,* ed. Edmund Burke III (Berkeley: University of California Press, 1993), 290–304.

48. Tibi, *Islam and Cultural Accommodation,* 70.

49. One such scholar was the Syrian-born Mohammad ibn Idris Shafi'i, who, living around the end of the eighth century, believed that the other foundations of Islamic science (*fiqh*) are the Koran, the Prophet's tradition (*sunna*), and analogical reasoning (*qiyas*). See Malise Ruthven, *Islam in the World* (Oxford: Oxford University Press, 1984), 151–55.

50. See chap. 2, note 75.

51. Issa Boullata, *Trends and Issues in Contemporary Arab Thought* (Albany: SUNY Press, 1990), 3–10.

52. See, for example, Ajami, *Arab Predicament,* 31.

53. On the same topic, Patai writes the following in *The Arab Mind:* "Just as the [Middle Eastern] student blames for his failure in exam not himself, but bad luck, the teacher, the difficult questions, the country, the system, and God, so the Arab nations blame the enemy, imperialism, betrayal, bad luck, and everything else, instead of penetrating to the roots of evil and extirpating it" (112).

54. Doreen Hinchcliffe, "Women and the Law in the United Arab Emirates," in *Arabia and the Gulf: From Traditional Society to Modern States,* ed. Ian Richard Netton (London: Croom Helm, 1986), 239.

55. The aim here is not to present a comprehensive examination of the women's issue in the Middle East, which would be beyond the reach of even an entire book, but to study the effects of the concept of manhood on cultural thought and social practice in the region.

56. Soraya Altorki, *Women in Saudi Arabia: Ideology and Behavior among the Elite* (New York: Columbia University Press, 1986), 23.

57. Fatima Mernissi, *The Veil and the Male Elite: A Feminist Interpretation of Women's Rights in Islam,* trans. Mary Jo Lakeland (Reading, Mass.: Addison-Wesley, 1991), 7–10.

58. Mervat Hatem, "Egypt's Middle Class in Crisis: The Sexual Division of Labor," *Middle East Journal* 42, no. 3 (Summer 1988):419. According to the figures that Hatem cites on page 417, for example, only 33.2 percent of veiled women in a survey in Egypt were willing to support a woman's unqualified right to work; 33.7 percent stated that women should work only if there is an economic need for it; 20.9 percent approved of women working in such traditional female occupations as medicine, teaching, and social work; and 9 percent opposed women's employment under any circumstances.

59. Oriana Fallaci, *Interview with History* (New York: Liveright, 1976), 271–72.

60. See, for example, Eliz Sanasarian, *The Women's Rights Movement in Iran: Mutiny, Appeasement, and Repression from 1900 to Khomeini* (New York: Praeger, 1982).

61. Quoted in Shaaban, *Both Right and Left Handed,* 113.

62. Barakat, *Arab World,* 111, 113.

63. Rugh, *Family in Contemporary Egypt,* 133.

64. Shaaban, *Both Right and Left Handed,* 118.

65. Maxine Molyneux, "The Law, the State, and Socialist Policies with Regard to Women: The Case of the People's Republic of Yemen, 1967–1990," in *Women, Islam, and the State,* ed. Deniz Kandiyoti (Philadelphia: Temple University Press, 1991), 241.

66. Hinchcliffe, "Women and the Law," 239.

67. Ahmad, "Arab Women," 32.

68. Hatem, "Egypt's Middle Class," 416.

69. Rugh, *Family in Contemporary Egypt,* 286.

70. Hatem, "Egypt's Middle Class," 420.

71. Rugh, *Family in Contemporary Egypt,* 286.

72. For a description of the *qisas* bill, see Mahmud Da'wati, "The Qisas Bill—Document," *Al-Tawhid: Quarterly Journal of Islamic Thought and Culture* 1, no. 4 (July 1984):136–66. For only the sections of the bill that specifically apply to women, see *In the Shadow of Islam: The Women's Movement in Iran,* ed. Azar Tabari and Nahid Yeganeh (London: Zed, 1982), 94–95.

73. Deniz Kandiyoti, "End of Empire: Islam, Nationalism, and Women in Turkey," in Kandiyoti, *Women, Islam, and the State,* 42.

74. Rohn Eloul, "Arab al-Hjerat: Adaptation of Bedouin to a Changing Environment," in *The Changing Bedouin,* ed. Emanuel Marx and Avshalom Shmueli (London: Transaction, 1984), 157.

75. For an example of the life of an "urban villager," see Joost Hiltermann, "Abu Jamal: A Palestinian Urban Villager," in Burke, *Struggle and Survival,* 364–76.

76. Mehdi Abedi and Michael Fischer, "An Iranian Village Boyhood," in Burke, *Struggle and Survival,* 323.

77. Patai, *Arab Mind,* 225. The author argues that the propensity for violence, or at least verbal argument, has been "part of the Arab personality since pre-Islamic days." He continues:

> At every level violence has always been present either actually or potentially. At the slightest provocation the fighting propensity surfaces, a quarrel ensues and easily degenerates into physical violence. In this connection, it appears that the readiness with which Arabs break into violent verbal abuse and threat is, in effect, a mechanism whose ultimate function is to prevent an oral dispute from leading to physical action.

Chapter 6. Political Culture

1. For some of the varying definitions of political culture, see Mehran Kamrava, *Understanding Comparative Politics: A Framework for Analysis* (London: Routledge, 1995), 58–59.

2. See Mehran Kamrava, *Politics and Society in the Third World* (London: Routledge, 1993), 136–38.

60 / NOTES FOR PAGES 202-205

3. Ibid., 144–45.

4. For a most interesting discussion of confessionalism in Lebanon, see Hilal Khashan, *Inside the Lebanese Confessional Mind* (Lanham, Md.: University Press of America, 1992).

5. While Islam has been widely discussed, it has not been examined from the angle taken in this chapter. For more on nationalism in the Middle East, see, among others, Elie Kedourie, *Politics in the Middle East* (Oxford: Oxford University Press, 1992), 291–306; Roger Owen, *State, Power, and Politics in the Making of the Modern Middle East* (London: Routledge, 1992), 81–107; and Bernard Lewis, *The Shaping of the Modern Middle East* (Oxford: Oxford University Press, 1994), 71–98. For more on the Palestinian question's role in various Middle Eastern countries, see Edward Said, *The Question of Palestine* (New York: Times Books, 1980); Laurie Brand, *Palestinians in the Arab World: Institution Building and the Search for State* (New York: Columbia University Press, 1988); Charles Smith, *Palestine and the Arab-Israeli Conflict*, 2d ed. (New York: St.Martin's, 1992), especially chaps. 4–10; and James Bill and Robert Springborg, *Politics in the Middle East*, 4th ed. (New York: HarperCollins, 1994), 356–58.

6. Bernard Lewis, *The Arabs in History* (Oxford: Oxford University Press, 1993), 40–41.

7. Recent publications on this subject are of vastly differing quality. For some of the more serious studies dealing with the emergence of recent trends in Islam, see, among others, Nazih Ayubi, *Political Islam: Religion and Politics in the Arab World* (London: Routledge, 1991); Alexander Cudsi and Ali Dessouki, eds., *Islam and Power* (London: Croom Helm, 1981); John Esposito, *The Islamic Threat: Myth or Reality?* (Oxford: Oxford University Press, 1992); Bernard Lewis, *Islam and the West* (Oxford: Oxford University Press, 1993); John Esposito, *Islam: The Straight Path* (Oxford: Oxford University Press, 1988); Malise Ruthven, *Islam in the World* (Oxford: Oxford University Press, 1984); Edmund Burke III and Ira Lapidus, eds., *Islam, Politics, and Social Movements* (Berkeley: University of California Press, 1988); Ernest Gellner, *Postmodernism, Reason, and Religion* (London: Routledge, 1992); and Sami Zubaida, *Islam, the People, and the State* (London: I.B. Tauris, 1993).

8. For more on the early years of the Islamic Republic of Iran, see Mehran Kamrava, *The Political History of Modern Iran: From Tribalism to Theocracy* (Westport, Conn.: Praeger, 1992), 81–116; and Hooshang Amirahmadi and Manoucher Parvin, eds., *Postrevolutionary Iran* (Boulder, Colo.: Westview, 1988).

9. *Constitution of the Islamic Republic of Iran,* trans. Hamid Algar (Berkeley, Calif.: Mizan Press, 1980), especially the preamble and Articles 1–14 and 107–10 (the latter articles were slightly amended later).

10. In the early 1970s, for example, Sadat courted the support of the Muslim Brotherhood and portrayed himself, albeit without much success, as a pious Muslim throughout his rule. Among the most widely distributed official photographs of Muammar Qaddafi and Saddam Hussein are those that show them praying, or in Saddam's case, visiting various mosques. Through elabo-

rate annual celebrations, the Saudis are reminded that their king is "the custodian of Islam's two holiest mosques." Even Turkey's virulently secular Türgot Özal tried to cultivate a pious image of himself in the early years of his administration.

11. For a concise account of parliamentary political openings to Islamic activists in Jordan, see Beverley Milton-Edwards, "A Temporary Alliance with the Crown: The Islamic Response in Jordan," in *Islamic Fundamentalisms and the Gulf Crisis: A Fundamentalism Project Report,* ed. James Piscatori (Chicago: University of Chicago Press, 1991), 88–108.

12. James Piscatori, "Religion and *Realpolitik:* Islamic Responses to the Gulf War," in *Islamic Fundamentalisms and the Gulf Crisis: A Fundamentalism Project Report,* ed. James Piscatori (Chicago: University of Chicago Press, 1991), 15–16.

13. For religiously inspired violence in Algeria, see Hugh Roberts, "A Trial of Strength: Algerian Islamism," in *Islamic Fundamentalisms and the Gulf Crisis: A Fundamentalism Project Report,* ed. James Piscatori (Chicago: University of Chicago Press, 1991), 131–54; and for Egypt, in the same volume, see Gehad Auda, "An Uncertain Response: The Islamic Movement in Egypt," 109–30. See also Michael Collins Dunn, "Fundamentalism in Egypt," *Middle East Policy* 2, no. 3 (1993):68–77.

14. See James Piscatori, ed., *Islamic Fundamentalisms and the Gulf Crisis: A Fundamentalism Project Report,* (Chicago: University of Chicago Press, 1991); Ayubi, *Political Islam;* Emmanuel Sivan, *Radical Islam: Medieval Theology and Modern Politics* (New Haven: Yale University Press, 1985); and Ram Swarup, *Understanding Islam through Hadis: Religious Faith or Fanaticism?* (Smithtown, N.Y.: Exposition, 1985).

15. Bill and Springborg, *Politics in the Middle East,* 61.

16. Fouad Ajami, *The Arab Predicament: Arab Political Thought and Practice since 1967* (Cambridge: Cambridge University Press, 1981), 187.

17. Ayubi, *Political Islam,* 158–59.

18. Ibid., 68.

19. For more on Heykal and Shariati, see Charles Smith, "The Intellectual, Islam, and Modernization: Heykal and Shariati," in *Comparing Muslim Societies,* ed. Juan R.I. Cole (Ann Arbor: University of Michigan Press, 1992), 163–92.

20. Ayubi, *Political Islam,* 69, 213.

21. Ali Shariati, *Bazgasht beh khish* (Return to the self) (Tehran: n.p., n.d.).

22. Ali Merad, "The Ideology of Islam in the Contemporary Muslim World," in *Islam and Power,* ed. Alexander Cudsi and Ali H. Dessouki (London: Croom Helm, 1981), 39.

23. Ibid., 39–40.

24. Kamrava, *Political History of Modern Iran,* 71–75.

25. Mehran Kamrava, *Revolution in Iran: The Roots of Turmoil* (London: Routledge, 1990), 12–13, 128–30.

26. Ibid., 124–26.

27. During the Iran-Iraq war, Syria was Iran's only Arab ally, and only Libya and Algeria remained neutral in the conflict. For a detailed account of the assistance given to Iraq by its Arab allies, see Dilip Hiro, *The Longest War: The Iran-Iraq Military Conflict* (London: Routledge, 1991), 75–81.

28. For a compelling account of Lebanon in the 1980s, see Thomas L. Friedman, *From Beirut to Jerusalem* (New York: Farrar, Straus and Giroux, 1989), especially 21–247. Equally impressive is Robert Fisk's *Pity the Nation: The Abduction of Lebanon* (New York: Simon and Schuster, 1990). For a less personal, more academic examination of Lebanon, see Samir Khalaf, *Lebanon's Predicament* (New York: Columbia University Press, 1987).

29. For an account of these and other developments, see Fisk, *Pity the Nation,* especially 199–643.

30. Piscatori, "Religion and *Realpolitik,*" 12.

31. Ibid., 6.

32. See, for example, *New York Times,* 28 March 1992, 28. As reported by the *New York Times,* 1 May 1993, 4, the U.S. State Department's annual report on terrorism named Iran as "the most dangerous sponsor of terrorism in 1992," although, especially since the late 1980s, the State Department or other U.S. government agencies have offered little factual evidence to substantiate this and other accusations of state-sponsored terrorism leveled against Iran's government. In recent years, the Sudan is said to be another sponsor of terrorism. See, for example, Sally Ann Baynard, "Fundamentalist Error," *Washington Post,* 29 August 1994, 21.

33. Khashan, *Inside the Lebanese Confessional Mind,* 13–15.

34. Said Amir Arjomand, "A Victory for the Pragmatists: The Islamic Fundamentalist Reaction in Iran," in Piscatori, *Islamic Fundamentalisms and the Gulf Crisis,* 52–69.

35. Bill and Springborg, *Politics in the Middle East,* 59.

36. See, for example, John Ruedy, *Modern Algeria: The Origins and Development of a Nation* (Bloomington: Indiana University Press, 1992), 252–56.

37. The references to *men* in the following paragraphs are intentional, since the various Middle Eastern leaders who have created cults of personality for themselves have all been male.

38. Achille Mbembe, "Power and Obscenity in the Post-Colonial Period: The Case of Cameroon," in *Rethinking Third World Politics,* ed. James Manor (London: Longman, 1991), 166–82.

39. J.M. Cook, "The Rise of the Achaemenids and Establishment of Their Empire," in *The Cambridge History of Iran,* vol. 2, ed. Ilya Gershetich (Cambridge: Cambridge University Press, 1985), 217.

40. Bill and Springborg, *Politics in the Middle East,* 157.

41. Quoted in H.C. Armstrong, *Grey Wolf: Mustafa Kemal* (London: Arthur Baker, 1936), 329.

42. Quoted in Bill and Springborg, *Politics in the Middle East,* 150.

43. Quoted in Jean Lacouture, *Nasser,* trans. Daniel Hofstadter (New York: Knopf, 1973), 186.

44. Gamal Abdul Nasser, *Egypt's Liberation: The Philosophy of the Revo-*

lution (Washington, D.C.: Public Affairs Press, 1955), 87–88, 114.

45. Anwar el-Sadat, *In Search of Identity: An Autobiography* (New York: Harper and Row, 1977), 206–7, 314–15.

46. Mohammad Reza Pahlavi, *Answer to History* (New York: Stein and Day, 1980), 175.

47. Quoted in Lewis Eigen and Jonathan Siegel, *The Macmillan Dictionary of Political Quotations* (New York: Macmillan, 1993), 351–52.

48. Former British Prime Minister Margaret Thatcher, for example, was often accused of launching a direct "assault" on democracy. See John Kingdom, *No Such Thing as Society? Individualism and Community* (London: Open University Press, 1992), 48.

49. Howard Wiarda and Harvey Kline, "The Pattern of Historical Development," in *Latin American Politics and Development,* ed. Howard Wiarda and Harvey Kline (Boulder, Colo.: Westview, 1990), 31–33.

50. For more on the "politics of a prophet," see Bill and Springborg, *Politics in the Middle East,* 138–50. See also Michael Cook, *Muhammad* (Oxford: Oxford University Press, 1983).

51. James Piscatori, *Islam in a World of Nation-States* (Cambridge: Cambridge University Press, 1986), 6–8.

52. Esposito, *Islam,* 30.

53. Hamid Enayat, *Modern Islamic Political Thought* (London: Macmillan, 1982), 28.

54. Esposito, *Islam,* 37–39.

55. Iliya Harik, "The Origins of the Arab State System," in *The Foundations of the Arab State,* ed. Ghassan Salame (London: Croom Helm, 1987), 23–24.

56. Alan Richards and John Waterbury, *A Political Economy of the Middle East: State, Class, and Economic Development* (Boulder, Colo.: Westview, 1990), 302–27.

57. Turkey and Lebanon, whose political systems may be best described as "quasi-democratic," seem to be exceptions to this rule, but they are not. In Turkey, Atatürk's cult of personality lives on and, under the rubric of Kemalism, continues to be central to the viability and legitimacy of the political system decades after his death. For an insightful and concise account of Atatürk's life and legacy, see Dankwart Rustow, "Atatürk as Founder of a State," in *Philosophers and Kings: Studies in Leadership,* ed. Dankwart Rustow (New York: George Braziller, 1970), 208–47. In Lebanon, instead of the cult of one leader, the country's confessional system has led to the budding of numerous smaller personality cults, each with a confessional leader trying to foster a cult of his own. But President Assad of Syria has bested them all, as represented by the size of his portrait at the Beirut airport, which is larger than that of the Lebanese president.

58. See Bill and Springborg, *Politics in the Middle East,* 176–227.

59. Sadat, *In Search of Identity,* 314–15.

60. Nazih Ayubi, "Government and the State in Egypt Today," in *Egypt under Mubarek,* ed. Charles Tripp and Roger Owen (London: Routledge,

1989), 12–13.

61. "Al-Hussein" was the name of a modified Scud missile with a longer range. Following the Gulf War of 1990–91, the Iraqi army was reported to have had fifty-one al-Hussein missiles, all of which were later destroyed pursuant to UN Resolution 687. International Institute for Strategic Studies, *The Military Balance 1991–1992* (London: Brassey's, 1991), 107.

62. See especially Samir al-Khalil, *The Monument: Art, Vulgarity, and Responsibility in Iraq* (Berkeley: University of California Press, 1991). For images and perceptions of Ayatollah Khomeini in Iran, especially in the years following the 1978–79 revolution, see Ervand Abrahamian, *Khomeinism: Essays on the Islamic Republic* (Berkeley: University of California Press, 1993), especially 1–12.

63. For an insightful account of contemporary populist and charismatic leaders in the Third World, see Barry Rubin, *Modern Dictators: Third World Coup Makers, Strongmen, and Populist Tyrants* (New York: McGraw-Hill, 1987).

64. Serif Mardin, "Religion and Politics in Modern Turkey," in *Islam in the Political Process,* ed. James Piscatori (Cambridge: Cambridge University Press, 1983), 139–42.

65. See Bill and Springborg, *Politics in the Middle East,* 153–54.

Chapter 7. Conclusion

1. John Waterbury, "Democracy without Democrats? The Potential for Political Liberalization in the Middle East," in *Democracy without Democrats? The Renewal of Politics in the Muslim World,* ed. Ghassan Salame (London: I.B. Tauris, 1994), 25.

2. Salame, *Democracy without Democrats?*

3. See Severine Labat, "Islamism and Islamists: The Emergence of New Types of Politico-Religious Movements," in *Islamism and Secularism in North Africa,* ed. John Ruedy (New York: St. Martin's, 1994), 103–21.

4. Typical high school "sciences," some of which have been introduced in earlier years, include algebra, geometry, trigonometry, calculus, anatomy, biology, physics, and chemistry. All are usually taught in the same week. Under the broad rubric of the "humanities," subjects include history, philosophy, and literature, and they are also all taught in the same week.

5. See, for example, Fatima Mernissi, *Islam and Democracy: Fear of the Modern World,* trans. Mary Jo Lakeland (Reading, Mass.: Addison-Wesley, 1992); *Islam and Democracy,* ed. Timothy Sisk (Washington, D.C.: U.S. Institute for Peace Press, 1992); John Esposito and James Piscatori, "Democratization and Islam," *Middle East Journal* 45, no. 3 (Summer 1991): 427–40; and Mohammed Abdelbeki Hermassi, "Islam, Democracy, and the Challenge of Political Change," in *Democracy in the Middle East,* ed. Yehuda Mirsky and Matt Ahrens (Washington, D.C.: Washington Institute for Near East Policy, 1993), 41–51.

6. For a fascinating treatment of this topic, see Fatima Mernissi, *Beyond the Veil: Male-Female Dynamics in Modern Muslim Society* (Bloomington: In-

diana University Press, 1987), especially vi–xxx and 11–85.

7. An example of such convenient labeling, even among intellectuals, is the tragic story of a Cairo University professor of Arabic literature, Dr. Nasr Abu Zeid, whose promotion from associate to full professor was blocked in 1993 by his peers, despite positive recommendations from outside reviewers, because of his critical analysis of Islamist discourse. The following year Abu Zeid was taken to court by Islamic militants who argued that since he had betrayed Islam, he could not be married to a Muslim woman and therefore had to divorce his wife. For more on the case, see Mustafa K. al-Sayyid, "A Civil Society in Egypt?" in *Civil Society in the Middle East,* ed. Augustus Richard Norton (Leiden: E.J. Brill, 1995), 277–80.

Bibliography

Abedi, Mehdi, and Michael M.J. Fischer. 1993. "An Iranian Village Boyhood." In *Struggle and Survival in the Modern Middle East,* ed. Edmund Burke III, 320–35. Berkeley: University of California Press.

Abrahamian, Ervand. 1982. *Iran: Between Two Revolutions.* Princeton: Princeton University Press.

———. 1993. *Khomeinism: Essays on the Islamic Republic.* Berkeley: University of California Press.

AbuKhalil, As'ad. 1992. "A New Arab Ideology? The Rejuvenation of Arab Nationalism." *Middle East Journal* 46 (1):22–36.

———. 1993. "Arab Intellectuals on Trial." *Middle East Journal* 47 (4):695–706.

Abu-Lughod, Lila. 1993. "Migdim: Egypt Bedouin Matriarch." In *Struggle and Survival in the Modern Middle East,* ed. Edmund Burke III, 269–392. Berkeley: University of California Press.

Adams, Michael. 1986. "One Yemen or Two?" In *Arabia and the Gulf: From Traditional Society to Modern States,* ed. Ian Richard Netton, 120–31. London: Croom Helm.

El-Affendi, Abdelwahab. 1991. "Studying My Movement: Social Science without Cynicism." *International Journal of Middle East Studies* 23 (1):83–94.

Afrasiabi, Bahram. 1985. *Iran va tarikh: Az koudetaq ta enqelab* (Iran and history: From the coup to the revolution). Tehran: Zarrin, 1364.

Aftandilian, Gregory L. 1993. *Egypt's Bid for Arab Leadership.* New York: Council on Foreign Relations Press.

Agah Institute. 1983. *Eelat va ashayer* (Clans and tribes). Tehran: Agah Institute, 1362.

Aghajanian, Akbar. 1994. "A New Direction in Population Policy and Family Planning in Iran." Paper presented at the annual meeting of the Middle East Studies Association of North America, Phoenix, Ariz.

Ahmad, Eqbal. 1993. "The Question of Iraq." *Nation,* 16 August, 178–82.

Ahmad, Feroz. 1993. *The Making of Modern Turkey.* London: Routledge.

Ahmed, Leila. 1991. "Arab Women." In *Women's Studies Encyclopedia,* vol. 3, ed. Helen Tierney, 28–32. Westport, Conn.: Greenwood.

Ajami, Fouad. 1981. *The Arab Predicament: Arab Political Thought and Practice since 1967.* Cambridge: Cambridge University Press.

Akhavi, Shahrough. 1980. *Religion and Politics in Contemporary Iran: Clergy-State Relations in the Pahlavi Period.* Albany: SUNY Press.

Ale-Ahmad, Jalal. 1962. *Gharbzadegi* (Westoxication). Tehran: Ravvaq, 1341.

———. 1978. *Dar khedmat va khiyanat-e roushanfekran* (On the service and disservice of intellectuals). Vols. 1–2. Tehran: Khawrazmi, 1357.

Almond, Gabriel. 1993. "Foreword: The Return to Political Culture." In *Political Culture and Democracy in Developing Countries,* ed. Larry Diamond, ix–xii. Boulder, Colo.: Lynne Rienner.

Altorki, Soraya. 1986. *Women in Saudi Arabia: Ideology and Behavior among the Elite.* New York: Columbia University Press.

Amirahmadi, Hooshang. 1990. *Revolution and Economic Transition: The Iranian Experience.* Albany: SUNY Press.

Amirahmadi, Hooshang, and Manoucher Parvin, eds. 1988. *Postrevolutionary Iran.* Boulder, Colo.: Westview.

Amjad-Ali, Charles. 1994. "Democratization in the Middle East Perspective." In *Building Peace in the Middle East: Challenges for States and Civil Society,* ed. Elise Boulding, 69–77. Boulder, Colo.: Lynne Rienner.

Amuzegar, Jahangir, and M. Ali Fekrat. 1971. *Iran: Economic Development under Dualistic Conditions.* Chicago: University of Chicago Press.

Anderson, Charles. 1992. "Toward a Theory of Latin American Politics." In *Politics and Social Change in Latin America: Still a Distinct Tradition?* ed. Howard Wiarda, 239–54. Boulder, Colo.: Westview.

Anderson, Lisa. 1987. "Lawless Government and Illegal Opposition: Reflections on the Middle East." *Journal of International Affairs* 42 (2):219–32.

———. 1991. "Absolutism and the Resilience of Monarchy in the Middle East." *Political Science Quarterly* 106 (1):1–15.

Anderson, Nancy Fix. 1993. "Benazir Bhutto and Dynastic Politics: Her Father's Daughter, Her People's Sister." In *Women as National Leaders,* ed. Michael A. Genovese, 41–69. Newbury Park, Calif.: Sage.

Ansari, Hamied. 1986. *Egypt: The Stalled Society.* Albany: SUNY Press.

Antoun, Richard T. 1989. *Muslim Preachers in the Modern World: A Jordanian Case Study in Comparative Perspective.* Princeton: Princeton University Press.

———. 1991. "Ethnicity, Clientship, and Class: Their Changing Meaning." In *Syria: Society, Culture, and Polity,* ed. Richard T. Antoun and Donald Quataert, 1–13. Albany: SUNY Press.

Arjomand, Said Amir. 1991. "A Victory for the Pragmatists: The Islamic Fundamentalist Reaction in Iran." In *Islamic Fundamentalisms and the Gulf Crisis,* ed. James Piscatori, 52–69. Chicago: University of Chicago Press.

Armbrust, Walter. 1994. "Watching Films in Egyptian Movie Theaters: Cinema as Secular Ritual." Paper presented at the annual meeting of the Middle East Studies Association of North America, Phoenix, Ariz.

Armstrong, H.C. 1936. *Grey Wolf: Mustafa Kemal.* London: Arthur Baker.

Ashraf, Ahmad. 1991. "State and Agrarian Relations before and after the Iranian Revolution, 1960–1990." In *Peasants and Politics in the Modern Middle East,* ed. Farhad Kazemi and John Waterbury, 277–311. Miami: Florida International University Press.

Askoy, Asu, and Haluk Sahin. 1993. "Global Media and Cultural Identity in Turkey." *Journal of Communication* 43:31–41.

Aslan, Ensar. 1989. *Atatürkcu dusunce sisteminde turk egitimi* (Turkish education Kemalist ideological system). Diyarbakir: Dicle Universitesi Press.

Auchterlonie, Paul. 1986. "Some Western Views of the Arab Gulf." In *Arabia and the Gulf: From Traditional Society to Modern States,* ed. Ian Richard Netton, 43–54. London: Croom Helm.

Auda, Gehad. 1991. "An Uncertain Response: The Islamic Movement in Egypt." In *Islamic Fundamentalisms and the Gulf Crisis,* ed. James Piscatori, 109–30. Chicago: University of Chicago Press.

Ayata, Sencer. 1991. "Traditional Sufi Orders on the Periphery: Kadiri and Naksibendi Islam in Konaya and Trabzon." In *Islam in Modern Turkey: Religion, Politics, and Literature in a Secular State,* ed. Richard Tapper, 223–53. London: I.B. Tauris.

Aydemir, Sevket Sureyya. 1969. *Tek adam: Mustafa Kemal* (The unique man: Mustafa Kemal). Vols. 1–3. Istanbul: Remzi Ketabevi.

Ayubi, Nazih. 1991. *Political Islam: Religion and Politics in the Arab World.* London: Routledge.

Azari, Farah, ed. 1983. *Women of Iran: The Conflict with Fundamentalist Islam.* London: Ithaca Press.

Azimi, Fakhreddin. 1993. "Amir Agha: An Iranian Worker." In *Struggle and Survival in the Modern Middle East,* ed. Edmund Burke III, 290–304. Berkeley: University of California Press.

Al-Azmeh, Aziz. 1986. "Wahhabite Policy." In *Arabia and the Gulf: From Traditional Society to Modern States,* ed. Ian Richard Netton, 75–87. London: Croom Helm.

———. 1994. "Populism contra Democracy: Recent Democratic Discourse in the Arab World." In *Democracy without Democrats? The Renewal of Politics in the Muslim World,* ed. Ghassan Salame, 112–29. London: I.B. Tauris.

Badran, Adnan, ed. 1989. *At the Crossroads: Education in the Middle East.* New York: Paragon House.

Baghi, E. 1991. *Barresi-ye enqelab-e Iran* (Analysis of the Iranian revolution). Tehran: Taffakor, 1370.

Bakhash, Shaul. 1989. "The Politics of Land, Law, and Social Justice in Iran." *Middle East Journal* 43 (2):186–201.

Banisadr, Abolhasan. 1976. *Kish-e shakhsiyyat* (Cult of personality). Paris: N.p.

———. 1978. *Eqtesad-e Tauhidi* (Tauhidi economics). Tehran: N.p.

Banuazizi, Ali, and Myron Weiner, eds. 1986. *The State, Religion, and Ethnic Politics.* Syracuse, N.Y.: Syracuse University Press.

Barakat, Halim. 1993. *The Arab World: Society, Culture, and State.* Berkeley: University of California Press.

Baram, Amatzia. 1991. "From Radicalism to Radical Pragmatism: The Shi'ite Fundamentalism Opposition Movements of Iraq." In *Islamic Fundamentalisms and the Gulf Crisis,* ed. James Piscatori, 28–51. Chicago: University of Chicago Press.

Batatu, Hanna. 1985. "Political Power and Social Structure in Syria and Iraq." In *Arab Society: Continuity and Change,* ed. Samih K. Farsoun, 34–47. London: Croom Helm.

Baxter, Craig. 1985. "Democracy and Authoritarianism in South Asia." *Journal of International Affairs* 38 (2):307–19.

Bayart, Jean-François. 1993. *The State in Africa: The Politics of the Belly.* London: Longman.

Bebler, Anton, and Jim Seroka, eds. 1990. *Contemporary Political Systems.* Boulder, Colo.: Lynne Rienner.

Beck, Lois. 1980. "Revolutionary Iran and Its Tribal Peoples." *Merip Reports* (May): 14–20.

———. 1990. "Tribes and State in Nineteenth- and Twentieth-Century Iran." In *Tribes and State Formation in the Middle East,* ed. Philip Khoury and Joseph Kostiner, 185–225. Berkeley: University of California Press.

———. 1993. "Rostam: Qashqa'i Rebel." In *Struggle and Survival in the Modern Middle East,* ed. Edmund Burke III, 305–19. Berkeley: University of California Press.

Behnam, Djamchid. 1985. "The Muslim Family and the Modern World: Papers from an International Symposium. The Tunis Conference." *Current Anthropology* 26 (5): 555–56.

Bellin, Eva. 1995. "Civil Society in Tunisia." In *Civil Society in the Middle East,* ed. Augustus Richard Norton, 120–47. Leiden: E.J. Brill.

Ben-Dor, Gabriel. 1988. "Ethnopolitics and the Middle Eastern State." In *Ethnicity, Pluralism, and the State in the Middle East,* ed. Milton Esman and Itamar Rabinovich, 71–92. Ithaca, N.Y.: Cornell University Press.

Berberouglu, Berch. 1990. *Political Sociology: A Comparative/Historical Approach.* Dix Hills, N.Y.: General Hall.

Berque, Jacques. 1974. *Cultural Expressions in Arab Society Today.* Translated by Robert Stookey. Austin: University of Texas Press.

———. 1983. *Arab Rebirth: Pain and Ecstasy.* Translated by Quintin Hoare. London: Al-Saqi.

Bhargava, Pradeep. 1989. *Political Economy of the Gulf States.* New Delhi: South Asia Publishers.

Bill, James, and Robert Springborg. 1994. *Politics in the Middle East.* 4th ed. New York: HarperCollins.

Binder, Leonard. 1978. *In a Moment of Enthusiasm: Political Power and the Second Stratum in Egypt.* Chicago: University of Chicago Press.

Birch, Anthony. 1993. *The Concepts and Theories of Modern Democracy.* London: Routledge.

Birks, J.S., and C.A. Sinclair. 1980. "Economic and Social Implications of Current Development in the Arab Gulf: The Oriental Connection." In *Social and Economic Development in the Arab Gulf,* ed. Tim Niblock, 135–60. London: Croom Helm.

Bonine, Michael E., and Nikki Keddie, eds. 1981. *Continuity and Change in Modern Iran.* Albany: SUNY Press.

Borthwick, Bruce M. 1979. "Religion and Politics in Israel and Egypt." *Middle East Journal* 33 (2): 145–63.

Boullata, Issa J. 1990. *Trends and Issues in Contemporary Arab Thought.* Albany: SUNY Press.

Bourdieu, Pierre, and James Coleman, eds. 1991. *Social Theory for a Changing Society.* Boulder, Colo.: Westview.

Bowen, Donna Lee. 1994. "Changing Contraceptive Mores in Morocco: Statistics, Trends, and Rumors." Paper presented at the annual meeting of the Middle East Studies Association of North America, Phoenix, Ariz.

Boyd, Douglas. 1993. *Broadcasting in the Arab World: A Survey of the Electronic Media in the Middle East*. 2d ed. Ames: Iowa State University Press.

Boyer, William W. 1992. "Reflections on Democratization." *Political Science and Politics* 25 (3):517–22.

Brand, Laurie A. 1988. *Palestinians in the Arab World: Institution Building and the Search for State*. New York: Columbia University Press.

———. 1995. "In the Beginning Was the State . . .: The Quest for Civil Society in Jordan." In *Civil Society in the Middle East*, ed. Augustus Richard Norton, 148–85. Leiden: E.J. Brill.

Bromley, Simon. 1994. *Rethinking Middle East Politics*. Austin: University of Texas Press.

Brown, Carl L. 1987. "The Middle East: Patterns of Change, 1947–1987." *Middle East Journal* 41 (1):26–39.

———, ed. 1973. *From Medina to Metropolis: Heritage and Change in the Near Eastern City*. Princeton: Darwin Press.

Brown, J.F. 1989. "The Military and Society: The Turkish Case." *Middle Eastern Studies* 21 (July): 387–404.

———. 1991. *Surge to Freedom: The End of Communist Rule in Eastern Europe*. Durham, N.C.: Duke University Press.

Brown, Nathan. 1991. "The Ignorance and Inscrutability of the Egyptian Peasantry." In *Peasants and Politics in the Modern Middle East*, ed. Farhad Kazemi and John Waterbury, 203–21. Miami: Florida International University Press.

Brumberg, Daniel. 1991. "Islamic Fundamentalism, Democracy, and the Gulf War." In *Islamic Fundamentalisms and the Gulf Crisis*, ed. James Piscatori, 188–208. Chicago: University of Chicago Press.

Brzezinski, Zbigniew. 1993. *Out of Control: Global Turmoil on the Eve of the Twenty-First Century*. New York: Charles Scribner's Sons.

Budge, Ian, and David McKay, eds., 1994. *Developing Democracy*. London: Sage.

Burke, Edmund III. 1991. "Changing Patterns of Peasant Protest in the Middle East, 1750–1950." In *Peasant and Politics in the Middle East*, ed. Farhad Kazemi and John Waterbury, 24–37. Miami: Florida International University Press.

———, ed. 1993. *Struggle and Survival in the Modern Middle East*. Berkeley: University of California Press.

Burke, Edmund III, and Ira M. Lapidus, eds. 1988. *Islam, Politics, and Social Movements*. Berkeley: University of California Press.

Burrill, Kathleen. 1988. "Modern Turkish Literature." In *The Cambridge Encyclopedia of the Middle East and North Africa*, ed. Trevor Mostyn, 202–3. Cambridge: Cambridge University Press.

Çakir, Rusen. 1994. *Ne Seriat ne demokrasi: Refah Partisini anlamak* (Neither Sharia nor democracy: The Refah Party analyzed). Istanbul: Siyabeyaz.

Carroll, Terrance J. 1986. "Islam and Political Community in the Arab World." *International Journal of Middle East Studies* 18 (2):185–204.

Chaney, David. 1987. "Sport as a Form of Mass Entertainment." In *Mass Culture, Popular Culture, and Social Life in the Middle East*, ed. George Stauth and Sami Zubaida, 47–63. Boulder, Colo.: Westview.

Chapman, Graham P., and Kathleen M. Baker, eds. 1992. *The Changing Geography of Africa and the Middle East.* London: Routledge.

Chirot, Daniel. 1994. *How Societies Change.* Thousand Oaks, Calif.: Pine Forge.

Choueiri, Youssef, ed. 1993. *State and Society in Syria and Lebanon, 1919–1991.* New York: St. Martin's.

Cole, Juan R.I. 1980. "Pastoral Nomads in a Rapidly Changing Economy: The Case of Saudi Arabia." In *Social and Economic Development in the Arab Gulf,* ed. Tim Niblock, 106–21. London: Croom Helm.

———. 1992. "Introduction." In *Comparing Muslim Societies: Knowledge and the State in a World Civilization,* ed. Juan R.I. Cole, 1–28. Ann Arbor: University of Michigan Press.

———, ed. 1992. *Comparing Muslim Societies.* Ann Arbor: University of Michigan Press.

Constitution of the Republic of Turkey. 1982. Ankara: Basan Matbaacilik Sanayi.

Cook, J.M. 1985. "The Rise of the Achaemenids and Establishment of Their Empire." In *The Cambridge History of Iran,* vol. 2, ed. Ilya Gershevitch. Cambridge: Cambridge University Press.

Cook, Michael. 1981. "Activism and Quietism in Islam: The Case of the Early Murji'a." In *Islam and Power,* ed. Alexander S. Cudsi and Ali E. Hillal Dessouki, 15–23. London: Croom Helm.

———. 1983. *Muhammad.* Oxford: Oxford University Press.

Costello, V.F. 1977. *Urbanization in the Middle East.* Cambridge: Cambridge University Press.

Cottell, Alvin, ed. 1980. *The Persian Gulf States: A General Survey.* Baltimore: Johns Hopkins University Press.

Cudsi, Alexander, and Ali Dessouki, eds. 1981. *Islam and Power.* London: Croom Helm.

Cunbur, Mujgan. 1981. *Atatürk ve melli kultur* (Atatürk and national culture). Ankara: Basbakanlik Basimevi.

Dabashi, Hamid. 1993. *Theology of Discontent: The Ideological Foundation of the Islamic Revolution in Iran.* New York: New York University Press.

Dahl, Robert. 1971. *Polyarchy.* New Haven: Yale University Press.

———. 1988. *Democracy and Its Critics.* New Haven: Yale University Press.

Davis, Eric. 1991. "Theorizing Statecraft and Social Change in Arab Oil-Producing Countries." In *Statecraft in the Middle East: Oil, Historical Memory, and Popular Culture,* ed. Eric Davis and Nicolas Gavrielides, 1–35. Miami: Florida International University Press.

Davis, Eric, and Nicolas Gavrielides, eds. 1991. *Statecraft in the Middle East: Oil, Historical Memory, and Popular Culture.* Miami: Florida International University Press.

Deegan, Heather. 1993. *The Middle East and Problems of Democracy.* Boulder, Colo.: Lynne Rienner.

Denoeux, Guilain. 1993. *Urban Unrest in the Middle East: A Comparative Study of Informal Networks in Egypt, Iran, and Lebanon.* Albany: SUNY Press.

Dessouki, Ali E. Hillal. 1981. "The Resurgence of Islamic Organization in Egypt: An Interpretation." In *Islam and Power,* ed. Alexander S. Cudsi and Ali E.

Hillal Dessouki, 107–18. London: Croom Helm.

Diamanouros, Nikiforos P. 1986. "Regime Change and the Prospects for Democracy in Greece: 1974–1983." In *Transitions from Authoritarian Rule: Southern Europe,* ed. Guillermo O'Donnell, Philippe C. Schmitter, and Laurence Whitehead, 138–64. Baltimore: Johns Hopkins University Press.

Diamond, Larry. 1993. "Causes and Effects." In *Political Culture and Democracy in Developing Countries,* ed. Larry Diamond, 411–35. Boulder, Colo.: Lynne Rienner.

———. 1993. "Introduction: Political Culture and Democracy." In *Political Culture and Democracy in Developing Countries,* ed. Larry Diamond, 1–33. Boulder, Colo.: Lynne Rienner.

Diamond, Larry, Juan Linz, and Seymour Martin Lipset, eds. 1990. *Politics in Developing Countries: Comparing Experiences with Democracy.* Boulder, Colo.: Lynne Rienner.

Di Palma, Giuseppe. 1990. *To Craft Democracies: An Essay on Democratic Transitions.* Berkeley: University of California Press.

Dixon, John. 1987. "Social Security in the Middle East." In *Social Welfare in the Middle East,* ed. John Dixon, 163–200. London: Croom Helm.

———, ed. 1987. *Social Welfare in the Middle East.* London: Croom Helm.

Doan, Rebecca Miles. 1992. "Class Differentiation and the Informal Sector in Amman, Jordan." *International Journal of Middle Eastern Studies* 24 (1):27–37.

Donohue, John J., and John L. Esposito, eds. 1982. *Islam in Transition: Muslim Perspectives.* Oxford: Oxford University Press.

Dorr, Steven R. 1993. "Democratization in the Middle East." In *Global Transformation and the Third World,* ed. Steven Dorr, Barry Shutz, and Robert Slater, 131–57. Boulder, Colo.: Lynne Rienner.

Dorr, Steven, Barry Shutz, and Robert Slater, eds. 1993. *Global Transformation and the Third World,* Boulder, Colo.: Lynne Rienner.

Dresch, Paul. 1990. "Imams and Tribes: The Writing and Acting of History in Upper Yemen." In *Tribes and State Formation in the Middle East,* ed. Philip S. Khoury and Joseph Kostiner, 252–87. Berkeley: University of California Press.

Dunn, Michael Collins. 1993. "Fundamentalism in Egypt." *Middle East Policy* 2 (3):68–77.

———. 1993. "Islamist Parties in Democratizing States: A Look at Jordan and Yemen." *Middle East Policy* 2 (2):16–27.

———. 1994. "The Al-Nahda Movement in Tunisia: From Renaissance To Revolution." In *Islamism and Secularism in North Africa,* ed. John Ruedy, 149–65. New York: St. Martin's.

Eaton, Gai. 1994. *Islam and the Destiny of Man.* Cambridge: Islamic Text Society.

Eickelman, Christine. 1993. "Fertility and Social Change in Oman: Women's Perspectives." *Middle East Journal* 47 (4):652–66.

Eickelman, Dale F. 1992. "The Art of Memory: Islamic Education and Its Social Reproduction." In *Comparing Muslim Societies,* ed. Juan R.I. Cole, 97–132. Ann Arbor: University of Michigan Press.

Eilts, Hermann Frederick. 1991. "The Persian Gulf Crisis: Perspectives and Prospects." *Middle East Journal* 45 (1):7–22.

Eisenstadt, S.N. 1966. *Modernization: Protest and Change.* Englewood Cliffs, N.J.: Prentice Hall.

———, ed. 1968. *Comparative Perspectives of Social Change.* Boston: Little, Brown.

Eloul, Rohn. 1984. "Arab al-Hjerat: Adaptation of Bedouin to a Changing Environment." In *The Changing Bedouin,* ed. Emanuel Marx and Avshalom Shmueli, 157–72. London: Transaction.

el-Enany, Rasheed. 1993. *Naguib Mahfouz: The Pursuit of Meaning.* London: Routledge.

Enayat, Hamid. 1982. *Modern Islamic Political Thought.* London: Macmillan.

Erkal, Mustafa. 1972. *Bolgeler arasi dengesizlik ve dogu kalkinmasi* (Regional imbalance and the development in the East). Istanbul: Samil Yayinevi.

Esman, Milton J., and Itamar Rabinovich, eds. 1988. *Ethnicity, Pluralism, and the State in the Middle East.* Ithaca, N.Y.: Cornell University Press.

———, eds. 1988. "The Study of Ethnic Politics in the Middle East." In *Ethnicity, Pluralism, and the State in the Middle East,* ed. Milton J. Esman and Itamar Rabinovich, 3–24. Ithaca, N.Y.: Cornell University Press.

Esposito, John L. 1988. *Islam: The Straight Path.* Oxford: Oxford University Press.

———. 1992. *The Islamic Threat: Myth or Reality?* Oxford: Oxford University Press.

———, ed. 1983. *Voices of Resurgent Islam.* Oxford: Oxford University Press.

Esposito, John L., and James Piscatori. 1991. "Democratization and Islam." *Middle East Journal* 45 (3):427–40.

Etzioni, Amitai, and Eva Etzioni, eds. 1964. *Social Change: Sources, Patterns, and Consequences.* New York: Basic Books.

Faghirzadeh, Saleh. 1982. *Sociology of Sociology.* Tehran: Soroush Press.

Falk, Richard. 1991. "The Cruelty of Geopolitics: The Fate of Nation and State in the Middle East." *Journal of International Studies* 20 (3):383–93.

Fallaci, Oriana. 1976. *Interview with History.* New York: Liveright.

Fargues, Phillippe. 1994. "Democratic Explosion or Social Upheaval?" In *Democracy without Democrats? The Renewal of Politics in the Muslim World,* ed. Ghassan Salame, 156–79. London: I.B. Tauris.

Farhang, Mansour. 1993. "Exchange." *Nation,* 8 November, 545.

Farsoun, Samih, ed. 1985. *Arab Society: Continuity and Change.* London: Croom Helm.

Farsoun, Samih, and Mehrdad Mashayekhi, eds. 1992. *Iran: Political Culture in the Islamic Republic.* London: Routledge.

Fathi, Asghar. 1994. "Communication Strategies for Social Change in Iran: Kasravi and Shariati." Paper presented at the annual meeting of the Middle East Studies Association of North America, Phoenix, Ariz.

Fawaz, Leila. 1993. "Sumaya: A Lebanese Housemaid." In *Struggle and Survival in the Modern Middle East,* ed. Edmund Burke III, 352–64. Berkeley: University of California Press.

Featherstone, Mike. 1987. "Consumer Culture, Symbolic Power, and Universalism." In *Mass Culture, Popular Culture, and Social Life in the Middle East,* ed. George Stauth and Sami Zubaida, 17–46. Boulder, Colo.: Westview.

Feiler, Gil. 1991. "Migration and Recession: Arab Labor Mobility in the Middle East, 1982–89." *Population and Development Review* 17 (1): 134–55.

———. 1993. "Palestinian Employment Prospects." *Middle East Journal* 47 (4):633–50.

Fields, Michael. 1985. *The Merchants: The Big Business Families of Saudi Arabia and the Gulf States.* Woodstock, N.Y.: Overlook Press.

Findley, Paul. 1989. *They Dare to Speak Out.* Chicago: Lawrence Hill Books.

Firouzan, T. 1983. "Darbare-ye tarkib va sazman-e eelat va ashayer dar Iran" (Concerning the composition and organization of tribes and clans in Iran). In *Eelat va ashayer* (Tribes and clans), ed. the Agah Institute, 7–62. Tehran: Agah Institute, 1362.

Firro, Kais. 1988. "The Druze in and between Syria, Lebanon, and Israel." In *Ethnicity, Pluralism, and the State in the Middle East,* ed. Milton J. Esman and Itamar Rabinovich, 185–97. Ithaca, N.Y.: Cornell University Press.

Fischer, Michael M.J. 1980. *Iran: From Religious Dispute to Revolution.* Cambridge, Mass.: Harvard University Press.

Fisk, Robert. 1990. *Pity the Nation: The Abduction of Lebanon.* New York: Simon and Schuster.

Fluehr-Lobban, Carolyn. 1990. "Islamization in Sudan: A Critical Assessment." *Middle East Journal* 44 (4):610–23.

Friedl, Erika. 1989. *Women in Deh Koh: Lives in an Iranian Village.* New York: Penguin.

Friedman, Thomas L. 1989. *From Beirut to Jerusalem.* New York: Farrar, Straus and Giroux.

Fuller, Graham E. 1991. *The Center of the Universe: The Geopolitics of Iran.* Boulder, Colo.: Westview.

Gause, F. Gregory III. 1994. *Oil Monarchies: Domestic and Security Challenges in the Arab Gulf States.* New York: Council on Foreign Relations.

Gellner, Ernest. 1969. "A Pendulum Swing Theory of Islam." In *Sociology of Religion,* ed. Roland Robertson, 127–40. New York: Penguin.

———. 1981. *Muslim Society.* Cambridge: Cambridge University Press.

———. 1988. *Plow, Sword, and Book: The Structure of Human History.* Chicago: University of Chicago Press.

———. 1990. "Tribalism and the State in the Middle East." In *Tribes and State Formation in the Middle East,* ed. Philip S. Khoury and Joseph Kostiner, 109–26. Berkeley: University of California Press.

———. 1991. "Islam and Marxism: Some Comparisons." *International Affairs* 67 (1):1–6.

———. 1992. *Postmodernism, Reason, and Religion.* London: Routledge.

———. 1994. *Conditions of Liberty: Civil Society and Its Rivals.* New York: Penguin.

Gerber, Haim. 1987. *The Social Origins of the Modern Middle East.* Boulder, Colo.: Lynne Rienner.

Gerner, Deborah J. 1994. *One Land, Two Peoples: The Conflict over Palestine.* Boulder, Colo.: Westview.

Gershetich, Ilya, ed. 1985. *The Cambridge History of Iran*. Vol. 2. Cambridge: Cambridge University Press.

Ghabra, Shafeeq. 1991. "Voluntary Associations in Kuwait: The Foundation of a New System?" *Middle East Journal* 45 (2):199–215.

Ghani, Ashraf. 1993. "Gulab: An Afghan Schoolteacher." In *Struggle and Survival in the Modern Middle East*, ed. Edmund Burke III, 336–51. Berkeley: University of California Press.

Gibb, H.A.R. 1947. *Modern Trends in Islam*. Chicago: University of Chicago Press.

———. 1962. *Mohammedanism*. Oxford: Oxford University Press.

———. 1962. *Studies in the Civilization of Islam*. Boston: Beacon Press.

Gibb, H.A.R., and Harold Bowen. 1963. *Islamic Society and the West*. Vols. 1–2. Oxford: Oxford University Press.

Giddens, Anthony. 1985. *Sociology: A Brief but Critical Introduction*. London: Macmillan.

Gillespie, Kate, and Gwen Okruhlik. 1988. "Cleaning Up Corruption in the Middle East." *Middle East Journal* 42 (1):59–82.

Ginat, Joseph. 1984. "Blood Revenge in Bedouin Society." In *The Changing Bedouin*, ed. Emanuel Marx and Avshalom Shmueli, 59–82. London: Transaction.

Giner, Savador. 1986. "Political Economy, Legitimation, and the State in Southern Europe." In *Transitions from Authoritarian Rule: Southern Europe*, ed. Guillermo O'Donnell, Philippe C. Schmitter, and Laurence Whitehead, 11–44. Baltimore: Johns Hopkins University Press.

Goldberg, Ellis. 1992. "Smashing Idols and the State: The Protestant Ethic and Egyptian Sunni Radicalism." In *Comparing Muslim Societies*, ed. Juan R.I. Cole, 195–236. Ann Arbor: University of Michigan Press.

Goldschmidt, Arthur. 1991. *A Concise History of the Middle East*. Boulder, Colo.: Westview.

Greenfeld, Liah. 1992. *Nationalism: Five Roads to Modernity*. Cambridge, Mass.: Harvard University Press.

Gresh, Alain, and Dominique Vidal. 1990. *A to Z of the Middle East*. London: Zed Books.

Guillaume, Alfred. 1956. *Islam*. New York: Penguin.

Gunter, Michael. 1993. *The Kurds of Iraq: Tragedy and Hope*. New York: St. Martin's.

Haeri, Shahla. 1989. *Law of Desire: Temporary Marriage in Iran*. London: I.B. Tauris.

Haidar, Aziz. 1988. "The Different Levels of Palestinian Ethnicity." In *Ethnicity, Pluralism, and the State in the Middle East*, ed. Milton J. Esman and Itamar Rabinovich, 95–120. Ithaca, N.Y.: Cornell University Press.

Haj Seyyed Javadi, Ali Asqar. 1978. *Bohran-e arzesh-ha* (Crisis of values). Tehran: Ravvaq, 1357.

Hakimi, Mohammad Reza. 1978. *Jahesh-ha* (Movements). Tehran: Nashr-e Farhang-e Islami, 1357.

Haley, P. Edward, and Lewis W. Snider, eds. 1979. *Lebanon in Crisis: Participants and Issues*. Syracuse, N.Y.: Syracuse University Press.

Halpern, Manfred. 1964. *The Politics of Social Change in the Middle East.* Princeton: Princeton University Press.

Harik, Iliya. 1974. *The Political Mobilization of Peasants: A Study of an Egyptian Community.* Bloomington: Indiana University Press.

Harik, Iliya, and Denis J. Sullivan, eds. 1992. *Privatization and Liberalization in the Middle East.* Bloomington: Indiana University Press.

Hatem, Mervat. 1988. "Egypt's Middle Class in Crisis: The Sexual Division of Labor." *Middle East Journal* 42 (3):407–22.

Havemann, Axel. 1991. "The Impact of Peasant Resistance on Nineteenth-Century Mount Lebanon." In *Peasants and Politics in the Modern Middle East,* ed. Farhad Kazemi and John Waterbury, 85–100. Miami: Florida International University Press.

Haynes, Jeffrey. 1993. *Religion in Third World Politics.* Boulder, Colo.: Lynne Rienner.

Hedley, R. Alan. 1992. *Making a Living: Technology and Change.* New York: HarperCollins.

Held, Colbert C. 1989. *Middle East Patterns: Places, Peoples, and Politics.* Boulder, Colo.: Westview.

Hermassi, Mohammed Abdelbeki. 1993. "Islam, Democracy, and the Challenge of Political Change." In *Democracy in the Middle East,* ed. Yehudah Mirsky and Matt Ahrens, 41–51. Washington, D.C.: Washington Institute for Near East Policy.

———. 1994. "Socioeconomic Change and Political Implications: The Maghreb." In *Democracy without Democrats? The Renewal of Politics in the Muslim World,* ed. Ghassan Salame, 227–42. London: I.B. Tauris.

Herzog, Hanna. 1988. "Political Ethnicity as a Case of Socially Constructed Reality: The Case of Jews in Israel." In *Ethnicity, Pluralism, and the State in the Middle East,* ed. Milton Esman and Itamar Rabinovich, 140–51. Ithaca, N.Y.: Cornell University Press.

Heykal, Muhammad Hussein. 1994. *Oktobr 1973: Selah wa siyasa* (October 1973: Guns and politics). Cairo: Al Ahram.

Hicks, Neil, and Ghanim al-Najjar. 1995. "The Utility of Tradition: Civil Society in Kuwait." In *Civil Society in the Middle East,* ed. Augustus Richard Norton, 186–213. Leiden: E.J. Brill.

Hillmann, Michael C. 1990. *Iranian Culture: A Persianist View.* Lanham, Md.: University Press of America.

Hiltermann, Joost. 1992. *Behind the Intifada: Labor and Women's Movements in the Occupied Territories.* Princeton: Princeton University Press.

———. 1993. "Abu Jamal: A Palestinian Urban Villager." In *Struggle and Survival in the Modern Middle East,* ed. Edmund Burke III, 364–76. Berkeley: University of California Press.

Hinchcliffe, Doreen. 1986. "Women and the Law in the United Arab Emirates." In *Arabia and the Gulf: From Traditional Society to Modern States,* ed. Ian Richard Netton, 238–44. London: Croom Helm.

Hinnebusch, Raymond A. 1991. "Class and State in Ba'athist Syria." In *Syria: Society, State, and Culture,* ed. Richard T. Antoun and Donald Quataert, 29–47. Albany: SUNY Press.

———. 1993. "State and Civil Society in Syria." *Middle East Journal* 47 (2):243–57.

———. 1995. "State, Civil Society, and Political Change in Syria." In *Civil Society in the Middle East,* ed. Augustus Richard Norton, 214–42. Leiden: E.J. Brill.

Hiro, Dilip. 1991. *The Longest War: The Iran-Iraq Military Conflict.* London: Routledge.

Hoffman, Lawrence A. 1986. "Introduction: Land of Blessing and 'Blessings of the Land.'" In *The Land of Israel: Jewish Perspectives,* ed. Lawrence A. Hoffman, 1–23. Notre Dame, Ind.: University of Notre Dame Press.

———, ed. 1986. *The Land of Israel: Jewish Perspectives.* Notre Dame, Ind.: University of Notre Dame Press.

Hopkins, Nicholas S. 1987. *Agrarian Transformation in Egypt.* Boulder, Colo.: Westview.

———. 1991. "Clan and Class in Two Arab Villages." In *Peasants and Politics in the Modern Middle East,* ed. Farhad Kazemi and John Waterbury, 252–76. Miami: Florida International University Press.

Hourani, Albert. 1954. *Syria and Lebanon.* Oxford: Oxford University Press.

———. 1962. *Arabic Thought in the Liberal Age.* Oxford: Oxford University Press.

———. 1980. *Europe and the Middle East.* Berkeley: University of California Press.

———. 1981. *The Emergence of the Modern Middle East.* Berkeley: University of California Press.

———. 1991. *A History of the Arab Peoples.* Cambridge, Mass.: Harvard University Press.

———. 1991. "How Should We Write the History of the Middle East?" *International Journal of Middle East Studies* 23 (2):125–36.

Hourani, Albert, Philip Khoury, and Mary C. Wilson, eds. 1993. *The Modern Middle East.* Berkeley: University of California Press.

Humphreys, R. Stephen. 1979. "Islam and Political Values in Saudi Arabia, Egypt, and Syria." *Middle East Journal* 33 (1):1–19.

Huntington, Samuel P. 1987. "The Goals of Development." In *Understanding Political Development,* ed. Myron Weiner and Samuel Huntington, 3–32. New York: HarperCollins.

———. 1991. *The Third Wave: Democratization in the Late Twentieth Century.* Norman: University of Oklahoma Press.

———. 1993. "The Clash of Civilizations." *Foreign Affairs* 72 (3):22–49.

Ibrahim, Saad Eddin. 1982. *The New Arab Social Order: A Study of the Social Impact of Oil Wealth.* Boulder, Colo.: Westview.

———. 1993. "Crises, Elites, and Democratization in the Arab World." *Middle East Journal* 47 (2):292–305.

———. 1995. "Civil Society and Prospects for Democratization in the Arab World." In *Civil Society in the Middle East,* ed. Augustus Richard Norton, 27–54. Leiden: E.J. Brill.

Ismael, Jacqueline S. 1993. *Kuwait: Dependency and Class in a Rentier State.* Gainesville: University Press of Florida.

Jabber, Paul. 1988. "Forces of Change in the Middle East." *Middle East Journal* 42 (1):6–15.

Jansen, G.H. 1979. *Militant Islam.* New York: Harper and Row.

Jansen, W. 1994. "Contested Identities: Women and Religion in Algeria and Jordan." Paper presented at the annual meeting of the Middle East Studies Association of North America, Phoenix, Ariz.

Joffé, George. 1993. *North Africa: Nation, State, and Religion.* London: Routledge.

Johnson, Nels. 1987. "Mass Culture and Islamic Populism." In *Mass Culture, Popular Culture, and Social Life in the Middle East,* ed. George Stauth and Sami Zubaida, 165–87. Boulder, Colo.: Westview.

Kaene, John, et al., eds. 1988. *Civil Society and the State.* New York: Verso.

Kamrava, Mehran. 1990. *Revolution in Iran: The Roots of Turmoil.* London: Routledge.

———. 1992. *The Political History of Modern Iran: From Tribalism to Theocracy.* Westport, Conn.: Praeger.

———. 1992. *Revolutionary Politics.* Westport, Conn.: Praeger.

———. 1993. "Conceptualizing Third World Politics: The State-Society See-Saw." *Third World Quarterly* 14 (4):703–16.

———. 1993. *Politics and Society in the Third World.* London: Routledge.

———. 1996. *Understanding Comparative Politics: A Framework for Analysis.* London: Routledge.

Kandiyoti, Deniz. 1991. "End of Empire: Islam, Nationalism, and Women in Turkey." In *Women, Islam, and the State,* ed. Deniz Kandiyoti, 22–47. Philadelphia: Temple University Press.

———. 1992. "Women, Islam, and the State: A Comparative Approach." In *Comparing Muslim Societies,* ed. Juan R.I. Cole, 237–60. Ann Arbor: University of Michigan Press.

———, ed. 1991. *Women, Islam, and the State.* Philadelphia: Temple University Press.

Karim-Hakkak, Ahmad. 1994. "The Alterity in the Subaltern: Two Recent Works by Two Iranian Women Writers." Paper presented at the annual meeting of the Middle East Studies Association of North America, Phoenix, Ariz.

Karsh, Efraim, and Inari Rautsi. 1991. *Saddam Hussein: A Political Biography.* New York: Free Press.

Katouzian, Homa. 1981. *The Political Economy of Modern Iran: 1926–1979.* New York: New York University Press.

Kazemi, Farhad. 1991. "Peasant Uprisings in Twentieth-Century Iran, Iraq, and Turkey." In *Peasants and Politics in the Modern Middle East,* ed. Farhad Kazemi and John Waterbury, 101–24. Miami: Florida International University Press.

Kazemi, Farhad, and John Waterbury, eds. 1991. *Peasants and Politics in the Modern Middle East.* Miami: Florida International University Press.

Kazziha, Walid. 1993. "Egypt in the Balance." In *Contemporary Egypt: Through Egyptian Eyes,* ed. Charles Tripp, 122–31. London: Routledge.

Keddie, Nikki. 1981. *Roots of Revolution: An Interpretive History of Modern*

Iran. New Haven: Yale University Press.

———. 1985. "Islamic Revival in the Middle East: A Comparison of Iran and Egypt." In *Arab Society: Continuity and Change,* ed. Samih K. Farsoun, 65–82. London: Croom Helm.

———. 1992. "Material Culture, Technology, and Geography: Toward a Holistic Comparative Study of the Middle East." In *Comparing Muslim Societies,* ed. Juan R.I. Cole, 31–62. Ann Arbor: University of Michigan Press.

Keddie, Nikki, and Beth Baron, eds. 1991. *Women in Middle Eastern History: Shifting Boundaries in Sex and Gender.* New Haven: Yale University Press.

Kedourie, Elie. 1992. *Democracy and Arab Political Culture.* Washington, D.C.: Washington Institute for Near East Policy.

———. 1992. *Politics in the Middle East.* Oxford: Oxford University Press.

Kedourie, Elie, and Sylvia G. Haim, eds. 1980. *Towards a Modern Iran: Studies in Thought, Politics, and Society.* London: Frank Cass.

Keen, Benjamin, and Mark Wassermann. 1988. *A History of Latin America.* 3d ed. Boston: Houghton Mifflin.

Kennedy, Hugh. 1986. "The Desert and the Town in Eastern Arabian History." In *Arabia and the Gulf: From Traditional Society to Modern States,* ed. Ian Richard Netton, 18–28. London: Croom Helm.

Kepel, Gilles. 1993. *Muslim Extremism in Egypt: The Prophets and the Pharaoh.* Translated by Jay Rothchild. Berkeley: University of California Press.

Kerr, Malcolm H., ed. 1975. *The Elusive Peace in the Middle East.* Albany: SUNY Press.

Khalaf, Samir. 1987. *Lebanon's Predicament.* New York: Columbia University Press.

Khalidi, Walid. 1989. "Lebanon: Yesterday and Tomorrow." *Middle East Journal* 43 (3):375–87.

Al-Khalil, Samir. 1989. *Republic of Fear: The Inside Story of Saddam's Iraq.* New York: Pantheon.

———. 1991. *The Monument: Art, Vulgarity, and Responsibility in Iraq.* Berkeley: University of California Press.

Khashan, Hilal I. 1992. *Inside the Lebanese Confessional Mind.* Lanham, Md.: University Press of America.

Kheirabadi, Masoud. 1991. *Iranian Cities: Formation and Development.* Austin: University of Texas Press.

Khosravi, Khosrow. 1981. *Mas'ale-ye arzi va dehghanan-e tohidast dar Iran* (The land issue and poor peasants in Iran). Tehran: Bidari, 1360.

Khoury, Philip S. 1991. "Syrian Political Culture: A Historical Perspective." In *Syria: Society, Culture, and Polity,* ed. Richard T. Antoun and Donald Quataert, 13–27. Albany: SUNY Press.

Khoury, Philip S., and Joseph Kostiner. 1990. "Introduction: Tribes and the Complexities of State Formation in the Middle East." In *Tribes and State Formation in the Middle East,* ed. Philip S. Khoury and Joseph Kostiner, 1–22. Berkeley: University of California Press.

Kimmerling, Baruch, and Joel S. Migdal. 1994. *Palestinians: The Making of a People.* Cambridge, Mass.: Harvard University Press.

Kislali, Ahmet Taner. 1994. *Kemalism laklik ve demokrasi* (Kemalism, secularism, and democracy). Ankara: Imge.

Knight, Caroline. 1992. "Traditional Influences upon Lebanese Politics." *Journal of Social, Political, and Economic Studies* 17 (3–4):328–29.

Korbani, Agnes. 1995. *The Political Dictionary of Modern Middle East.* Lanham, Md.: University Press of America.

Kramer, Gudrun. 1994. "The Integration of the Integrists: A Comparative Study of Egypt, Jordan, and Tunisia." In *Democracy without Democrats? The Renewal of Politics in the Muslim World,* ed. Ghassan Salame, 200–226. London: I.B. Tauris.

Kressel, Gideon M. 1984. "Changes in Employment and Social Accommodations of Bedouin Settling in an Israeli Town." In *The Changing Bedouin,* ed. Emanuel Marx and Avshalom Shmueli, 125–54. London: Transaction.

Kuniholm, Bruce. 1980. *The Origins of the Cold War in the Near East: Great Power Rivalry and Diplomacy in Iran, Turkey, and Greece.* Princeton: Princeton University Press.

Kuran, Timur. 1989. "On the Notion of Economic Justice in Contemporary Islamic Thought." *International Journal of Middle Eastern Studies* 21 (2):171–91.

Kurian, Gregory Thomas, ed. 1992. *Encyclopedia of the Third World.* Vols 1–3. 4th ed. New York: Facts on File.

Labat, Severine. 1994. "Islamism and Islamists: The Emergence of New Types of Politico-Religious Movements." In *Islamism and Secularism in North Africa,* ed. John Ruedy, 103–21. New York: St. Martin's.

Lacouture, Jean. 1973. *Nasser.* Translated by Daniel Hofstadter. New York: Knopf.

Lapidus, Ira M. 1990. "Tribes and State Formation in Islamic History." In *Tribes and State Formation in the Middle East,* ed. Philip S. Khoury and Joseph Kostiner, 25–47. Berkeley: University of California Press.

Leca, John. 1994. "Democratization in the Arab World: Uncertainty, Vulnerability, and Legitimacy. A Tentative Conceptualization and Some Hypotheses." In *Democracy without Democrats? The Renewal of Politics in the Muslim World,* ed. Ghassan Salame, 48–83. London: I.B. Tauris.

Lechner, Norberto. 1991. "The Search for Lost Community: Challenges to Democracy in Latin America." *International Social Science Journal* 129 (3):541–52.

Legrain, Jean-François. 1991. "A Defining Moment: Palestinian Islamic Fundamentalism." In *Islamic Fundamentalisms and the Gulf Crisis,* ed. James Piscatori, 70–87. Chicago: University of Chicago Press.

Lerner, Daniel. 1958. *The Passing of Traditional Society: Modernizing the Middle East.* London: Free Press.

Lesch, Ann Mosley. 1991. "Contrasting Reactions to the Persian Gulf Crisis: Egypt, Syria, Jordan, and the Palestinians." *Middle East Journal* 45 (1): 30–50.

Lewando-Hundt, Gillian. 1984. "The Exercise of Power by Bedouin Women in the Negev." In *The Changing Bedouin,* ed. Emanuel Marx and Avshalom Shmueli, 83–124. London: Transaction.

Lewis, Bernard. 1963. *Istanbul and the Civilization of the Ottoman Empire.*

Norman: University of Oklahoma Press.

———. 1964. *The Middle East and the West*. Bloomington: University of Indiana Press.

———. 1968. *The Assassins: A Radical Sect in Islam*. New York: Basic Books.

———. 1968. *The Emergence of Modern Turkey*. Oxford: Oxford University Press.

———. 1982. *The Muslim Discovery of Europe*. New York: Norton.

———. 1986. *Semites and Anti-Semites*. New York: Norton.

———. 1991. *The Political Language of Islam*. Chicago: University of Chicago Press.

———. 1992. "Rethinking the Middle East." *Foreign Affairs* 71 (4):99–119.

———. 1993. *The Arabs in History*. Oxford: Oxford University Press.

———. 1993. "Islam and Liberal Democracy." *Atlantic Monthly* 271 (2):89–94.

———. 1993. *Islam and the West*. Oxford: Oxford University Press.

———. 1994. *The Shaping of the Modern Middle East*. Oxford: Oxford University Press.

———, ed. 1974. *Islam from the Prophet Muhammad to the Capture of Constantinople*. New York: Harper Torchbooks.

Lijphart, Arend. 1990. "Democratic Political Systems." In *Contemporary Political Systems*, ed. Anton Bebler and Jim Seroka, 71–86. Boulder, Colo.: Lynne Rienner.

Lindholm, Charles. 1992. "Quandaries of Command in Egalitarian Societies: Examples from Swat and Morocco." In *Comparing Muslim Societies*, ed. Juan R.I. Cole, 63–94. Ann Arbor: University of Michigan Press.

Lipset, Seymour Martin. 1992. "The Centrality of Political Culture." In *Parliamentary versus Presidential Government*, ed. Arend Lijphart, 207–11. Oxford: Oxford University Press.

Lockman, Zachary. 1994. "Introduction." In *Workers and Working Classes in the Middle East: Struggles, Histories, Historiographies*, ed. Zachary Lockman, 71–109. Albany: SUNY Press.

———, ed. 1994. *Workers and Working Classes in the Middle East: Struggles, Histories, Historiographies*. Albany: SUNY Press.

Luciani, Giacomo. 1994. "The Oil Rent, the Fiscal Crisis of the State, and Democratization." In *Democracy without Democrats? The Renewal of Politics in the Muslim World*, ed. Ghassan Salame, 130–55. London: I.B. Tauris.

Lustick, Ian S. 1988. *For the Land and the Lord: Jewish Fundamentalism in Israel*. New York: Council on Foreign Relations.

McMurray, David. 1993. "Haddou: A Moroccan Migrant Worker." In *Struggle and Survival in the Modern Middle East*, ed. Edmund Burke III, 377–93. Berkeley: University of California Press.

Magnus, Ralph. 1980. "Societies and Social Change in the Persian Gulf." In *The Persian Gulf States: A General Survey*, ed. Alvin Cottrell, 369–413. Baltimore: Johns Hopkins University Press.

Maisels, Charles Keith. 1993. *The Emergence of Civilization*. London: Routledge.

Makiya, Kanan (Samir al-Khalil). 1993. *Cruelty and Silence: War, Tyranny, Uprising, and the Arab World*. New York: Norton.

Manor, James, ed. 1991. *Rethinking Third World Politics.* London: Longman.

Mardin, Serif. 1983. "Religion and Politics in Modern Turkey." In *Islam in the Political Process,* ed. James Piscatori, 138–59. Cambridge, Mass.: Cambridge University Press.

Marx, Emanuel. 1984. "Economic Change among Pastoral Nomads in the Middle East." In *The Changing Bedouin,* ed. Emanuel Marx and Avshalom Shmueli, 1–16. London: Transaction.

Marx, Emanuel, and Avshalom Shmueli, eds. 1984. *The Changing Bedouin.* London: Transaction.

Maxwell, Kenneth. 1986. "Regime Overthrow and the Prospects for Democratic Transition in Portugal." In *Transitions from Authoritarian Rule: Southern Europe,* ed. Guillermo O'Donnell, Philippe C. Schmitter, and Laurence Whitehead, 109–37. Baltimore: Johns Hopkins University Press.

Merad, Ali. 1981. "The Ideology of Islam in the Contemporary Muslim World." In *Islam and Power,* ed. Alexander S. Cudsi and Ali E. Hillal Dessouki, 37–48. London: Croom Helm.

Mernissi, Fatima. 1987. *Beyond the Veil: Male-Female Dynamics in Modern Muslim Society.* Bloomington: Indiana University Press.

———. 1991. *The Veil and the Male Elite: A Feminist Interpretation of Women's Rights in Islam.* Translated by Mary Jo Lakeland. Reading, Mass.: Addison-Wesley.

———. 1992. *Islam and Democracy: Fear of the Modern World.* Translated by Mary Jo Lakeland. Reading, Mass.: Addison-Wesley.

Migdal, Joel. 1988. *Strong Societies and Weak States: State-Society Relations and State Capabilities in the Third World.* Princeton: Princeton University Press.

Milani, Farzaneh. 1992. *Veils and Words: The Emerging Voices of Iranian Women Writers.* Syracuse, N.Y.: Syracuse University Press.

Miller, William Green. 1968. "Political Organization in Iran: From Dowreh to Political Party." *Middle East Journal* 23 (2):159–67.

Mirsky, Yehuda, and Matt Ahrens, eds. 1993. *Democracy in the Middle East.* Washington, D.C.: Washington Institute for Near East Policy.

Moaddel, Mansoor. 1991. "Class Struggle in Postrevolutionary Iran." *International Journal of Middle East Studies* 23 (3):317–43.

Moghadam, Valentine. 1987. "Industrial Development, Culture, and Working Class Politics: A Case Study of Tabrizi Industrial Workers in the Iranian Revolution." *International Sociology* 2, no. 2 (June): 165.

———. 1993. *Modernizing Women: Gender and Social Change in the Middle East.* Boulder, Colo.: Lynne Rienner.

Molyneux, Maxine. 1991. "The Law, the State, and Socialist Policies with Regard to Women: The Case of the People's Democratic Republic of Yemen, 1967–1990." In *Women, Islam, and the State,* ed. Deniz Kandiyoti, 237–71. Philadelphia: Temple University Press.

Moore, Barrington Jr. 1966. *Social Origins of Dictatorship and Democracy.* New York: Penguin.

Moosa, Matti. 1994. *The Early Novels of Naguib Mahfouz: Images of Modern Egypt.* Gainesville: University Press of Florida.

Mortimer, Edward. 1991. "Christianity and Islam." *International Affairs* 67

(1):7–13.

Mostyn, Trevor, ed. 1988. *The Cambridge Encyclopedia of the Middle East and North Africa*. Cambridge: Cambridge University Press.

Moussalli, Ahmad S. 1995. "Modern Islamic Fundamentalist Discourses in Civil Society, Pluralism, and Democracy." In *Civil Society in the Middle East*, ed. Augustus Richard Norton, 78–119. Leiden: E.J. Brill.

Mumcu, Ugar. 1986. *Terorsuz ozgurluk* (Freedom without terror). Istanbul: Tekin Yayinevi.

Mumford, Lewis. 1961. *The City in History: Its Origins, Its Transformation, and Its Prospects*. New York: Harcourt, Brace and World.

Muravchik, Joshua, et al. 1993. *Democracy in the Middle East: Defining the Challenge*. Washington D.C.: Washington Institute for Near East Policy.

Muslih, Muhammad. 1993. "Palestinian Civil Society." *Middle East Journal* 47 (2):258–74.

———. 1995. "Palestinian Civil Society." In *Civil Society in the Middle East*, ed. Augustus Richard Norton, 243–68. Leiden: E.J. Brill.

Muslih, Muhammad, and Augustus Richard Norton. 1991. "The Need for Arab Democracy." *Foreign Policy* 83:3–19.

Nadoushan, Mohammad Ali. 1990. *Sokhan-ha ra beshnaveem* (Listening to speeches). Tehran: Enteshar, 1369.

Nafi, Zuhair Ahmad. 1983. *Economic and Social Development in Qatar*. London: Francis Pinter.

Nagi, Mostafa H. 1986. "Migration of Asian Workers to the Arab Gulf: Policy Determinants and Consequences." *Journal of South Asian and Middle Eastern Studies* 9 (3):19–34.

Nahas, Maridi. 1985. "State-Systems and Revolutionary Challenge: Nasser, Khomeini, and the Middle East." *International Journal of Middle East Studies* 17 (4):507–27.

Al-Naqeeb, Khaldoun Hasan. 1990. *Society and State in the Gulf and Arab Peninsula: A Different Perspective*. Translated by L.M. Kenny. London: Routledge.

Nashat, Guity, ed. 1983. *Women and Revolution in Iran*. Boulder, Colo.: Westview.

Nasser, Gamal Abdul. 1955. *Egypt's Liberation: The Philosophy of the Revolution*. Washington, D.C.: Public Affairs Press.

Nelson, Joan M. 1987. "Political Participation." In *Understanding Political Development*, ed. Samuel Huntington and Myron Weiner, 103–59. New York: HarperCollins.

Netton, Ian Richard, ed. 1986. *Arabia and the Gulf: From Traditional Society to Modern States*. London: Croom Helm.

Niblock, Tim. 1993. "International and Domestic Factors in the Economic Liberalization Process in Arab Countries." In *Economic and Political Liberalization in the Middle East*, ed. Tim Niblock and Emma Murphy, 55–83. London: British Academic Press.

———, ed. 1980. *Social and Economic Development in the Arab Gulf*. London: Croom Helm.

Niblock, Tim, and Emma Murphy, eds. 1993. *Economic and Political Liberaliza-*

tion in the Middle East. London: British Academic Press.

Norton, Augustus Richard. 1993. "The Future of Civil Society in the Middle East." *Middle East Journal* 47 (2):205–16.

———. 1995. "Introduction." In *Civil Society in the Middle East,* ed. Augustus Richard Norton, 1–26. Leiden: E.J. Brill.

———, ed. 1995. *Civil Society in the Middle East.* Leiden: E.J. Brill.

Omran, Abdel R., and Farzaneh Roudi. 1993. *The Middle East Population Puzzle.* Washington, D.C.: Population Reference Bureau.

Oncu, Ayse. 1994. "Packaging Islam: Cultural Politics on the Landscape of Turkish Commercial Television." *New Perspectives on Turkey* 10:13–16.

Osseiran, Sanaa. 1994. "The Democratization Process in the Arab-Islamic States of the Middle East." In *Building Peace in the Middle East: Challenges for States and Civil Society,* ed. Elise Boulding, 79–90. Boulder, Colo.: Lynne Rienner.

Ostle, Robin. 1991. *Modern Literature in the Near and Middle East.* London: Routledge.

Owen, Roger. 1985. *Migrant Workers in the Gulf.* London: Minority Rights Group.

———. 1992. *State, Power, and Politics in the Making of the Modern Middle East.* London: Routledge.

———. 1994. "Socioeconomic Change and Political Mobilization: The Case of Egypt." In *Democracy without Democrats? The Renewal of Politics in the Muslim World,* ed. Ghassan Salame, 183–99. London: I.B. Tauris.

Pahlavi, Mohammed Reza Shah. 1968. *Mission for My Country.* London: Hutchinson.

———. 1980. *Answer to History.* New York: Stein and Day.

Palmer, Monte, Ali Leila, and El Sayed Yassin. 1988. *The Egyptian Bureaucracy.* Syracuse, N.Y.: Syracuse University Press.

Parker, Richard. 1988. "Anti-American Attitudes in the Arab World." *Annals of the American Academy of Political and Social Sciences* 497:46–57.

Parry, Geraint, and Michael Moran, eds. 1994. *Democracy and Democratization.* London: Routledge.

Patai, Raphael. 1973. *The Arab Mind.* New York: Charles Scribner's Sons.

Pazzanita, Anthony G. 1994. "Morocco versus Polisario: A Political Interpretation." *Journal of Modern African Studies* 32 (2):265–78.

Perin, Cevdet. 1987. *Atatürk, kultur devrimi* (Atatürk, cultural revolution). 3d ed. Istanbul: Inkilap Kitabevi.

Perthes, Volker. 1994. "The Private Sector, Economic Liberalization, and the Prospects of Democratization: The Case of Syria and Some Other Arab Countries." In *Democracy without Democrats? The Renewal of Politics in the Muslim World,* ed. Ghassan Salame, 243–69. London: I.B. Tauris.

Pinkney, Robert. 1993. *Democracy in the Third World.* Boulder, Colo.: Lynne Rienner.

Pipes, Daniel. 1990. *Greater Syria: The History of an Ambition.* Oxford: Oxford University Press.

Piscatori, James. 1986. *Islam in a World of Nation-States.* Cambridge: Cambridge University Press.

————. 1991. "Religion and *Realpolitik:* Islamic Responses to the Gulf War." In *Islamic Fundamentalisms and the Gulf Crisis: A Fundamentalism Project Report,* ed. James Piscatori, 1–27. Chicago: University of Chicago Press.

————, ed. 1983. *Islam in the Political Process.* Cambridge: Cambridge University Press.

————, ed. 1991. *Islamic Fundamentalisms and the Gulf Crisis: A Fundamentalism Project Report.* Chicago: University of Chicago Press.

Polk, William R. 1991. *The Arab World Today.* Cambridge, Mass: Harvard University Press.

Posusney, Marsha Pripstein. 1994. "Collective Action and Workers' Consciousness in Contemporary Egypt." In *Workers and Working Classes in the Middle East: Struggles, Histories, Historiographies,* ed. Zachary Lockman, 211–46. Albany: SUNY Press.

Pridham, B.R. 1986. "Oman: Change or Continuity?" In *Arabia and the Gulf: From Traditional Society to Modern States,* ed. Ian Richard Netton, 132–55. London: Croom Helm.

Quandt, William B. 1981. *Saudi Arabia in the 1980s: Foreign Policy, Security, and Oil.* Washington D.C.: Brookings Institution.

Quandt, William B., Fuad Jabber, and Ann Mosely Lesch. 1973. *The Politics of Palestinian Nationalism.* Berkeley: University of California Press.

Quataert, Donald. 1991. "Rural Unrest in the Ottoman Empire, 1830–1914." In *Peasants and Politics in the Modern Middle East,* ed. Farhad Kazemi and John Waterbury, 38–47. Miami: Florida International University Press.

Rabbani, Mouin. 1994. "Unmasking Makiya: Iraq and Arab Intellectuals." *Third World Quarterly* 15 (12):342–50.

Rabinovich, Itamar. 1988. "Arab Political Parties: Ideology and Ethnicity." In *Ethnicity, Pluralism, and the State in the Middle East,* ed. Milton Esman and Itamar Rabinovich, 155–72. Ithaca, N.Y.: Cornell University Press.

Randall, Susan C., and Hermann Strasser. 1981. *An Introduction to Theories of Social Change.* London: Routledge and Kegan Paul.

Reid, Donald Malcolm. 1993. "The Postage Stamp: A Window on Saddam Hussein's Iraq." *Middle East Journal* 47 (1):77–89.

Rejali, Darius. 1994. *Torture and Modernity: Self, Society, and State in Modern Iran.* Boulder, Colo.: Westview.

Rezun, Miron. 1992. *Saddam Hussein's Gulf Wars: Ambivalent Stakes in the Middle East.* London: Praeger.

Richards, Alan. 1993. "Economic Imperatives and Political Systems." *Middle East Journal* 47 (2):217–27.

————. 1995. "Economic Pressures for Accountable Governance in the Middle East and North Africa." In *Civil Society in the Middle East,* ed. Augustus Richard Norton, 55–78. Leiden: E.J. Brill.

Richards, Alan, and John Waterbury. 1990. *A Political Economy of the Middle East: State, Class, and Economic Development.* Boulder, Colo.: Westview.

Rieff, Philip, ed. 1970. *On Intellectuals.* Garden City, N.Y.: Anchor Books.

Robbins, Philip. 1993. "The Overlord State: Turkish Policy and the Kurdish Issue." *Journal of International Affairs* 69, no. 4 (October): 657–76.

Roberts, Hugh. 1991. "A Trial of Strength: Algerian Islamism." In *Islamic Fun-*

damentalisms and the Gulf Crisis, ed. James Piscatori, 131–54. Chicago: University of Chicago Press.

Robertson, Ronald, ed. 1969. *Sociology of Religion.* New York: Penguin.

Rodinson, Maxine. 1979. *The Arabs.* Translated by Arthur Goldhammer. Chicago: University of Chicago Press.

Rosberg, James. 1994. "Causes and Consequences of Judicial Independence in Contemporary Egypt." Paper presented at the annual meeting of the Middle East Studies Association of North America, Phoenix, Ariz.

Roy, Oliver. 1994. "Patronage and Solidarity Groups: Survival or Reformation?" In *Democracy without Democrats? The Renewal of Politics in the Muslim World,* ed. Ghassan Salame, 270–81. London: I.B. Tauris.

Ruedy, John. 1992. *Modern Algeria: The Origins and Development of a Nation.* Bloomington: Indiana University Press.

———, ed. 1994. *Islamism and Secularism in North Africa.* New York: St. Martin's.

Rugh, Andrea B. 1984. *Family in Contemporary Egypt.* Syracuse, N.Y.: Syracuse University Press.

Rugh, William A. 1987. *The Arab Press.* Syracuse, N.Y.: Syracuse University Press.

Rustow, Dankwart, ed. 1970. *Philosophers and Kings: Studies in Leadership.* New York: George Braziller.

Ruthven, Malise. 1984. *Islam in the World.* Oxford: Oxford University Press.

el-Sadat, Anwar. 1977. *In Search of Identity: An Autobiography.* New York: Harper and Row.

Saeed, Javaid. 1994. *Islam and Modernization: A Comparative Analysis of Pakistan, Egypt, and Turkey.* Westport, Conn.: Praeger.

Safran, Nadav. 1988. *Saudi Arabia: The Ceaseless Quest for Security.* Ithaca, N.Y.: Cornell University Press.

Said, Edward W. 1978. *Orientalism.* New York: Vintage Books.

———. 1980. *The Question of Palestine.* New York: Times Books.

———. 1981. *Covering Islam: How the Media and the Experts Determine How We See the Rest of the World.* New York: Pantheon Books.

———. 1993. *Culture and Imperialism.* New York: Knopf.

Said, Edward W., and Christopher Hitchens, eds. 1989. *Blaming the Victims.* London: Verso.

Saktanber, Ayse. 1991. "Muslim Identity in Children's Picture Books." In *Islam in Modern Turkey: Religion, Politics, and Literature in a Secular State,* ed. Richard Tapper, 171–88. London: I.B. Tauris.

Salame, Ghassan. 1994. "Introduction: Where Are the Democrats?" In *Democracy without Democrats? The Renewal of Politics in the Muslim World,* ed. Ghassan Salame, 1–22. London: I.B. Tauris.

———. 1994. "Small Is Pluralistic: Democracy as an Instrument of Civil Peace." In *Democracy without Democrats? The Renewal of Politics in the Muslim World,* ed. Ghassan Salame, 84–111. London: I.B. Tauris.

———, ed. 1987. *The Foundations of the Arab State.* London: Croom Helm.

———, ed. 1994. *Democracy without Democrats? The Renewal of Politics in the Muslim World.* London: I.B. Tauris.

Salibi, Kamal. 1993. *The Modern History of Jordan.* New York: St. Martin's.

Saltoff, Robert. 1993. *The Politics of Change in the Middle East.* Boulder, Colo.: Westview.

Samuel, Edwin. 1969. *The Struggle of Society in Israel.* New York: Random House.

Sanasarian, Eliz. 1982. *The Women's Rights Movements in Iran: Mutiny, Appeasement, and Repression from 1900 to Khomeini.* New York: Praeger.

Sargent, Lyman Tower. 1993. *Contemporary Political Ideologies.* Belmont, Calif.: Wadsworth.

Sartori, Giovanni. 1987. *The Theory of Democracy Revisited.* Vols. 1–2. Chatham, N.J.: Chatham House.

Sayeed, Khalid Bin. 1985. *Western Dominance and Political Islam.* Albany: SUNY Press.

Al-Sayyid, Mustapha K. 1993. "A Civil Society in Egypt." *Middle East Journal* 47 (2):228–42.

———. 1995. "A Civil Society in Egypt?" In *Civil Society in the Middle East,* ed. Augustus Richard Norton, 269–93. Leiden: E.J. Brill.

Schirazi, Asghar. 1993. *Islamic Development Policy: The Agrarian Question in Iran.* Boulder, Colo.: Lynne Rienner.

Schmidt, Dana Adams. 1974. *Armageddon in the Middle East.* New York: John Day.

Schmitter, Philippe C. 1986. "An Introduction to Southern European Transitions from Authoritarian Rule: Italy, Portugal, Spain, and Turkey." In *Transitions from Authoritarian Rule: Southern Europe,* ed. Guillermo O'Donnell, Philippe C. Schmitter, and Laurence Whitehead, 3–10. Baltimore: Johns Hopkins University Press.

Schumpeter, Joseph. 1947. *Capitalism, Socialism, and Democracy.* 3d ed. Harper and Brothers.

Seale, Patrick. 1989. *Assad of Syria: The Struggle for the Middle East.* Berkeley: University of California Press.

———. 1991. "Assad: Between Institutions and Autocracy." In *Syria: Society, Culture, and Polity,* ed. Richard T. Antoun and Donald Quartaert, 97–110. Albany: SUNY Press.

Seccombe, Ian J. 1986. "Immigrant Workers in an Emigrant Economy: An Examination of Replacement Migration in the Middle East." *International Migration* 24 (2):377–89.

Seddon, C. 1993. "Algerian Civil War." *New Statesman and Society* 6 (3 December): 11.

Seddon, David. 1993. "Austerity Protests in Response to Economic Liberalization in the Middle East." In *Economic and Political Liberalization in the Middle East,* ed. Tim Niblock and Emma Murphy, 88–112. London: British Academic Press.

Sfeir, George N. 1988. "Source of Law and the Issue of Legitimacy and Rights." *Middle East Journal* 42 (3):436–46.

Shaaban, Bouthaina. 1988. *Both Right and Left Handed: Arab Women Talk about Their Lives.* Indianapolis: Indiana University Press.

Shah, Nasra M., and Sulayman S. al-Qudsi. 1989. "The Changing Characteristics of Migrant Workers in Kuwait." *International Journal of Middle Eastern Studies* 21 (1):31–55.

Shambayati, Hootan. 1994. "The Rentier State, Interest Groups, and the Paradox of Autonomy: State and Business in Turkey and Iran." *Comparative Politics* 26 (3):307–31.

Sharabi, Hisham. 1985. "The Dialectics of Patriarchy in Arab Society." In *Arab Society: Continuity and Change,* ed. Samih K. Farsoun, 83–104. London: Croom Helm.

———. 1988. *Neopatriarchy: A Theory of Distorted Change in Arab Society.* Oxford: Oxford University Press.

Shariati, Ali. 1980. *Marxism and Other Western Fallacies: An Islamic Critique.* Translated by R. Campbell. Berkeley: Mizan Press.

———. 1983. *Hobut dar kavir* (Creation in the desert). Tehran: Taqveem, 1362.

Sharoni, Simona. 1994. "Gender Issues in Democracy: Rethinking Middle East Peace and Security from a Feminist Perspective." In *Building Peace in the Middle East: Challenges for States and Civil Society,* ed. Elise Boulding, 99–110. Boulder, Colo.: Lynne Rienner.

Shibutani, Tamotsu, and Kian M. Kwan. 1965. *Ethnic Stratification: A Comparative Approach.* New York: Macmillan.

Shoaee, Rokhsareh. 1987. "The Mujahid Women of Iran: Reconciling 'Culture' and 'Gender.'" *Middle East Journal* 41 (4):519–37.

Sisk, Timothy D., ed. 1992. *Islam and Democracy.* Washington D.C.: U.S. Institute of Peace Press.

Sivan, Emmanuel. 1985. *Radical Islam: Medieval Theology and Modern Politics.* New Haven: Yale University Press.

Sklar, Richard L., and Mark Strege. 1992. "Finding Peace through Democracy in Sahelian Africa." *Current History* (May):224–29.

Smith, Charles D. 1992. "The Intellectual, Islam, and Modernization: Heykal and Shariati." In *Comparing Muslim Societies,* ed. Juan R.I. Cole, 163–92. Ann Arbor: University of Michigan Press.

———. 1992. *Palestine and the Arab-Israeli Conflict.* 2d ed. New York: St. Martin's.

Sorenson, Georg. 1993. *Democracy and Democratization.* Boulder, Colo.: Westview.

Stephens, John D. 1989. "Democratic Transition and Breakdown in Western Europe, 1870–1939: A Test of the Moore Thesis." *American Journal of Sociology* 94 (5):1019–77.

Strauth, George, and Sami Zubaida, eds. 1987. *Mass Culture, Popular Culture, and Social Life in the Middle East.* Boulder, Colo.: Westview.

Strum, Philippa. 1992. *The Women Are Marching: The Second Sex and the Palestinian Revolution.* Chicago: Lawrence Hill Books.

Sullivan, Soraya, trans. 1991. *Stories by Iranian Women since the Revolution.* Austin: Center for Middle Eastern Studies at the University of Texas.

Sunar, Ilkay, and Sabri Sayari. 1986. "Democracy in Turkey: Problems and Prospects." In *Transitions from Authoritarian Rule: Southern Europe,* ed. Guillermo O'Donnell, Philippe Schmitter, and Laurence Whitehead. Baltimore: Johns Hopkins University Press.

Swarup, Ram. 1985. *Understanding Islam through Hadis: Religious Faith or Fanaticism?* Smithtown, N.Y.: Exposition.

Tabari, Azar, and Nahid Yeganeh, eds. 1982. *In the Shadow of Islam: The Women's Movement in Iran.* London: Zed.

Tapper, Richard. 1990. "Anthropologists, Historians, and Tribespeople." In *Tribes and State Formation in the Middle East,* ed. Philip S. Khoury and Joseph Kostiner, 48–73. Berkeley: University of California Press.

———. 1991. "Introduction." In *Islam in Modern Turkey: Religion, Politics, and Literature in a Secular State,* ed. Richard Tapper, 1–27. London: I.B. Tauris.

Tapper, Richard, and Nancy Tapper. 1991. "Religion, Education, and Continuity in a Provincial Town." In *Islam in Modern Turkey: Religion, Politics, and Literature in a Secular State,* ed. Richard Tapper, 56–83. London: I.B. Tauris.

Taylor, Alan, 1988. *The Islamic Question in Middle East Politics.* Boulder, Colo.: Westview.

Tester, Keith. 1992. *Civil Society.* London: Routledge.

Tetreault, Mary Ann. 1993. "Civil Society in Kuwait: Protected Spaces and Women's Rights." *Middle East Journal* 47 (2):275–91.

Al-Thakeb, Fahed T. 1985. "The Arab Family and Modernity: Evidence from Kuwait." *Current Anthropology* 26 (5):575–80.

Thornburg, Max Weston. 1964. *People and Policy in the Middle East.* New York: Norton.

Tibi, Bassam. 1990. *Islam and the Cultural Accommodation of Social Change.* Translated by Clare Krojzl. Boulder, Colo.: Westview.

———. 1990. "The Simultaneity of the Unsimultaneous: Old Tribes and Imposed Nation-States in the Modern Middle East." In *Tribes and State Formation in the Middle East,* ed. Philip Khoury and Joseph Kostiner, 127–52. Berkeley: University of California Press.

Tierney, Helen, ed. 1991. *Women's Studies Encyclopedia,* vol. 3. Westport, Conn.: Greenwood.

Tolley, George S., and Vinod Thomas, eds. 1987. *The Economics of Urbanization and Urban Policies in Developing Countries.* Washington, D.C.: World Bank.

Tripp, Charles, ed. 1983. *Contemporary Egypt: Through Egyptian Eyes.* London: Routledge.

Tripp, Charles, and Roger Owen, eds. 1989. *Egypt under Mubarak.* London: Routledge.

Tschirgi, Dan, ed. 1994. *The Arab World Today.* Boulder, Colo.: Lynne Rienner.

Tucker, Judith E., ed. 1993. *Arab Women: Old Boundaries, New Frontiers.* Bloomington: Indiana University Press.

Tuma, Elias. 1987. *Economic and Political Change in the Middle East.* Palo Alto, Calif.: Pacific Books.

Turabi, Hasan. 1993. "Islam, Democracy, the State, and the West." *Middle East Policy* 1 (3):49–61.

Turan, Ilter. 1991. "Religion and Political Culture in Turkey." In *Islam in Modern Turkey: Religion, Politics, and Literature in a Secular State,* ed. Richard Tapper, 31–55. London: I.B. Tauris.

Ucok, Bahriye. 1985. *Atatürk'un izinde bir arpa boyu* (A barley's length after Atatürk). Ankara: Turk Tarih Kurumu Basimevi.

Van Dam, Nikolaos. 1978. "Sectarian and Regional Factionalism in the Syrian Political Elite." *Middle East Journal* 32 (2):201–10.

Vandewalle, Dirk. 1988. "From the New State to the New Era: Toward a Second Republic in Tunisia." *Middle East Journal* 42 (4):602–20.

———. 1991. "Qaddafi's 'Perestroika': Economic and Political Liberalization in Libya." *Middle East Journal* 45 (2):216–31.

Van Hear, Nicholas. 1992. "Update: Migrant Workers in the Gulf." *Migrant Workers in the Gulf*. London: Minority Rights Group.

Vatikiotis, P.J. 1981. "Islamic Resurgence: A Critical View." In *Islam and Power*, ed. Alexander S. Cudsi and Ali E. Hillal Dessouki, 169–96. London: Croom Helm.

Vatin, Jean-Claude. 1981. "Religious Resistance and State Power in Algeria." In *Islam and Power*, ed. Alexander S. Cudsi and Ali E. Hillal Dessouki, 119–57. London: Croom Helm.

Vergin, Nur. 1985. "Social Change and the Family in Turkey." *Current Anthropology* 26 (5):571–74.

Viorst, Milton. 1994. *Sandcastles: The Arabs in Search of the Modern World*. New York: Knopf.

Waardenburg-Kilpatrick, Hilary. 1988. "Modern Arabic Literature." In *The Cambridge Encyclopedia of the Middle East and North Africa*, ed. Trevor Mostyn and Albert Hourani, 198–200. Cambridge: Cambridge University Press.

Waterbury, John. 1991. "Peasants Defy Categorization (as Well as Landlords and State)." In *Peasants and Politics in the Modern Middle East*, ed. Farhad Kazemi and John Waterbury, 1–23. Miami: Florida International University Press.

———. 1991. "Twilight of the State Bourgeoisie?" *International Journal of Middle East Studies* 23 (1):1–17.

———. 1994. "Democracy without Democrats? The Potential for Political Liberalization in the Middle East." In *Democracy without Democrats? The Renewal of Politics in the Muslim World*, ed. Ghassan Salame, 23–47. London: I.B. Tauris.

Webster, Roger. 1986. "Human Resources in the Gulf." In *Arabia and the Gulf: From Traditional Society to Modern States*, ed. Ian Richard Netton, 188–201. London: Croom Helm.

Weiner, Myron, and Samuel Huntington, eds. 1987. *Understanding Political Development*. New York: HarperCollins.

White, Jenny B. 1994. *Money Makes Us Relatives: Women's Labor in Turkey*. Austin: University of Texas Press.

Wiarda, Howard, ed. 1992. *Politics and Social Change in Latin America: Still a Distinct Tradition?* Boulder, Colo.: Westview.

Wiarda, Howard, and Harvey Kline, eds. 1990. *Latin American Politics and Development*. Boulder, Colo.: Westview.

Wikan, Unni. 1980. *Life among the Poor in Cairo*. Translated by Ann Henning. London: Tavistock.

Wilkinson, J.C. 1980. "Changes in the Structure of Village Life in Oman." In *Social and Economic Development in the Arab Gulf,* ed. Tim Niblock, 122–33. London: Croom Helm.

Williams, John Alan, ed. 1982. *Themes of Islamic Civilization.* Berkeley: University of California Press.

Wright, Robin. 1986. *Sacred Rage: The Wrath of Militant Islam.* New York: Simon and Schuster.

———. 1991. "Unexplored Realities of the Persian Gulf Crisis." *Middle East Journal* 45 (1):23–29.

Zahlan, Rosemarie Said. 1989. *The Making of the Modern Gulf States: Kuwait, Bahrain, Qatar, the United Arab Emirates, and Oman.* London: Unwin Hyman.

Zakaria, Rafiq. 1991. *Muhammad and the Quran.* Penguin.

Zubaida, Sami. 1987. "Components of Popular Culture in the Middle East." In *Mass Culture, Popular Culture, and Social Life in the Middle East,* ed. George Stauth and Sami Zubaida, 165–87. Boulder, Colo.: Westview.

———. 1993. *Islam, the People, and the State: Political Ideas and Movements in the Middle East.* London: I.B. Tauris.

Index

Abbasis, rule of, 173
Abdu, Shaykh Mohammad, 175
Abu Dhabi, oil exports of, 135
Afghani, Jamaladdin, 175
Ajami, Fouad, 63–64, 72
Alabedin Ben Ali, Zein, 219
Al Ahram, 74
Algeria: anti-Islamic backlash in, 205;
   coup d'état in, 47; and reverse of de-
   mocratization, 29–30; revolution in,
   158, 160; state-led capitalism in, 44, 45
Amin, Samir, 72
Anti-Westernism, and cultural authentic-
   ity, 181–82
Arabic language, and cultural authenticity,
   180, 181
Arab socialism, 44, 45
Arafat, Yasir, 203, 223
Argentina: civil society in, 17; democratic
   consolidation in, 16
Assad, Hafez, 60, 62, 223; and cult of per-
   sonality, 218; and Western values, 142
Atatürk, Mustafa Kemal, 9, 30, 62,
   158–59, 219; and cult of personality,
   213, 214–15, 218
Authentication, legitimizing function of,
   178–79
Authenticity: call to, 207; search for cul-
   tural, 179–82
Authority, distrust of secular, 198
Autocracy, as social force, 40, 42, 79, 80
Averroës, 176
al-Azhar, 175

Ba'athist regime, 60
Ba'ath Party, 218
Bahrain: oil exports of, 134–35; popula-
   tion of, 102; society of, 113; urban pop-
   ulation of, 118; wealth of, 106
Bandaranaike, Sirimavo, 7–8
Bandaranaike, Solomon, 7–8

Bangladesh: democratic consolidation in,
   17; family dynasties in, 8; lack of civil
   liberty in, 7
Barakat, Halim: on Arab society, 177–78;
   on identity, 177
Base Ecclesiastical Communities, 20, 61
Beard, adoption of, 172
Beck, Lois, 56
Bedouins, 54, 55; incorporation of, into
   modern society, 120, 121; nomadic,
   128; and sociocultural contradictions,
   155
"Beer Drinkers' Party," 25
Bendjedid, Chadli, 29
Berbers, 56
Bhutto, Benazir, 7, 8
Bhutto, Zulfikar Ali, 7
Bill, James: on Kemalism, 158–59; on
   peasants, 125
Binder, Leonard, 43; on "second stratum,"
   122, 123–24
Blame, refusal to accept, 188–89
Bourguiba, Habib ibn Ali, 62, 219; and
   Western values, 142
Boyd, Douglas, 143–44
Brazil: civil society in, 17; democratic con-
   solidation in, 17
Bride price, 194
British mandatory rule, 221
Bureaucracy: contradictions in, 43; profes-
   sional ethos of, 43

Capitalism, state-directed, 44–45
Career politicians, in quasi democracies, 7
Catholic Church and Catholicism: and
   democratic transition, 21, 25; reorienta-
   tion of, 61
CEBs, 28
Child marriage, 194
Chile, democratic consolidation in, 17
Christian Phalangists, 209

Çiller, Tansu, 194
"City of the Dead," 98
Civic Forum, 20, 24, 27
Civil society, 25–30; components of, 25; and cultural uniformity, 28–30; and democratic transition, 15–16; impediments to Middle Eastern, 38–39; in Middle East, 33–39; political function of, 26; as preceding political crafting, 16, 17; as requirement for democracy, 225; and viable democracies, 5
Civil Society in the Middle East (Norton), 33
Civil-society organization, and democratic goals, 20–21
"Clash of Civilizations?, The," (Huntington), 11–12, 32, 224
Class(es): development of concept of, 83–84; social/cultural differences among, 99–101
Class consciousness: development of, 82–83; political repression of, 84–85
Colombia, democratic consolidation in, 17
Colonialism, 221
Colosio, Luis, 8
Communist Manifesto, The (Marx), 83
Compromise, inability to, 187–88
Confederacy, definition of, 53
Confessionalism, 202
Confucianism, as nondemocratic culture, 11–12
Consensus democracies, 4
Consociational democracies, 4
Contractors, and government contacts, 110
Controlled (guided) democracies, 226
Costa Rica, democratic consolidation in, 17
Costello, V.F., 137
Cultural schisms, 183–84, 189
Cultural schizophrenia, 13
Culture(s): clash of, 176; democracy and, 30–31
Czechoslovakia, civil society in, 17

Dahl, Robert, 2
Dar al-Harb, 171
De-Islamization, process of, 62
Demiral, Süleyman, 8
Democracy: and culture, 30–31; definitions of, 2–4; key ingredients for, 225;

in Middle East, 31–39; necessary conditions for, 4, 5, 9, 10, 168; as political crafting, 13–14; and political culture, 10–13; social component of, 14; varieties of, 4–9
Democratic consolidation, task of, 17–18
Democratic norms, internalization of, 28
Democratization: catalysts for, 14; chronological order of, 26; and political crafting, 9–16; social actors and, 23–25; stages of, 21–22; waves of, 10–11
Denoeux, Guilain, 46
Dhofar revolution, 127
Dhows, 119
DiPalma, Giuseppe, 10: on democracy as political crafting, 13–14, 31; on role of military, 28–30
Diplomacy, as unifying force, 169
Direct democracy, 4
Divorce, 193; summary, 194
Dress, and cultural liberation, 183
Dubai, 106, 113; oil exports of, 135

Economic priorities, rational, 43
Education: Middle Eastern, as obstacle to democracy, 228–29; and political socialization, 69–74; state-controlled social science, 228–29
Educational establishments: need for overhaul of, 229; as social institutions, 79
Egypt, 45; anti-Islamic backlash in, 205; bureaucratic growth in, 44; and civil society, 35; economic growth of, 135; and constitutional position on family, 50; female employment in, 194; informal employment in, 51; tourism in, 144; urban population of, 137
Elite(s): democratically committed, 225; and democratic consolidation, 17–18; replacement of, 14; rural, and national politics, 123–24; social/political, in Gulf states, 103–6
Elite-dominated democracies, 4
Elitism, in quasi democracies, 6–7
Empathy, definition of, 147
Entrepreneurs, in oil-dependent economies, 107, 109–10
Ethnic groups, image of, 60
Ethnic homogeneity, 59
Ethnicity, 56–60; elusive nature of, 59–60;

manipulation of, 58, 80; as social institution, 56; as source of identity, 80
Ethnic pluralism, as norm, 59
Ethnocentrism, 202
Escapism, of Middle Eastern youth, 183–84
Erbakan, Necmettin, 8
Expatriate factor, 113–17
Expatriates: division of labor among, 115–16; influence of, on local population, 154–55; isolation of, 58; marginalization of, 226; from outside Middle East, 154
Extended family: breakup of, 52; as social institution, 79. See also Family(ies)

Face, 186–87
Fahd (king of Saudia Arabia), 219
Familism, as social pattern, 49–50
Family(ies), 49–53; corporate interests of, 51–52; economic functions of, 51; legal reforms regarding, 194; as political liability, 52–53; social changes within, 161–62
Family dynasties, in quasi democracies, 7
Farmers, small, as rural social class, 124
Farouk (king of Egypt), 174, 215
Farsi language, and cultural authenticity, 180, 181
Fasting, importance of, 171
Father, as patriarch, 50
Father-child relationship, on national level, 80
Femininity, Middle Eastern ideal of, 190, 191
Fields, Michael, 107
Firdawsī, 76, 180
FIS. See Islamic Salvation Front
Folklore, importance of, 197–98
Foucault, Michel, 178

Gandhi, Indira, 7
Gandhi family, 7
Gathering places, as social institutions, 74–78, 79
Gecekondus, 98
Gellner, Ernest, 25–26, 28; on cultural rediscovery, 64–65; on Islam, 170; on tribes, 55–56
Gemayel, Amin, 8
Gemayel, Bashir, 8

Gender: changes in notion of, 190; and division of labor, 190, 191
Grassroots movement: as civil-society organizations, 18; and democratic transitions, 24. See also CEBs
Greece, civil society in, 16
Guevara, Che, 227
Gulf states: middle class in, 36; ruling families of, 103–6; welfare coverage of, 135, 152–53. See also Oil-dependent economies
Gulf War, 208; and Islam's politicization, 209

Hair, dyeing of, as cultural liberation, 183
Halab-abads, 98
Halpern, Manfred, 147–48
Hanafi, Hasan, 72
Harik, Iliya, 217
Hashemites, 221
Hassan (king of Morocco), 174; and personality cult, 218–19, 223; and Western values, 142
Havana Cafeteria, 76
Havel, Václav, 24, 227
Held, David, 3
Heykal, Muhammad Hussein, 69, 72, 73, 74, 206
Historical events, as unifying force, 169–70
Hitler, Adolf, 9
Honor, 185–86; differing notions of, 186
Hungary, as civil society–driven viable democracy, 18, 30
Huntington, Samuel, 224; on "clash of civilizations," 11–12, 32; on democracy, 2–3; on political culture, 10–13, 14–16; on role of military, 28–30
Hussein (king of Jordan), 174, 223; and Western values, 142
Hussein, Saddam, 62, 203, 208, 209; and cult of personality, 214, 215–16, 218, 219, 223; as father figure, 37; and Western values, 142

Ibn-Khaldūn, 53
Ibrahim, Saad Eddin, 34; on bedouins, 120, 121; on entrepreneurs, 110
Identity, psychological dilemma regarding, 176–79
Imperialism, cultural effects of, 85–86

Industrial workers, as social class, 95–98
Informality, of Middle Eastern society, 43, 45, 46–47, 79
Integrated economies: social class composition in, 119–24, 129–30; urban classes in, 90–102
Intellectual activity, preconditions for, 72–73
Intellectual climate, Middle Eastern, 80–81
Intellectuals: vs. expatriates, 71–72; as social actors, 23, 24–25; as social force, 79; social role of, 71
Intelligentsia: in integrated economies, 92–93; particular characteristics of, 27
Intifada, Palestinian, 164, 165
Iran, 45; as Empire, 214; informal employment in, 51; intellectual tradition in, 73; and Islamic repoliticization, 204; Islamic Republic of, 204–5, 207, 211; maternity leave law in, 163; oil as export of, 134; political Islam in, 210, 211; revolution in, 47, 158, 160, 208, 212, 213; state-led capitalism in, 45; urban population of, 137; White Revolution in, 158, 159
Iran-Iraq war, 208
Iraq, 45; Ba'athist revolution in, 160; economic development in, 44, 45; and economic sanctions, 210; and invasion of Kuwait, 208; maternity leave law in, 163; urban population of, 137
Irrigation system, and social organization, 122
Islam, 170–76, 204–13; as antidemocratic, 39, 80; and change, 172–76; and daily life, 170–72; as impediment to democracy, 228, 229–30; intellectual rediscovery of, 206; as nondemocratic culture, 11–12; as obstacle to democratization, 226; pervasiveness of, 175–76, 198–99; political element of, 204–7; politicization of, 171; and recurrence of personality cults, 216–17; repoliticization of, 61, 204; resurgence of, 65–66, 179–80; as social institution, 62–64, 79; and socialism, 160; as source of political legitimacy, 222–23; and the state, 207–13; as traditional core, 141
Islamic dress code: adoption of, 70, 164, 172; observance of, as symbol, 64

Islamic fundamentalism, 13, 61, 205, 211
Islamic phrases, frequent use of, 171, 172
Islamic radicalism, and refutation of Westernization, 142
Islamic reformism, 175; and Islamic populism, 173
Islamic Salvation Front (FIS), 29, 227
Islamists, Egyptian, 174
Ismael, Jacqueline, 106
Israel: rural culture in, 196; schisms in, 66

Jamaat Islami, 227
Jangali movement, 126
Jordan: open-door economic policy of, 135; political Islam in, 205; social security in, 163
Judaism, as social institution, 66–67

Kasravi, Ahmad, 180
Kemal, Yasar, 73
Kemalism, 158–59
Kenya, democratic consolidation in, 17
al-Khalifah family, 106
Khashoggi, Adnan, 107
Khomeini, Ayatollah Ruhollah, 173; and cult of personality, 213, 214, 218, 219, 223; as father figure, 37
Kinfolk, reliance on, 43, 45
Kinship, tribal, 54
Kulthoum, Umm, 143, 178
Kumaratunga, Chandrika, 8
Kurds and "Kurdish problem," 56, 73; Turkey's, 7, 9; and Turkomans, 60
Kuwait: and laws on female status, 194; oil exports of, 135; population of, 102; restrictive citizenship of, 114; social security in, 163; society of, 113; urban population of, 118

Labor, gender and division of, 190, 191
"Labor aristocracy," 96
Land, attachment to, in rural culture, 197; ownership of, and class, 122–23
Land reform, as tool for class neutralization, 117
Language: and cultural authenticity, 180–81; as unifying force, 169
Lebanese Muslims, 209
Lebanon: democratic consolidation in, 17; disintegration of, 208–9; political Islam in, 210, 211; as quasi democracy, 8; ur-

ban population of, 137
Lerner, Daniel: on Westernization, 140; on subcategories of Middle East society, 147, 151
Liberation: authenticating function of, 178–79; cultural, 182–84
Libya: economic development in, 44; maternity leave law in, 163
Lijphart, Arend, 4
Lineage: reliance on, 43, 45; tribal, 54
Literacy rates, of women, 164
Local customs, neglect of, 144–45
Lockman, Zachary, 97
Louis XIV (king of France), 219
"Love marriages," 193
Lower-middle class, in integrated economies, 95
Lumpen proletariat, 98–99; vs. industrial workers, 96–97

Madagascar, democratic consolidation in, 17
Mahfouz, Naguib, 73, 74, 76, 178, 227
"Managed liberalization," state-led process of, 34
Manhood, Middle Eastern ideal of, 190, 191
"Manly" societies, 91–93
Marriage, age at, 164, 193
Marx, Karl, 83
Mass-dominated democracies, 4
Media, as source of cultural diffusion, 142–44
Mehdi, Imam, 214
Merad, Ali, 207
Merchant class, in oil-dependent economies, 107–9
Mernissi, Fatima, 164
Mexico, as elite-dominated democracy, 8
Middle class: in integrated economies, 93–95; in oil-dependent economies, 110–11; politically autonomous, 35–36
"Middle Eastern exceptionalism," 224
Migdal, Joel, 157
Migration, and urban growth, 137–40
Migrants: exile of, 116; female, 116; non-Palestinian, 115–17; physical segregation of, 136–37, 153–54; as urban villagers, 196. See also Expatriates
Military, role of, in democratic transitions, 28–30

Mobility, political/economic, 43, 45
Modern, connotation of, 101
Modernity: definition of, 128; vs. traditionalism, 113
Moghadam, Valentine, 162, 163, 164
Monarchies, family-based, 42
Moore, Wilbert, 131, 132
Morocco: foreign borrowing by, 135; informal employment in, 51; and political Islam, 205; tourism in, 144
Mosca, Gaetano, 122
Mosque: as place of worship, 59; as social institution, 74, 77–78, 172
Mothers, reverence for, 195
Mubarak, Hosni, 62; and cult of personality, 214, 218; and Western values, 142
Muhammad: and cult of personality, 214; as founder of socialism, 160; leadership style of, 42; lineage of, 219
Muslim Brotherhood, 174, 210
Mustazafan, Iran's, 210

al-Nahda, 227
al-Naqeeb, Khaldoun, 156
Nasreen, Taslima, 7
Nasser, Gamal Abdel, 62, 203, 219; and cult of personality, 213, 215, 223; and economic development projects, 44; semitotalitarianism of, 158, 159–60
Nationalism: and political culture, 202, 203, 222; as social force, 48–49
Nehru, Jawaharlal, 7
Neopatriarchy, 85, 148, 151
Nepotism, 45
New Forum, 24
Nomads, and allegiance to state, 127–28
Norton, Augustus Richard, 33, 34, 35
Nostalgia, and cultural authenticity, 180–81
Nuclear families, prevalence of, 161. See also Family(ies)

Oil, and economic growth, 134–35
Oil-dependent economies: social class composition in, 121–28, 129–30; urban classes in, 102–13
Oman and Omanis: and control of change, 152–53; in Kuwait, 58; population of, 102
Open Sesame, 143
Ottoman Empire, 174

Pahlavi, Mohammad Reza, 62, 221; and cult of personality, 215; semitotalitarianism of, 158, 159; rule of, 174, 218

Pahlavi family, state-directed capital projects of, 44

Pakistan: democratic consolidation in, 17; family dynasties in, 8; lack of human rights in, 6–7

Palestinian Authority, creation of, 114

Palestinian issue, 202, 203, 222

Palestine Liberation Organization. *See* PLO

Palestinians: in Jordan, 58; as politicized, 113–14, 116

Patai, Raphael, 181

Patriarchal family structure, 80

Patronage, of ruling families, 104

Peasants: and potential opposition to state, 126–27; landless, as rural social class, 125; shuttle, 126

People's Democratic Republic of Yemen (PDRY), 163; marital law reform in, 194

Perón, Juan, 9

Personality cults, 202, 213–22; displays of, 218–19; and leader's personal power, 217; social/cultural resonance of, 216, 221–22

Petrodollars, effects of, 112

Piscatori, James, 209–10

PLO (Palestine Liberation Organization), 114

Poland, civil society in, 17; as civil society–driven viable democracy, 18, 30

Polisario movement, 127

Political crafting, and civil society, 16

Political culture, 201–23; aspects of, 202; definitions of, 201–2; components of, 5

Political economy, Middle Eastern, 35–36

Political Islam, 73, 208; disenchantment with, 210–11; growing strength of, 211–13

Political rule, as unifying force, 169

Political systems, classification of, 217

Polyarchies, 2

Polygamy, decline of, 193

Population growth, in cities, 136

Portugal, civil society in, 16

Poverty, as obstacle to democratic development, 11

Praying, importance of, 171

Prejudice, 168

Primordialism: in Middle East, 42, 48–49; as social force, 79–80

Procedural formalism, 43

Procedures/rules, aversion to, 189

Professional organizations, and civil society, 34

Protocols of the Elders of Zion, 72

Qabus, 156

Qaddafi, Muammar, 203, 219; and cult of personality, 214, 223; as father figure, 37; and Western values, 142

Qatar: oil exports of, 135; population of, 102; urban population of, 118

Qisas, law of, 195

Qom, 175

Quasi democracies, 3–4, 226; in Central and Latin America, 6–7; in Third World, 5

Rahman, Ziaur, 8

Rashid, Sheikh, 106

Regimes, types of, 220

Religion: politicization of, 205–6; in rural culture, 197; as social institution, 61–68, 79; as source of identity, 80; as unifying force, 169

Religious change, state-initiated, 174, 175

Religious minority, societal role of, 67–68

"Rentier states," 103, 226

Representative democracy, 4

Restricted democracies, 4

Revolutionary Guards, 209

Revolutionary Institutional Party (PRI), 8

Revolutions: from above, 158–60; from below, 160–61; as social change, 132–33

Reza, Mohammad, 62

Richards, Alan: and Middle East states' classification, 217; on Middle East economy, 135

Rituals, as social reality, 172

Rugh, Andrea, 195

Rugh, William, 143

Ruling families: as social/political elite, 103; and sociocultural change, 156–57

Rural classes: in integrated economies, 118, 121–28; in oil-dependent economies, 118, 119–21

Rural culture, 196–98

Rushd, Ibn, 175
Rushdie, Salman, 208

al-Sabah family, 103, 221
Sabra refugee camp, 209
Sadat, Anwar, 62, 208; assassination of,
    47; and cult of personality, 214, 215,
    218; as father figure, 37; and Western
    values, 142
Said, Edward, 72, 85
Said, Sheikh, 126
Said, Sultan, 156
al-Saud, house of, 208, 219
Saud, Ibn, 103
Saudi Arabia: economic growth of, 135;
    and Islamic repoliticization, 204; popu-
    lation of, 102; urban population of, 118
Saudi Development Plan, 153
Schumpeter, Joseph, 2
"Second stratum," 122, 123–24
Segmentary, Middle Eastern societies as,
    32
Selfish individualism, 187–89
Semitotalitarianism, Middle Eastern, 158
Sephardi-Ashkenazi, influence of, 59
Shah, Mohammad Reza. See Pahlavi, Mo-
    hammad Reza
Shah Nameh (Firdawsī), 76, 180
Shame (Nasreen), 7
Sharabi, Hisham, 72; on effects of imperi-
    alism, 85–86; on neopatriarchy, 148,
    151
Shari'a, 163, 173
Shariati, Ali, 73, 175, 206, 207
Sharjah, oil exports of, 135
Shatila refugee camp, 209
Shia(s): activists of, 60; Iranian, 213; Leba-
    non's, 210, 211
Shiism, 77
Social actors, kinds of, 21
Social change, 131–67; causes of, 134–45;
    definition of, 131; and gender relations,
    164–66; in Gulf monarchies, 151–57;
    manifestations of, 145–66; in Middle
    East, 147–51, 157–66; negative ramifi-
    cations of, 166–67; paradoxes in, 225;
    patterns of, 132–33; self-generated, 161;
    unintentional, 154; and urbanization,
    136–40; and Westernization, 140–42
Social class(es), 82–130; definition of, 86;
    in integrated economies, 87, 88; non-

traditional, 86; in oil-dependent econo-
    mies, 89; rural, 87, 88–89, 117–28; as
    socioculturally differentiated, 111–13,
    128–29; traditional vs. modern, 86,
    148–51; urban, 87, 88, 90–117, 145–46
Social engineering, state-sponsored,
    158–60
Social forces: in Middle Eastern society,
    41–49; and priorities of society, 79–80;
    state resistance to, 43
Social formations, as contradictory, 47–48
Social institutions 49–78; as actors, 21;
    definition of, 49; and education, 69–74;
    ethnicity and, 56–60; family as, 49–53;
    gathering places as, 74–78; religion
    and, 61; tribalism as, 53–56
Social norm, state manipulation of, 37
Society: institutional cornerstones of, 225;
    nontraditional, 178; sociocultural/eco-
    nomic composition of, 149–51; tradi-
    tional, 178; transitional, 178
Solidarity, 20, 21, 24, 25, 28
Sorensen, Georg, 3, 4
Soroush, Abdulkarim, 74
Sources of identity, as social force, 79, 80
South Africa, as civil society–driven viable
    democracy, 18
South Korea, democratic consolidation in,
    17
Spain, civil society in, 16
Sports club, role of, 78
Springborg, Robert, 125, 158–59
Sri Lanka, democratic consolidation in,
    17; family dynasties in, 7–8; persecu-
    tion of Tamil in, 7
State: political institutions of, 225; as prae-
    torian, 19, 26; and secular changes,
    174; and social forces, 42–43; society's
    lack of links with, 19–20
State institutions, as social actors, 21
State-society relationship, 221, 223; and
    democratic political system, 4–9; gap
    in, 81, 226–27; in Middle East, 157–61;
    and social change, 133, 134
Status, Middle Eastern preoccupation
    with, 199–200
Student(s), politicization of, 70–71
Sudan: economic development in, 44; so-
    cial security in, 163
Sultanism, 219
Sunni(s), 60, 77, 78

Syria: and civil society, 35; economic growth of, 44, 135; maternity leave law in, 163
Syrian Social National Party, 72

Taiwan, democratic consolidation in, 17
Taleghani, Ayatollah Mahmud, 175
Tamil, persecution of, 7
Tanzania, democratic consolidation in, 17
Taxation, in Middle East, 36–37
Teahouses, as social institutions, 74, 75–77, 78, 79
Technological innovation, and change, 174
al-Thani family, 103
Thornburg, Max, 170
Tibi, Bassam: on cultural chauvinism, 187; on identity, 177; on Islam, 170–71, 173, 175
Tolerance, need for, 227
Tourism, as source of cultural diffusion, 142, 144–45
Tourist visas, restrictions on, 153
Tradition: role of, in Gulf states, 152; in rural culture, 197–98
Transitional, Middle Eastern society as, 147, 151
Transplacements, 14
Tribes and tribalism, 53–56; chieftain, 53, 54–55; and city, 56; as cultural force, 202; definition of, 53; disappearance of, 53; and ethnicity, 56–58; evolution of, 53; factors influencing, 55; manipulation of, 80; as social institution, 54; solidarity of, 54; as source of identity, 54; and state, 54
Tunisia: bureaucratic growth in, 44; and civil society, 35; foreign borrowing of, 135; informal employment in, 51; personal status laws in, 163; tourism in, 141
Turkish language, and cultural authenticity, 180–81
Turkey: civil society in, 16–17; democratic consolidation in, 17; foreign borrowing by, 135; importance of family in, 50; informal employment in, 51; Kurdish problem in, 7, 9; open-door economic policy of, 135; personal status law in, 163; as quasi democracy, 8–9
"Tyranny of the face," 95

United Arab Emirates: population of, 102; urban population of, 118; wealth of, 106
Upper classes: in integrated economies, 91–92; in oil-dependent economies, 102–6
Upper-middle classes: in integrated economies, 92–93; in oil-dependent economies, 108–9
Upward mobility, 101–2
"Urban bias," 90
Urban classes: in integrated economies, 90–102; in oil-dependent economies, 102–13
Urbanization: and development of new social classes, 145–46; and social change, 136–40; and tribalism, 54

Veil, women's use of, 172
Venezuela, democratic consolidation in, 17
Viable democracies, 3–4; and civil society, 5; civil society–driven, 18–19
Virginity, expectation of, 193

Walesa, Lech, 227
Waterbury, John, 126, 135, 217
Wealth, sources of, in Gulf states, 104–6
Webster, Roger, 153–54
Weimar Republic, 9
Westernization, 140–42
White Revolution, 158, 159
Women: economic disadvantage of, 194; and education, 163–64; legal status of, 153, 155; mass effort to improve conditions of, 195–96; in revolutionary periods, 164–65; and sexuality, 190; and *shari'a*, 163; societal ambivalence of, 165–66; sociocultural roles of, 192–93; and workforce, 162

Yemen, experiment with democracy in, 226

Zakariyya, Fouad, 72, 73
Zambia, democratic consolidation in, 17
Zedillo, Ernesto, 8
Zia, Khaleda, 8
Zionism, 66

About the Author

MEHRAN KAMRAVA teaches in political science at California State University, Northridge. Born in Iran, he received a Ph.D. in Social and Political Sciences from Cambridge University. He is the author of a number of books, including *Revolutionary Politics; Revolution in Iran: The Roots of Turmoil;* and the forthcoming *Cultural Politics in the Third World.*